To Scott

A Great East Yorker

EAST YORK:
1924-1997
Toronto's
Garden of Eden

 FriesenPress

Suite 300 - 990 Fort St
Victoria, BC, V8V 3K2
Canada

www.friesenpress.com

Copyright © 2018 by Alan Redway
First Edition — 2018

The author acknowledges the support he received from the East York Foundation
The work of Anna Malandrino in typing the text and preparing the index
The image editing by Tracy Chow of tcdesktopservices@gmail.com
The front cover design by Valentine De Landro

ISBN
978-1-5255-2937-5 (Hardcover)
978-1-5255-2938-2 (Paperback)
978-1-5255-2939-9 (eBook)

1. HISTORY, CANADA, POST-CONFEDERATION (1867 TO PRESENT)

Distributed to the trade by The Ingram Book Company

Inside...

INTRODUCTION

Many long-time East Yorkers—and I am one of them—describe East York as a small town in a big city. When I tell people who live in other parts of Toronto where I live, they often respond, "East York is different, isn't it." That's a statement not a question. A long-time local East York barber told me of a conversation he had with a customer who had recently moved to East York. "This place is special," his customer said. "Don't let anyone else know about it. Let's keep it to ourselves."

East York is different. It is special. It truly has had, and I hope it always will have, that small town in a big city feeling. It is a clean, safe, and friendly community in which the residents care about each other and are concerned for the well-being of their neighbours.

I grew up in a part of the former Borough of East York; the Town of Leaside. When the former Town of Leaside was merged with the former Township of East York in 1967 to create the Borough of East York, many residents of both the former town and the former township thought that the people on the other side of the bridge spanning the Don Valley were somehow different from themselves. The truth, of course, was quite the opposite. They had more in common than they ever imagined.

In 1972, I was elected to the borough council, serving for ten years, six of them as mayor of East York. It was immediately evident to me how similar the two formerly separate communities really were. Perhaps they realized it as well, but did not want to admit they had been wrong.

Together, they demonstrated the characteristics, as I describe them, of a small town in a big city. The Borough of East York prided itself on being clean, safe, and a friendly community in which the residents cared about each other and were concerned for the well-being of their neighbours.

Just as they had formerly been as separate communities, all the borough residents were watchful of the way their council spent their hard-earned tax dollars, demanding excellent local services at the least possible cost. No matter where they lived in the borough, whether they had to cross the Woodbine or the Leaside Bridge or come from Dawes Road to do so, East York residents from every part of the community would always come in force to council and committee meetings to hold their councillors' feet to the fire, to make sure they got the message and looked after the residents' interests. That can't happen in a big city where, because of size and distance, residents are forced to leave matters in the hands of the city council, and the councillors in turn leave many matters in the hands of the city staff.

Both before and after the Province of Ontario created the Municipality of Metropolitan Toronto in 1954, the thirteen municipalities that then composed Metro, including the Township of East York and the Town of Leaside, had well-defined boundaries, which had created in each a real sense of being a small-town community. In 1967, when the Province of Ontario merged East York and Leaside, the new Borough of East York had different but still defined boundaries, which allowed it to create a new but real sense of a small town community. In 1998, when the Province of Ontario amalgamated the six Metro municipalities to form the megacity of Toronto, the clearly defined boundaries of the Borough of East York were erased. Understandably, the staff of the new megacity wanted to eliminate the old local loyalties that residents of the former Metro municipalities, including East York, had for their own communities and create in them a new loyalty solely to the megacity. So far, that has not worked in East York. However, as time passes, the lack of the defined boundaries together with the impact of new residents who never knew East York as it was before amalgamation, the regular revisions of federal and provincial riding and municipal ward boundaries, and the focus on Toronto as a world-class rather than a livable city, reinforce the megacity staff's efforts to undermine the old loyalties. This helps to weaken, if not eliminate, that sense of living in a small town within a big city.

I have written this book because I believe that it is essential that we record the East York story before it disappears from living memory. The long-time Commissioner of Parks and Recreation, Stan Wadlow, always referred to East York as the Garden of Eden. It is my fervent hope that the future residents of the former Borough of East York will never lose the sense that they live in the Garden of Eden of Toronto—a small town within a big city.

Toronto's Garden of Eden

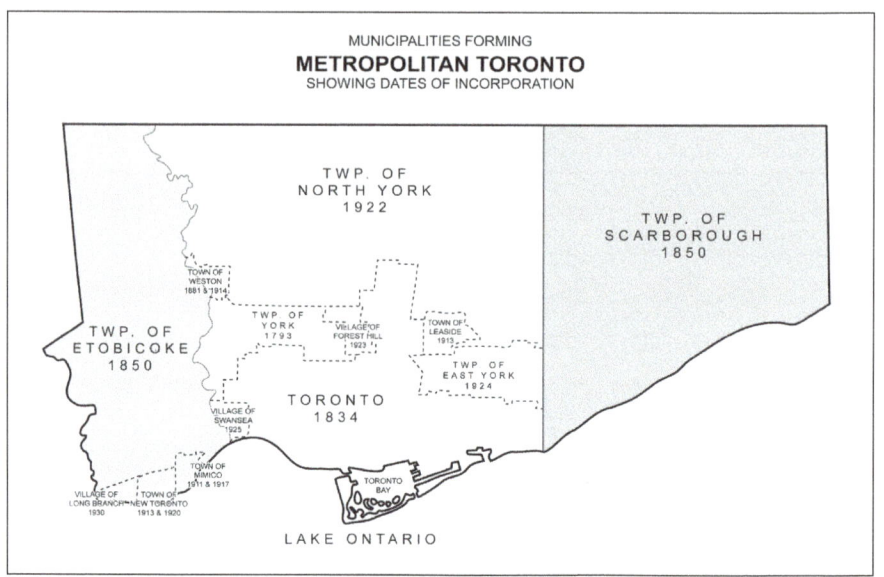

East York in 1924
(Source: Valentine De Landro)

Taylor Creek Park

– Chapter 1 –

THE GENESIS

In the year 1900, as the twentieth century dawned, East York did not exist, but a small hamlet on the heights overlooking the Don River known as Todmorden did. That year, the Todmorden District School Board hired William Diefenbaker to teach twenty-eight students in its one-room Plains Road Schoolhouse. Among them were four boys who later, in 1942, were destined to sit together in the Canadian House of Commons in Ottawa as Conservative Members of Parliament.

One of those four boys was R.H. (Bob) McGregor, who began his adult life as a market gardener and later founded the Malvern Construction Company that built the Woodbine Bridge and several apartment buildings on Dawes Road. He also served on York Township Council, then the first East York Township Council, as deputy reeve and later as reeve, before his election to the House of Commons in Ottawa as the York East Member of Parliament, where he served for thirty-six consecutive years from 1926 to 1962. A second boy, Joe Harris, whose family owned the abattoir at Danforth and Coxwell Avenues, known to local residents as the "glue factory," played the key role in the founding of the Toronto East General Hospital (now known as the Michael Garron Hospital). He negotiated the purchase of the land and assembled the original financing, serving as the hospital's chairman of the board of governors from 1926 until 1952. Harris was elected to parliament in 1933, where he served continuously until his death in 1952. The third lad, George Tustin, moved from Todmorden to Napanee, Ontario, where after a successful career as a local business owner, he was elected as the mayor of Napanee before becoming the Member of Parliament for Napanee, serving continuously for twenty-two years, from 1935 to 1957. The last of those four boys was the teacher's son, John Diefenbaker, destined to become a future prime minister of Canada from 1957 to 1963. Prime Minister John Diefenbaker appointed the first woman to serve in the federal cabinet, Ellen Fairclough, as his Minister of Immigration. He gave the vote for the first time ever to Canada's indigenous people, and appointed the first indigenous person to sit in the parliament of Canada, Senator Akay Na Muka (James Gladstone). He also enacted the Canadian Bill of Rights, the forerunner to the Canadian Charter of Rights and Freedoms. Later, each of the four boys, now men, would credit their teacher at Plains Road School, William Diefenbaker, as their inspiration to serve in public life.[1]

Prior to 1924, East York was part of the Township of York, the traditional territory of the Huron-Wendat, the Seneca of the Iroquois Confederacy (Haudenshanees), the Ojibwa of the Anishinaabe, and

R.H. (Bob) McGregor MP	Joe Harris MP	George Tustin MP
(Source: google.ca)	*(Source: wikipedia.org)*	*(Source: Lennox Addington Museum & Archives)*

---

1. Diefenbaker, John G., *One Canada; The Crusading Years 1895 to 1956*, MacMillan of Canada, 1975, 10, 12, 17–18

Prime Minister RT Hon.
John G. Diefenbaker
(Source: EY Advocate)

George Tustin, Joe Harris, R.H. McGregor,
John Diefenbaker (front)
(Source: East York Foundation)

1941 Plains Rd School Reunion
(Source: East York Foundation)

most recently, the Mississauga of the New Credit. It was subsequently settled by United Empire Loyalists fleeing the USA after the American Revolution, soon followed by others, mostly from the British Isles, who mainly devoted themselves to farming and market gardening. When the farms and market gardens along parts of the southern boundary of York Township gave way to housing, they were being annexed by an expanding City of Toronto (originally the Town of York, founded by Governor John Graves Simcoe, it was incorporated as the City of Toronto in 1834). By 1921, however, other parts of York Township, North York, East York,

Swansea, and Forest Hill were also on the verge of becoming separate municipalities.[2]

In that same year, one of William Diefenbaker's students, R. H. (Bob) McGregor, now a market gardener and a member of York Township Council, negotiated on behalf of School Section Seven of the York Township Public School Board the purchase of five acres of Billy McKay's farm at the northwest corner of Coxwell and Sammon Avenues for the sum of $35,707. When the school built on that site was completed, it was named R.H. McGregor Public School in his honour. [3]

As the farm lands and market gardens gave way to housing, more and more of the residents were living in the York Township but working in the City of Toronto. Many of the city streets were extending north across the township boundary[4] and ratepayer associations such as Todmorden, Greenwood, Woodbine Heights, Danforth Park, and Dentonia Park were springing up in the southeast part of York Township. Residents on streets listed in Schedule A were petitioning York Township Council for concrete sidewalks, surfaced roads, water mains, street lighting, and firefighting equipment.[5] These residential streets, which had existed long before, would soon become part of East York.

By the year 1921, there were only 6,000 residents of York Township living on farms, while some 75,000 were now effectively urban dwellers. The farm population was stable and not growing. North York was a community of farmers, but the York Township Council was stacked against them. None of the five council members was considered a farmer. The North York farmers were paying 23% of the property taxes, but the York Township Council was spending almost 100% of the money on local improvements in the urban parts of the township.[6]

Immediately following World War I, Canada experienced what was called "a farmers' revolt." The United Farmers of Alberta, Saskatchewan,

---

2. Boylen, J.C., *York Township, an Historical Survey 1850 –1954*, Municipal Corporation of the Township of York, Toronto, 1954, 259

3. Deed of Land dated May 20, 1921, registered July 25, 1921 in the Registry Office for the Registry Permission of the East and West Ridings of the County of York as Instrument Number 137776 York

4. Boylen, J.C., *York Township, an Historical Survey 1850 –1954*, Municipal Corporation of the Township of York, Toronto, 1954, 260

5. Township of York Council Minutes, 1922

6. Boylen, J.C., *York Township, an Historical Survey 1850 –1954*, Municipal Corporation of the Township of York, Toronto, 1954, 261

Manitoba, and Ontario were all elected as the provincial government of their respective provinces. In 1919, the United Farmers of Ontario, headed by E.C. Drury as premier, formed the government of this province. Spurred on by the farmers' provincial revolt and subsequent victory, the North York farmers revolted as well, petitioning the Ontario Legislature for the right to secede from York Township. Their petition was granted and, following a successful plebiscite held only in that part of the township requesting secession, the Township of North York was incorporated as a separate municipality on June 13, 1922.[7]

That presented the remainder of York Township with a dilemma. Southeast York was now cut off from the rest of the township. Special public meetings of residents and councillors were held to consider the options. Some suggested instituting a ward system, and some suggested incorporating York as a city. Others suggested doing nothing. In the result, however, the Township of York Council passed the following resolution:

"That the solicitor be requested to prepare a petition requesting the Legislature of the Province of Ontario at the present siting to divide the Township of York into East and West Townships."

That motion, moved by Dennis McCarthy and seconded by John Galbraith, was passed on a four to one vote. R. H. (Bob) McGregor voted against the motion. It is interesting to note that at the time, three of the five members of York Township Council—McCarthy, Galbraith, and McGregor—all resided in what was to become the Township of East York. They were all destined to become members of the inaugural Council of the Township of East York. McGregor would later become the reeve of East York and go on to become the long-serving Member of Parliament for York East.[8]

On February 28, 1923, a petition from the Township of York Council was presented in the Ontario Legislature, "praying that an Act may pass to detach certain portions of the Township to be called the Township of East York." The bill to incorporate East York was presented to and guided through the Legislative Assembly by George S. Henry, then the MPP for

---

7. Hart, Patricia W., *Pioneering in North York, a History of the Borough*, General Publishing Company Limited Toronto, 1968, page 259
8. Township of York Council Minutes, 1922

York South, which included what was to become the Township of East York. Later, Henry was to become a Conservative premier of Ontario.[9] The Act of Incorporation having passed, it received the required royal assent from the lieutenant governor of Ontario on May 8, 1923. That same day, the Legislature was prorogued by Premier E.C. Drury.[10] In the provincial election that followed that year, the United Farmers of Ontario government that held office when the bill incorporating East York was enacted went down to defeat.[11]

George S. Henry MPP   Premier E.C. Drury
(Source: wikipedia.org)   *(Source: wikipedia.org)*

As with the act incorporating North York, the one incorporating East York required only the electors living in that part of York Township "bounded on the north by the Township of North York, on the east by the Township of Scarborough, on the south and on the west by the City of Toronto, to vote on the question:

"Are you in favour of the incorporation of the eastern part of the Township of York as set out in the Act of the Legislature of Ontario passed in 1923, as the Township of East York?"

9. Proceedings of the Ontario Legislative Assembly, February 28, 1923, Statues of Ontario, 12–14 George V c.99, 398

10. Johnston, Charles M., Drury, E.C., *Agrarian Idealist*, University of Toronto Press, Toronto, 1986, 202

11. Johnston, Charles M., Drury, E.C., *Agrarian Idealist*, University of Toronto Press, Toronto, 1986. 191

The results of the vote, held on July 7, 1923, were as follows:

Number of votes cast in the Affirmative	448
Number of votes cast in the Negative	102
Majority in favour of Incorporation	346 [12]

Thus, on January 1, 1924, the Township of East York came into existence as a separately incorporated municipality.[13]

No doubt, many of those who voted in the negative hoped that the south east part of York would be annexed by the City of Toronto. As recently as 1920, the city had annexed ninety-four acres on the north side of the Danforth, followed the next year by eighteen acres of the Davies' Estate (formerly Taylor family lands). Before World War I, in spite of a resolution protesting an annexation proposal passed by a meeting of well over a thousand Todmorden residents,[14] City Council had agreed to do just that. They planned to annex Todmorden, but the plan died when the war broke out. After it ended, even though they were now residents of the Township of East York, the businessmen of Todmorden asked City Council to complete the annexation approved in 1914. However, when residents south of the Danforth objected, the idea died.[15]

While 1923 legislation creating the Township of East York described the boundaries as North York on the north, Scarborough on the east and the City of Toronto on the south and west, there was no mention of the Town of Leaside, incorporated in 1913. The future would bring some further changes to that vague southern and western border description.

---

12. Minutes of East York Township Council, first meeting, 1924
13. Statues of Ontario, 12-14 George V c.99 page 398
14. *Toronto Star,* July 23, 1914
15. Report on the Government of the Metropolitan Area of Toronto to the Hon. David Croll, Minister of Municipal Affairs in the Province of Ontario by A.F.W. Plumtre, Department of Political Science and Economics, University of Toronto, June 20, 1935

Schedule A

Barker Avenue, Chisholm Avenue, Coleridge Avenue, Gowan Avenue, Gamble Avenue, Bee Street, Chilton Avenue, Woodycrest Boulevard, Cedarvale Avenue, Don Mills Road, Nealon Avenue, Sammon Avenue, King Edward Avenue, Meagher Avenue, Warland Avenue, Wolverton Avenue, Hopedale Avenue, Pape Avenue, Stanhope Avenue, Sibley Avenue, Fulton Avenue, Frater Avenue, LeRoy Avenue, Greenwood Avenue, Mortimer Avenue, McKay Avenue, Queensdale Avenue, Woodmount Avenue, Holborne Avenue, Woodbine Avenue, Bungalow Avenue, Minton Place, Monarch Park Avenue, Peplar Avenue, Secord Avenue, Palmer Avenue, Dawes Road, Lumsden Avenue, Glebemount Avenue, and Goodwood Park Crescent.

– Chapter 2 –

"AND THE LORD GOD PLANTED A GARDEN EASTWARD IN EDEN."[1]

What did Toronto's Garden of Eden look like before its incorporation as a separate municipality?

Although only 550 persons cast a ballot in the plebiscite that created the new Township, East York's actual population at the time was 19,849.[2] The residents were mainly centred on two unincorporated communities, Todmorden in the southwest and Little York in the southeast.[3]

With the arrival of the United Empire Loyalists and other Europeans in the late eighteenth and early nineteenth centuries, a favoured few, including the Anglican Church, were given large grants of crown lands including in the area destined to become East York.[4] However, prior to 1924, most had been sold and resold by their owners. By the time it was incorporated, with the exception of the 4000 acres owned by the Taylors,[5]

---

1. Good News Bible, Canadian Bible Society 1976, Ch.2, Verse 8
2. East York Public Library, Fascinating Facts about East York, 1996, 2
3. Davidson, True, *The Golden Years of East York*, Centennial College Press, Toronto, 1976, 45, 46
4. Davidson, True, *The Golden Years of East York*, Centennial College Press, Toronto, 1976, 28
5. Guthrie, Ann, *Don Valley Legacy, A Pioneer History*, The Boston Press, 1986. 15

the 240-acre Dentonia Park farm, owned by the Masseys,[6] the Anglican Church's Clergy Reserves, and the hamlets of Todmorden and Little York, the new township was made up of small farms and market gardens.[7]

The market gardens had been developed to meet the ever-increasing needs of the city of Toronto's growing population. The market gardeners themselves were small-scale producers growing their fruits and vegetables on five to sixteen-acre lots. Most of them developed their own customer base, selling directly to the consumer at their farm gate or going door to door with a horse and wagon or a push cart. [8] According to Pat Burford, her uncle Red Hogan, who lived at 327 Mortimer Avenue, was one of the most well-known of them.[9] George English, a long-time resident of Woodville Avenue, told me that one of his first jobs was selling fruit and vegetables door to door for Red Hogan.[10] Other market gardeners sold their produce to grocery stores or at the St. Lawrence Market.[11]

Many of the East York market gardeners started in Leslieville and Riverdale, then suburbs of Toronto, moving north as their land was sold and divided into building lots. Other market gardeners such as the Papes, Logans, and Greenwoods stayed put, but streets bearing their names continued to be extended north into East York.[12]

The 1920 city directory identifies the great many market gardeners in East York (Schedule B). They were mainly located along Pape Avenue, Donlands Avenue (formerly Leslie Street), Sammon Avenue, Gardeners Lane (now Mortimer Avenue), Cosburn Avenue (formerly Bee Street), Plains Road, and St. Clair Avenue East. [13]

Prominent East York market gardeners included: A.H & J.E. (Joe) Jennings with fifteen acres at Greenwood and Sammon; Charles McKay, north of Sammon and east of Greenwood; Joseph Fitzgerald, east of

---

6. Davidson, True, *The Golden Years of East York*, Centennial College Press, Toronto, 1976, 30

7. Davidson, True, *The Golden Years of East York*, Centennial College Press, Toronto, 1976, 28

8. Doucette, Joanne, *Pigs, Flowers and Bricks; a history of Leslieville to 1920*, Self–Published, 2011, 75

9. Interview with Pat and Jay Burford, January 26, 2016

10. Interview with George English, December 29, 2015

11. Doucette, Joanne, *Pigs, Flowers and Bricks; a history of Leslieville to 1920*, Self–Published, 2011, 75

12. Doucette, Joanne, *Pigs, Flowers and Bricks; a history of Leslieville to 1920*, Self–Published, 2011, 226

13. Lister, Jim, *East York Incorp.: 1924 An Illustrated History*, Self–Published, 1983, 175

Woodbine; William Sammon on Gardners Lane; the Dart family on Don Mills Road; Robert Barker on Gardners Lane east to Woodbine; John Somers on Donlands; the Squires family on Dawes Road at St. Clair; and the Cosburn family with twelve acres between Donlands and Woodbine. Many East York Streets are named for them. In all, there were forty-four market gardeners in East York, but all were gone after 1927.[14]

Housing development invaded East York, just as it had earlier in Leslieville and Riverdale, forcing the market-gardener families to move once again. During my six years as mayor of East York (1977–1982), I was invited to open the Markham Fair. It is organized each year by the Markham and East York Agricultural Society. At that time, the president of the society was a member of the Cosburn family. When the Cosburns and other market gardeners left East York, they moved to Scarborough and later to Markham, as once again they were overtaken by housing development. Most of these former East York families are no longer in the business, but apparently, the Squires family are still market gardening in the Milton area.[15]

Market Gardeners 1
(Source: East York Foundation)

---

14. Riverdale Library Local History Collection
15. Doucette, Joanne, Interview, December 14, 2015

Market Gardeners 2
(Source: East York Foundation)

Delivery of Market Garden Produce
(Source: East York Foundation)

Bell family market gardeners home 269 Donlands (Leslie Street)
(Source: East York Foundation)

Todmorden

Why did Todmorden and Little York become centres of population prior to the incorporation of the Township? The simple answer is jobs.

Todmorden has been called Toronto's earliest industrial village. Hovering on the cliffs overlooking the Don Valley, it was named by early settler John Eastwood after his birthplace in Yorkshire, England, because the scenery along the Don River reminded him of his former home.

In the late eighteenth century, Parshall Terry and the Skinners had established both a grist mill and a saw mill in the Don Valley. Then in the early nineteenth century, John Eastwood and Colin Skinner converted the grist mill to a paper mill. About the same time, the Helliwells opened a brewery and distillery, but it wasn't until the arrival of the Taylor family in 1826 that the Todmorden industrial village really took off.[16]

The Taylors acquired the Eastwood paper mill and developed two additional mills in the valley. The upper mill located north of the forks of the Don River made rag newsprint for the Toronto Globe. The middle mill at the foot of Beachwood Drive would later become a unit of the Howard Smith Paper Mills producing fine quality paper, and later still a division of Domtar. But the lower mill located at the foot of Todmorden Road (now Pottery Road), turned out coloured paper and paper bags. Together, these three mills, when owned by the Taylor family, employed a work force of sixty-two men, women, and some children.[17]

The Taylors didn't stop there. They also founded the Don Valley Pressed Brick Works and the Sun Brick Company. Later, Robert Davies, a son-in-law of the Taylors, bought these brickyards.[18] Bill Lewis, who grew up in the Todmorden neighbourhoods, remembers the eighty-five foot deep quarry pool at the Sun Brick Company site, which was ideal for swimming in the summer and skating in the winter. Eventually, this quarry was completely filled in with East York garbage.[19] The Don Valley Brick companies produced some twelve million bricks a year. Most were

---

16. Darke, Eleanor, *A Mill Should be Built, an early history of Todmorden Mills*, National Heritage, Toronto, 1995, 85, 86

17. Sauriol, Charles, *Remembering the Don*, Consolidated Amethyst Communications, 1981, 54, 55

18. Sauriol, Charles, *Remembering the Don*, Consolidated Amethyst Communications, 1981, 128, 129

19. Interview with Bill Lewis, November 9, 2015

used in Toronto but many were exported to the United States. Getting the heavily-loaded wagons of brick up the Pottery Road hill was a major problem for the brick yards.[20] Percy Bustin recalled that a man with a team of horses frequently had to reinforce the regular wagon teams for the difficult climb up the hill. Shades of today's tow trucks. But Percy said, "We have no idea whether he was an enterprising bloke making a few bucks for himself, or if the team belonged to one of the brickyards."[21]

Besides the paper mills and the brick yards, the Taylors operated a saw mill in Taylor's Bush. During 1914 alone, the mill cut a million and a half board feet of white pine.[22]

The mills, brickyards, farms, and market gardens provided the jobs that drew people to Todmorden. The community developed originally along Don Mills Road (now Broadview Avenue) from Todmorden Road (now Pottery Road) to what is now O'Connor Drive. In 1880, Don Mills Road was described by a Todmorden resident: "A dirt road smooth with packed down snow from sleigh runners in the winter, ankle-deep mud in spring, and thick with fine dust in summer. At the intersections, boards were laid for the crossings. On each side of the road were deep ditches, their sides lush in summer with tall grasses, wild rose bushes, buttercups, daisies and meadowsweet. Along one side of the road ran a boardwalk while in places great trees—among them magnificent chestnuts spread over in summer shade. There were a very few homes in the valley at that time most were built along the sides of Don Mills Road. These houses were either red brick or white frame, their front yards usually enclosed by picket fences. They were scattered singly in groups or rows separated by fields of grass and clover or by vacant lots."[23] Not much had changed by 1924.

Todmorden Road ran across the valley in a north westerly direction rising to Moore Avenue and Bennington Heights. Later, it was renamed Pottery Road for Burns Pottery, which was located near the bridge where the road crosses the Don River. There, Burns made good use of the valley clay.[24]

---

20. Sauriol, Charles, *Remembering the Don*, Consolidated Amethyst Communications, 1981, 128
21. Bustin, Percy, *Memories: The Early Days of East York*, Self –Published, 1976, 1
22. Sauriol, Charles, *Remembering the Don*, Consolidated Amethyst Communications, 1981, 135
23. Guthrie, Ann, *Don Valley Legacy, A Pioneer History*, The Boston Press, 1986, 120
24. Sauriol, Charles, *Remembering the Don*, Consolidated Amethyst Communications, 1981, 84

Soon houses were being built on other Todmorden streets such as Burgess Avenue (now Mortimer), Nash Avenue (now Westwood), Gowan, Gamble, Torrens, Woodville, and Bee (now Cosburn), all running east from Don Mills Road to Pape Avenue.[25] The writer Robert Thomas Allen described the area at the time as "a flat suburb of English, Irish, and Scotch cops, TTC motormen, and T. Eaton Company tie clerks." Electric street lighting of a sort was introduced to the Toronto area in 1880, soon followed by the telephone two years later.[26]

By the time the township was incorporated, the King Street car line had been extended north on Broadview to the Danforth, and the Bloor Danforth Viaduct (Prince Edward Viaduct) had been completed. That made it much easier for East Yorkers to access the many jobs across the border in the city of Toronto. However, that easier access to more jobs also brought with it the beginning of drastic change spearheaded by land speculators focused on turning East York's farms and market gardens into housing developments. [27]

A prize example of this was the plan to develop a subdivision of high-end Rosedale housing on the lands north of O'Connor to the edge of the Don Valley from Beechwood Drive to Leslie Street (now Donlands Avenue). This land had, until then, been a pig farm. Don Hough told the story of his family's experience with this proposed subdivision.

"When my mother would walk to church, she would see this house [later to become 26 Chilton Rd.] abandoned and with no roof because the subdivision was never approved, being too like Rosedale, with its confusing streets. Finally, my uncle bought it and we moved into it. When we moved to Chilton Road, our house and the pavilion on Rivercourt were the only buildings in ninety acres. Originally, the stone gates at Rivercourt and O'Connor were further east, in line with the pavilion. Our house faced west and a thirty-four-foot verandah. When the registered plan was changed and Chilton Road came into existence, our back door was facing the street. My father then had to put a thirty-four-foot verandah on the east side of the house, facing the street. An early plan showed a north-south

25. Davidson, True, *The Golden Years of East York*, Centennial College Press, Toronto, 1976, 46

26. Doucette, Joanne, *Pigs, Flowers and Bricks; a history of Leslieville to 1920*, Self–Published, 2011, 222

27. Guthrie, Ann, *Don Valley Leaside, A Pioneer History*, The Boston Press, 1986, 5

street, slightly to the east of Rivercourt Blvd., named Don Way Cres., and two east-west streets called Blackthorn Road and Thorncliffe, and two half-moon streets called Rivercourt Cres. and Edgecliffe Cres." The stone gates intended to mark the entrance to "East York's Rosedale" still exist at the corner of O'Connor Drive and Rivercourt Blvd. (originally called Bungalow Road).[28]

What Don Hough calls "the pavilion," Bill Lewis calls "the Mexican House." Originally, the real-estate sales office for the proposed subdivision was located there, at 39 Rivercourt Blvd. Later, it became a dance hall. The former East York reeve, Rupert Leslie, lived at 22 Rivercourt Blvd. [29] According to his grandson, Marshall Leslie, the stone gates, or the pillars as he calls them, at Rivercourt and O'Connor Drive (then Don Mills Road) were his grandfather's idea.[30]

Both before and after the township was incorporated, residents of the Todmorden area shopped at Jay Burford's grandparents' store at the corner of Torrens and Broadview,[31] as well as at Bater's General Store and Post Office located on Broadview near Westwood. According to George English, Bater's carried everything you could want. The Todmorden Masonic Lodge met in the room above the store. Nearby was the Todmorden Hotel.[32] Long-time resident Elsie Hallam Curtis had vivid memories of it: "A lot of men worked at the Don Valley Brick Works. On pay day, some of the wives would line up at the top of Pottery Road to snatch their pay envelopes before the men could cross over to the Todmorden Hotel."[33] Behind the hotel was Hughie Reid's blacksmith shop, where you could get your horse shod while you were in the hotel having a beer. When milk and bread were home-delivered by horse and wagon, Hughie's best customers were the dairies, the bread men, and the brickyards.[34]

Long-time resident Gord Haslett, whose father was a teamster when that meant a man with a horse and wagon, told me that one of his chores

---

28. Hough, D.S., *Some of My Memories of East York*, The East York Historical Society, 1992, 8
29. Interview with Bill Lewis, November 9, 2015
30. Interview with Marshall Leslie, March 23, 2017
31. Interview with Jay and Pat Burford, January 26, 2016
32. Interview with George English, December 29, 2015
33. Miller, Lorne S., *Our Danforth*, Lorne Miller & Associates Inc., Toronto, 2008, 2
34. Davidson, True, *The Golden Years of East York*, Centennial College Press, Toronto, 1976, 46

as a kid was to drive the horses from his Linsmore Crescent home to the Hughies' blacksmith shop whenever they needed new shoes.[35]

Percy Bustin recalled:

"Many of those early settlers who came from the British Isles were skilled in the building trades, and built their homes brick by brick and board by board as the cash became available. While the home was being built, the family lived in the basement. Since Father was no doubt working in one of the mills or the brickyards all day, the home building had to be done in the evenings and on weekends. Bill Curtis, one of East York's old-timers, liked to tell about the mother who, in the evenings while Dad laid brick, held up an oil lantern so that he could see what he was doing. There were some who, for some reason or another, never did accumulate enough cash to finish their homes, and the writer can remember when families were still living in roofed-over basements even as late as the thirties, and out-houses were still in vogue at the end of the garden. One cannot help but shudder when one thinks of the unpleasant trip it must have been on a cold winter's night when one had to answer the call of nature."[36]

One of those houses still stands today, although substantially renovated, at 343 Sammon Avenue. Nora Curran, who lives in the house, a young ninety-five years of age when I met her, told me that her father, a silversmith by trade, arrived here from Ireland in 1917 with no experience in construction, and immediately began to build the home in stages, starting with excavating the basement by hand. Nora was born in the house in 1922.[37]

Most of the homes were built by the owners themselves, but there were exceptions. The Taylor family built and rented a number of houses on Hassard, Woodville, Torrens, Gamble, and Bee Avenues for the families of men that worked at their mills and brickyards. They also built a number of mansions for themselves, including at 20 Beechwood Drive, built in 1840; the oldest privately-owned house in East York,

---

35. Interview with Gord Haslett, February 13, 2013
36. Bustin, Percy, *Memories: The Early Days of East York*, Self –Published, 1976, 2
37. Interview with Nora Curran, June 5, 2017

Chester Park (now demolished) at 1132 Broadview; Bellehaven, also now demolished, at 1068 Broadview; Fernwood at 2 O'Connor Drive, formerly the Ina Grafton Gage seniors residence, presently the Sisters of St. Joseph convent; Four Oaks Gates at the corner of Don Mills Road and O'Connor Drive; and the original Taylor home, Thorn Cliff, built in what is now the Thorncliffe Park community. [38]

Joyce Crook used to play at Bellehaven with her friends and Earl Kitchener School classmates, Barbara Stewart and Ann Lambert. Ann was one of the Taylor grandchildren. She later became Ann Guthrie and authored the book *Don Valley Legacy* concerning the early history of the Taylor family. One day back in the orchard hidden from view, Anne offered Joyce and Barbara a cigarette. Joyce says that was the first and the last time she ever smoked.[39] When the Taylors sold Bellehaven, "The purchaser was James Fransceschini, the president of the Dufferin Construction Company, who wanted a place to dump fill from the excavation for Eaton's College Street store, and as part of the sale he allowed the Taylors to live in the house, rent free, for as long as they lived. The fill was dumped into the Don Valley and was hidden from view by a hedge of flowering shrubs. Little did Mr. Fransceschini realize when he made the deal that William Taylor would live to the age of eighty-seven and his wife Isabella would not die until 1951, when she was ninety-four."[40] For a period of time Nora Curran and her husband operated a craft shop in the former Bellehaven stables.[41]

38. Guthrie, Ann, *Don Valley Legacy, A Pioneer History*, The Boston Press, 1986, 205
39. Interview with Joyce Crook, November 12, 2015
40. Guthrie, Ann, *Don Valley Legacy, A Pioneer History*, The Boston Press, 1986, 206
41. Interview with Nora Curran, June 5, 2017

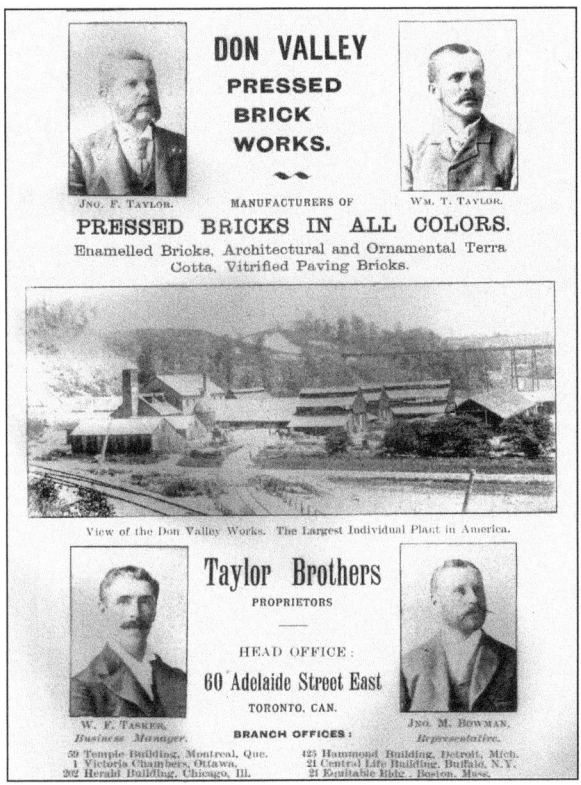

Brick Works Taylor Brothers
(Source: East York Foundation)

Brickworks Excavation #3
(Source: Toronto Archives)

Don Mills north from Gamble
(Source: Toronto Archives)

Bloor Viaduct Under Construction
(Source: Toronto Archives)

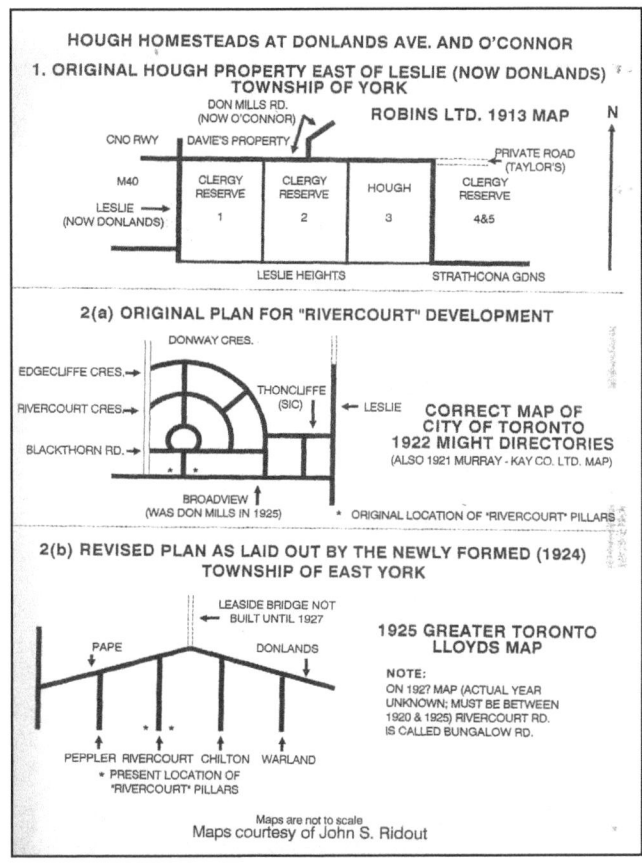

Rivercourt Development
(Source: Don Hough)

Rivercourt Pillars
(Source: Margaret McRae)

Todmorden Hotel
(Source: East York Foundation)

Blacksmith Shop
(Source: East York Foundation)

Gord Haslett
(Source: Panchetta Barnett)

Percy Bustin
(Source: East York Foundation)

358 Donlands (Leslie Street) 1910
(Source: East York Foundation)

358 Donlands (Leslie Street) Today
(Source: Margaret McRae)

12-14 Hassard Built by The Taylors
(Source: Margaret McRae)

Woodville Ave Looking West From Pape
(Source: East York Foundation)

Little York

In 1924, East York's other population and employment centre was Little York. Situated in the southeastern part of the new township, it was located in the area just north of the intersection of Dawes Road and the Danforth.

Dawes Road, named after the farmer and hotel keeper Clem Dawes, was only a cow path until the mid-nineteenth century, when it was officially recognized as a public road. Starting at Kingston Road near Main Street, it ran north across the Danforth, extending on an angle to Moffats Corners at St. Clair Avenue East and then farther north to L'Amoreaux at Finch Avenue in Scarborough. Victoria Park Avenue did not run north of the Danforth at that time. Later, when it was extended, Victoria Park was called the Township Line or the Boundary Line with Scarborough. [42]

In the late nineteenth century, the Grand Trunk Railway, whose line ran parallel to but south of the Danforth, established a round house and marshalling yard for as many as 420 railway cars in the Dawes Road area near its flag stop station of York, from which Little York derives its name. Settlement in Little York was of course spurred on by the jobs created by the Grand Trunk Railway nearby.

South of Little York was Coleman's Corner, a small settlement named for the first postmaster, Charles Coleman. Although it had several hotels and small shops, its proximity to Little York meant that they were usually considered one village. Ultimately, however, Coleman's Corner (but not Little York) was absorbed by its neighbour south of the Danforth, the Village of East Toronto. That was later annexed by the City of Toronto, leaving Little York in the Township of York, soon to become part of the new Township of East York. As the population of Dawes Road and the Secord area grew around it, Little York would soon lose its distinctive identity.[43]

The farms, market gardens, and brickyards in the area as well as the Grand Trunk freight depot provided jobs for the residents of Little York, Dawes Road, and Secord. The Chapman family and their cousins,

---

42. Milanish, Melanie, *Dawes Road: a Shortcut to the Market and a Natural Resource Base*, Self–Published paper, February 14, 2011
43. Brown, Ron, *Toronto's Lost Villages*, 40

the Newmans, started most of the brickyards. Phippen and Field bought the Chapman brickyard, where the Park Vista apartments stand today. J.E. DeLaplante purchased the Chapman yard north of that but Halsey Chapman continued to operate a brickyard on the present site of George Webster Public School at Cedarcrest and Gower, while the Newmans had a similar business where the Dentonia Park Golf course is now. [44]

More jobs became available when the farm implement manufacturer Walter Massey developed the 240-acre farm, which he named Dentonia Park farm, for his wife, Susan Denton. It extended from Dawes Road on the west to Pharmacy Avenue on the east and from the Danforth on the south to what became Crescent Town on the north. Here, Massey carried on the agricultural experiments that led to his discovery and production of a safe milk supply for the people of Toronto, milk which he distributed through his own company, City Dairy. Massey kept his herds of pedigreed cattle in a four-storey barn on the farm. All the milking attendants were required to wear white coats, while music was piped in to soothe the cows as they were being milked.[45] Verna King, a daughter of Cecilia Murphy, who grew up in a house at 13 Midburn Avenue, which was moved there from Jarvis Street, has vivid memories of the "Massey Estate before WWII, including the rose gardens and the beautiful goldfish pond. The fish were very big. Several of our neighbours on Midburn worked for the Massey family; the head gardener, an assistant to the head gardener, the chauffeur, and the nurse for the children."

Like Todmorden's Plains Road School, Little York had a school as well, roughly where Victoria Park Elementary School stands today. It had a student at this time who was destined to become the first governor general born in Canada, Vincent Massey.

Additional railway jobs were created when McKenzie and Mann's Canadian Northern Railway laid its rails through the Taylor Creek ravine, opening a ticket office on Midburn Avenue in the early years of the twentieth century. The extension of the Danforth streetcar line from Broadview to Luttrell Avenue was another impetus to population growth in the area because it provided easier access to jobs in Toronto. A lady who lived on Eastdale Avenue told me that before the streetcar line was

---

44. Dawes Road Library files on Dawes Road and Secord
45. Davidson, True, *The Golden Years of East York*, Centennial College Press, Toronto, 1976, 30

extended, she use to walk from Eastdale to Broadview every morning to catch the King streetcar to go to work downtown, and then do the same every evening when she came home.[46] The streetcar line made it much faster and much easier to get to work downtown or to the jobs at William Harris' Abattoir, known to East Yorkers as the "glue factory," at Danforth and Coxwell. In 1966, the street car line was replaced by the Bloor-Danforth Subway.

Still more jobs were created in the area by the Toronto Type foundry and the Toronto Hosiery Company on Balfour Avenue. [47] Then in 1921, the Ford Motor Company opened its assembly plant in the only part of East York south of the Danforth, west of Victoria Park Avenue. Later, Ford sold this plant to American Motors for the assembly of the Nash and the Rambler motor vehicles. This site, of course, was destined to become Shoppers World Danforth.[48]

Percy Bustin recalls, "In the early days, any idea of planning, or how the community should grow and develop in the future, was completely unthought of. When someone wanted to build a house, a store, a stable, or even a small factory, he just built it wherever he took the notion to build it. All a chap had to do was give old Joe Davis, the building inspector of those days, $2.00 for a building permit, and he could build wherever he liked, providing of course that it was not in the middle of the street. A good example of this is Dawes Road, which became a conglomeration of businesses and workshops, interspersed here and there with modest homes and small shops."[49]

The first streets to build-up in the Dawes Road area were Gower, Donora, Brenton, and Midland (now Midburn) Avenues. Halsey and Chapman Avenues are named after Halsay Chapman's brickyard, still operating in that location when East York was incorporated in 1924. Streets bounded by Sibley and Victoria Park Avenues, from Dentonia Avenue to the Danforth, were also built up around the same time. The earliest streets in the Secord area were Lumsden, Eastdale, Secord, Barrington Avenues, and Main Street.

---

46. Brown, Ron, *Toronto's Lost Villages*, 40
47. Dawes Road Library files on Dawes Road and Secord
48. Dawes Road Library files on Dawes Road and Secord
49. Bustin, Percy, *Memories: The Early Days of East York*, Self –Published, 1976, 8

In the middle of the nineteenth century, Danforth Avenue hotel owner Charles Gates developed the Newmarket Race Course in the area between the now Oak Park and Chisholm Avenues. The Queen's Plate was held at the Newmarket Race Course in 1868. Early residents of the Secord area "remember the race track still being in existence until 1920. At this time, it was either called Seagram's track or Newmarket Race Track. We believe, however, that Mr. Gates owned the track and let Seagrams stable and train their horses there."[50] According to others, Gates sold his race course to the whiskey distillers Seagram Bros. when the Woodbine Race Track was opened. Seagram's turned it into a racehorse stable with a miniature race track. "There was room for thirty to forty horses, which were being trained on the mile-long track. Jockey Alfi Nicholi used to exercise the horses."[51] The existence of the race track here explains why the present streets in that area—Newmarket, Epsom, Gatwick, Doncaster, and Crewe—are all named for famous race courses in England.[52]

The Secord area got its name "sometime between 1913 and 1923, when it was suggested that Johnson Street be renamed since there were already two other Johnson Streets in the city. This was causing confusion in the mail. Dave Harris, the assessor of the township, took a petition around to the neighbours suggesting they have the streets name changed to Laura Secord Avenue. The petition was signed and the name was changed. Many other street names were changed around this time. We can assume that the Secord Area, at that time, was just a collection of small homes and wooden houses. Inside, some were covered with tarpaper and most just had bare boards and studs." [53]

50. Dawes Road Library files on Dawes Road and Secord
51. Interview with Tom Carter, January 30, 2017
52. Interview with Tom Carter, January 30, 2017
53. Fagan, Lu Ann, *The Secord Area*, East York Board of Education, 1974, 30

Clem Dawes
(Source: google.ca)

Little York Station
(Source: Derek Bales-Toronto Railway Historical)

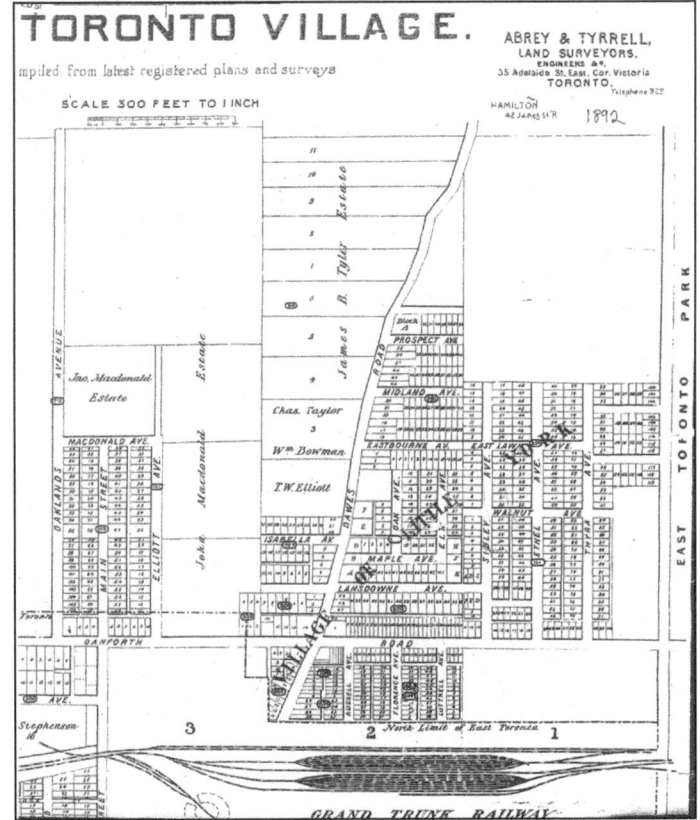

Map of Little York
(Source: Toronto Archives)

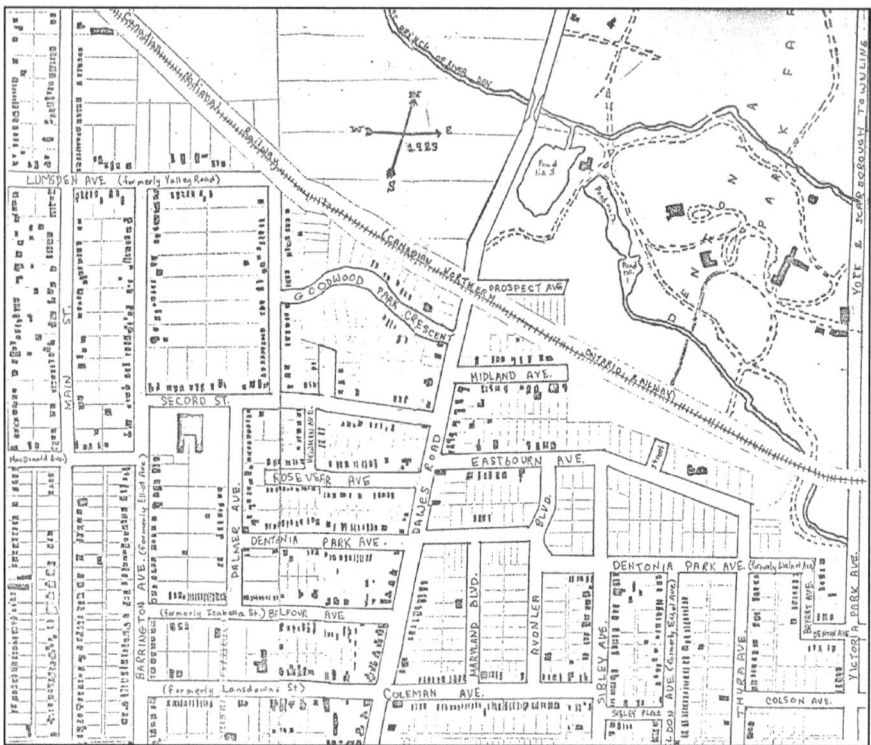

(Source: Lu Anne Fagan)

Dentonia Park Farm
(Source: East York Foundation)

City Dairy Delivery Horse and Covered Wagon
(Source: East York Foundation)

Massey Employee Home 6 Midburn
(Source: Margaret McRae)

William Newman_Sophie became Mrs Wooley 147 Dawes
(Source: East York Foundation)

The Centre

"Between these two built-up areas, Todmorden and Secord, the center of the township was still market gardens and vacant land yet to be subdivided for the thousands of homes to come. Coxwell Avenue came to a dead end at Sammon Avenue, where to the north, Billy McKay had a twenty-nine acre farm.

"Plains Road was the only through street to the north and was lined with market gardens. O'Connor Drive was yet unheard of and was the location of the Taylor family farm stretching all the way from Don Mills Road to Woodbine Avenue. It was not unusual to see fat pigs wallowing in mud holes close to the roadway."[54]

This was East York both prior to and at the time of its incorporation as a municipality.

---

54. Bustin, Percy, *Memories: The Early Days of East York*, Self –Published, 1976, 7

Schedule B

Market Gardeners in East York – 1920

Robert Barker	477 Cosburn Avenue
Joe Barron	
William Bell	269 Donlands Avenue
Robert Bell	269 Donlands Avenue
James Bell	269 Donlands Avenue
Len Bourne	
Tom Brayman	
John S. Bunce	15 Plains Road
Joe Byers	
Carwardine Bros.	988 Pape Avenue
James F. Clarke	
Fred J. Collins	328 Donlands Avenue
Cosburn Bros.	299 Donlands Avenue
George H. Curtis	85 Woodville Avenue
Herb L. Daniels	
William Daniels	
George Dart	
Joe Dart	302 Donlands Avenue
John Dart	8 Plains Road
William H. Dunn	
Ernest Elston	
William H. Jennings	289 Sammon Avenue
Chris Leaman	
Harold Magee	
James McCauley	1221 Donlands Ave. this may be an old Leslie Street number
R.H. McGregor	2 Cosburn Ave. & 261 Donlands Ave.
James Saunders	
James W. Sims	
Edward Smith	473 Sammon Avenue
Frank Smith	473 Sammon Avenue
Bernardo Somers	118 Donlands Avenue
William Stephenson	
William G. Tustin	639 Don Mills Road
William Ward	170 Aldwych Ave. and Don Mills
Percy Westwood	982 Broadview Avenue

– Chapter 3 –

LET THERE BE LIGHT – AND THE LIGHT APPEARED – THAT WAS THE FIRST DAY[1]

On New Year's Day, 1924, the first day that the brand-new township came into existence, rather than staying in bed to recover from their New Year's Eve celebrations, the voters of East York went to the polls to elect their first municipal council. Fourteen men ran for five council positions. Four of those elected that day had served previously on the Township of York Council: Reeve Robert Barker, First Deputy Reeve Robert H. (Bob) McGregor, Second Deputy Reeve John Galbraith, and Third Deputy Reeve Dennis McCarthy. The fifth person elected that day as councillor was Halsey W. Chapman, who at the time owned a brick yard where George Webster School stands today. He was the only new face. The election of Bob McGregor as first deputy reeve was immediately challenged and later set aside by a court order. The following was recorded in the minutes of the council meeting of March 3, 1924: "Pursuant to the order

---

1. Good News Bible, Chapter 1, Versc. 345

of the Master in Chambers which declared the seat of First Deputy Reeve vacant, as was noted in the minutes of February 14th. Statuary notice was given to the ratepayers for the filing of this office by the posting up of notices, etc., and nominations were received to fill the vacant office on February 23rd, 1924, which resulted as follows: Amos Allpress, John McDonald, R.M. Leslie and R.H. McGregor.

Messers, R.M. Leslie and J. McDonald resigned but there still being more candidates nominated than were required, a poll was opened on the 1st of March, which resulted as follows:

Number of votes cast for Mr. Allpress	130
Number of votes cast for Mr. McGregor	1096

Mr. McGregor being elected by a majority of 966."[2]

After the election, the councillors got right down to business. Meeting at 40 Jarvis Street, where the York Township Council also met, the new East York Council took up exactly where the York Township had left off the previous year by receiving petitions for better roads and sidewalks and for the installation of water mains, sewers, and street lighting.

Shortly after that first meeting, Council approved moving the Township Office to 443 Sammon Avenue, formerly the location of one of the Township of York's municipal works yards but now the yard of the newly incorporated Township of East York. It had a water tower, which made it readily identifiable to the residents. Later, this became the site of St. Aloysius Catholic School, later a Montessori School. Council also approved the standing bull-dog surrounded by a wreath of maple leaves as the township crest, but rejected the suggestion that the corporate status of the township should be changed to that of a town and that its name should be changed to Eastdale.[3] However, there were other more practical problems for the council to face. Where was the new township to get its water and hydro supply, and where could it dispose of its sewage? The city of Toronto was a logical answer, but when negotiations with

---

2. East York, Council Minutes, January 1924
3. East York, Council Minutes, January 1924

the City fell through, East York was forced to construct its own sewage disposal plant, establish its own hydro system, and buy its water from Scarborough.[4]

477 Cosburn_Reeve Robert Barker Home 1910 demolished 1950s
(Source: East York Foundation)

Council 1925
(Source: East York Foundation)

---

4. Davidson, True, The Golden Years of East York, Centennial College Press, Toronto, 1976, 67

Council 1926
(Source: East York Foundation)

Council 1927
(Source: East York Foundation)

EY original municipal office formerly Township of York's Works Yard
(Source: East York Foundation)

Water Tower Sammon Ave
(Source: East York Foundation)

Township Coat of Arms
(Source: East York Foundation)

During the short five-year period from the time of its incorporation until the 1929 crash, the new township experienced a period of rapid growth and incurred significant infrastructure expenditures in connection with the construction of the Todmorden and Leaside Bridge, East York Collegiate Institute, the Toronto East General Hospital, and the Woodbine Bridge.

A 1922 edition of the *Toronto Star* showed a sketch of a structure that would bridge the Don River from Leaside to Todmorden with an accompanying article under the sketch reading, "The above viaduct as large as the Bloor Street Bridge connecting Todmorden and Leaside may be erected by the Township of York. Last night the county engineer, Frank Barber, presented estimates of the cost of such a viaduct to a meeting of Todmorden taxpayers. The cost would be $870,000. Mr. Barber said the building of the viaduct would permit the development of a corner of Toronto's immediate suburbs sixteen miles in extent. It would connect the workmen of Todmorden with the factories of Leaside if Leaside was to become a great manufacturing district." [5]

Three years later, the East York Council approved the construction of the bridge based on an agreement that the cost was to be shared by five governments: the Province, the County of York, the City of Toronto, the Town of Leaside, and the Township. East York's share was to be 15%, which Council hoped to recover from land owned by Thorndale Securities Limited on the other side of the Don Valley.[6] Thorndale Securities didn't come through but the York Land Company, owner of a great deal of Leaside land, made a contribution to ensure that the bridge from which the company was sure to benefit, actually got built.[7] At the time, both Pape and Donlands Avenues came to a dead end at Don Mills Road (now O'Connor Drive), so both were extended north through the Smith farm to meet at the bridge, which was then constructed by Roger Miller and Sons Limited.[8] When it opened in 1927, the TTC celebrated the occasion by running double-decker buses back and forth across the span.[9]

---

5. Hough, D.S., *Some of My Memories of East York*, The East York Historical Society, 1992, 4
6. East York, Council Minutes, June 1925
7. Davidson, True, *The Golden Years of East York*, Centennial College Press, Toronto, 1976, 68
8. East York, Council Minutes, May 1926
9. Hough, D.S., *Some of My Memories of East York*, The East York Historical Society, 1992,

While the Todmorden and Leaside Bridge was under construction, the new township started to incur capital costs for its first secondary school, East York Collegiate Institute. The cornerstone of the school was laid in 1926 in a farm field that is now the north-east corner of Coxwell and Cosburn Avenues. It was built on five acres of Clergy Reserve land purchased for $3,800 an acre.[10] The lands from the present-day Donlands to Woodbine Avenues and from the present O'Connor Drive to Cosburn Avenue had been set aside as Clergy Reserve to be rented until sold.[11] The Clergy Reserves were tracts of land in both Upper and Lower Canada (now Ontario and Quebec) reserved for the support of Protestant clergy by legislation of the British Parliament called the Constitutional Act in 1791. These lands ultimately became provincial crown lands. Those in East York remained undeveloped for years, despite the fact that many homes were built right beside them. Before the collegiate opened, high school classes were held in the basement of Danforth Park School (now D.A. Morrison Middle School).[12] Billy McKay's farm was immediately south of the collegiate. Sometimes, he would discharge his rifle over the heads of students cutting across his fields to get to school.[13]

The 110-bed Toronto East General Hospital (now the Michael Garron Hospital) opened for business in 1929. It was built on five acres of land that Billy McKay had sold to the City of Toronto in 1924 for $8,000 an acre.[14] Since the land was located in East York but owned by the City, the Township agreed to allow Toronto to annex the five-acre site, which then became a virtual city island surrounded by East York.[15] Joe Harris, Member of Parliament, one of the Plains Road School boys taught by William Diefenbaker, spearheaded the hospital fund-raising drive. He negotiated the purchase of the property from Billy McKay and served as chairman of the hospital board for the next twenty years.[16] Joe Harris' father owned the "glue factory" at the corner of Coxwell

10. Hough, D.S., *Some of My Memories of East York*, The East York Historical Society, 1992, 6
11. Hough, D.S., *Some of My Memories of East York*, The East York Historical Society, 1992, 6
12. Hough, D.S., *Some of My Memories of East York*, The East York Historical Society, 1992, 12
13. Hough, D.S., *Some of My Memories of East York*, The East York Historical Society, 1992, 13
14. Bullard, Jason, *The Biggest Little Hospital East of the Don River: The History of the Toronto East General & Orthopedic Hospital Inc.*, Toronto East General Hospital Public Relations. 1994, 2, 3
15. East York Council Minutes, April 1927
16. Bullard, Jason, *The Biggest Little Hospital East of the Don River: The History of the Toronto East General & Orthopedic Hospital Inc.*, Toronto East General Hospital Public Relations. 1994, 5, 6, 4

and the Danforth, well known to East Yorkers at the time because of the odour that permeated the township air when the wind blew from the south.

Construction on the Woodbine Bridge started in 1929. Like the Todmorden-Leaside Bridge, it was built by the County of York. However, since it was entirely within East York, the township contributed a substantial share of the cost. The bridge was constructed by R.H. (Bob) McGregor's Malvern Construction Company. It was not until 1931 when the bridge was nearing completion that East York acquired actual road access to it when the Taylor family donated the land necessary to extend O'Connor Drive from Don Mills Road to the south end of the bridge. At the same time, the township also acquired the land necessary to extend Woodbine Avenue from Cosburn Avenue to meet O'Connor Drive at the new bridge. The road running east and north of the bridge was initially named the Woodbine Highway, but that was later changed to O'Connor Drive. When the Woodbine Bridge was planned, the Township Council expected it would immediately touch off new development north and east of the bridge, but because it opened for traffic during the Great Depression in 1932, development of the area was delayed considerably. The one exception, however, was the Woodbine Golf and Country Club, which was constructed shortly after the bridge opened in what is now Woodbine Gardens.[17]

Leaside Bridge Building
(Source: East York Foundation)

_____

17. Dolbey, Michael P., *A History of Woodbine Gardens*, Self-published. 2015

1311 Pape_Pine Grove Pk N of OConnor property divided to extend
Pape and Donlands (Leslie St) home still exists
(Source: East York Foundation)

Leaside - Bridge Opening
(Source: East York Foundation)

East General Hospital
(Source: wikimedia.org)

Woobine bridge
(Source: East York Foundation)

Bridges, high schools, and hospitals aside, what was life like for the people of East York during the 1920s?

Don Hough, who grew up in the Todmorden area during the 1920s, said, "On Plains Road, where I was born, and on Chilton Road, where we moved when I was two years old, we had no hydro, running water, sidewalks, or sewers until 1926... My brother and I slept in the cold attic... In the winter time, my father would heat up bricks in the oven, and then wrap them up in newspaper to put in our beds. We had no furnace. This worked fine until one night the bricks were too hot and the newspaper started burning. Saturday night was bath night, and the old tub was hauled into the kitchen and filled with pots heated on the stove and from a small water tank attached to the end of the stove. Being the youngest, I was always last and generally had to share the water used previously by another member of the family. I remember one summer day my mother was doing the washing on what would later be our front lawn, in a wooden washing machine, powered by hand. After the bluing had been put in and the last rinsing had been completed, she gathered me in her arms, as I had been playing in the mud, undressed me, and put me in the machine for a bath."[18]

Lawrence Main grew up at 254 Glebemount. His family emigrated from Scotland in 1919, settling in East York. During the next few years, his parents lived in rented houses on King Edward, Gledhill, Gamble, and

---

18. Hough, D.S., *Some of my memories of East York*, The East York Historical Society, 1992, 9

back to King Edward before buying a small bungalow at 254 Glebemount at the corner of Holbourne, where they stayed for the rest of their lives.[19] Bill Lewis had a similar experience growing up. His family moved every two years when they learned of a house with a lower rent.[20]

The two-bedroom bungalow, which housed the six members of the Main family, had no conveniences. Their outhouse was inside their garage because they had no car; that was better in the winter time and the neighbours thought they had indoor plumbing. All around their home at the time were open fields and bush land. Clothes were handed down from one of the boys to the other and were resewn to fit by Lawrence's mother. Across the street was a grocery store, where the Mains and their neighbours shopped every day because there was no refrigeration. But milk, bread, ice, and tea were delivered to their door by horse and sleigh in the winter and horse and wagon the rest of the year.

Since there were no school buses, everyone walked to school no matter how far away. If you wanted to bring your lunch to school, you had to have a note from home as to why. Otherwise, you walked home for lunch.

Lawrence remembers the large, open-air ice-skating rink at the corner of Woodbine and Cosburn. "The weather in those days was so cold that the township dumped a large load of horse manure from one of the many dairy horse barns at the side of the rink. When the skaters' feet got cold, they would sink their skates into the warm manure. Those skates had to be left outside for a day or two after an evening on the rink."

Lawrence would often accompany his mother to the township offices at Sammon Avenue to pay their tax and hydro bills. That meant they had to avoid Billy McKay's horses when they walked across his fields.[21] Lawrence and his mother weren't the only ones to have a run in with Billy McKay's horses. In 1924, a half hour after Percy Bustin, later an East York Councillor, opened his new drug store at the south-east corner of Sammon and Coxwell Avenues, he heard someone entering his shop. Happily, he went out front to greet his first customer, but instead he found a horse had stuck its head in the front door.[22] Stray horses were still a problem two years later when the Greenwood Woodbine Horticultural

---

19. Main, Lawrence G., *Growing Up in Old East York Township*, Self–published, 2013, 1
20. Interview with Bill Lewis, November 9, 2015, 4
21. Main, Lawrence G., *Growing Up in Old East York Township*, Self–published, 2013, 3
22. Bustin, Percy, *The Early Days of East York*, Self –Published, 1976, 1

Society complained to East York Council that the animals were destroying the lawns in the area.[23]

In those days, the Ontario Government created a "penny bank" for school children, located in downtown Toronto and open only on Saturdays. Lawrence's mother would take her children to the bank by streetcar to deposit their pennies in their accounts.[24] The Main children weren't the only ones making use of the penny bank. Joyce Crook, who grew up on Dilworth Crescent and attended the Earl of Kitchener Public School (later a teachers' college, still later part of Centennial College's East York campus but now town houses) at Pape and Mortimer, has vivid memories of it. She recalls lining up once a week with her classmates to give her teacher the pennies to deposit for them. On one occasion, Joyce handed her teacher a $10 bill given to her by her uncle. Her teacher was shocked and telephoned Joyce's mother for a satisfactory explanation.[25]

In the 1920s, flooded cellars were the norm rather than an exception. Every spring, the streets were a sea of mud. There was a joke that went around at the time like this: "When walking along Woodbine Avenue one spring day, one man passed another, and all he could see was the man's head and shoulders. 'Rough walking,' he said to the passerby. 'Walking!' replied the bloke. 'Who's walking? I'm riding a horse.'" [26]

After World War I, the southeast communities of East York, Little York, and Secord grew rapidly because of the demand for building lots by returning veterans. Some veterans were given their lots for free.

"Most built their own homes. Usually the owner would dig a basement, put a roof on it, and live in the basement until they could afford to add a first floor. Neighbours helped each other. They would build at night and on the weekends. A group of neighbours would start working in the morning to put up a temporary house. One of them would bring over a keg of beer to ease the job along. These temporary houses had only four rooms, made of wood and tarpapered inside and out. By 6:00 p.m. that same day, the family could move in. The houses were built at the rear of the lot because that left room for a permanent home to be built in stages at the front of the lot. Then the building in the rear could be converted to

23. East York Council Minutes, November 1926
24. Main, Lawrence G., *Growing Up in Old East York Township*, Self–published. 2013, 3
25. Interview with Joyce Crook by John Michailidis, East York Historical Society, Tidbits
26. Bustin, Percy, *The Early Days of East York*, Self –Published, 1976, 2

a garage. Sometimes a house was moved from one location to another on rollers pulled up the street by horses. There were very few brick houses built so the area was referred to as 'shacktown.'

"There were no sewers until the late 1920s, so these houses had outside toilet facilities. Often, three families would use the same outside pump for their water supply, but some were lucky enough to have a pump inside by the kitchen sink. Most houses had electric lighting but if not, they used gas or coal-oil lamps. Their stoves burned gas or coal. There were few telephones, so if you didn't have one, you visited a neighbour who did.

"There were a great number of corner and mid-block stores mixed in with the residential homes. They were mainly grocers, butchers, and confectionaries. Some people opened stores in the front portion of their homes. If it didn't succeed, they reconverted it. Many families lived above their store.

"Since there was no refrigeration, the iceman delivered huge blocks of ice cut from Lake Simcoe in the winter hauled by wagons drawn by two rather than one horse because of the weight of the ice. In the summer, because the ice melted more quickly, deliveries were every day. The dairies made similar deliveries with one-horse wagons most of the year, but with sleighs in the winter snow. They delivered not only milk but butter, eggs, and cheese as well. Everyone had a vegetable garden and used the road horse droppings as fertilizer.

"Until paved in the late 1920s, the roads were oiled to keep down the dust from the sand and gravel. Frequently, boys would come home covered in oil. The sidewalks were double wooden planks. If you slipped off, you became mired in thick, grey mud.

"The mailman delivered daily, including on Saturdays and Christmas Day.

"Surprisingly, there was a day-care facility for the children of women who had to work after losing their husbands in the war. Called the Danforth of East Toronto Day Nursery, it was located on Main Street in the building used by the Church of the Nazarene and provided care and hot meals for the children."[27]

---

27. Fagan, Lu Ann, *The Secord Area*, Self–Published, A Study under "Experience '74," sponsored by the Ontario Ministry of Education, 1974, 38

Another surprising event occurred at that time when the provincial Public Highway Department approved the placing of stop signals at the intersection of Victoria Park and Danforth Avenues, on condition that the light was to be in operation only on market days or on such days as there was heavy congestion of traffic. The cost was to be borne by the municipalities of East York and Scarborough. [28]

In 1929, Plains Road was the only street running across the township to Woodbine Avenue north of Cosburn. O'Connor Drive still ended at Don Mills Road. Coxwell Avenue came to a dead-end at Sammon Avenue, blocked from proceeding further north by Billy McKay's twenty-nine acre farm and by the Clergy Reserve.[29] Woodbine Gardens was farm land,[30] as was Topham Park, apart from the greyhound race track located there while Parkview Hills was still a Taylor family farm.[31]

Isolated on the west side of the Don Valley, linked to the rest of East York only by Pottery Road, was the farm land, market gardens, and orchards of Governor's Bridge and Bennington Heights. Governor's Bridge (formerly Rosedale Annex) derived its name from the residence, now demolished, of the Ontario lieutenant governor, just across the bridge in Chorley Park, north Rosedale. Although subdivided in 1912, it wasn't until 1923 that the first fifty homes were built there.[32] Governor's Manor, the grand, Elizabethan-style two-storey apartment building, constructed in the shape of a U on Douglas Crescent, was built in 1928.[33]

Although a young lawyer, Thomas Weatherhead, built a home there for his new bride Evelyn Bennington and himself in 1925, years passed before many more homes were built to replace the farms, orchards, and market gardens of Bennington Heights (formerly called Rosemount, then Moore Park Annex). Weatherhead became an East York school trustee and subsequently the solicitor for the township board of education. He persuaded East York Council to change the name of his street to Bennington Heights Drive in honour of his wife. Today, the entire area is known as Bennington Heights.[34]

---

28. East York Council Minutes, November 1929

29. Bustin, Percy, Memories: *The Early Days of East York*, Self –Published, 1976, 6

30. Dolbey, Michael P., *A History of Woodbine Gardens*, Self–published. 2015

31. Main, Lawrence G., *Growing Up in Old East York Township*, Self–published, 2013, 4

32. Interview with Gordon Sherk, February 19, 2014

33. Interview with Peter Weatherhead, April 5, 2013

34. Interview with Peter Weatherhead, April 5, 2013

The 1920s were good years for the township, but unbeknownst to East Yorkers, as the decade ended, extremely tough times were about to begin.

Coal Delivery
(Source: East York Foundation)

Ice Delivery
(Source: East York Foundation)

Moore Avenue Looking West From Bayview
(Source: East York Foundation)

– Chapter 4 –

THE LEAN YEARS

The Depression descended on the entire world like a prolonged eclipse of the sun. Unemployed East Yorkers who had purchased new homes with first, second, and even third mortgages were now in desperate straits.

The suffering of the residents in the Secord area was typical of that endured by the people of East York throughout the dirty thirties. Lu Ann Fagan described it as follows:

Perhaps the most difficult time the Secord Area has ever had to survive is the Depression. The Depression, which occurred between 1929 and 1939, was ten years of poverty for most people in this area.

The Depression began on October 29, 1929, in the New York Stock Exchange. For some reason, a panic occurred and people began to sell huge numbers of stocks. Nobody would buy the stocks so companies began to collapse as the money which had supported them, was taken away. As a result, there was a great scarcity of money all over the world. East York was very badly hit because most of its people were quickly laid off work. The City of Toronto had a general policy, such that it must try hardest to keep its own residents employed. Most East York people went into the *city to work and they were laid off before city residents. This community became poverty stricken with the majority of its workers unemployed. This terrible unemployment situation lasted for ten years.*

East York had to supply welfare to the unemployed and their families so a large burden was placed upon those people who were still working and who had to pay higher taxes. Those working also suffered a cut in income and lengthened hours.

During this time of hardship, people organized groups to protect their rights. There were groups of taxpayers, businessmen, workers, and home-owners. These groups were all very vocal at East York township meetings and thus, made these meetings lively affairs.

In April and May 1930, newspapers reported that the people of East York wanted the City of Toronto to annex the Township. This was quite a change from East Yorkers' former desire to be independent. It was based, however, on a desire to help the unemployed find jobs and to prevent further unemployment by making it impossible for the city companies to lay off East York men because they did not live in the city. But the City did not want the extra burden of supporting this very poor municipality with its high unemployment rate, and so, refused.[1]

In 1926, both the Townships of York and East York had demonstrated the desire of their residents to be independent by obtaining provincial legislation to prevent amalgamation with or annexation by the City of Toronto. But after the Depression struck, as their financial situation continued to deteriorate, their attitudes changed drastically because then both East York and York initiated negotiations for annexation by the city. East York's negotiator was its comptroller, Bill Heaton. In the end, however, the negotiators were unable to agree on terms acceptable to all parties. [2]

Lu Ann Fagan continues: "Welfare in those days was called 'relief,' and it was much less than today. People had to work for their relief checks. Two or three days' work would get a single man a relief voucher for a grocery order. Relief vouchers could not be used for alcohol or cigarettes. He would take this voucher to a storekeeper who would mark the items down and send a bill to the Township of East York.

---

1. Fagan, Lu Ann, *The Secord Area*, East York Board of Education, 1974, 90
2. Redway, Alan, *Governing Toronto: Bringing back the city that worked*, Friesen Press, 2014, 9, 10

"One man caught in the Depression unemployment recalls working at the Secord garbage dump. Men were paid twenty cents per day to shovel wheel-barrows of sand over the garbage. Although this was a ridiculously small sum, men were glad to work for so little. Pride would not allow them to accept relief without working in return. Today, the Stan Wadlow Club House is built on this same garbage dump. The actual dump was east of the arena about half way to Halden Avenue." [3]

There were many other garbage dumps in East York at the time. One was near Goodwood Park Crescent on which, tragically, babies were found lying dead because there was no money to bury them.[4]

Lu Ann Fagan goes on: "Where possible, men did relief work related to their trade. A shoemaker, for example, would repair the shoes of all the people on relief as his relief job, and a barber would cut their hair. One interesting measure taken by the township was to give men on relief plots of land near Oak Park School for gardens. These vegetable plots had two purposes: to cut down food costs, and to occupy the time of the unemployed men who otherwise felt useless, restless, and ashamed because they were taking relief money but had nothing to do. Gardens covered most of the backyards as well.

"This was a time of very low spirits among the people for the men were out of work for as long as ten years. People saw everything they had worked for so hard all their lives disappear. Houses remained half built because their owners could not buy building materials. Many people lost most of their savings when the Home Bank went bankrupt and could only pay its customers 25% of the money it owed them. The bank building still stands on the south-west corner of Main and Danforth. It is easily recognized, for the name 'The Home Bank' is inscribed in the stonework. A moratorium had to be called on all mortgages. This meant that homeowners had only the interest to pay, not the principal. But even so, many people could not pay and therefore lost their homes. Most had worked all through the 1920s to raise enough money to build these homes. To lose them was heartbreaking. Houses were left vacant while many houses contained two families, sharing the rent, because neither family could afford to live alone. Some men who had had a trade before

---

3. Fagan, Lu Ann, *The Secord Area*, East York Board of Education, 1974, 91
4. Davidson, True, *The Golden Years of East York*, Centennial College Press, 1976, 75

the Depression gave it up and never went back to it, because all energy had been drained from them. Families were commonly evicted from their homes. All in all, it was a dreadful time.

"People did survive all this by learning to 'make do' with what they had. Junk men collected old bits of garbage and put together gadgets and parts to sell second-hand to people who could not afford better things. People learned to repair cars and household items themselves, rather than call a repairman. Because relief only granted a small amount of heating coal, it was impossible to heat all the rooms in the house. Thus, much of daily living took place in the kitchen in winter as it was heated by the stove. In the cold of the morning, the family ran quickly downstairs from their icy bedrooms to the warm kitchen. Some unemployed men set up tarpaper shacks and lived in Taylor Creek Valley.

"If one member of a family had work, the income was stretched to feed everyone. The poverty shared by all created a sense of generosity in the people. People showed great goodwill, sharing and helping each other. This was the only way they could manage to get through and retain their good spirits. So there were some good times as well as some good deeds during the Depression. Secord Ladies Auxiliary raised money through card parties, and used it to supply clothing, boots and shoes to school children who otherwise could not have gone to school. Money was raised through many social occasions."

One shopkeeper of the 1930s was well known for his generosity. He sent his employees out to take food orders, because people could not afford telephones. Then the orders were made up and delivered. Each order had a free bag of candies as a Sunday treat for the children, who did not have many luxuries. Kids did not have things we would take for granted, like bicycles or summer camp, or even winter boots. As the Depression got underway, people began to charge all their groceries, and soon some people owed this grocer $200. Considering that a family of five could buy food for five dollars a week, this meant a family could buy forty weeks' worth of food on credit. Families from as far as Scarborough came to his store because their grocers did not have this policy. The grocer took out mortgages on homes and grew wealthy because he fed the people in this time of crisis.

During the Depression a strong atmosphere of co-operation existed. Everyone had a common problem or cause. Each person could sympathize with every other person to some extent. Even the sharp dividing line between the rich and the poor was weakened, for it would appear that the wealthy Massey family was affected by the Depression. Although the actual date has not been found, it seems that sometime around 1930, Mrs. Massey gave away a good deal of land to the City of Toronto, which she had previously planned to subdivide and sell for houses. Likely she gave it away because she could not sell during the Depression and it was a financial burden to her. To maintain the land and pay its taxes cost a lot of money and no one could raise enough to buy it. The City made the land into Dentonia Park. Mrs. Massey eventually sold the entire estate to a private boy's school called Crescent School. Crescent Town is on the property today.

So the wealthy Masseys and their servants probably had this much in common; that the effects of the Depression had changed the lives of both. A similar bond made it possible for wandering men, who travelled the country to seek employment, to ask for food at any back door. One lady tells how her mother never turned a hungry man away, even if it meant that her own family would be hungry. The spirit of sharing, of supporting others, was so strong that people denied themselves, and made meaningful sacrifices. This is one reason people can recall happy memories of the Depression. It was a time of warmth and caring.

As one man describes it, the Depression was a combination of good times and sadness. One of the saddest things was the feeling of shame people had when they were forced to go on relief. Attitudes were different at that time from those we hold today. A man took great pride in working to earn what he needed to support his family. Without work, he was ashamed to take money which, he felt, he did not deserve. Thus, people tried to hide, as much as possible, the fact that they were on relief.

As one lady told Lu Ann Fagan: "They felt disgraced by it. It was a disgrace." It was a disgrace, because unfortunately those lucky enough to be employed sometimes looked down at those on relief. Being on relief was referred to as being "On Pogie." The western part of the Secord Area was called "Pogie Palace," because there was cheap housing, and thus many families on relief lived there. It is very sad to think that aside from their great poverty, many people suffered from social disgrace, simply because they were unemployed." [5]

---

5. Fagan, Lu Ann, *The Secord Area*, Self–Published, A Study under "Experience '74," sponsored by the Ontario Ministry of Education, 1974, 94

Lawrence Main remembers "one family on Virginia Avenue who received an eviction notice. This fellow was a WWI veteran with a family of young children and the Legion Vets arrived that day dressed in their Legion uniforms, circled the house, and would not let the sheriff's men carry out the eviction. That's how desperate were those dark days." [6]

Another source told John Michailidis, "The veterans draped a Union Jack over the front door and sang 'God Save the King.' What choice did the bailiff have but to leave without evicting the family?"[7]

Jim Lister was born and grew up in a home built by his father Bill, a WWI veteran, at 270 Gledhill Avenue. His parents never told Jim until years later that, unable to pay their mortgage or taxes, they had lost ownership of the home to their mortgage company, Eaton's, in 1930. Jim never learned the truth at the time because the Lister family—father, mother, and six children—continued to live in that house until 1944 by renting it from Eatons for $15 a month.[8]

Johnny Brans, who made concrete blocks at the corner of Savoy and Cedarvale Avenues across the street from where Stan Wadlow Park and the Kiwanis Swimming Pool are today, was ineligible for relief because he had a business. Johnny, who immigrated to Canada from Holland, had the consul general of the Netherlands intervene on his behalf to request the Township Council to reconsider his case. Council refused to do so.[9] When Jack Freer, the barber at the corner of Woodbine and Cosburn Avenues, learned of Johnny's dire straits, he lent him $5,000 with interest at 8% on merely a handshake, no promissory note, nothing in writing at all. After the economy improved, Johnny repaid Jack the entire amount plus interest at 8.5%. [10]

In addition to the Secord Ladies Auxiliary, many other East York organizations provided help to families on relief, including the Danforth Park Welfare Association, the Todmorden Welfare Association, the McGregor Welfare Association, the Donlands Cosburn Business Men's Association, the East York Business Men's Association, Branch 10 Royal Canadian Legion Ladies Association, the Branch 11 Royal Canadian

---

6. Main, Lawrence, *Growing Up in Old East York Township*, Self–published, 2013
7. Michailidis, John, East York Historical Society, Tidbits, September 2006
8. Interview with Jim Lister, October 19, 2015
9. East York Council minutes, December 1937
10. Interview with Jack Freer, August 18, 2016

Legion Ladies Association, Branch 22 Royal Canadian Legion Ladies Association, and the Dawes Road Veterans and Ratepayers Association.[11]

While East Yorkers were suffering in this way, the Township was going bankrupt. East York Council had been going merrily along building new roads, sewers, and schools and financing them by borrowing secured by debentures (municipal bonds). Now the township was forced to default on its debenture payments.

On November 14, 1933, East York Council applied for the appointment of a board of supervisors. That was a polite way of saying that East York was bankrupt. It was not alone. During the Great Depression of the 1930s that followed the stock market crash, thirty-six Ontario municipalities were bankrupt, including Scarborough, Leaside, Long Branch, Mimico, New Toronto, Etobicoke, York Township, North York, and Weston. Each had defaulted on their debt payments and all applied to the Ontario Municipal Board to appoint a committee of supervisors to manage their financial affects. The City of Toronto, Forest Hill Village, and the Village of Swansea were the only Toronto area municipalities to escape bankruptcy at that time.[12]

By 1935, 46% of the property owners in the Township of East York were unemployed and receiving relief (welfare) assistance paid to the recipients not by the federal government nor by the provincial government, but rather from the real estate property taxes of the municipality in which the unemployed worker resided. It goes without saying that these unemployed home owners were unable to pay their property taxes, so in the case of East York, 54% of the home owners were paying for 100% of municipal services, including relief for the 46% unemployed. No wonder East York went bankrupt.[13]

The time spent under provincial supervision was not easy. On one occasion, one of the township school boards threatened to resign en masse rather than cut teachers' pay another 6.5% as ordered by the Board of Supervisors after having been required the previous year to cut the teachers 7% and their other employees 10%. The savings from that additional pay reduction would have amounted to only fifty cents per

11. East York Council minutes, 1929-1939
12. Redway, Alan, *Governing Toronto: Bringing back the city that worked*, Friesen Press, 2014, 40
13. Redway, Alan, *Governing Toronto: Bringing back the city that worked*, Friesen Press, 2014, 11

person. On another occasion, Council was forced to discontinue some small extra payments to the unemployed in order to get the Board of Supervisors to release pay cheques for township employees. [14]

As time went on and the situation worsened, a feeling of panic set in. In response to this dreadful situation, two hundred people met in a local school and founded the East York Workers Association a few months later. [15] The association membership, which reached 1600, was bolstered by the day to day contacts of relief recipients in the welfare office and by socialists such as Arthur Williams, who became the president of the organization in 1933.[16]

From then on, Williams was the East York Workers Association. Its main business of course, was the never-ending struggle for food, clothing and shelter. Endless deputations to the Township Council complained that the heating allowance was inadequate; that the hydro was being cut off to relief recipients in arrears of their bills; that the clothing depot would give each person only one suit of underwear; that the only dental treatment allowed relief recipients was extractions; and that the relief investigator had rotten manners.[17]

Percy Bustin described some of those council meetings this way: "Deputations both vociferous and boisterous often packed the chamber, with more standing than sitting, and never was this more so than during the Depression of the thirties. To the deputation's way of thinking, the council, and the council alone, were responsible for all their troubles and for the state of the country in general. On many occasions, the reeve threatened to call the police, located next door in the same building, and have the deputation thrown out onto the street. On one occasion, it actually became necessary to read the Riot Act." [18]

Bustin doesn't identify when or where the Riot Act was read, but Reee Rupe Leslie's grandson Marshall says that it took place at the reeve's home on Rivercourt Boulevard. He had received a warning

---

14. Davidson, True, *The Golden Years of East York*, Centennial College Press, 1976, 82
15. Schulz, Patricia V., *The East York Workers' Association: A Response to the Great Depression*, New Hogtown Press, Toronto, 1975
16. Schulz, Patricia V., *The East York Workers' Association: A Response to the Great Depression*, New Hogtown Press, Toronto, 1975, 4
17. Schulz, Patricia V., *The East York Workers' Association: A Response to the Great Depression*, New Hogtown Press, Toronto, 1975, 4
18. Bustin, Percy, *Memories: The Early Days of East York*, Self –Published, 1976, 8

from a Rivercourt neighbour, the brother of Tim Buck, the leader of the Communist Party of Canada, that a lynch mob was headed to his house aimed at hanging the reeve. According to Marshall Leslie, his grandfather and three of his children, two boys and a girl, all armed with four-inch wrenches because Reeve Leslie was a plumber by trade, stood on his front porch and faced the mob, which disbursed quietly after the reeve read the Riot Act. [19]

The Riot Act is a proclamation set out in the Canadian Criminal Code that can be used when twelve or more people engage in an unlawful assembly that has begun to disturb the peace tumultuously and violently. It can be delivered by a justice, mayor, reeve, sheriff, or head of a correctional facility. That person is required to step as near as is safe before the crowd, and after determining that a riot is in progress, in a loud voice command silence and then read the proclamation: "His Majesty the King charges and commands all persons being assembled to disperse and peaceably to depart to their habitation or their lawful place of business on pain of being guilty of an offense for which on conviction they may be sentenced to imprisonment for life. God Save the King." Originally, the penalty was death. The crowd had thirty minutes to disburse or face the penalty.[20]

One might wonder why Tim Buck's brother would warn Reeve Leslie. Marshall Leslie says that his grandfather looked after the plumbing at the Communist Party's headquarters on Cecil Street in Toronto. As such, the reeve, although not a party member himself, was well acquainted with all the leading members of the Canadian Communist Party.[21] After Tim Buck was released from jail in 1934, he stayed at 181 Glebemount, Bob Murphy's grandfather's home. Bob's grandfather, Edward Murphy, picked Buck up that day and drove him to his home in East York, where he was welcomed by two boys, Bob's father and a neighbour's lad, singing the Communist anthem, "The Internationale." The future East York Councillor George Treadway lived next door at 183 Glebemount at that time.[22]

---

19. Interview with Marshall Leslie, March 23, 2017
20. The Canadian Criminal Code, 1933
21. Interview with Marshall Leslie, March 23, 2017
22. Interview with Bob Murphy, May 31, 2017

"Municipal elections were a free-for-all, citizens turned out by the hundreds and blew off steam. We remember one time an irate citizen threatened to mount the platform and tear a candidate apart, and the chairman banged his gavel so hard, its head flew off and just missed the bloke raising the rumpus. The pay for councillors those days was $4.00 per meeting, and the joke around town was that whenever they ran short of cash they called a meeting." [23]

In the squeeze between rising relief costs, pressure for increased benefits, and an insufficient tax base, the East York Council tried to cut costs. At first, they proposed a reduction of 10% in wages for all township employees who earned over $35 a week. That plan was dropped at that time but, two years later when the financial situation became desperate, all salaries were cut by 10%.

Next, Council tried to reduce costs with a plan to have the Township employees share the existing work by laying off thirty workers and rotating one thousand unemployed men through the thirty jobs. That would have averaged 1.2 hours of work per week for each man. Later, Council proposed laying off all of the township garbage collectors and roads employees and replacing them with relief recipients, to be paid only their relief allowances. The savings would have been substantial because the higher levels of government would have contributed eighty of the cost. However, the East York workers' representatives on Council opposed this, on the basis that not only would working people lose jobs, but working for the paltry relief was totally unjust. That plan was dropped.

Another source of pressure on the Township Council was the bank, which periodically threatened to close out their overdrafts. In January 1933, the Township overdraft amounted to $294,000. The bank would only allow that to continue if the Township practiced stringent economies. East York debentures (bonds) were trading on the market at this time from 35–65 cents on the dollar. The major source of pressure came from the Province through its appointed supervisor, A. J. B. Gray. He had to approve every expenditure East York Council made, and he was tough.

A Provincial technique for cost cutting was to tell the East York Council to persuade its unemployed to leave the township. There were several such provincial schemes. One was the back-to-land movement.

---

23. Bustin, Percy, Memories: *The Early Days of East York*, Self –Published, 1976. 8

The land selected for the East York participants in this provincial project was near Cochrane, midway between Sudbury and Moose Factory. The settlers hoped, after three years of work, to have title to eighty acres of land. Twenty-five families left the township. The men went first to build the log cabins for their families. Farming there was a disaster. Some came back almost immediately, only to be condemned as quitters by those who stayed.

Another problem for the Township during the "dirty thirties" involved the 450 men living in the brick kilns on the Don Flats. Some were transients riding the rails from place to place who stayed there only because the camp was close to the railroads. Others lived there for longer periods. A group of Finlanders joined the camp when the construction jobs that brought them to Toronto failed to materialize. After the township ordered the destruction of the camp, most of the men left for the highway construction camps up north, although a few were moved to Exhibition Grounds. The police broke up the brick huts and burned the wooden structures. One tree house was demolished, along with shelters built in the trestles of the Governor's and Moore Avenue bridges. Two weeks later, a group of Bulgarians tried to resettle the area. "The only one who could speak English told the officers they had no place to go and had been turned down for work on the Trans-Canada Highway, but the police told the men they could not remain so they packed and left." Leaving the township was a potential solution for only a small minority of families, but judging by the experiences of those that did leave, it was not an attractive alternative. For those who remained in the township, the struggle for survival went on.[24]

From the western edge of the Don Valley in Governor's Bridge, Gordon Sherk, who lived there most of his life, recalls, "In the ravine on the east side of the tracks the valley housed a well-known and well established 'Hobo Jungle.' The residents had their own village set up— shelters built from tar paper, packing boxes, and bits of lumber. The train travelling in cold weather required a lot of coal to get up enough steam for the steep grade ahead. The train workers managed to 'spill coal' onto the tracks near the hobo village and the villagers would soon have fires going.

---

24. Schulz, Patricia V., *The East York Workers' Association: A Response to the Great Depression*, New Hogtown Press, Toronto, 1975, 6

The hobos would come up the hill and receive sandwiches and other food from the residents. My mother was a participant—until my father's shirts went missing from the clothes line." [25]

"The Workers Association tried to persuade East York Council to change relief payments from vouchers to cash. The Province pressured municipalities to issue vouchers for food and goods instead of providing relief recipients with cash. With vouchers, the Province believed that relief recipients would make better use of their assistance by obtaining basic food, clothing, and shelter necessities and not frivolous items. The Workers Association favoured cash relief payments because it would provide recipients more choice to purchase goods from any retailer they thought fit. Relief vouchers were accepted by a handful of retailers and the relief recipients frequently complained that such retailers did not offer the best prices or quality products. In addition, the Association argued that cash relief was a more dignified method of purchasing products and paying in cash boosted the morale and self-worth of relief recipients.

"In November 1935, after consulting with the Province, the Township Council agreed to change relief payments from vouchers to cash, but the cash payments were at a reduced rate, effectively reducing the amount of products a family could purchase. Upset with the Township's decision to reduce relief payments, the Workers Association called a strike of employable relief recipients. To receive relief, employable males were required to work at the Township's parks. The work involved shovelling dirt from one end of a park and the next day shovelling the dirt back." [26]

Jim Lister, a young boy at the time, remembers that well. "One of the projects was leveling the grounds of Cedarvale Park (now Stan Wadlow Park). Small steel buckets on wheels were run on tracks and when filled with dirt, were dumped over the side of the valley, into the present Park area. There was a wading pool at the bottom of the hill, and during the early 1950s the whole side of this hill slid down into the Park burying the wading pool." [27]

East York Council's response to the strike was to revert to the voucher system for relief benefits. The Workers Association introduced another

---

25. Interview with Gordon Sherk, February 19, 2014

26. Michailidis, John, East York Historical Society, Tidbits, September 2006

27. Interview with Jim Lister, October 19, 2015

tactic to pressure the Township to revert to cash relief. The association asked its members to pull their children out of school in the township. At that time, the Province's education grants were based on the number of students attending school each day. With thousands of families pulling kids from school, the Township would receive less Provincial money for education. On November 13, 1935, the council reluctantly reinstated cash relief. However, before it could be implemented, the bank stepped into the fray. The Bank of Nova Scotia refused to grant a loan to the Township without the province guaranteeing the loan payments. Without the guarantee, the Township could not receive a loan; thus, it did not have the money to provide cash relief. That spelled the end of the program.

Although the cash instead of voucher strike was a failure, the action of the Workers Association did draw enough sympathy for the unemployed to have the Association's president, Arthur Williams, elected reeve of the township in December 1935.

Since Williams was more than three months in arrears of his rent, the first task of the newly elected reeve was to defend his right to the office. In April 1935, a few months before the December municipal elections, the Provincial government passed legislation prohibiting anyone from holding public office who was more than three months in arrears of their rent. Many of the township's residents were enraged at the thought of holding another election for reeve. The issue was settled when another election was scheduled, but since no one but Williams declared their intent to run, a second election was not held and Williams was acclaimed reeve of the township. It's not certain how the Province sidestepped its own law prohibiting Williams to hold public office." [28]

Arthur Williams' time as reeve was short lived, however. One year later, he was defeated at the polls by the same reeve that he defeated the year before, Jack Warren.[29]

Don Hough remembered Arthur Williams this way: "Arthur Williams was elected as reeve, and was a Socialist. He had two low-cost houses built on the west side of Pape Ave. between Woodville and Torrens, and another one at the southeast corner of Greenwood and Memorial Park.

---

28. Michailidis, John, East York Historical Society, Tidbits, September 2006
29. East York Council Minutes, 1934, 1935, 1936

The latter was occupied by Fred Brown, disposal plant foreman. During this period, the Conservatives were turfed out of power in East York."[30]

By the end of 1937, the Township's relief rolls dropped by nearly half from 8,000 in December 1936 to 4,700 in December 1937. With the end of the Depression in sight, the need for the Workers Association dwindled.[31] "The Depression ended with the onset of the Second World War in 1939. Most of the younger unemployed men were needed to be soldiers. Their wives received money from the government and great spending sprees took place. In fact, labour became scarce."[32]

Unemployed Workers Shack on Don Valley
(Source: East York Foundation)

---

30. Hough, D.S., *Some of My Memories of East York*, The East York Historical Society, 1992, 4

31. Michailidis, John, East York Historical Society, Tidbits, September 2006

32. Fagan, Lu Ann, *The Secord Area*, Self–Published, A Study under "Experience '74," sponsored by the Ontario Ministry of Education, 1974, 94

Unemployed Workers Shack on Don Valley
(Source: East York Foundation)

Makeshift Dwellings 2
(Source: East York Foundation)

Jim Lister
(Source: Jim Lister)

24 Savoy Ave. owned by Johnny Brans
(Source: East York Foundation)

Council c1930
(Source: East York Foundation)

Tim Buck (C L) at Maple Leaf Gardens
(Source: Toronto Archives)

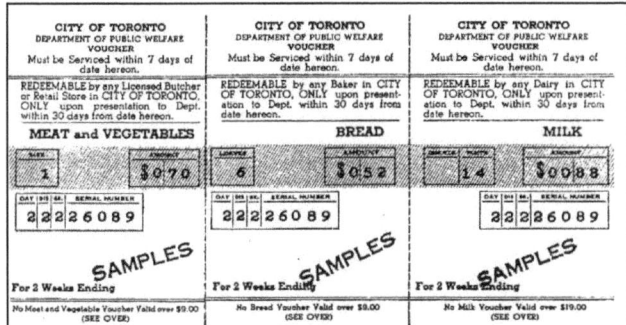

CITY OF TORONTO	CITY OF TORONTO	CITY OF TORONTO
DEPARTMENT OF PUBLIC WELFARE	DEPARTMENT OF PUBLIC WELFARE	DEPARTMENT OF PUBLIC WELFARE
VOUCHER	VOUCHER	VOUCHER
Must be Serviced within 7 days of date hereon.	Must be Serviced within 7 days of date hereon.	Must be Serviced within 7 days of date hereon.
REDEEMABLE by any Licensed Butcher or Retail Store in CITY OF TORONTO, ONLY upon presentation to Dept. within 30 days from date hereon.	REDEEMABLE by any Baker in CITY OF TORONTO, ONLY upon presentation to Dept. within 30 days from date hereon.	REDEEMABLE by any Dairy in CITY OF TORONTO, ONLY upon presentation to Dept. within 30 days from date hereon.
MEAT and VEGETABLES	BREAD	MILK
1 $0.70	6 $0.52	14 $0.88
22 22 26089	22 22 26089	22 22 26089
SAMPLES	*SAMPLES*	*SAMPLES*
For 2 Weeks Ending	For 2 Weeks Ending	For 2 Weeks Ending
No Meat and Vegetable Voucher Valid over $9.00 (SEE OVER)	No Bread Voucher Valid over $8.00 (SEE OVER)	No Milk Voucher Valid over $19.00 (SEE OVER)

By 1935 over 45% of East York's population
was on relief. The Workers' Association
won a major victory in forcing a change
from vouchers, such as these, to a
direct cash food allowance.

The CCF caucus of the Ontario legislature in 1943. Arthur Williams, a
president of the East York Workers'
Association and reeve of the township
in the 1930s, is in the middle.

CCF Caucus 1935; 2nd row centre – Arthur Williams
(Source: google.ca)

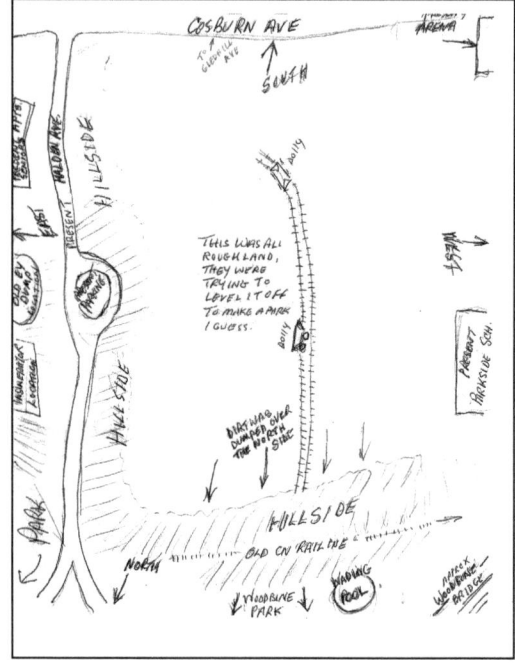

Jim Lister Map
(Source: Jim Lister)

Jim Lister Work Dollys
(Source: Jim Lister)

East York Council - 1938-39
(Source: East York Foundation)

Governor's Bridge Community 1939
(Source: Toronto Archives)

– Chapter 5 –

BILLY McKAY

During the Great Depression of the 1930s, the Township of East York acquired ownership of a great deal of land because the previous owners, now unemployed, could not afford to pay their property taxes. Billy McKay's farm made up a substantial part of the land that the Township claimed for unpaid taxes.[1]

Billy raised pigs and horses on the three parcels of farm land he had purchased from Mr. Clendennan, Mr. McMichael, and the Manufacturers Life Insurance Company in 1891.[2] In 1921, because of the need for a school in the area, R.H. (Bob) McGregor (one of William Diefenbaker's students at Plains Road school, now the Secretary-Treasurer of Section Seven of the York Township Public School Board), arranged on behalf of the board to purchase one entire parcel (Block A) from Billy for the sum of $35,707. The school subsequently built on that land was named the R.H. McGregor Public School.[3] Soon after, Billy sold another small

1. Bustin, Percy, *The Early Days of East York*, Self –Published, 1976, 4
2. Michailidis, John, Research, 2006
3. Deed dated May 20, 1921, registered July 25, 1921 as Instrument 13776, York

strip of his land to the Township of York to be used to extend and widen Mortimer Avenue as far as its present intersection with Coxwell Avenue.[4] At that time, Coxwell dead-ended at Sammon Avenue.[5] The extension of Mortimer essentially allowed access to the new school from both Mortimer and Sammon Avenues.

The area also lacked a hospital as there wasn't one east of the Don River at that time. Therefore, a number of the residents east of the Don formed the Toronto East General Hospital Association, chaired by Joe Harris, another one of William Diefenbaker's students at Plains Road School, now a Member of Parliament. In 1925, after Mr. William Hill had passed away, leaving his entire estate of $40,000 to be used for the construction of a hospital in the east end of the city, Joe Harris persuaded the city of Toronto to buy and Billy McKay to sell 5.029 acres of his farm north and east of Sammon at the dead end of Coxwell Avenue for $8,000 an acre.[6] At the same time, Billy donated a further 1.5 acres of his farm land to the city for the hospital site.[7]

The remainder of Billy's farm, 45.10 acres, composed of blocks B, C, and lot 9, lay smack in the centre of the township of East York between Little York and Secord on the east and Todmorden on the west. In 1926, Billy appealed an increase in the assessment on his farm. The Township Council, presided over by Reeve R.H. (Bob) McGregor, sitting as a court of assessment revision, refused his appeal. Then Billy offered to sell the land to the township for $1,000 an acre. Deputy Reeve Rupe Leslie immediately took him up on the offer. Council had a resolution drawn up and a cheque made out to buy the land, but Billy backed out and refused to sell.[8]

Frustrated, not only on this occasion but on numerous others as well, by Billy's refusals to accept the Township's offers to buy at least enough of his land to extend Coxwell Avenue from its dead end at Sammon Avenue north to Cosburn, East York Council reassessed Billy's farm as industrial land, resulting in a significant increase in his taxes. Understandably, Billy

---

4. Deed dated July 12, 1921, registered August 16, 1921 as Instrument 138503, York

5. Bustin, Percy, Memories: *The Early Days of East York*, Self–Published, 1976, 5

6. Spalding, Jean, *Sunrise to Sunset, The History of TEGH*, School of Nursing, Centennial College Press, 1978, 2

7. Deed dated November 24, 1924, registered December 20, 1924 as Instrument 3180, Township of East York

8. *Toronto Daily Star,* May 22, 1926

considered this unjust and refused to pay his property taxes, even after they had gone into default.[9]

According to the widely believed story (or hearsay), Billy fell in love with a Miss Gowan, a teacher at Plains Road School.[10] Although he didn't know her, he built a red brick house for her on the north side of Sammon, west of Knight Street, and bought her a diamond ring.[11] Billy went up to Miss Gowan, telling her that they were going to be married that Saturday. Shocked, of course, she turned him down.[12] Apparently, he was equally shocked at her refusal and never moved into that house, but instead moved into the barn behind it. It was said that the rejection of marriage changed Billy from a friendly and generous person who loved children to one who would chase kids cutting across his property on their way to school, threatening them with his shotgun.[13]

Miss Anne Brown described her encounter with Billy this way: "As a small child, I crossed his fields to go to R.H. McGregor School. He gave a right-away for a dirt road, to be used for access to the school. We were warned to stay on the road only. My only encounter with Billy was when I took a short cut to school. The other children using the road were shouting and pointing. When I got to the top of the rise, there was Billy, crouched by the fence with his rifle across his arm. Walking past him, my heart pounding, he said to me, 'You better run, little girl, or you will be late for school.' I never ran so fast in my life."[14]

From that time on, Billy could be seen wandering the township looking like a tramp in old overalls, work boots, and hat. He neglected his farm and refused to pay his property taxes so the township claimed his land for the arrears.[15]

The Toronto Humane Society took Billy to court for ill-treating his horses and pigs. An inspector testified at the hearing as to the filth and neglect of his animals. Billy requested an adjournment, telling the court, "I have been sick and my boy is sick." The magistrate, having granted

---

9. *Toronto Daily Star*, June 27, 1937
10. Interview with Colleen Peacock, January 31, 2017
11. Michailidis, John, Research, 2006
12. Interview with Colleen Peacock, January 31, 2017
13. Michailidis, John, Research, 2006
14. Letter to Colleen Peacock, 160 Queensdale Avenue from Mrs. Anne Brown, 100 Dunkirk Road, dated December 11, 2000
15. Michailidis, John, IResearch, 2006

him four previous adjournments, refused his request and gave him a suspended sentence.[16]

Finally, his neighbours reported to the township health officials that there was a horrible smell coming from his barn. The Toronto East General Hospital superintendent said the atmosphere was unbearable whenever there was an east wind and that they had been putting up with it for seven or eight years.[17] In the past, according to the health department, when they tried to enter his property, Billy had chased them away with pitchforks, but this time they found him asleep in the barn beside a pile of manure and a dead horse. Another horse had to be shot dead and five other malnourished ones were sent to the Humane Society.[18] Although rumour had it that Billy was dead, he was actually admitted to the Lakeshore Psychiatric Hospital in New Toronto.[19] Shortly after, before health officials could demolish it, his barn mysteriously burned down.[20]

Now that Billy was in a psychiatric hospital, the Ontario government's public trustee had the responsibility to administer his assets. Almost immediately, they commenced discussions with East York Council concerning Billy's farm. But the township that had defaulted on its own debt four years earlier, was then under bankruptcy supervision by Alfred Gray of the Ontario Department of Municipal Welfare and could make no financial decisions without Mr. Gray's approval. As a result, one Ontario government department was discussing Billy's farm with another Ontario government department.[21]

The public trustee asked the municipality to delay any action with respect to Billy's farm for three months and possibly longer in order that it could investigate the possibility of selling the farm and paying the outstanding property taxes. Mr. Gray, however, was emphatic that two parcels, block B and lot 9, had been registered in the name of the Township over a year ago. Billy, having failed to arrange a settlement of his tax arrears during that year, had in accordance with the provincial legislation, lost all right to redeem and regain ownership of those parcels of land.

16. *Toronto Daily Star*, December 8, 1936
17. *Globe and Mail*, May 18, 1937
18. *Globe and Mail*, May 18, 1937
19. *Globe and Mail*, May 18, 1937
20. Michailidis, John, research
21. Internal Memorandum of the Public Trustee dated June 21, 1937

In addition, Mr. Gray told the public trustee that he was instructing East York Council to immediately register on title a plan to extend and widen Coxwell to Cosburn; to widen Mortimer west of Coxwell; and to register block C in the township's name for property tax arrears. He concluded there was no hope of a compromise of any sort with Mr. Gray, who was proceeding strictly in accordance with Ontario government law.[22] However, Gray did agree to let the public trustee have the opportunity to buy back the property on behalf of Billy if satisfactory arrangements could be made.[23] The public trustee tried to sell block C, but could not find a buyer.[24] It must be remembered that these events were happening during the Great Depression of the 1930s and that Mr. Gray's mandate from the Ontario government was to put the Township on a sound financial footing as quickly as possible.

Reeve John Warren and the Township Council wasted no time in complying with Mr. Gray's instructions, including his instructions to prepare and register a plan for subdividing the property as well as closing Lumsden Avenue and opening and extending Mortimer to Glebemount.[25] A month and a half after that, the township registered the Notice of Tax Arrears.[26]

Five years later, in 1942, according to a report received by the Public Trustee:

All property which was owned by Billy McKay has been built up and cut up into new streets and extension of other streets, and also a portion at the rear of the East General Hospital has been taken in to their grounds, extending their property to Mortimer Avenue. On the North West corner of Coxwell Avenue and Mortimer Avenue, the Township of East York has set aside a large block consisting of probably four or five acres for a new park. This has been planted with shrubs and trees and they have their sign on it. All to the North and East of Coxwell Avenue and on Coxwell Avenue, it is practically built up solid with new houses,

22. Internal Memorandum of the Public Trustee dated June 23, 1937

23. Letter to D. Tucker, Acting Clerk of the Township from the Assistant to the Supervisor, Alfred Gray, dated June 26, 1937

24. Letter to the Public Trustee from George A. Lister Real Estate Appraiser dated March 10, 1938

25. *Toronto Daily Star*, June 27, 1937

26. Note of Registration addressed to Wm. McKay c/o of Public Trustee, Osgoode Hall, Toronto dated August 11, 1937 signed by D. Tucker acting Treasurer

the majority of which are four and five roomed bungalows, probably built on the Government Plan. The only vacant land left which was owned by the above noted is a small section at the north end of Coxwell Avenue, just South of Cosburn Avenue and they are now building in the district at the present time. New houses are extending up Coxwell Avenue and will eventually take in this vacant property. The only piece that appears to have been left alone is the small piece of land east of the East General Hospital, fronting on Sammon Avenue, where the patient lived in the old barn which was demolished by the East York township Department. At the rear of this site was his sand pit which is now being filled in. This property may still be in the name of East York. Block "C" which is composed of 16.65 acres at the corner of Glebemount and Sammon Avenues has all been built in solid. Apparently all the property belonging to the patient has been disposed of except the small portion east of the East General, which was used by the patient as living quarters.[27]

Billy McKay's red brick house, later demolished, became the intern's residence at the East General. [28]

Percy Bustin, the pharmacist at the south-east corner of Coxwell and Sammon, later an East York Councillor, wrote in 1976, "The opening of Coxwell Avenue North was, however, a boon for some smart home-builders, who were able to buy building lots fronting on the new street for fifteen dollars a foot, unbelievable but true. Today, the same frontage is worth fifty times that much."[29]

According to the East York Council minutes, the township sold those building lots to four different members of the Lankins family, A. J. Baldwin, W. H. Brown, T. W. Oliver, G. Robertson, F. Turton, Pugh Brothers, and a dozen others. These were the "smart home-builders" referred to by Percy Bustin.[30] George English told me that the Pugh Brothers built homes on Woodville Avenue before the beginning of the war.[31] The Pughs also built all the homes on Athlone south of Plains Road,

---

27. Internal Memorandum of the Public Trustee dated November 13, 1942
28. Spalding, Jean, *Sunrise to Sunset, The History of TEGH*, School of Nursing, Centennial College Press, 1978, 12
29. Bustin, Percy, Memories: *The Early Days of East York*, Self –Published, 1976, 6
30. East York Council minutes 1942
31. Interview with George English, December 29, 2015

according to Mrs. Hill, who moved into their model home at 28 Athlone in 1945.[32] Jean Hivala's parents moved into one of nine new homes built by Fred Baldwin Jr. on Glenwood Crescent in 1948 or 1949.[33] Soon, East York led all municipalities in Canada for home building.[34]

Billy died in 1943, still a resident of the Lakeshore Psychiatric Hospital. His death notice stated he was an indigent.[35]

No photo exists of
Billy McKay

R.H. McGregor School
(Source: East York Foundation)

32. Interview with Mrs. Hill, April 10, 2017
33. Interview with Jean Hivala, March 4, 2017
34. Bustin, Percy, Memories: *The Early Days of East York*, Self –Published, 1976, 6
35. Michailidis, John, Research

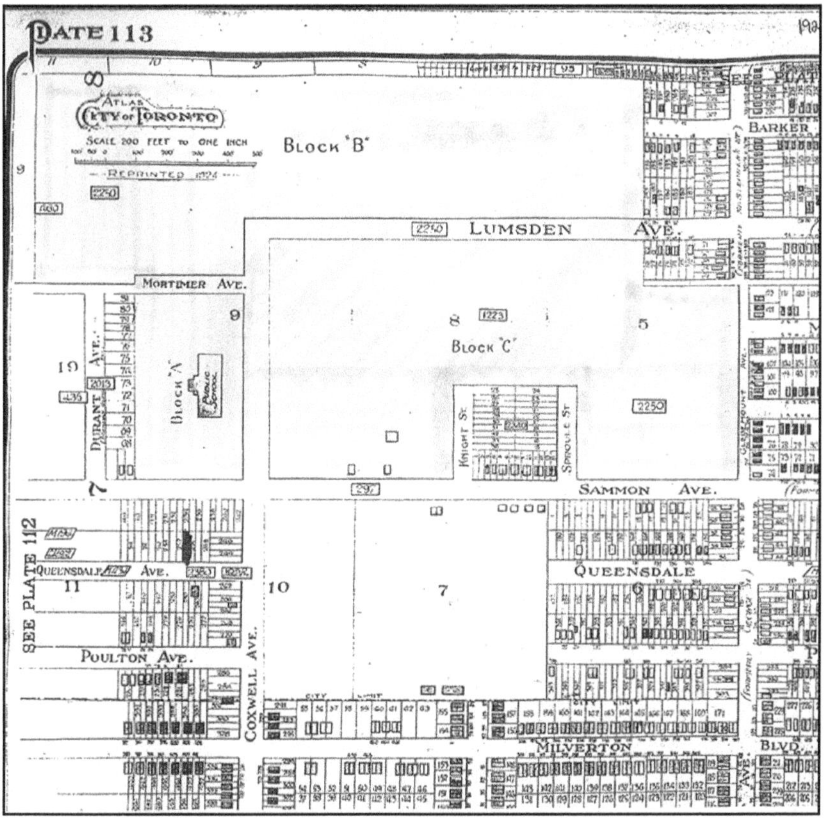

Block A B C
(Source: Toronto Archives)

Billy McKay's House
(Source: East York Foundation)

East General Hospital
(Source: Jim Lister)

East York aerial 1930 looking south
(Source: Jim Lister)

* East York aerial picture in 1930 looking north from Sammon Avenue
(Source: Jim Lister)

Cosburn Looking East
(Source: East York Foundation)

Durant Looking North From Mortimer   William McKay Headstone
(Source: East York Foundation)   *(Source: Colleen Peacock)*

– Chapter 6 –

WORLD WAR II

On September 10, 1939, Canada declared war on Germany. That changed everything, not only in East York but in our entire country. Suddenly there were an unlimited number of job openings in the army, navy, air force, and war industries. East Yorkers joined the armed forces in huge numbers. Toronto-based militia units such as the Queens Own Rifles, the Royal Regiment of Canada, the 48th Highlanders, the Toronto Scottish, and the Irish Regiment were popular choices. George English recalls that all the young men on his street (Woodville Avenue), including his brothers, joined the Royal Regiment, which took part in the Dieppe Raid on the coast of France on August 19, 1942.[1] Because so many East Yorkers participated in that raid, four months later, the Township Council named the park site on Cosburn Avenue, formerly the Smith Property, Dieppe Park in honour of the East York men who fought and gave their lives in that battle or became prisoners of war for the duration of the Second World War. Of the 4963 Canadians who participated in that raid, only 2211 returned and 1944 became POWs.

---

1. Interview with George English, December 29, 2015

A plaque in East Sussex, England, reads:

"Is it nothing to you, all ye who pass by a tribute to the memory of those gallant goodhearted Canadian boys who passed on fighting for us on the Dieppe Raid, August 19, 1942 knowing what ought to be done and doing it at all costs. They were worthy of their country. They shall be greatly remembered for God proved them and found them worthy of himself." [2]

Two years later on D-Day, June 6, 1944, East Yorkers went ashore in the first wave of assault troops with the Queen's Own Rifles of Canada, including Sammy Hall of 11 Cadorna Avenue and Willie McBride of 84 Dunkirk Road serving in Company A of the regiment. Both were killed that day.[3] Rolf Jackson of Roosevelt Avenue went ashore with Company B. He was wounded but survived the war.

George English walked down to the army recruiting office on the Danforth the day he turned eighteen and joined up. He wanted to join the Royal Regiment as his brothers had, but he was assigned to the Queen's Own. When he got to Europe, he asked for a transfer to the Royal Regiment but was sent into battle with the Lincoln and Welland Regiment instead. Dug in behind a dyke in Holland with artillery shells going over head, he began to wonder what he had gotten himself into.[4]

Lawrence Main's brother Robert joined the Royal Canadian Signal Corps. Another brother, Bill, and his sister, Isabel, both joined the R.C.A.F. while Lawrence joined the Toronto Scottish Regiment. His school friend Norm Betts was killed in Italy and his friend Eddie Cooper was shot down in a bomber raid.[5]

Don Hough joined the Royal Canadian Engineers but was sent overseas with the Royal Canadian Artillery attached to the Canadian Intelligence Corps. He was mentioned in despatches during the war.[6]

Many East York schools have plaques on their walls listing the names of their students who served in World War II. The Secord Public

2. Michailidis, John, East York Tidbits, East York Historical Society, June 2006
3. Martin, Charles C., Battle Diary, Dundurn Press, 1994, Appendix E
4. Interview with George English, December 29, 2015
5. Main, Lawrence, *Growing Up in the Old Township of East York*, Self-published, 2013, 18
6. Hough, Don, *Some of My Memories of East York*, The East York Historical Society, 1992, 37

School plaque names thirty-nine former students who were killed in action, while the Danforth Park Public School plaque (now D.A. Morrison Middle School) lists the names of thirty-five former students, including the Sealey brothers, Albert and Harold, as well as Jim Lister's brother, Bill, who made the supreme sacrifice.

In 1945, as the war was ending, 17½ year-old Jim Lister joined the Navy after hearing Jim Hunter on radio station CFRB asking for recruits. He didn't get to fight the enemy but he saw the world with the Navy before returning to East York to get a job with the township a short time later.[7]

George English
(Source: Margaret McRae)

Bill Lewis was a twelve-year-old student at William Burgess School when the war began. He has vivid memories of the air raid siren on the school roof and of the prisoner of war camp in the Don Valley. The POWs were mainly German merchant seamen docked in Canadian ports when the war was declared. In order to identify them as POWs, they wore blue clothes with a red stripe on their trousers and a red dot on the back of their jackets. The POWs were kept busy digging clay for the brickyards in the valley while they were interned. Bill and his friends would often go down to the camp, where the POWs would ask the boys to buy them cigarettes. Bill and his friends would oblige them. There was no age restriction for

---

7. Interview with Jim Lister, October 19, 2015

buying cigarettes in those days. On one occasion, Bill recalls a POW breaking out in a fit of laughter after making a mock Nazi salute.[8]

Gordon Sherk, who grew up in Governor's Bridge on the far west side of the township, remembers that the German POWs were also housed in the garages at the former lieutenant-governor's residence across Governor's Bridge at Chorley Park, where they would whistle at the girls passing by.[9] After VE Day (Victory in Europe Day), the camp was abandoned. Later, it was vandalized and burned to the ground.[10]

Meanwhile, the war industries were desperate for workers. East York's young men were in the armed forces, so a great many East York women, who had heretofore always been homemakers, now went to work for paying jobs in the war industries. Life would never be quite the same again.

Small local businesses converted to war industries. York Knitting Mills on Coleman Avenue became an ammunitions factory. The Hollinger Bus Line took a great many East Yorkers from the southeast community to work each day at another ammunitions manufacturer, the General Engineering Company (GECO), located in what later became known as Scarborough's Golden Mile.[11] George English told me labour was so scarce during the war that his grandfather came out of retirement to take a job at the Sangamo plant in Leaside.[12] East Yorkers also worked at Canada Wire and Cable and Research Enterprises in the Leaside industrial area. They would cross the Leaside Bridge each day to go to work, then many would re-cross it at noon to have their lunch at Todmorden Branch 10 of the Royal Canadian Legion at Pape and Woodville Avenues. The Canada Wire and Cable plaque, commemorating its employees who served in the armed forces and paid the supreme sacrifice, now hangs on the wall in the Branch 10 canteen.[13]

With the war came rationing. Sugar was rationed in July 1942, tea and coffee in August, butter in December, meat the following March, and

8. Interview with Bill Lewis, November 9, 2015
9. Interview with Gordon Sherk, February 19, 2014
10. Interview with Cathy Andrews, RCL Branch 10, September 6, 2016
11. Fagan, Lu Ann, *The Secord Area*, Self–Published, A Study under "Experience '74," sponsored by the Ontario Ministry of Education, 1974, 94
12. Interview with George English, December 29, 2015
13. Interview with Jay and Pat Burford, RCL Branch 10, January 26, 2016

finally gasoline. Round blue tokens were issued to each family for meat and ration books with coupons in them for everything else. Next came price, wage, and rent controls administered and enforced across Canada by the Wartime Prices and Trade Board, all in the name of the war effort. Food was considered a war weapon. With Britain cut off from traditional food sources on the European continent, Canadian food exports provided an essential lifeline to people in the British Isles.[14]

East Yorkers did their part growing their own vegetables in "victory gardens" allotted on vacant municipal land. Many of the school students pitched in collecting household fats and bones for the war effort. Don Forsey, who lived on Donlands Avenue at the time, remembers bringing his family's collection to William Burgess School. According to government advertising, one pound of fat provided enough glycerine for 150 rounds of Bren gun bullets, while bones were essential for making industrial glue.[15] The war ended in 1945 and the boys and girls came home, but rationing continued until 1947.[16]

Bill Lewis
(Source: Panchetta Barnett)

POW Camp c1940
(Source: East York Foundation)

14. National War Services, RG 44, Vol 10, History of Voluntary and Auxiliary Services Division, Appendix 6, Reports of Citizens Committee and Co-ordinating Councils

15. Interview with Don Forsey, January 8, 2016

16. National War Services, RG 44, Vol 10, *History of Voluntary and Auxiliary Services Division*, Appendix 6, Reports of Citizens Committee and Co-ordinating Councils

EY Women's Army Corp
(Source: East York Foundation)

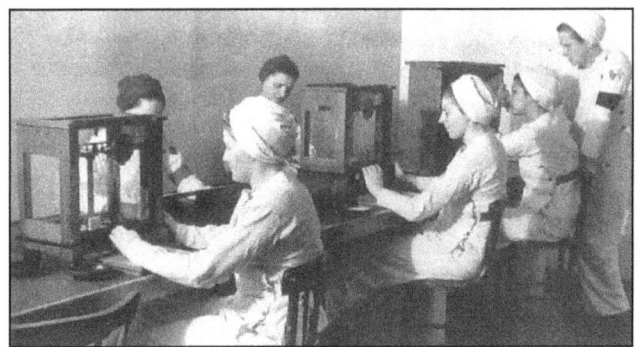

Geco Workers
(Source: Archives of Ontario)

Collecting Scrap
(Source: East York Foundation)

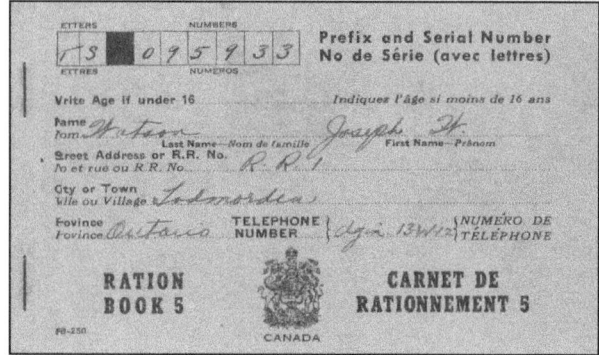

Ration Book Cover
(Source: East York Foundation)

Ration Book Coupons
(Source: East York Foundation)

The Royal Canadian Legion

Immediately after World War I, known to its veterans as the Great War, returning service men formed veterans associations. By the time East York was incorporated, there were four of these in the township: the Todmorden Great War Veterans Association, the East Toronto Great War Veterans Association, the Woodbine Heights Great War Veterans Association, and the Dawes Road Veterans Association. Later, a fifth appeared, the Jubilee Branch of the Canadian Legion British Empire Soldiers Legion, but just as quickly disappeared.[17] All but the

17. East York Council minutes, 1945

Jubilee later became branches of the nationwide Royal Canadian Legion. Great numbers of East York Great War veterans became Legion members. Membership soared again after World War II, augmented still later by veterans of the Korean War, peacekeeper missions, and family members.

Branch 22

Woodbine Heights Branch 22 originated after the end of the First World War as a men's club meeting at the Church of the Resurrection (then located on the east side of Woodbine south of its present location on the west side of the street). Most were returned war veterans who registered with the Great War Veterans Association. In the fall of 1921, one of their members, Robert Barker, then a York Township Councillor and later the first reeve of East York, donated property on Barker Avenue to the branch for a Legion Hall.

"Members, their friends and neighbours dug the cellar using a member's horse-drawn scoop. Something was added to the construction every week. When the roof went on the building, it was a cause for celebration with home brew. Everyone made their own in those days but Frank Inwood later a Branch president, ran a home-brew store on Sammon Avenue.

"Members would vie for the best in quality, while some was good and some was better and some did not reach its destination because the contents of the bottles could not stand the shaking necessary in transportation. Tops would fly off and what was saved had to be drunk behind someone's out house or backyard barn. However, sufficient did reach the intended destination and a goodly time was had by all.

"Someone who had done time in the trenches in France punched holes in a bucket to make a brazier, coal was supplied from somewhere, a table and some chairs were found and a slop pail went in the corner, it was rough but we all had lived in far worse conditions, at least it was dry under foot. Reminds me of the song we used to sing, 'Far, Far from Ypres I want to be, Where German snipers can't get at me, Cold is my dugout, Damp are my feet, Listening to whisbangs that sing me to sleep.' By 1925, a hole had been dug out in the back wall and an added cellar was begun, built and covered by much the same hands that built the first stage.

Bill Hull, Wally Wood, and another Reed, Bill Lister, The Hearst brothers and many others, a cement floor was laid and Mrs. VanKoughnet supplied a billiard table and later a piano. A furnace was built in the old part and plans went ahead to build the hall proper.

"In 1926, a start was made and the sports committee ran a field day in (Woodbine Park) now Taylor Park. They raised $1,500.00 from the enterprise; a fairly large sum in those days. The money almost paid all our debts, put a roof on the hall and laid a good floor. Williamson Lumber Co on Woodbine Ave forgave us the balance and we were on solid ground again.

"We operated these field days for three years with variable success. We would have boxing and wrestling exhibitions, a mini midway with rides for the children, a beauty contest —almost everyone in the Branch had a duty and all worked enthusiastically to make the day a success.

"One incident marred the last year, 1930. The wooden foot bridge crossing the railway tracks, which is now a footpath on the south side of the valley, gave way as the crowd was leaving. Several people, some of them children, received serious injuries.

"The next year we engaged a circus. The Legion were to get a percentage of the take and we operated a few of our own money-making booths. The land was a vacant area north of Sammon and west of Woodmount.

"The effort, although moderately successful, was made exciting due to opposition groups (mostly young men who were out of work) who threatened to do damage to circus property, causing a number of Branch members to assist East York Police in guarding the area well into the night.

"These were the early days of the Depression Years and the Township eventually made work available. The area, which is now Cedarvale Park, was a deep ravine with another deep depression just around the Public School on Cedarvale. All this was filled in partly with garbage but mostly by hand shovel by an army of men.

"These were also the times when members gathered in force to prevent an eviction —many stories could be told in this regard.

"Our Poppy Fund was distributed by a committee of three, the President being the convenor and a meeting was called when a request was presented. This was hardly necessary because there were so many applicants that a date was set for applications to be received and a day for distribution. The whole amount, except for a very small sum, was divided almost evenly among the applicants.

"There was no money to save evictions. Water, heat and light were the first consideration —the remainder, usually $2.00 each, was the hand-out. The township looked after food and clothing.

"The year 1926 was a turning point for the War Veteran Clubs. Sir Douglas Haig had been invited to visit Canada to bring numerous War Veteran groups together into one body.

"The Convention of War Veteran Clubs met in Winnipeg in Oct. 1926 and the Canadian Legion was founded.

"Charlie Webb (at his own expense) represented Woodbine Heights C.W.V.A. at the convention and came home as the Representative of Branch 22, Canadian Legion, Ontario Command." [18]

"The Branch formed a Building Committee early in the 1940s and called it the 'New Building Committee,' when they could see that lots of ex-service men and women would be returning home soon. They even had a committee to meet discharging service men at the CNE grounds to recruit new members. Anyway the need for a larger hall was seen very early on, before the war ended. They even planned on a membership of 500. At least that was what they estimated it would require a meeting hall to seat.

"The old Barker Hall, was in need of repairs and upkeep. The Branch put an extension on just prior to the war, but the hall itself was not in the most desirable location, especially after they built homes to the west of Binswood Ave. towards Coxwell Ave. Of course there was no parking lot and it was not really needed, in the thirties and forties.

"Comrade George Treadway was a big help in finding a lot to build on, as he was a business man (Insurance), also Comrade Walter Stewart was a contact in the township Council.

"The Branch bought a building lot at Cosburn Avenue and Woodmount Avenue. They had some problem there, so they bought another at Roblin Avenue. But that was a bust too, as the neighbors took up a petition, they didn't want a Legion near them. Looking at Roblin Avenue today, you can

---

18. Falkner, Len, *Early Days of Branch 22*, Self–Published, 1981, 1–11

hardly blame them. There was also a lot on Woodbine Avenue at Sammon Avenue, but what happened there is not recorded. Finally, the money they made on the sale of land they were able to invest in the present location. Reeve Harry Simpson laid the corner stone.

"Just the day-to-day operation and fund raising to keep the bills paid took hours and days of people's personal time. I am sure that lots of the members could not have done as well without the ladies' support. Reading the minutes it can be seen that the Ladies Auxiliary, besides helping during social events and catering, also put hard cash into the Branch. They never got the same recognition, but I am sure the officers and members all have the ladies to thank for supporting the efforts of the men. It was called the "men's Branch": how it has changed."[19]

Branch 22
(Source: Anna Malandrino)

---

19. Lister, Jim, *Building of Branch 22 Royal Canadian Legion 70th Anniversary*, 1996, 1, 2, 3

Branch 11

In its early years beginning in December 1918, the members of Branch 11 of the Royal Canadian Legion met in members' homes and then at Secord School. They were veterans mostly from Danforth Avenue, Woodbine Avenue, and Dawes Road. Branch 11 likely absorbed the members of the Dawes Road Veterans Association. In 1924, the branch purchased the original McPherson Presbyterian Church at 65 Dawes Road for its own Legion Hall. When that hall was extended, the municipal address changed to 103 Coleman Avenue. Branch 11 moved to its 9 Dawes Road location south of the Danforth in 1971. Although the Legion Hall is not located in East York, Branch 11 and its Ladies Auxiliary have always maintained a close connection first with the township and later with the borough, especially contributing to True Davidson Acres nursing home and East York baseball, as well as many other programs for seniors and young people.[20]

Legion Branch 11
(Source: google.ca)

---

20. Royal Canadian Legion, Branch 11, Website

Branch 10

After WWI, the Todmorden Great War Veterans Association—now Todmorden Branch 10 of the Royal Canadian Legion—was one of the first veterans organizations to be formed anywhere in Canada. Its first meetings were held in a double garage on Gowan Avenue behind the Bank of Nova Scotia at the corner of Pape and Gowan Avenues before moving to the basement of William Burgess School. Branch 10's present location at 1080 Pape Avenue on the northeast corner of Woodville Avenue across from William Burgess School was built in 1927. Additions were added in the thirties, fifties, and seventies. It is said that the branch building at 1080 Pape is haunted. Strange noises and lights have been seen there on a number of occasions, although no one was in the branch at those times. To date, it's an unsolved mystery. The branch has held a Remembrance Day memorial service every year since 1919. It sponsors the 330 Air Cadet Squadron as well as many local sports teams.[21]

Legion Branch 10
(Source: Margaret McRae)

---

21. Interview with Cathy Andrews, RCL, Todmorden Branch 10, September 6, 2016

Branch 345

Brigadier O.M. Martin Branch 345 of the Royal Canadian Legion was not established by veterans of WWI but rather by those of WW II. Initially, membership was restricted to veterans who had actually served overseas but that has changed with the passage of time.[22] East York Council donated land at 81 Peard Road to the Branch in 1945. Its Legion Memorial Hall later expanded and was opened on March 4, 1949.[23]

Branch 345 was named after a prominent East Yorker described by one of his former pupils, Don Hough, as follows:

"The principal of Danforth Park School was a six-nation Indian, Mr. O.M. Martin. He went overseas as a brigadier, and it was my pleasure to meet him when he visited a camp where I was stationed. He returned to Canada and built a new house on the north side of O'Connor, just west of Woodbine. He then became Magistrate Martin. One day in court, a man was raving about another, referring to him as a foreigner. Magistrate Martin immediately interrupted him and told him that everyone in the court except the magistrate himself, were foreigners." [24]

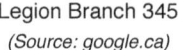

Legion Branch 345	Brigadier O.M. Martin
(Source: google.ca)	*(Source: google.ca)*

---

22. Michailidis, John, East York Tidbits, East York Historical Society, June 2006

23. Interview with Christopher Salmond, RCL Branch 345, December 3. 2015

24. Hough, Don, *Some of My Memories of East York*, The East York Historical Society, 1992, 12

On November 11 every year, the four East York Legions organize the annual Remembrance Day Service in the Memorial Gardens at the East York Civic Centre.[25] Over the years, these four Legion branches have played a significant role in shaping both the character and the community spirit of Toronto's Garden of Eden.

Dedication of Memorial Gardens 1948
(Source: East York Foundation)

25. Royal Canadian Legion, Todmorden Branch 10, Website

Now, with the war over, East York was about to grow up.

PROCLAMATION

FEBRUARY 23, 1997

**Corporation of the
Borough of East York**

WHEREAS;   on 17 August 1948 the Central Council of Veterans requested that the Council of the Township of East York consider erecting a War Memorial in front of the new municipal offices;

AND WHEREAS;   this request was granted by the Council of East York and the new cenotaph was built and unveiled on 12 September 1948;

AND WHEREAS;   at the official unveiling Reeve John Warren dedicated in perpetuity the cenotaph and the lands around it which contained the park and sunken gardens to the men and women who had fought and died for Canada during the Second World War and to those who had returned to build our community;

AND WHEREAS;   the name of this park from that time onward has been Memorial Gardens;

AND WHEREAS;   the Royal Canadian Legion continues to lay wreaths at the cenotaph and continues to maintain vigil over the property dedicated in perpetuity to their members;

AND WHEREAS;   the Council of the Borough of East York has consulted with and sought the permission of the Royal Canadian Legion for every modification to the grounds including the new municipal building, the rededication of the cenotaph and the building of the Early Childhood Education Centre;

AND WHEREAS;   the Council is desirous to rededicate the cenotaph and grounds in perpetuity lest it be forgotten that a solemn pledge was made in 1948 which must always be honoured;

THEREFORE BE IT RESOLVED THAT the Council of the Borough of East York rededicates in perpetuity the Cenotaph and Memorial Gardens to the care of the Royal Canadian Legion and its members so that it will serve as a lasting remembrance to all of those who so bravely served our country and our municipality in times of war and in times of peace.

Borough of East York,
February 1997.

Canada's Only Borough

MICHAEL D. PRUE,
Mayor.

Memorial Gardens Proclamation 1997
(Source: East York Foundation)

– Chapter 7 –

GROWING UP

The extension of Coxwell Avenue through what had been Billy McKay's farm was the catalyst that touched off an East York house-building boom.

In earlier days, a great many families in Little York, Secord, and Todmorden built their own homes. Now, however, a number of individuals started to build homes not for themselves but to sell to others. In the central part of East York, builders would start by purchasing lots laid out on the plan put prepared by the township engineer.[1] In some cases, after finishing a house, the builder's family would move into it themselves while he was building another house on another lot. When that was finished, the family would move into the new house and the builder would sell the first one using the proceeds of sale to buy another lot on which to build another house, and repeat the process.

---

1. East York Council minutes 1942-1948

The Taylor family owned the property at the north end of Coxwell. Percy Bustin, writing in 1974, described what happened to it:

"As was the case with Billy McKay, the Taylor family were also caught in the squeeze of rising taxes, and in 1930 they were forced to subdivide and sell their farm. The writer remembers buying the first two acres of the farm from the Taylor Estates for the sum of $600.00 an acre, and reselling it two or three years later for the sum of $3,600.00 an acre, not a bad profit, but at a modest estimate those same two acres to-day are worth from seventy thousand to eighty thousand dollars an acre, plus the value of the homes now standing on the property. Should the same property ever be rezoned to permit the building of apartments, its value would jump to well over $100,000.00 an acre. Who would have believed it forty years ago: Certainly not the writer.

"Until the year 1932, the most northerly crosstown street running from Pape to Woodbine was Plains Road, lined with market gardens. O'Connor Drive was as yet unheard of, and was the location of the Taylor family farm stretching all the way from Don Mills Road to Woodbine Avenue. It was not unusual to see fat pigs wallowing in mud holes close to the roadway. It was not until the new Woodbine Bridge was built that O'Connor Drive was constructed a block farther north (of Plains Road). To permit the then-dirt road to be widened to four lanes (only two of them paved) the Taylor family were induced by the council of the day, to turn over to the Township several feet frontage of their farmland, which they did at a very reasonable price. The opening of the new bridge (built by R.H. (Bob) McGregor's Malvern Construction Company) gave access to that section of East York north of the valley to Sunrise Avenue, (The North York border), which heretofore had remained open fields totally undeveloped. What is now Parkview Hills was a part of the Taylor farm, and the writer remembers buying the first four, three hundred foot deep lots for $40.00 a foot frontage, a bargain even in those days. On the east side of O'Connor and north of St. Clair, there was a golf course covering 188 acres, and many an old timer will tell you, its clubhouse was a favorite meeting place in those days. Still farther north on the east side was a farm with huge sheds in which they grew mushrooms.

"With the opening of the bridge the area developed rapidly, and the council designated north of Parkview Hills an industrial area.

Some of the first firms to locate there were Peek Frean's, the famous biscuit makers; Yardley's, makers of toilet goods and cosmetics; and the Kendall Company, manufacturers of surgical dressings. On Victoria Park Avenue to the north, was Maryville Farm of Frank O'Connor, a candy manufacturer and founder of the Laura Secord Candy Shops, and a personal friend of the then-premier, Mitchell Hepburn. Since the Province had assisted financially in building the bridge, the council granted the premier's request: that the new road be named O'Connor Drive."[2]

Home building began to pick up steam in the late 1930s and the early years of World War II. By 1942, East York led all municipalities in Canada with 1500 homes built in a three-year period. It slowed down, however, when building materials were rationed, and then came to a complete stop when building materials dried up altogether because they were needed for war-related projects.[3] Once the war ended, the builders were off to the races again on both sides of the Woodbine Bridge.

The golf course east of the Woodbine Bridge that Percy Bustin refers to was originally named the Woodbine Golf and Country Club. In 1938, the township claimed the entire golf course property for unpaid property taxes. A short time later, East York resold the property to a new owner, who changed the name of the golf course to Gleneagles. Under the new owner, it not only featured golf in the warmer months of the year but skiing and tobogganing in the winter. Gleneagles operated until 1949 when the clubhouse was destroyed by fire. After the fire, the township again reclaimed the golf club property for unpaid taxes, then sold most of it but retained a small triangle of land along O'Connor and St. Clair.

A short time later, the City of Toronto got the bright idea that this former golf course would be an excellent location for a new Toronto zoo to replace the one then in Riverdale Park. That idea went over in East York like a lead balloon.[4]

---

2. Bustin, Percy, *Memories: The Early Days of East York*, Self –Published, 1976, 6

3. Grant, Suzanne, DiAnne & Bert C., *With a Box of Tools: a History of Crestview and the Grant Family*, Crestview Investment Corporation, 2014, 35

4. Dolbey, Michael, *A History of Woodbine Gardens*, Self–published, 2015, 10

Michael Dolbey's well-researched and excellent history of Woodbine Gardens takes up the story from there:

"The only area in which housing development had begun before the end of WWII was Glenwood Crescent west of O'Connor Drive opposite the entrance to the Gleneagles Golf and Country Club. This development is on a small triangle of high land between the Taylor Creek ravine and the Curity Creek ravine.

"When the Township of East York sold the former Woodbine Golf & Country Club property to Eddie Rudd and associates in 1940 they retained ownership of a portion of the property along O'Connor Drive and St. Clair Avenue. A plan of a subdivision was created and submitted by Doris Tucker, Secretary of the Township, as owners of the property. It was submitted on May 28, 1941 and finally approved and filed in the Registry Office as Plan 3054 on Oct 27, 1941. The plan extended Glenwood Crescent east of O'Connor drive and created Gleneagles Avenue parallel to and south of St. Clair Avenue. Gleneagles Avenue was later changed to an extension of Glenwood Crescent.

"The first house to be built in the new subdivision was "the Mary Pickford Bungalow" at 90 Glenwood Crescent. A newspaper article at the time stated, "Miss Pickford expects to raise upwards of $250,000 for the combined British charities through the sale of shares in the Mary Pickford bungalow project, a handsome $15,000 home located at O'Connor Drive and Glenwood Crescent in East York, a suburb of Toronto. This project was made possible by Miss Pickford's donation of $5,000 through the sale of her mother's house in Toronto. Shares for the bungalow are being sold by the Lion's clubs throughout Canada and through stores and offices in all major Canadian cities. The shares sell for $1 each." The Gerrard Business Men's Association partnered with the Lions club in this project. The proceeds went to the Lions British Child War Victim's Fund (50%), the Evening Telegram British War Victim's Fund (40%) and the Malta Relief Fund Society of Toronto (10%) Mary Pickford was at the official opening of the bungalow on May 26, 1943 ensuring great publicity for ticket sales. Mr. George Ellis of Scarborough won the draw made by Ontario Premier George Drew at the 'Fair for Britain' in Riverdale Park on August 26, 1943. Mr. Ellis immediately put the house up for sale." [5]

---

5. Dolbey, Michael, *A History of Woodbine Gardens*, Self–published, 2015, 11

Woodbine Golf club
(Source: google.ca)

Premier Mitchell Hepburn	Senator Frank OConnor	Mary Pickford
(Source: Archives of Ontario)	*(Source: google.ca)*	*(Source: East York Foundation)*

Before the war, on the north side of St. Clair Avenue East where Selwyn Public School stands today, there was a dog-racing track where Jim Balmer's father raced his Hall of Fame champion greyhound, Gallant Warrior.[6] On the same site, between 1944 and 1946, the Wartime Housing Company, a subsidiary of the federal Department of Munitions and Supply, later merged with Canada Mortgage and Housing Corporation (CMHC), developed and built 197 prefabricated homes for veterans[7] called the

---

6. Interview with Jim Balmer, October 13, 2016
7. Canada Mortgage and Housing Corporation Archives

Topham Park War Veterans Community. When built, these homes were rented to veterans and their families, but later they were given the option to buy and many did. Stan French refers to these homes as "temporary wartime housing." He says that he believes East York "insisted that these homes were to have concrete basements. My wife, Emily, lived in a four-room wartime home in Montreal and they had no basements and they're all gone decades ago." Not so with the frequently renovated Topham Park homes in East York. Although they were built originally as on an assembly line, three each day,[8] they are still going strong to this day. At the time, the area was commonly known as "Sunshine Valley." According to Don Hough, one of the first veterans to move in:

"After WWII his [John Hollinger's] bus ran up O'Connor to Tiago Avenue, and we people living in the Wartime Housing would trudge through the mud to a bus stop on O'Connor; remove our rubber boots and pile them in the corner, and put on our shoes – hoping to find our own rubber boots at night when we returned. The bus driver, Mac used to sing 'All out for Sunshine Valley,' and that is how the area got that name. We were the first people to move onto Topham Road No. 8." Don was the founding president of the Sunshine Valley Community Association, which dismantled a TTC Ladies Powder Room Building at Wychwood and St. Clair and re-assembled it in Topham Park. When East York Council named the park in 1948 it voted $250.00 to assist the renovation of the building and R.H. McGregor's Malvern Construction put in the heating and plumbing for free." [9]

The Topham Park building was later taken over by the Board of Education and classes were held in it. The area was named by East York Council in honour of Corporal Frederick George (Toppy) Topham, a medical orderly with the 1st Canadian Parachute Battalion, a recipient of the Victoria Cross during World War II.[10]

---

8. Interview with Stan French, November 24, 2015

9. Hough, Don, *Some of My Memories of East York*, The East York Historical Society, 1992, 6

10. East York Council minutes, 1948

His citation read as follows:

On 24th March 1945 Corporal Topham, a medical orderly, parachuted with his Battalion onto a strongly defended area east of the Rhine. At about 1100 hours, whilst treating casualties sustained in the drop, a cry for help came from a wounded man in the open. Two medical orderlies went out to this man in succession but both were killed as they knelt beside the casualty.

Without hesitation and on his own initiative, Corporal Topham went forward through intense fire to replace the orderlies who had been killed before his eyes. As he worked on the wounded man, he was himself shot through the nose. In spite of severe bleeding and intense pain, he never faltered at his task. Having completed immediate first aid, he carried the wounded man slowly back through continuous fire to the shelter of a wood.

During the next two hours Corporal Topham refused all offers of medical help for his own wound. He worked most devotedly throughout this period to bring in wounded, showing complete disregard for heavy and accurate enemy fire. It was only when all casualties had been cleared that he consented to his own wound being treated.

His immediate evacuation was ordered, but he interceded so earnestly on his own behalf that he was eventually allowed to return to duty.

On his way back to his company he came across a carrier which had received a direct hit. Enemy mortar bombs were still dropping around, the carrier itself was burning fiercely and their own mortar and ammunition was exploding. An experienced officer on the spot warned all not to approach the carrier.

Corporal Topham, however, immediately went out alone in spite of the blasting ammunition and enemy fire, and rescued the three occupants of the carrier. He brought those men back across the open and although one died almost immediately afterwards, he arranged for the evacuation of the other two, who undoubtedly owe their lives to him.

This N.C.O. (Non-Commissioned Officer) showed sustained gallantry of the highest order. For six hours, most of the time in great pain, he performed a series of acts of outstanding bravery and his magnificent and selfless courage inspired all who witnessed it.[11]

---

11. Department of National Defence, Ottawa, 3rd August 1945

The Victoria Cross is the highest military decoration awarded for "valour in the face of the enemy" to members of the armed forces in the Commonwealth. In Canada, it takes precedence over all other orders, decorations, and medals.

Streets in Sunshine Valley were named Vicross and Valor to recognize the importance of the Victoria Cross to the veterans that moved into this neighbourhood. Three other streets were named for Victoria Cross recipients: Barron Road for Corporal Colin Barron, who won the Victoria Cross for his bravery during the WW I battle of Passchendaele in Belgium;[12] Merritt Road for Cecil Merritt, who won the Victoria Cross while commanding his battalion, the South Saskatchewan Regiment, in the Dieppe Raid on August 19, 1942; and of course, Topham Road for Frederick "Toppy" Topham.[13]

Fred Topham VC
(Source: wikipedia.org)

Donald Sinclair Hough
(Source: East York Foundation)

---

12. Richard Longley, Past President, Architectural Conservancy, Ontario
13. Gordon A. *Brown Middle School students History of the Topham Park Community,*
    Self–Published, 1

Topham Park
(Source: East York Foundation)

Topham Community Centre
(Source: East York Foundation)

Topham Park Home Building
(Source: East York Foundation)

Galbraith Avenue
(Source: East York Foundation)

Today, the area is known as the Topham Park Community.

Postwar home building south of St. Clair and west of Victoria Park took place from east to west beginning with another subdivision developed by the director of the federal Veterans Land Act known as Vetland and described by Michael Dolbey as follows:

"The earliest post-war plan submitted by G. Murchison, Director of the Veterans Land Act adjacent to Dawes Road, Plan 3294, approved on April 24, 1946, named Ferris Road and Squires Avenue as well as Vetland Road (later changed to Glencrest Boulevard) and Stephney Avenue (later changed to Glenburn Avenue). Unlike the Topham Park veteran's housing development, all the proposed lots were quite large, typically ½ acre (110' frontage x 225' deep or 75' frontage x 300' deep). This was because the mandate of the Veteran's Land Act was to settle veterans on full-time farms or part-time small holdings. However, as building progressed, many of the large lots were subdivided. A central section containing 11 of the original large lots was bought and subdivided by Plan 4357, approved on April 23, 1953, adding Youngmill Drive and 36 small house lots." [14]

Now came the large-scale private builders, starting with Robert McClintock, as described by Michael Dolbey.

---

14. Dolbey, Michael, *A History of Woodbine Gardens*, Self–published, 2015, 14

"On April 30, 1947 East York builder Robert McClintock bought the land at auction. Over the next few years he developed the area under subdivision plans M-573, (1947-04-17), M-591 (1947-09-11), M-598 (1949-03-18), 3878 (1949-03-18) and M-605 (1949-10-25). Glencrest Boulevard and the east side of Plaxton Drive were developed first while a major culvert crossing was constructed at the south end of Plaxton Drive to extend Ferris Road to the south side of the deep Ferris Creek ravine. The area south of the Ferris Creek ravine was then developed including Ferris Road, Ferris Crescent, Glen Albert Drive (believed to be named for Albert Starmer, a painter who worked for McClintock) and Curran Drive (named after McClintock's bookkeeper/office manager, Henry T. Curran, the father of former CBC traffic reporter Jim Curran; the Currans bought a house in the development off Plaxton Crescent). The last area to be developed was the north-west portion, which was cut into by several small tributary ravines of Ferris creek. Three short cul-de-sacs, Glencrest Blvd, Plaxton Crescent, and Glen Robert Drive (believed to be named for Robert McClintock) exit off the west side of Plaxton Drive to provide access to the tableland between the ravines. When they were built, homes at the end of these three roads looked westward over the Woodbine Golf Club.

While some lots in Morningside Park were sold to individuals who wanted to build their own homes, the majority were built by McClintock. Small brick bungalows and 1 ½ storey houses of standard design predominated. It is believed that the bricks were obtained from the local brick works on Dawes Road that continued to operate until the early 1950s. Shortly after the end of WWII building materials were in short supply. It is said that after the war, Robert McClintock bid on and won a contract to remove the military barracks that had been built on the CNE grounds. His crews disassembled the barracks and reused the material to build houses in Morningside Park. He may also have gotten material from the removal of barracks at Camp Borden.

Robert McClintock had been a builder before and during the war constructing many houses in East York south of Taylor Creek. He lived at 206 Woodycrest Avenue near Pape and Mortimer Avenues. It is said that as a young man he was a hard-drinking man. However, his wife became very ill and he vowed to give up drink if she survived. His wife did survive and Robert McClintock joined the congregation of the Calvary Church on Pape Avenue just north of Danforth Avenue. In Morningside Park in 1947, he built the Morningside Park Gospel Church on the south-east corner of St. Clair Avenue and Glenfield Crescent. It was a "daughter work" of McClintock's Calvary Church. His company went on to develop the area south of Eglinton Square and later, many other areas further north in Scarborough. In each area that he developed he donated land for a church. The Bridlegrove Bible Church and Gracepoint Baptist Church, both near Pharmacy and Sheppard Avenues, are built on such land. McClintock was devoted to his church and was a quiet philanthropist. He is memorialized in the name of McClintock Manor, a Christian-oriented high-rise apartment building for seniors that is beside, and associated with, Calvary Church in East York.

The Morningside Gospel Church continued in operation until the late 1980s. In 1967, the Reverend Dr. Gerald Griffiths became the Pastor at Calvary Church. At this time, Robert McClintock was the church's senior elder. McClintock helped the Griffiths with accommodation by providing them with a house he had bought on Taylor Driver where the Griffiths still live. Dr. Griffith's wife, Kitty Anna Griffith, a teller of Bible stories, began radio broadcasts of a program called "Bible Stories with Mrs. G," and later "A visit with Mrs. G." Demand for the program expanded rapidly resulting in it being broadcast in English on hundreds of weekly releases. The stories have been published in books, audio and digital media and they have been translated into many foreign languages. Since Dr. Griffith's retirement in 1990, he and Kitty Anna have operated their business. A Visit with Mrs. G Ministries Inc., from the former Morningside Park Gospel Church building at 2851 St. Clair Avenue East in the Woodbine Gardens area of Toronto.

The next area to be developed was the land formerly occupied by the Woodbine (Gleneagles) Golf Club. The name "Woodbine Gardens," created by its developer, was later applied to the whole area now known by that name.

As previously told, the Golf Course lands, originally developed by Mr. Harold Beatty's Woodbine Development Company, had been seized in 1939 by the Township of East York for default of tax payments. The Golf course was sold to Eddy Rudd who attempted, unsuccessfully, to breathe new life into it. In 1943, it was again seized by the Township of East York and, in 1944, it was sold to Mr. G. Clifford Green. Mr. Green was the manager of the Imperial Bank at the corner of Adelaide and Victoria

Streets in Toronto and he lived on Eastmount Avenue on the east edge of the Don Valley just north of the Prince Edward Viaduct. By 1950 he had moved to Chilton Avenue in East York. In 1951 Clifford Green sold the Woodbine Golf Club property to Farlinger Development Ltd., which developed most of Woodbine Gardens west of Rexleigh Drive over the next few years. Alex W. Farlinger who lived on Dinnick Crescent in North Toronto operated the Farlinger Realty Company during the Depression and the war years. After the war, his company had expanded with a number of offices including one at 727 Coxwell Avenue in East York. After the war he founded Farlinger Development Limited, which bought the Woodbine Golf Club property from Green in 1951. Later Farlinger Development Limited went on to develop the Clairlea area north of St. Clair between Victoria Park and Warden Avenues and Bayview Village in North York. Alex Farlinger's son, William A. Farlinger, culminated a long career in commerce and finance as chairman and CEO of the accounting firm Ernst and Young. After retiring he served as chairman of Ontario Hydro/Ontario Power Generation during the Conservative government of Mike Harris.

The first area to be developed in Farlinger's Woodbine Gardens' development was the area between Glenwood Crescent on the north and Ferris Ravine to the south described as subdivision plan M-623 (1951-05-29). Farlinger lost no time in promoting his development with an article in the Toronto Star on May 19, 1951; "A.W. Farlinger real estate reports 400 lots in the 163-acre former Woodbine golf course in Scarboro [sic] are going fast with 141 houses under construction. The houses will run from $15,000 to $30,000. Plans include five acres for apartment houses, and 25 acres for industrial development: 35 acres have been allotted for park use in accordance with plans of the Don Valley Conservation association. The development will have roads, sidewalks, curbs and sewer and water facilities."

Short roads such as Hale Court, Leander Court, Glen Gannon Drive, and Glen Eden Crescent were necessary to develop the tableland between the many small tributary ravines off Ferris Creek. After developing the infrastructure, Farlinger Developments sold many of the lots to other builders, who constructed houses. This resulted in a more diverse mix of house styles and sizes than in some other areas. The area labelled Block A in the SW corner of the plan was reserved for apartment buildings that were built later at 127 Glenwood Drive and 5-7-9 Stag Hill Drive.

The next area of the golf course lands to be developed was between the Ferris Ravine on the north, Taylor Creek Ravine on the south and the west boundary of Lot 3 on the east, described as subdivision plan M-630 (1952-05-08).

Until Rexleigh Drive was extended south across the Ferris ravine, the area could only be accessed from the east by Ferris Drive and Glen Albert Drive. The Rexleigh Drive crossing of the Ferris Ravine was a major undertaking requiring tributaries to the north, the installation of storm sewers, and the filling of the ravine—at this point approximately 200m (670') wide—to a depth of approximately 6m (20'). It has been estimated that 380,000 cubic meters (500,000 cubic yards) of soil were moved in the area.

Plan M-630 shows three large blocks on each side of Rexleigh Drive at the Ferris Ravine crossing, separated by narrow blocks under which the stream culverts run. These blocks were intended for future shopping and apartment developments. It is interesting to note that in the proposed southern extension of Rexleigh Drive across the Taylor-Massey Creek Valley to intersect with Hampstead Avenue just west of Main Street, a four-acre school block was reserved adjacent to the proposed road between the south side of Taylor Creek and the former railway tracks. This development was approved before 1954's Hurricane Hazel caused a change in thinking about the appropriate uses of valley bottom land. Neither the Rexleigh Drive extension nor the school was built.

Block R on the western end of Plan M-630 was developed as single-family housing shortly after as Plan M-632, by Farlinger Developments Limited. Block J, in the south-east corner of Plan M-630 adjacent to Dawes Road, was first laid out as ten large house lots along Evenrude Road. Later, the road was renamed Park Vista Drive and became the site of the Park Vista Estates apartments and condominiums.

The last part of the area to be developed was the south-east corner adjacent to Dawes Road, as it had been occupied by the Chapman Brick Company Ltd. since its incorporation in 1911. The brick works are believed to have operated until the early 1950s. The George Webster Public School, which opened in 1954, and the adjacent George Webster Park were built on the site of the brickworks. Most of the houses in this area are duplexes or multiplexes. Halsey and Chapman Avenues are named after Halsey Chapman, the owner of the brickworks and a former East York Council member.

The first plan in this area was registered in 1923 by the Chapman Brick Company and it created Chapman Avenue with fourteen building lots, mainly on its south side. However, a few lots were built on before the end of WWII. The east end of Halsey Avenue was laid out in Plan 3626, approved in November 1948. The west end of Halsey and Chapman Avenues with Avis Crescent between them were laid out in Plan M-780 approved in October 1958 and Munford Crescent was not developed until October 1967." [15]

Glenwood Cres
(Source: East York Foundation)

St.Clair West Looking East Toward Dawes Rd
(Source: East York Foundation)

15. Dolbey, Michael, *A History of Woodbine Gardens*, Self–published, 2015, 1

1949 Vic Pk_St Clair
(Source: Jim Lister)

Glen Roberts 1947
(Source: East York Foundation)

Dawes Rd Looking North
(Source: East York Foundation)

Woodbine Golf Course Subdivision
(Source: East York Foundation)

Chapmans Brick Yard
(Source: East York Foundation)

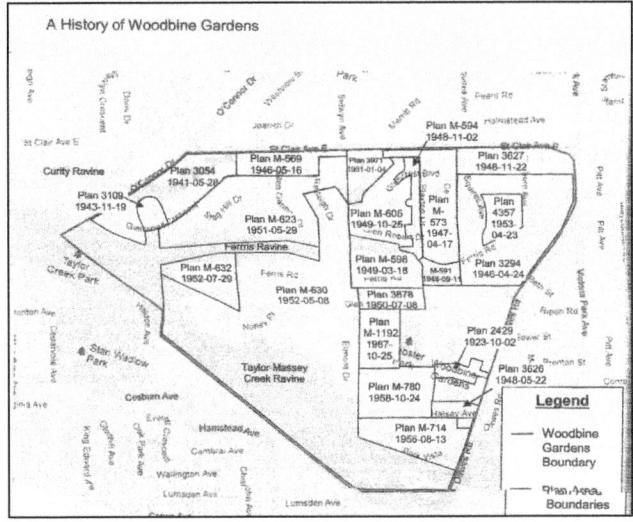

Map History of Woodbine Gardens
(Source: Michael Dolbey)

Cedarvale Park
(Source: East York Foundation)

Cedarvale Park 1
(Source: East York Foundation)

Before World War II, Parkview Hills, where Jim Balmer flew model airplanes,[16] was farmland and a garbage dump. It was owned by the Taylor family at that time but by 1947, the Taylor brothers were selling off land and getting into the development business. Together with Roy Pearson, William Pugh, George Lankin, Robert McClintock, and Mr. Hiscock to name a few, they each built a half a dozen homes in Parkview Hills.

"Other individuals came in, bought the land themselves and built their own homes. Three hundred feet-deep lots were selling for approximately $40.00 a frontage foot when the subdivision first opened. One could purchase a three-bedroom bungalow in 1949 for approximately $9,950.00.

It is believed that many of the streets were named by the Taylor Brothers. The streets of White Pine, Hackberry, Alder, and Aspen were named after the trees that grew in the area. Presteign Avenue derived its name from the Welsh town of Presteign, believed to be the hometown of builder William Pugh. He also donated the land on which Presteign Woodbine United Church now stands, on condition that it too be named after his birthplace. Marilyn and Doris are believed to be named after daughters or family relations of the Pughs.

The foundations for the homes were dug using teams of horses. Residents with cars had to leave them at Sandra, since roads did not exist at the time. As it was new subdivisions, mud was a commodity that was always in abundance until the roads were paved beginning in 1950. Mrs. Mary Lankin, a long-time Parkview Hills resident (1948) and wife of the late George Lankin, builder of some of the two-storey homes in Parkview Hills, recalls the milkman's horse getting stuck up to its belly in the mud at the corner of Alder and Parkview Hill Crescent. The tenacious mud was also a trap later for the tractor-trailer trucks that would get lost in the neighbourhood, their drivers not realizing St. Clair was not a through street. Mr. Tom Potter reminisced how as a child he and friends swam and fished in the creek (a practice subsequently discouraged in 1955 when the waters were deemed polluted).

The neighbourhood was full of young families, recalls Mrs. Helen Hinds. Most did not own cars so shopping meant coordinating oneself

---

16. Interview with Jim Balmer, October 13, 2016

and trying to find some transport to the Danforth. It often meant hitching a ride in whatever was available (including the milk truck). Shopping and mobility became much easier once the Hollinger Bus Lines started their service across the bridge. It is easy to forget how far east the neighbourhood was back then when all we see around ourselves is the city. For the inhabitants in the area it was a different situation; they shared their backyards with farm fields and cattle.

Acknowledgements: Sandy Evan-Jones, Mary Lankin, Helen Hinds, Mr. and Mrs. E.J. Parker, Margaret Mulholland, Jean Farnell, Mr. and Mrs. Neal and Tom Potter." [17]

Post-war veterans housing was also built south-west of the Woodbine Bridge. Although Joyce Crook's father was a returning service man, veterans with fewer than two children did not qualify for the wartime housing built in Sunshine Valley. Since Joyce was an only child in 1959, the family moved into one of the six houses on Memorial Park Avenue just west of Greenwood Avenue, built under the Veterans Land Act. Joyce, who has lived there ever since, told me that she was happy that the Crook family never moved to Sunshine Valley because the houses built there were only intended to last for ten years.[18] According to Mrs. Bickle, who lives nearby on Frankdale Avenue, her house and all those on Frankdale from Memorial Park south to Mortimer Avenue were built in 1947 under the Veterans Land Act, exclusively for the families of returning service men, such as her late husband, Arthur.[19] When Isabel Montgomery returned to East York after duty in England with the RCAF, she and her husband, who had seen action with the Canadian Armoured Corps in Italy, purchased a home on Inwood Avenue north of Mortimer Avenue. Theirs one of an entire block of homes also built under the Veterans Land Act exclusively for those who had served in the war.[20]

17. Van Dette, Justin, Parkview Hills Community Association, November 2013
18. Interview with Joyce Crook, November 12, 2015
19. Interview with Mrs. Bickle, March 3, 2017
20. Interview with Isabel Montgomery nee Main, December 2, 2015

Broadview and Cosburn
(Source: East York Foundation)

Across the Don Valley, homes were being built in Governors Bridge (formerly the Rosedale Annex) and Bennington Heights (formerly known both as Rosemount Heights or the Moore Park Annex) as well. The Governors Bridge, which spans the Moore Park Ravine from Toronto to East York, derives its name from the lieutenant governor of Ontario, whose official residence in Chorley Park was just across the bridge in Rosedale. According to Gordon Sherk, a long-time resident of the neighbourhood, when the bridge was opened in 1923, the lieutenant governor's wife used to walk their dogs, Salt and Pepper, across the bridge to what became East York's Governor's Bridge neighbourhood.[21]

Although it was subdivided in 1912 and Governor's Manor, an Elizabethan-style two-storey "U"-shaped apartment, had been constructed in 1928,[22] only fifty houses were built before World War II and some lost their homes for unpaid taxes. Gordon told me, "Some neighbours who could no longer afford their rent just fled. I understand that some neighbours would switch items in the abandoned homes if they liked them better than their own."

Gordon recalls, "We kids had a wonderful place to grow up. We could move through the woods to the Brickworks and watch the mining taking place. My family home was made of Brickwork's brick—they still have the stamp, Don Valley."

---

21. Interview with Gordon Sherk, February 19, 2014
22. Interview with Peter Weatherhead, April 5, 2013

The Township of East York sold off the lots and houses claimed for unpaid taxes starting in 1932, but home building in Governor's Bridge didn't start in earnest until after the war. Original street names were changed: Southview Avenue became Nesbitt Drive, Oakdale Crescent became Douglas Crescent, and Hawthorne Avenue became Governor's Road.

Early on, says Gordon, "the neighbourhood was referred to as 'Little Hollywood' because some of the early houses featured Spanish architectural accents. The area did house movie stars, but mostly it was popular with doctors, professors, lawyers, and business men because of our close proximity to downtown."[23] Ursula Franklin, CBC personality Joyce Davidson, and garden expert Art Drysdale were some of the well-known residents.

On the heights overlooking the Governor's Bridge neighbourhood was Bennington Heights. Although the area had been laid out in building lots as early as 1890, it remained mainly as farm land and market gardens until the early 1940s.

When he married Evelyn Bennington in 1925, Thomas Weatherhead built a house there, but few others were constructed until after World War II. Housing development brought with it street name changes here as well: Hillside Road became Brendan Road, Foy Avenue became Burnham Road, and Clarence Avenue became Heath Street East. Thomas Weatherhead, who became an East York school trustee and later the school board's solicitor, persuaded East York Township Council to change his street name to Bennington Heights Drive in honour of his wife, so Erminie and Mallory Avenues became Bennington Heights Drive.

It was also Thomas Weatherhead who chose the site for Bennington Heights School at the end of Bennington Heights Drive. For a time, the area was known as the Moore Park Annex, but since both the school and the longest street were named Bennington Heights, the local real estate agents began to refer to the entire area as Bennington Heights.

Many well-known people have lived there over the years, including the authors Margaret Atwood, who grew up there and has written books about her neighbours, and another well-known author, James Bacque.

---

23. Interview with Gordon Sherk, February 19, 2014

Others included Norman McLeod, the first and long-time principal of Leaside High School; Manley MacDonald, the Ontario landscape artist who painted many Bennington scenes in the 1930s; Lotta Dempsey, a *Toronto Star* columnist; Frank Trumpane, a *Toronto Telegram* columnist; Bruce Brown, the architect for many churches; and Thomas Weatherhead's son David, who served as a Liberal Member of Parliament for Scarborough West.[24]

In 1949, Bert Grant's Lawrence Construction Company, purchased ten acres of the former Murray farm in Bennington Heights east of Pottery Road, where it constructed twenty-two low rise apartment buildings of eight to ten units each, totalling 180 units, together with a number of detached bungalows.[25] Much of the land on which the new streets of Mallory Crescent and Leacrest Road were created by this development had been used during the war as victory gardens by nearby residents, including my own family.

Crestview Apts 1951
(Source: Crestview Investment Corp)

24. Interview with Peter Weatherhead, April 5, 2013

25. Grant, Suzanne, DiAnne & Bert C., *With a Box of Tools: a History of Crestview and the Grant Family*, Crestview Investment Corporation, 2014, 49

Before World War II, the Township of East York had been slowly evolving. After the war ended, it was quickly becoming Toronto's Garden of Eden.

East York Council 1950
(Source: East York Foundation)

– Chapter 8 –

METROPOLITAN TORONTO

As East York grew up, it lost the character of a rural community and took on its character as a small town within a big city. The Township had survived the threat of amalgamation with the City of Toronto, but now it had to face the threat of massive apartment development.

In 1940, East York was finally able to make a deal with its debenture holders to reduce the interest payments and shorten the repayment time on the debt. That allowed the township (which had been under provincial financial supervision since 1933 because of its inability to make interest payments on those debentures) to obtain an Ontario Municipal Board Order returning the council to full control of its financial affairs.[1] This gave new life to the ability of East York Council to provide municipal services to its residents. What were the township's municipals services like up to this time?

Percy Bustin, who opened his drugstore at the corner of Coxwell and Sammon Avenues in 1924 and later served on the Township Council from 1952 to 1962, tells the story:

---

1. East York Council minutes, March 1940

"Ever since its incorporation in 1924, the Township municipal offices together with its works yard has been located on Sammon Avenue (later the site of St. Aloysius Separate School and later still a French school). Now with the population increasing and with residents working and paying taxes there was an immediate need to provide better services which was not possible from these facilities. So in 1941, Council approved a plan to layout a Memorial Park at the corner of Coxwell and Mortimer on a portion of Billy McKay's farm acquired for unpaid property taxes. Seven years later, the Township offices moved to their new location with the opening of the new Municipal Building in Memorial Park." The park was to provide a constant reminder of those brave men and women of the community who paid the supreme sacrifice either in the First or Second world wars. In that regard, Percy added, "The Memorial Garden was so beautifully laid out, and which in our opinion, should never, but never be encroached upon in the future."[2]

The move to the new building gave the township space to improve and add to local municipal services. In the 1940s, a new Cosburn Fire Hall was built. The East York Kiwanis Club leased land in Cedarvale Park (now Stan Wadlow Park), where they constructed a swimming tank (now called the Kiwanis Pool). The East York Leaside Health Unit was established, the first Public Library Board was appointed, and the Don Valley Conservation Committee was formed. Approval was given to the East York Hydro Commission for its building in the Memorial Park, and the East York Community Centre Council was established.[3]

East York Municipal Building 1948-1990
(Source: East York Foundation)

2. Bustin, Percy, Memories: *The Early Days of East York*, Self –Published, 1976, 6
3. Township of East York in the Heart of Metropolitan Toronto, 1959-60

By 1950, however, the threat of amalgamation with the city of Toronto had reared its head again. All of the Toronto daily newspapers had been advocating total amalgamation for years. East York had faced this threat before. At one point, when the Township defaulted on its debenture payments during the Great Depression, it had actually courted annexation by the City. East York had joined the township of York, at that time, in an attempt to negotiate annexation. Bill Heaton, the township's comptroller known to the council as Mr. Everything, led the negotiations for East York. The city negotiator was R.C. Harris, the man for whom the R.C. Harris Water Filtration Plant on the Lake shore is named and the same man who had the foresight to add the second deck to the Prince Edward Viaduct, making it possible for the Bloor-Danforth subway line to be built years later. In the end, the negotiators agreed to disagree and the matter died for the time being.

By the end of World War II, the Greater Toronto Area had changed dramatically. Prosperity had returned. The population of the Toronto region fuelled by immigrants from Britain and Europe was growing rapidly. The sole exception, however, was the city of Toronto itself. The city was completely built up with virtually no vacant land within its pre-war boundaries. In fact, the city population was actually declining somewhat. The increasing population of the region, however, created housing, transportation, water supply, and sewage treatment problems for many of the other twelve municipalities surrounding the city. So on February 2, 1950, Toronto City Council voted to apply to the Ontario Municipal Board for complete amalgamation of the thirteen municipalities, one of which, of course, was East York.

The Ontario Municipal Board, made up of a three-man panel, was chaired by Lorne R. Cumming, Q.C. Before the hearings on the subject began, the OMB denied a request by the suburbs for an order requiring the City Council's application for amalgamation to be put to a vote of its taxpayers. The hearings themselves lasted from June 19, 1950, to June 7, 1951. During that time, the board members received three hundred written submissions and listened to three million words of oral testimony from eighty-five witnesses. Although the hearings ended in mid-1951, the board did not release its ninety-two page decision, soon known as the Cumming Report, until January 20, 1953.

All the witnesses on behalf of the City of Toronto supported amalgamation, emphasizing the efficiency and cost savings of one big government. Of course, the three Toronto daily newspapers did so as well. On the other hand, the suburbs emphasized the errors, extravagance, and inefficiencies of the city in handling its own problems, claiming these would only increase with amalgamation and result in higher overall taxation without any improvement in services. The suburbs placed heavy emphasis on public access to local government. Small-scale governments were more accessible to the taxpayers and more familiar with their local problems, they said. Former Swansea Reeve Elmer Brandon, now a Member of Provincial Parliament, put forward the idea that the city of Toronto should be split up into a number of smaller municipalities because larger cities get further away from the people. East York and the Township of York, reflecting the views of their residents, were insistent on maintaining their own identities, their frugal administrations, and their fiscal prudence while also recalling how in 1931, the City had said no to them during their time of need.

After Cumming had identified the main options, he met with Ontario Premier Leslie Frost and other Provincial government officials at least ten times to discuss the content of the OMB report before it was finally made public.

"Amalgamation," Cumming wrote, "would result in increased taxes due to bringing all the suburban wages, salary scales, and working conditions up to city levels… Costs would increase with the size of the municipality because of the larger number of employees per unit of population and per capita costs in general tend to increase with the size of the municipality. A large city is able to pay more than a small one and to afford an almost endless list of desirable but unnecessary expenditures. It is unrealistic to expect any single council to give sufficient consideration to the many difficult problems in an area of more than 240 square miles and over one million people. The need for reform does not justify complete amalgamation. The loss of local autonomy would mean domination of the central city through their concentrated voting power. An amalgamated city might be strong, efficient and well organized but it would not be local government." He went on to say, "Local government, in a democracy however, at least to the majority of Ontario people means a government which is very close to the local residents and is carried on by duly elected local leaders who offer their services from time to time in the interests of their local community and who learn at the same time something of the duties and responsibilities of public office... In the judgement of the board, these problems cannot be resolved by further reliance upon the process of voluntary inter municipal co-operation with its apparent inevitable delays. Apart from the interminable controversies involved in the method it would appear to be practically impossible to hope for unanimous approval of thirteen sets of local government when projects involving heavy capital expenditures, although located within some of the municipalities must be financed by combining the resources of all."

Instead of amalgamation or the status quo, Cumming recommended a federation in the best tradition of the British North American Act that created Canada in 1867. A new Metropolitan Toronto Council was to be created by the provincial legislature to be concerned with capital projects, property assessment, debenture borrowing, major trunk sanitary sewers, public transit, arterial roads, and regional planning. Meanwhile, the thirteen municipalities continuing to exist within their present boundaries would provide for policing, fire protection, licensing, libraries, local planning, and tax collection.

On February 25, 1953, Premier Frost personally moved first reading of Bill 80 in the Ontario Legislature, implementing the Cumming recommendations to establish the Municipality of Metropolitan Toronto.

Metropolitan Toronto Council was composed of the twelve mayors or reeves of the suburban councils, plus the mayor and two controllers receiving the most votes in the city together with the nine city aldermen who led the polls in their wards. The chairman of Metropolitan Toronto Council was to be appointed initially for a two-year term by the lieutenant governor in council, i.e. by the premier himself, and thereafter to be elected by Metro Council members. The chairman was not required to be one of the elected members of Metro Council. This left East York with one representative, the reeve, on a council of twenty-five. It is interesting to note in the light of current remuneration that the chairman's pay was not to exceed $15,000 per year; that the Metro Council members pay was not to exceed $1,800 per year, and that a committee chair's pay was not to exceed $100.

Fred Gardiner was appointed chairman and in doing so gave up an income of $50,000 a year practicing law for the job paying only $15,000, but he agreed to serve for two years only. He stayed on much longer than two years and became known as the "Big Daddy of Metro." In years to come, he was to face another tough customer in East York's True Davidson, whom I discuss in more detail later.

The Township of East York had now become an incorporated municipality within the incorporated Municipality of Metropolitan Toronto. The East York Council would deal with local issues, while its representative on the Metropolitan Toronto Council, the reeve, would deal with Metro-wide issues crossing the boundaries of the thirteen Metro area municipalities. [4]

Premier Leslie Frost (L) OMB Chairman Lorne Cumming (R)
(Source: Globe and Mail Feb 26, 1953)

The Thirteen Metro Police Forces Merge

While East York escaped total amalgamation in 1954, two years later, the East York Police did not. The township had its own police force from the day it was incorporated. "Before incorporation in 1924, East York was supervised by the York County Police Force. The Force used the Don Jail on Gerrard Street in the city of Toronto." After the incorporation, the new township police department consisted of the chief constable and five men.

---

4. Redway, Alan, *Governing Toronto: Bringing back the city that worked*, Friesen Press, 2014, Ch.2, 18, 34

People remember policemen riding on their bicycles. They also walked the beat. In those days, their equipment was very poor. In 1935, the then-sixteen-man force possessed only one car, so the men travelled on motorcycles, which didn't even have windshields. In the bitter cold winter, an officer would pad his knees and cover his face with brown paper. One officer use to stand at night in the horse manure at Silverwood's Dairy to warm his frozen feet.

There were other difficulties on the police force. The force's radio station was constantly breaking down. Since there were no cells in the tiny station, they had to use jails in other areas. In this area, they used the Main Street Jail.

In those early days, when the area was not densely populated, there was a good feeling between the police and the community. Officers had to live in the area to even be considered for the job. They knew and chatted with many people personally, and a much friendlier attitude existed than today. The police and the community were more like neighbours. Superintendent Walmer tells of spending most of his summer days in the Depression asking people to turn off their lawn sprinklers, and on hot nights walking through streets where people slept on lawns or wheeled cranky babies.[5]

East York Police Inspector James Warren told the story this way:

"Police history of the Township of East York dates back to 1923 when following the secession of the present Township of East York from the Township of York, Thomas McCann was appointed chief constable to maintain law and order in the new municipality.

"The chief constable's office at this time was in his residence on Gamble Ave. In the same year, William Wilken, originally a member of the County of York Police Force, severed his connections with that force to serve under Chief McCann, and a short time later was promoted to the rank of sergeant. Upon the death of Chief McCann in 1934, Wilken was appointed to chief constable, a position he held until his death a year later.

"At this time the personnel of your police force consisted of a chief constable, sergeant, and six constables as from 1923 to 1929 six men had been added to the force in the following order: Walter Mulock, who

---

5. Bustin, Percy, *Memories: The Early Days of East York*, Self –Published, 1976, 10

took charge of the force on the death of Chief Wilken (until the arrival of Ernest Old from York Township in 1936). Walter served under Chief Old as Deputy Chief until 1937 when he resigned to take up farming.

William Creighton who was retired on pension after twenty-five years' service.

William Masters, Sergeant, who passed away in 1945 after twenty-nine years' service.

Herbert Darnborough and Robert McKay, who resigned in 1935, and James Warren, now inspector.

"Two more constables were added in 1931. Henry Smith, the present chief constable, and Harold Haden, who died in 1951 after resigning due to ill-health.

"In those early days, the hours of duty consisted of twelve-hour shifts, six a.m. to six p.m. days and six p.m. to six a.m. nights with no days off, only summer vacations. The equipment at that time was comprised of one automobile and four motorcycles. In the early part of 1929 we received our orders from the chief's residence and we reported by telephone to his house every hour when on duty; when off-duty, if required, the chief would contact us at our respective residences. (It is here that I would like to say a word of appreciation to a lady who is still residing in our municipality. I refer to the first Chief Constable's wife, Mrs. McCann. Her manner, patience, and understanding during the period of phoning her home for orders, I am sure was appreciated by all the old members of the force – as one of them I personally say, "Thank you very much.")

"Late in the year 1929, a one-room police station with a small switchboard was installed at 443 Sammon Ave., the municipal offices. This was the headquarters for both police and fire departments.

"As previously stated, Ernest Old was appointed chief constable in 1936, and served in that capacity until 1949 when he died suddenly while on duty. In July of this same year, Deputy Chief Smith was appointed to rank of chief constable.

"With the tremendous increase in population, particularly during the past ten to twelve years, the need for a much larger force was apparent, and has resulted in new members being added to the strength of the department each year, until now the force comprises an over-all personnel of forty, all ranks, which includes the chief constable, two inspectors, four sergeants, one patrol sergeant, one sergeant of detectives, one detective, three plainclothesmen, twenty-six uniform constables and one clerk (civilian). There are four radio-equipped cars, and three motorcycles.

"There is every indication that 1952 will see the appointment of more new members as the population of the township will be close to 65,000 people residing and carrying on business throughout its seven square miles. With continued additions to the force, the need for larger quarters was much in evidence and the staff as a whole looked forward to the time when they would be located in a modern police station large enough to meet the requirements of an ever-expanding force and a rapidly growing community. The fall of 1948 saw the need fulfilled when the new Municipal Building was opened at Coxwell and Mortimer Avenues, of which the Police Dept. occupies the whole west wing, consisting of a main front office, chief constable's office inspector's office, orderly room, detective office, storeroom, and a cell-block of four separate units, which has been a great asset to the department, as previously all prisoners had to be taken to a city police station. This is a brief history of your police department, members of which are the defenders of your civil liberties, as the Honourable A.W. Roebuck, Q.C., so ably put it in an address, "Civil Liberty is the right of the citizen to live in freedom, unmolested by the Crown, the Government or any other citizen. Such freedom of each individual must of course be limited by the equal rights of all citizens band themselves together in communities and engage policemen and organize police forces, and charge them with the duty of maintaining an ordered society, regulated by the rule of law, the only possible form of society in which conditions of freedom can exist."

"To the citizens of East York, both old and new: this is your police department—we belong to you. Identify yourself as conscientious, community-minded, law abiding citizens by extending to us your good-will and cooperation. For without the good-will and cooperation of the people the efficiency of any police department is limited. Our sole purpose is not always to prosecute but rather to perform our duty so that the citizens of the community under our jurisdiction may live under the full protection of the laws and freedoms which we as a free nation are blessed with the liberty to enjoy." [6]

---

6. Souvenir Program, East York Police Association – First Annual Circus, 1952

The township had had its own Police Commission since 1936. In 1952, the commission was composed of the Reeve Harry Simpson, County Court Judge Ian Macdonnell, and Magistrate O.M. Martin. The force also had its own union, the East York Police Association and the association of its East York Police Ladies' Auxiliary.[7]

To read Inspector Warren's history of the East York Police Department, one would get the impression that there were no criminals and no crime in the township, but of course, that was not the case. Bruce Horner's father, Bert Horner, joined the East York Police Department in 1950. He was one of two police constables called to the scene of a suspected break and enter on Mortimer Avenue near Woodbine. The *Toronto Telegram* reported it as follows: "Cornered in the house the suspect dived head first through a window and a storm window landing in a shower of glass then raced ahead of the officers who fired several shots at him, wounding him once. He was captured half a block away after he had scaled ten back fences." [8]

One of Canada's most notorious bank robbers, Edwin Alonzo Boyd, grew up in East York. As a boy, Boyd lived with his family in a duplex on Bee Street (now Cosburn Avenue) but later moved to 160 Chisholm Avenue and then to 31 Glebemount Avenue. He attended Gledhill and Secord Public Schools before serving overseas in World War II. After the war ended, and while unemployed, Eddie Boyd turned to robbing banks for a living. Between 1949 and 1951, he and his accomplices held up at least six banks, one of which was in East York, directly involving the Township police department.

In January 1950, Boyd held up the Canadian Bank of Commerce on O'Connor Drive at St. Clair Avenue East. "One of the first police officers to join the chase was East York Constable Cecil Caskie, who by chance checked Don Mills Road and noticed the blue Meteor on the side road. "I found the engine of this car very warm and the keys in the ignition still swinging." The police were certain the bandit had fled into the heavy brush of the adjoining swampy ravine, near what is now Taylor Creek Park and the Don Valley. By two p.m., in a swirling snowstorm, about seventy-five uniformed officers and detectives from East York, Toronto, and surrounding departments were combing the six square-mile area

---

7. Souvenir Program, East York Police Association – First Annual Circus, 1952
8. Interview with Bruce Horner, January 31, 2017

from four different directions. Roadblocks had been set up on all streets leading in and out of the ravine, and police were canvassing nearby homes along Don Mills Road, O'Connor Drive, and St. Clair Avenue. They were stopping and searching freight trains on the CNR line running through the ravine. The police dragnet was for nothing. "Boyd had been in the bush only long enough to remove his disguise, walk quickly to a rented garage a few blocks south of O'Connor Drive where his panel truck was waiting, and left the area."[9] Pat Burford, whose uncle, Red Hogan, lived in the area at the time, says that Boyd hung out at 6 Torrens Avenue and hid his cars in the garage there.[10]

Eddie Boyd got away that time but a year later, after he had escaped from the Don Jail for a second time, members of the East York Police were among the parade of police armed with machine guns and shotguns who ultimately captured him and his gang in an abandoned barn off rural Don Mills Road. One of those East York police officers was Constable Bert Horner.[11]

In 1956, the thirteen area municipalities' police forces were amalgamated. Shades of things to come. The East York police force was integrated into the metropolitan police force. East York police force Chief Harry Smith became one of five deputy chiefs on the Metro force[12] and Bert Horner became a Metro police officer at 54 Division, stationed initially at the East York Municipal building and later on Cranfield Road. [13]

East York Police
(Source: Charlotte Balmer)

---

9. Vallee, Brian, Edwin Alonzo Boyd: *The Story of the Notorious Boyd Gang*, Doubleday Canada 1997, 86–89

10. Interview with Pat Burford, January 26, 2016

11. Interview with Bruce Horner, January 31, 2017

12. Interview with Charlotte Balmer, October 13, 2016

13. Interview with Bruce Horner, January 31, 2017

Bert Horner
(Source: Bruce Horner)

Cole Brothers Circus on Woodville 1931
(Source: East York Foundation)

Chief Smith
(Source: Charlotte Balmer)

Magistrate O.M. Martin
(Source: East York Foundation)

Reeve Harry Simpson
(Source: East York Foundation)

East York Police Department
(Source: Bruce Horner)

Edwin Boyd.
(Source: theglobeandmail.com)

Hunt for Edwin Alonso Boyd_Haystack
(Source:Bruce Horner)

The township had survived, at least for the time being, the threat of amalgamation with the city of Toronto, but now it had to face the apartment war.

– Chapter 9 –

THE APARTMENT WAR

If Farlinger Developments Limited had stuck to building single-family detached homes, all would have been well, but when it started to build apartment buildings, everything hit the fan. It was the beginning of the "Developers vs the Ratepayers" war. There were a number of battles and a great many skirmishes, but the hostilities really began with the battle of Rexleigh Drive.

East York has always been a community of home owners. The early settlers had an intense loyalty to their detached-home family neighbourhoods as opposed to apartment buildings. The war was touched off in 1957 when word got around that Farlinger planned to build apartment buildings on both sides of Rexleigh Drive north of Ferris Road in what was then designated ravine or valley lands.

Like any war, this one was shaped by events that preceded the outbreak of hostilities, specifically in this case, the election of Jack Allen to East York Council.

In his history of Woodbine Gardens, Michael Dolbey describes how the war began.

"Jack R. Allen first ran for East York Council in December 1953 at the age of thirty-four. He and his family had lived in East York all his life. His grandfather, Samuel Allen, had been East York's health officer for three years. Jack Allen was a veteran of five years' RCAF service, a graduate of the Niagara Parks Commission School of Horticulture, and was working as a landscape architect. He was a member of the Toronto Board of Trade and the East York Rotary club. He ran on a platform of park development, street improvement, and improvements in sewage and garbage disposal facilities. In his first election, Jack led the six-member council race with 5745 votes, out-distancing many former council members to become vice chairman of council. During his first one-year term, he was chairman of the Works Committee, which was responsible for parks.

At the next election in December 1954, Jack Allen ran for the position of reeve against Harry G. Simpson, who had held the post for the past five years (1949-1954) and John Warren, former reeve for fifteen years (1935-49). Harry Simpson won his sixth term and Allen was out of office, but not for long. In mid-1955, Councillor John McGivney resigned his seat because he was moving to Windsor. At the 1954 election, a resolution to change to a two-year term had been approved and it was reported that, unlike city councils, townships were not allowed to appoint members to fill vacancies between regular elections. As a result, a by-election was called for September 17, 1955. Six candidates ran for the position with Jack Allen winning a majority of 2,367 votes cast—a small 8% turnout. Much was made of the fact that the election cost taxpayers $4.22 per vote.

In March 1956, the issue of apartment buildings in East York was raised by Dentonia Investments Limited, who had purchased land between the south edge of Taylor Creek Ravine and Dentonia Park. It intended to build a 1500-unit apartment building but claimed it had purchased a right of way across the park that it would use if the Township did not provide other suitable access. Jack Allen favoured issuing the building permit. All other councillors had a variety of reservations. In the end, they voted to toss the question in the lap of Metro Parks Committee."

In the next Township elections on December 3, 1956, Harry G. Simpson, reeve for the previous six years, stepped down. Jack Allen ran for reeve and defeated C. Howard Chandler, a business executive and East York Councillor for the previous five years. Allen had campaigned on a platform of improved transportation, keeping taxes down, and retaining the township's park areas.

In March 1957, Reeve Jack Allen announced a plan to extend Cosburn Avenue east through Taylor Creek Valley to Victoria Park Avenue. The "handsome two-mile parkway winding through lush greenbelt park" could be linked to Dawes Road and the proposed north-south Rexleigh Drive to Main Street connection. The road was needed, Allen said, to relieve the rush-hour congestion at the corner of O'Connor Drive and Woodbine Avenue. No mention of apartment buildings was made at this time but plans were quickly developed for them around the proposed Cosburn Extension. True Davidson later claimed that Reeve Allen had hired an apartment architect named Sulio Venchiarutti as a planning consultant and that they "saw East York's future as one great apartment city, spreading from an arterial road in Taylor Creek valley, up both sides of the ravine."

Mike Dolbey
(Source: Panchetta Barnett)

Rexleigh Drive Looking South From Glenwood
(Source: East York Foundation)

Jack R Allen (Reeve)
(Source: East York Foundation)

Looking North From Hamstead
(Source: East York Foundation)

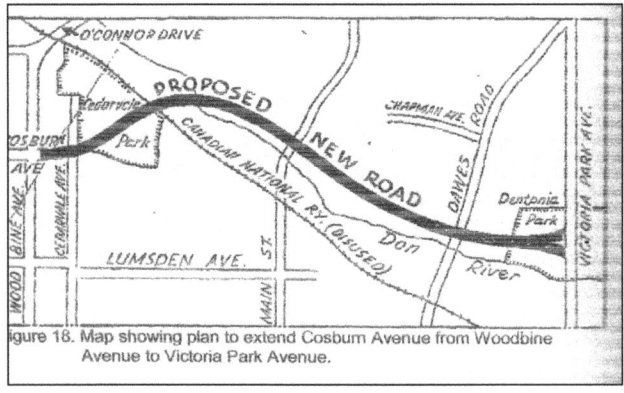

Figure 18. Map showing plan to extend Cosburn Avenue from Woodbine Avenue to Victoria Park Avenue.

Looking North From Hamstead
(Source: East York Foundation)

The Proposed Cosburn Avenue Extension

The plan was not received well by conservation groups that wanted the Don Valley and Taylor-Massey Creek valley lands preserved as natural areas. Allen pushed his plan through the Township Council's Planning Committee but Council rejected the plan and on November 4, 1957, enacted a freezing by-law (#6438) to prevent any changes in the township's zoning structure until a new township plan was approved unless Council passed a by-law asking the Ontario Municipal Board (OMB) to free specific areas for rezoning. The OMB held a hearing about this by-law on December 9, 1957, and recommended certain changes that were subsequently adopted by East York's Council with the passing of by-law #6464 amended freezing by-law on December 31, 1957.

Planning in the township was at an impasse. As the 1958 elections approached, the development of parklands became a central issue in the campaign. A group called the Don Valley Conservation association wanted the Township to donate the valley lands to the Metro Region Conservation Authority for the development of a green belt. Allen claimed that development firms were prepared to pay $2,000,000 for the apartment lands after the township provided services costing $500,000, and that East York needed the increased assessment. Reeve Allen described the "green belters" as "a bunch of birdwatchers who don't know what they are meddling in." The issues were heatedly discussed at an all-candidates meeting before the Woodbine Gardens–Morningside Park Ratepayers Association held at George Webster School.

Despite the controversy, Jack Allen was re-elected reeve of East York in December 1958. Former councillors Percy Bustin, Norman Cheeseman, and Norman McKay were re-elected with three new councillors, True Davidson, Royden Brigham (both former school trustees), and Willis Blair. Reeve Allen was known to be pro-development and former councillors Bustin, Cheeseman, and McKay were generally against high rise or ravine development. The new councillors Davidson, Brigham, and Blair were supporters of ratepayers' views on less development and preservation of green-space. The variety of views portended a stormy term for Council.

At the inaugural meeting of the new council in January, Reeve Allen stated that a master plan to control development and ensure orderly industrial and residential construction would be put in place in 1959 and that the township was looking forward to providing better park facilities with more swimming pools for children. His hope that the apartment-development controversy would fade away was shattered in February when members of the Woodbine Gardens and Morningside Park Ratepayers Association discovered that on December 5, 1958, the former council, in response to a request from Farlinger Development Ltd, had amended the freezing by-law to permit the construction of apartment buildings in the Ferris ravine on Rexleigh Drive. It was reported that the developer intended to erect three high-level apartment buildings and a shopping centre on the site. More than two hundred members of the ratepayers association jammed the February 16 council meeting, demanding that the by-law of the previous council be reversed. When this was not approved, they demanded that Council agree to inform the OMB that they were not in favour of the unfreezing by-law passed by the previous council. The council finally passed resolution 6825: "Council goes on record as being not necessarily in favour of by-law 6574 as submitted to the OMB."

Leading the Woodbine Gardens and Morningside Park Ratepayers Association were James A. (Jim) McConaghy, president, and Jack Christie, secretary. Jim McConaghy, the general manager of a manufacturing firm, lived at the west end of Glen Robert Drive. When he bought his property in Morningside Park and built his home in the late 1940s, it overlooked the Ferris ravine creek and the Woodbine golf course. McConaghy had run unsuccessfully for East York Council in the 1958 election. Jack Christie had been active in organizing community baseball and hockey teams and was by this time secretary of the Ontario Minor Hockey Association. He lived on the south end of Glen Eden Crescent in Woodbine Gardens just to the north of the Ferris Ravine. Their association claimed that the proposed apartment complex would significantly affect views and property values in their area. They claimed that Farlinger Developments had misled buyers in their area, saying that circulars promoting the development promised that ravine lands would be maintained as parklands. They believed that it was inappropriate to erect tall apartment buildings in the midst of a large area of single family dwellings. Mr. Farlinger denied that his circulars mentioned a greenbelt and stated that the land had been zoned for apartments as far back as 1954 when the development plan had been submitted to Council for approval.

At the next council meeting on March 2, 1959, Jim McConaghy, on behalf of the ratepayers association, urged Council to take no action to support further developments on Rexleigh Drive. Lawyers for Farlinger Development Corporation and other parties urged Council to allow these developments. It was unanimously agreed by Council that no action be taken. The developers were unhappy with this decision and on April 16 gave notice that they would appeal the freezing by-law to the OMB. The appeal was successful but the township still did not issue the permits. On September 10, lawyers for the developer served notice that they would apply to the Supreme Court of Ontario for an order of mandamus, requiring the Township of East York to issue permits to build two multiple-suite apartment buildings on the Rexleigh Drive site.

Meanwhile, Reeve Allen introduced a master zoning plan that had been developed by consultant Sulio Venchiarutti and his firm, Urban Planning Consultants. It recommended massive apartment-complex developments both in the Taylor Creek Ravines and to the east of Woodbine Avenue between Oak Park and Lumsden Avenues. It was debated in Council on April 29, 1959, amid cheers and boos from ratepayers, who jammed the council chamber. After heated debate, a resolution made by Councillor Percy Bustin to turn down the plan as unacceptable was passed. Demands that the contract of the planning consultants be terminated were resisted by Reeve Allen but the firm resigned a month later. This was seen as a victory for the Woodbine Gardens and Morningside Park Ratepayers Association, who had demanded their removal.

On September 22, 1959, Mr. Justice Walsh of the Supreme Court of Ontario ordered the Township of East York to issue building permits for the Rexleigh Drive developments despite the freezing by-laws that were in place. Council met on September 30, 1959, and instructed the township's solicitor to draft a new temporary zoning by-law that incorporated new building standards that limited building height in areas of single family dwellings. The new by-law 6688 was passed on October 8, 1959, and Council resolved to issue building permits to all requests that met the new by-law. Within a month, the township had received forty-four requests for permits for apartment development and it was reported that ten had been accepted. Council was again considering ways of curtailing all construction until approval of zoning restrictions. During this period, Reeve Allen used his influence to obtain a building permit for the Hampton Park Apartments in the Governor's Bridge area of East York on land that the previous council had designated as green belt. This became the infamous "Bayview Ghost," the story of which has been told elsewhere. In early November, it was reported that the Ontario Department of Municipal Affairs had launched an investigation of East York's financial affairs and Reeve Allen spent seventy minutes behind closed doors with Minister Warrender. No outcome of the investigation has been found and there is no mention of an investigation in the township minutes.

In mid-November 1959, at a meeting of the Woodbine Gardens and Morningside Park Ratepayers Association, Reeve Jack Allen was asked to explain the township's apartment-building policy and the meeting finished with demands that the reeve and his council resign. Allen then blamed groups such as the ratepayers association for causing the rejection of his earlier proposed official plan saying, "If the first official plan had been accepted, we wouldn't be in this predicament today."

Construction of the two six-storey apartment buildings on Rexleigh Drive, for which permits had been ordered by the Supreme Court, proceeded during late 1959 and 1960. Though not high by later standards, they towered over the homes of Jim McConaghy, Jack Christie, and their neighbours. All the other apartment blocks built later along the Ferris ravine crossing of Rexleigh Drive were only two storeys high, suggesting that the building standards incorporated in the new zoning by-laws passed in October 1959 had been effective. No subsequent reports about this apartment controversy have been found in the press.

At the end of 1959, as the municipal elections approached, True Davidson was convinced to run for reeve by representatives of almost all of the ratepayers groups and particularly by Jack Christie, who had worked closely with her to implement the East York Canada Day celebrations that True had instituted. In later life, True Davidson introduced Jack Christie to a friend as "the person who got me elected as reeve the first time." Jim McConaghy ran for council and campaigned on closer liaison between council and ratepayers, vacant land retained for parks, and preservation of a green belt. It was reported that most candidates were "railing against the Ontario Municipal Board for its slowness in handling the township's master zoning plan."

A record 40% of voters turned out for the 1960 East York municipal elecion, the highest in the township's history. True Davidson won a clear victory, defeating Jack Allen by more than 1600 votes. Elected councillors were Leslie Saunders (former mayor of Toronto), Willis Blair, James McConaghy, Percy Bustin, Norman Maughan, and Norman McKay.[1]

Jack Christie, in his memoirs, *The Generation of Changes*, explains why he got involved in the war and how others helped to fight it.

The doorbell rang at our Glen Eden Crescent residence one evening in 1957. A man who introduced himself as Percy Green was about to issue an invitation that would start us walking on a completely different path.

He and I had never met, but when I invited him in to explain the reason for his visit, my garden suddenly expanded. Unknown to him, or to me, the door was opening for an opportunity to service the community in which I lived. I didn't realize it at the time, and I certainly harboured no such aspirations. But my course was being changed and I had no control over that. I was about to start down a new and unknown path but never alone. I would do what was expected of me and things would turn out all right.

Percy Green was an East York citizen, a resident in a bungalow at the northeast corner of Ferris Road and Rexleigh Drive. He had learned that developers planned to build apartment buildings on both sides of Rexleigh Drive, north of Ferris Road in what was then designated, ravine or valley lands. Percy Green feared such development. As it turned out, Percy was opposed to the point of obsession. His fears were well founded.

His purpose in knocking at my door was to request our support by having us sign a petition to be presented to council, expressing the community's opposition to such development.

When Dorothy and I both agreed to sign (the buildings would overlook and shadow our garden) he invited us to attend a Sunday evening meeting at the home of Reeve Jack Allen. Because I had never seen a local reeve, much less been in the home of a reeve, we accepted the invitation. "Reeve" was the rural equivalent of mayor. Once again my self-styled trait of being 'a sucker for anything I've never done before' came to the forefront and I said we would love to attend. That was a decision destined to change our lives.

---

1. `Dolbey, Michael, History of Woodbine Gardens, Self–published, 2015, 21, 27

There were about fifty people seated in the basement recreation room of Reeve Allen's house at Ferris Road and Notley Drive. The reeve stood behind his bar and spoke to the people. Various members of the audience responded or asked questions. I was surprised when the reeve answered every question vaguely, or avoided answering the question at all. Finally I couldn't keep quiet any longer, I stood up and repeated the previous question and got the same type of answer. So I re-phrased the question, same result. I started to walk slowly along the front of the bar, thinking of a different way to ask the same question. This went on for some time, and I was getting no closer to an answer. All the while one gentleman (I learned later he was a lawyer engaged by one of the residents) kept motioning for me to continue. It felt like a Perry Mason (remember him?) type exchange. I persisted, and finally I said, "Mr. Reeve, will you please tell us, are you going to help the people, or are you on the side of the developers?" This time he said, "I will support whatever is best for the people of East York," which told us he had no intention of supporting our position. The rebuffed assembly left his home.

Another meeting was arranged for a few nights later at the home of Jim and Grace McConaghy on Glen Robert Drive. At that meeting a committee was appointed to form, or re-organize, the Woodbine Gardens and Morningside Park Ratepayers Association. A week or so later a public meeting was held at George Webster School and I assumed my first public office.

Mr. McConaghy became the first president and Jack Christie was elected secretary. My "big mouth" at the Reeve's home had identified me for office, once again the office of secretary.

All of that activity only set the stage for what was to come. We were able to recognize that the reeve was in favour of the development and would be of no help to us. He actually was opposed to our position. We learned later that one of the developer officials was a close personal friend of the reeve.

We made arrangements to appear before the Township Council at its next meeting. We were aware that Council had already passed an amendment to the zoning by-law to permit the development. We requested that Council rescind the by-law because it had been passed without any public consultation. Despite the fact that we were supported by a group of residents large enough to pack the Council chambers, we didn't have much success. We appeared to have the sympathy of most councillors, but not enough for them to rescind an act that had been passed by that same council. The session adjourned without resolving our problem.

During the Council meeting, Reeve Allen had been openly hostile. In one remark he made fun of "Penny collector McConaghy" because of Jim's business operating Penny Gum machines in various shops and banks. He also addressed me and said, "You are the leader of a few rabble-rousers in a small area and I (Allen) represent the whole municipality." He had no way of knowing that his remark would spark the organization of the largest and strongest ratepayer movement East York has ever known.

Mr. McConaghy as president and I as secretary were joined by Marg Anderson as treasurer, Jack Manley, Cy Reader, Edris McKay, Wally Scott, Alex Best and Jack Irwin as officers of the Woodbine Gardens and Morningside Park Ratepayers' Association. There was another ratepayers' association in the south end of our area known as the Secord Ratepayers' Association and we decided to contact them.

The meeting of the minds of the two organizations resulted in the resolve to start a federation of ratepayers' associations in East York. But first there had to be more associations organized. We set up a committee consisting of McConaghy, Christie, Jack Manley, Cy Reader, and Jack Irwin from our association along with Jim Edmonds and Joe Bartley from the Secord Association. We drew up a plan to organize a ratepayers' association around every public school in the municipality. Within a few months we had done that. We now had a total of thirteen community groups organized. Among the thirteen there were our first two groups as well as the Parkview Hills association, Collegiate Community, Hartman Jones, Broadview area, Governors Bridge, Bennington Heights, William Burgess and Selwyn St. Clair associations. All had agreed to unite under one umbrella organization, the Federation of Ratepayers' Associations of East York.

Jim McConaghy and I were unanimously elected founding president and secretary of the new federation. Once again I was into something I had never done before. In this case, it had never happened before in East York. Thus it was that when we next appeared before Council I was able to address them with an opening statement: "Mr. Reeve, like you I now represent the whole municipality." That didn't have much effect on the reeve but we could see that Council members were quite impressed and True Davidson obviously enjoyed the situation. So did the people I represented.

Although Council members made themselves appear to be sympathetic towards our cause, they declined any action that would rescind the motion. Sensing the trend, I hurriedly scribbled out a note and passed it to one of the councillors I felt might support us. It read something like "Although Council doesn't wish to rescind the proposed amendment this Council does go on record as being not necessarily in favour of the development as proposed." Councillor Brigham read it and nodded. He then proposed a motion worded as I had suggested and True Davidson seconded it. It passed with only Reeve Allen opposed.

Armed with that much, we prepared to oppose the proposal when it was being considered at the Ontario Municipal Board. We had engaged a lawyer, a Mr. Newman, whose wife was a well-respected controller on the Council of the City of Toronto. We had several meetings with Mr. Newman. At one of those meetings I told him I had read an article in a newspaper that made me doubt our Council's right to have passed the zoning amendment during the period in which it had been approve, just before an election.

I had read of a case in New Brunswick in which the courts had upset a Council action because the decision had been taken in the period between nomination day and Election Day. The same situation applied to East York. Mr. Newman said nothing but made a note of my comment, as he had done with anything any of our group had said.

Then came the O.M.B. meeting. It started at 9:30 a.m. and lasted all day. At the opening meeting the East York Council's lawyer rose to read the motion I had scribbled and Council had passed. The chairman of the board reacted angrily. He almost shouted, "If Council can apply here for approval of a zoning amendment and then send along another motion that they do not necessarily approve, they're crazy. They cannot pass their responsibility to this board. We shall proceed to hear the original application."

The East York solicitor responded by saying, "Yes sir, but representing the wishes of Council, I am unable to say anything in support of the application." We had gained at least that much and had defused Council support of the application. We then spent the rest of the day hearing various lawyers from the companies involved in the development and from a couple of residents who opposed it. Finally, our lawyer was called to rebut the various lawyers. He very calmly rose and said, "Sir, with all due respect, I don't think we should even be here today."

The chairman, quite surprised, asked why he would say such a thing.

Mr. Newman then explained that the amendment for which the hearing was being held was the product of a "rump council." He cited the New Brunswick case I had raised and elaborated by quoting half a dozen others, even a couple in Britain in the 1700s.

A disgusted chairman asked, 'Why didn't you tell us that at 9:30 this morning?' Mr. Newman replied, "Sir, it's quite possible we may be back here sometime and I thought it would be useful if I heard what they had to say." The chairman then asked the developers lawyers if they had any response, and they responded negatively except for a couple of Latin quotes I didn't understand. The chairman said, "You're reaching with that" and ruled the application rejected, the by-law voided. We were the winners. We thought!

When we left the offices of the Ontario Municipal Board that day, we thought that democracy had prevailed. The people had spoken and the people had won out over the developers. But justice does take some surprising turns and we were about to experience one. The lawyers for the developers appealed to the courts, asking that the court direct East York to issue a building permit. They based their petition on a case in which a developer had challenged the validity of the zoning by-law of the Township of Scarborough and had won. East York's zoning by-laws was similar, and the judge accepted the Scarborough case as a precedent and ruled in favour of our antagonists. The Township had no course but to issue the building permits when requested to do so.

The builder almost immediately applied for permits but for only two of the four buildings he planned to build. Restricting himself to two at that time turned out to be a mistake because eventually it would be to our benefit.

Jim McConaghy and I, as president and secretary of both our own association and of the federation, had many occasions to visit with and talk to the various council members. Jim and I were in full agreement that the associations under our leadership would be "different" from the traditionally radical rate-payer groups. We advocated a peaceful approach to Council as opposed to the antagonistic "storm the ramparts" tactics of most ratepayer groups. We were successful. So much so that the more radical individuals in the movement called us "McConaghy and Christie, the great pacifists." We reasoned that Council as our friends would do more for us than if we were enemies. We believed that as soon as they realized that we were opposed to them as politicians, they no longer had to fear us because they had already lost our votes. Our beliefs prevailed and one day as I was leaving True Davidson's home (after having secured indications of her support) she said to me, "You are a breath of fresh air in our political atmosphere." That may have been because, in this field new to me, I was again the naïve beginner. I was just doing my job and things were working out. That wasn't the last nice thing she said to or about me.

Our pacifist, or friendly, approach didn't mean that we never demonstrated our strength. When one of us was scheduled to represent our association at a council or committee meeting, resident supporters filled the council chambers. The difference was that they were quiet and orderly and did nothing to disturb the decorum of the meeting. I feel that our cause was helped by this approach and by our evident control over those who were there to support us.[2]

This one was at least a partial victory for the developers but it had ignited a raging fire in the ratepayers' right across East York. Council seemed to get the message.

| Jim McConakey | Jack Christie | True Davidson 1959-60 |
| *(Source: East York Foundation)* | *(Source: Jack Christie)* | *(Source: google.ca)* |

---

2. Christie, Jack, *The Generation of Change,* Self–published, Ch. 17, 175, 176, 180

The Bayview Ghost

The second battle in the war, that of the Bayview Ghost, took place in the Governor's Bridge area at the extreme west end of the township on land Council had originally designated as green belt. Reeve Jack Allen was involved in this one up to his neck as well.

The ghost, also known to some as the white elephant, was a derelict apartment building that stood on the table lands south of Nesbitt Drive overlooking the Bayview Extension where a subdivision of detached homes stands today. The tale of the ghost began in 1953 when the developers purchased twenty-eight acres of land mainly in the Don Valley. Shortly after, however, Metro Toronto expropriated seventeen acres of the land to construct both the Don Valley Parkway and the Bayview Extension.

Six years later, in 1959, the developers applied to the Township of East York for a permit to construct two seven-storey apartment buildings on their remaining table land, which they intended to be the first phase of eleven similar buildings on that site. Ignoring a prior commitment to consult with the nearby East York residents of Governor's Bridge and Bennington Heights before making any decision, the Township Council went ahead and rezoned the site for apartments without providing for municipal sewer services. The building inspector then issued the permit, which later, it was alleged, had been done under duress from the Township reeve, Jack Allen. Once the building permit was issued, construction began immediately and continued non-stop under floodlights well into the night.

A storm of protests from the local residents caused the council to reverse itself by passing resolutions prohibiting sewer construction and revoking the building permit. That brought construction to a halt but not before the walls and floors of a seven-storey building had been erected.

Between 1960 and 1976, numerous unsuccessful attempts were made to bring down the ghost structure. The township zoned the site for detached homes but the Ontario Municipal Board (OMB), unwilling to decide whether the building permit had been issued illegally, referred the matter to the courts to decide the issue by way of a stated case in which all parties had to agree on the facts in advance of the court hearing. Because the township, the developers, and the residents could never agree on the facts, the courts never heard the case. Next, East York asked Metro Toronto to expropriate the property, but Metro refused. Then East York, now the Borough of East York, declared the ghost to be an unsafe structure, but the developers immediately repaired it. When the borough tried to claim the ghost for unpaid taxes, the developers promptly paid up in full.

The matter was brought to a head in 1979 when the borough obtained a special act of the Ontario Legislature authorizing it to enter the site, tear down the ghost, and charge the demolition costs to the developers. After failing to have the courts block the borough from proceeding under this legislation, the developers went straight to the Ontario Municipal Board with an entirely different plan. Prior to the OMB hearing, the developers made a deal with Metro Toronto to give up their still unpaid $1.7 million claim for the seventeen acres Metro had expropriated back in 1953 in exchange for the right to build cloverleaf access from the site of the ghost to the Bayview Extension. At the OMB hearing that followed, the developers presented their new plan for 880 high rise and townhouse units. The borough, supported by the local residents, countered with a plan for a sixty-six detached home subdivision. Mysteriously, rather than choosing one of the two plans before it, the board pulled its own plan out of thin air and approved 440 townhouse units for the site. The borough then appealed that strange decision to the Ontario Provincial Cabinet. With the enormous help of our local MPPs Bob Elgie, Dennis Timbrell, and Margaret Scrivener, all three of whom were Provincial Cabinet ministers (the cabinet was also under the pressure of a provincial election campaign), overturned the OMB and approved the borough's plan.

That brought the developers to the negotiating table. When East York Mayor Alan Redway met with them, they outlined two options; either they could build according to the borough plan or wait and do nothing until Redway was no longer the mayor and then try again to have their plan approved. They had been around for years before Alan Redway was mayor, they said, and they would still be here long after he was gone. Finally, however, a peace treaty was agreed upon for exactly what East York had asked for at the OMB: the demolition of the ghost at the developer's expense and the construction of a detached home subdivision.

In November 1981, the twenty-two-year-old ghost was finally demolished, but construction of the subdivision did not proceed for some time after the demolition. Access to the site under the approved plan required the construction of a bridge over the railroad right-of-way, the ownership of which was claimed by both the original owner, the Ontario and Quebec Railway and the CPR. They had been using the right-of-way under a ninety-nine-year lease from the old Ontario and Quebec Railway, which was about to expire. Now, of course, the Ontario and Quebec Railway was claiming ownership in order to sell it back to the CPR for a huge profit. The case went all the way to the Supreme Court of Canada, which finally decided in favour of the CPR. Shortly after that decision was handed down, the bridge was approved and the houses were built. Today, where the Ghost stood for twenty-two years, there is a detached home subdivision in keeping with the character of the nearby neighbourhoods. Score this one for the ratepayers.[3]

Bayview Ghost
(Source: Bayviewnews.com)

---

3. Redway, Alan, Recollections, 1972–1994

Alan Redway at Bayview Ghost
(Source: John Mahler Tor Star)

Robert Elgie
(Source: The Globe and Mail)

Dennis Timbrell 2017
(Source: Dennis Timbrell)

The Battle of Mallory Crescent

Although Reeve True Davidson and her council seemed to have learned the lesson from the battle of Rexleigh Drive, ten years later, shades of Jack Allen, they apparently had forgotten it entirely.

Cadillac Developments and Belmont Construction had applied to rezone 10.5 acres of land including the Mallory Crescent road allowance itself (south of Moore Avenue and east of Bayview Avenue) in order to permit the construction of three twenty-two-storey and two twenty-nine-storey apartment buildings. That proposal would have replaced forty-six existing single family homes with 1382 new apartment units.

At that time, 1966, Mallory Crescent was located in Bennington Heights in the Township of East York bordering on the Town of Leaside. As a result of the Goldenberg Royal Commission report, the Ontario Legislature had passed legislation effective January 1, 1967, merging the town with the township to create the Borough of East York. The Mallory Crescent battle was fought at the same time as merger discussions were going on between East York and Leaside.

The fight began when East York Council approved the development over the objections of Leaside Council. After receiving representations from the area ratepayers, Leaside Council agreed to oppose the rezoning when it came before the OMB for approval.

Despite that and despite receiving a letter from Reeve True Davidson of East York lauding the benefits of the project, the ratepayers collected and delivered petitions and hundreds of letters of opposition to East York Council. Leaside and Bennington Heights homeowners then packed a public meeting held at East York Collegiate aimed at selling the merits of the proposal to the residents. The next day, a Toronto newspaper called it a stormy session that accomplished nothing. In fact, however, it served to strengthen the ratepayers' resolve to oppose the rezoning. The residents then launched a fund-raising drive culminating with another packed public meeting at Leaside High School. This resulted in the formation of the Leaside-Bennington Heights Association, which with the support of the Leaside Property Owners Association took the lead opposing the rezoning.

At the OMB hearings, which lasted ten days, the application for approval of the rezoning by East York Council was opposed by the Leaside-Bennington Heights Association—represented by one ratepayer from Leaside (Donald Anderson) and one ratepayer from Bennington Heights (Eric Moore)—the Leaside Property Owners Association, Leaside Council, and a number of individuals appearing in person. The board's decision was a victory for the residents. Not only was the rezoning application dismissed, but legal costs were awarded against both the developers and the township for the first time.

The developers appealed to the provincial cabinet but it was rejected. One month later, Leaside and East York merged to become the Borough of East York. The battle of Mallory Crescent set a precedent in the history of community action.[4]

Jack Christie, as a member of the Township Planning Board, played a role in this one as well:

Mallory Crescent was another East York area that came into prominence during my tenure. An application had been made for approval of a plan to demolish the homes and low-rise apartment buildings and replace them with high-rise. The site seemed to be an ideal site for such a development, set to one side from Leaside proper and over-looking the Don Valley Parkway. The approval hearings spread through several Planning Board meetings and we never had any representation from the public. The Planning Board recommended approval and the matter proceeded to council. It was then that the public uproar started. As a result, Council arranged to have a public meeting at East York Collegiate. The eight-hundred-seat auditorium was packed, and many members of the public had their say, as did Reeve Davidson, members of Council, Planning Board members, and the developers' lawyers. I was one of the last to speak. I tried to be honest and outlined the various Planning Board meetings, reminding the people that there had been no public opposition at any time during that process. I told them that I had voted for the development and that under the same circumstances, I would vote yes again. But I did tell them that if they thought we were wrong they should appear at the Ontario Municipal Board hearings and try to convince the board that we were wrong. I also assured them that if the board ruled in their favour, I would support them in their opposition of the development. To my surprise, they enthusiastically applauded. In retrospect, that applause probably triggered the end of my membership on the East York Planning Board.

The Municipal Board supported the objecting ratepayers and refused approval of the Mallory Crescent development. That fall my term on the board would expire and I, or someone else, would be appointed for the next three-year term. I was not re-appointed.

I received a nice letter from True Davidson thanking me on behalf of the community for my great contribution to planning and to East York. It didn't mention re-appointment nor expiration of my term. Just "thank-you" and in effect, goodbye from the board.

---

4. Redway, Alan, Recollections, 1972–1994

About ten years later, while visiting some East Yorkers in Florida, I was told the reason why I hadn't been re-appointed. My informant was Howard Chandler, an alderman who had been involved. He told me that True had approached him and was concerned because I appeared to be developing a position from which I could run for mayor, and that besides being strong in my own ward I had the complete backing of Leaside residents. She also was planning to retire and was afraid that I would be "a shoo-in" for a vacant mayoralty chair. This didn't fit with her plans. She considered Willis Blair as the right man for the job and she wanted him to succeed her. That also meant removing anyone who might stand in the way. Removal from the Planning Board would reduce my exposure.[5]

Crescent Town

One massive apartment development that sparked little if any ratepayer opposition was that of Crescent Town because it complied with the Township of East York's 1962 Official Plan. This large-scale apartment development was built on the thirty-three acre site of Crescent School, formerly part of the Dentonia Park Farm between Victoria Park Avenue and Dawes Road. Crescent Town consists of fourteen buildings containing 2,737 suites in six apartment buildings and many townhouses, some of which are rented and the others have condominium ownership. The complex developed by Howard Investments and built in 1970 by Belmont Construction Company Limited includes a school, shopping plaza, medical offices, and a recreation social centre with a swimming pool, all linked to the subway by a skywalk.[6]

Crescent Town
(Source: East York Foundation)

5. Christie, Jack, *The Generation of Change,* Self–published, 183, 184
6. The *East Yorker,* September 1969

Laird and Eglinton

In 1972, George Goldlist submitted a plan to redevelop the Sangamo factory site at the southeast corner of Laird and Eglinton for high rise apartments. Goldlist had built many of the high-rise apartment buildings in Thorncliffe Park including the forty-two-storey Leaside Towers at 85 and 95 Thorncliffe Park Drive, which when built, were the tallest in the British Commonwealth. The Thorncliffe Park apartments complied with Leaside's Official Plan (OP), but this site was designated industrial in the OP. That sent the residents of the former Town of Leaside, now merged with the township as part of the Borough of East York, up the wall. More mass meetings were held. Fortunately, the Borough Council turned down the project three years later with little debate. It appeared that East York Council had finally gotten the message, so a potential major battle turned into a minor skirmish.[7]

Thorncliffe Park Development
(Source: East York Foundation)

---

7. Redway, Alan, Recollections, 1972–1994

Woodbine and O'Connor

The last major battle in the apartment war ended in 1977, but it had started eleven years earlier. At that time, Peter Dimitroff (who had previously constructed a high-rise apartment building, called the Citadelle, on Don Mills Road adjacent to the North York boundary with no opposition) proposed an apartment development on the north side of O'Connor Drive, just west of the Woodbine Bridge.

Approval of his proposal made in the name of Hemus Developments must have appeared to Mr. Dimitroff to be a forgone conclusion. After all, The Trillium, a high-rise apartment built on the site of the old Hollinger Bus line garages at 1501 Woodbine Avenue, had already been constructed on the east side of Woodbine just south of the bridge. But he hadn't taken into account the Collegiate Community Ratepayers Association under the able leadership of Gladys Lane. By 1972, the Hemus Developments proposal had been rejected by the Borough Council, the OMB, and the Ontario provincial cabinet. However, that didn't stop Peter Dimitroff; he came back a year later under the name of Claverly Developments with a large townhouse proposal for the same site. Although Council initially approved the Claverly proposal, it was subsequently reversed following the next election on the initiative of a new ward Alderman John Flowers, a member of the Collegiate Community Ratepayers Association. Again, the Dimitroff proposal was rejected at the OMB. But Peter Dimitroff believed that if at first you don't succeed, try, try, and try again, which he did with the Trimontium proposal for a detached-home subdivision for the same site.

This time, the ratepayers agreed with the idea but opposition now came from the Toronto Field Naturalists led by Helen Juhola, who pointed out that many proposed houses were too close to the edge of the Don Valley, possibly destroying the old-growth trees and unique flora and fauna. Finally, after the plan was modified, those issues were resolved and the development went ahead.[8] It was another victory for ratepayer persistence and action. The East York spirit was alive and well.

The apartment war launched East York's True Davidson Era.

---

8. East York Council minutes, 1976

726 O'Connor home of R.H. Bob McGregor (demolished for Trimontium)
(Source: Jim Lister)

Gladys Lane (C) Stan Wadlow (L) Judge Blake Lane (R)
(Source: Stan Wadlow)

John Flowers
(Source: East York Foundation)

– Chapter 10 –

THE TRUE DAVIDSON ERA

True Davidson is an icon, and her name is synonymous with East York.

True was born Jean Gertrude Davidson in 1901 at Hudson, Quebec. Before moving to East York in 1947 at the age of forty-six, she had lived in four provinces; graduated from Normal School in Regina; taught elementary and high school; graduated with both a BA and a MA from Victoria College, University of Toronto; worked for a book publisher; and as the municipal clerk for the Village of Streetsville (now part of Mississauga). When she left Streetsville and moved to a three-room cottage on Linsmore Crescent in East York (which she later described as a combination egg-crate), she was broke, lonely, and depressed. However, True didn't stay down for long. Soon she was organizing a kindergarten at her own home for the local children. It made such an impression on her neighbours that they urged her to run for the school board. Thus, five years after moving to East York, True's career in the public life of the township had begun.

Eleanor Darke describes this era in her book, *Call ME True*:

"Within two years after her election as a school trustee, East York had a kindergarten programme renting whatever extra space required. Then she began to fight for special classes for the hard of hearing, the retarded, the rapid learners, and for bigger playgrounds, instrumental music, and better library facilities. She felt strongly that Canada had its own literature and that the schools should be teaching more of it. In his tribute at her funeral, Dalton A. Morrison, then director of education for East York said, 'True's mark is on the community's education development. She pushed for programs to recognize individual differences...academic excellence... music and the arts...scholarship fund...student government...improved educational climate...competitive working conditions for staff...library resource centres...trustee workshops...In educational circles it has been said that women are overlooked. True broke this mould in 1952 to become the first woman to chair the East York Board of Education and again to chair the finance committee of the Metropolitan School Board.'"[1]

During True's time as a school trustee, Cosburn and St. Clair (now Gordon A. Brown) Junior High Schools were completed and Victoria Park, Presteign Heights, Selwyn, George Webster, and Parkside Public Schools were built.

"But the school board did not pay a living wage." Emily Smith talked about how True never had any money. "She managed so many things so well for a person who had as little money as she had...She made do with more things than I ever knew anybody to. I didn't know that kind of – I was going to say—poverty. It was poverty." After True sold her little house on Linsmore, she "moved several places, paying rent. She really had to have a very low rent-rate in order to have a place of her own. For a while, she lived here in our recreation room. It was always a matter of being able to pay the rent." Jack Christie remembered True "living in a basement apartment on Cosburn Avenue and other than her bed all her furniture was orange crates covered in fabric," and that "she never had much money. Half the time she was on the Hydro Commission she was behind in her rates." Willis Blair recalled, "True was frugal in every way. She had to be. She had no money. When she'd go to school-board conventions—she went to every one she could—she'd take the money that was required for train fare or plane fare, whatever, and she'd take a cheaper route and use the difference to eat on."[2]

---

1. Darke, Eleanor, *Call Me True, A Biography of True Davidson*, Dundurn Press, 1997, 57
2. Drake, Eleanor, *Call Me True, A Biography of True Davidson*, Dundurn Press, 1997, 66

True topped the polls in her first run for council, receiving 5,772 votes out of a possible 40,000. Her nearest competitor was more than 600 votes behind. She enthused to the reporters: "It's unbelievable, it's wonderful. I'll serve ten years on council like the last ten years I had on the board of education." She spoke of how she had decided to run because it was time for a change and because she believed that East York needed a master plan of zoning bylaws. "East York should have planned development such as they have in European cities. We are small, compact, and cohesive, and we could do a planning job that could be the envy of Canada. Her decision to run certainly wasn't for the money. Willis Blair elected the same year, remembered that "we got $1,450 for our first year on Council"—although, even this sum was more than what True had been receiving as a school board trustee.

Although settlement in the East York area can be traced back to the 1790s, the municipality itself was only thirty-four years old when True joined Council. As True later wrote, East York "was hardly old enough to be well established in 1929 when we entered the chill days of depression. Growth was impossible and even hope was hard to maintain. Only after blood was pumped back into the veins of our economy by terrible surgical processes of war did we become what from the beginning we had in us to be." She described the members of Council in those days as "individual giants" who ran things their way, but who ran them well. "I remember coming home from the Annex area of Toronto one snowy night when the Bloor cars were running a stub line along the single cleared track. I crossed hopelessly to the Hollinger bus depot and found to my amazement, East York's buses buzzing merrily backwards and forwards along fully cleared highways. Of course, John Hollinger was on Council." She said, "The Kiwanians ran East York in those days. Bill Heaton and Percy Muir ruled the elected officials with a firm hand. Walter Stewart built libraries out of nothing with the help of the Kiwanians and collected paintings of A.Y. Jackson...George Curtis and Wilf Turner strove mightily in the interests of music, and Norman Tuckwell's collegiate orchestra...started many able students on the way to musical excellence."

In her first term on Council, True became chairman of the Works Committee and began agitating to dispose of some of the unnecessary land owned by the municipality which she described as "a liability to us in their present condition." When she became reeve in 1960, she followed through on this idea, deeding 245 acres of valley land to the Metropolitan Toronto and Region Conservation Authority as part of its flood control and water conservation scheme. The local paper claimed that this was the largest single block of land ever donated to the Authority by a member municipality. Willis Blair approved since East York, with a population of only 72,000 couldn't afford to develop the lands into parks.

Another of her early contributions to the municipality was the creation of the Dominion Day celebrations. This was one of Jack Christie's first experiences with True. He remembered that the reeve, Jack Allen, opposed the idea, saying, "Who's going to stay in town on Dominion Day for a little parade?" But True never did give up. She demanded that it happen and it did. Jack Christie believes that East York had the first Dominion Day parade in Metropolitan Toronto, a claim also made by True. She took equal pride in her establishment of the Simcoe Day celebrations. "We led the way with Simcoe Day celebrations also, and this example, too, is being followed elsewhere." Doris Tucker remembered that it was through True's prompting that "we started celebrating Dominion Day on a grand scale. In my recollection, a great deal of planning went into this project under the enthusiastic efforts of both the recreation director...and [True]. The celebration was a daylong event, starting off with a parade... followed by official opening ceremonies...then entertainment, and athletic contests, etc. throughout the day. In the evening there was dancing under the stars...followed by the grand finale, which was a beautiful display of fireworks. The parade...was always quite an attraction with its bands, decorated floats and many marching groups...The reeve rode in a special car near the front of the parade. For the occasion (True) wore a new outfit, topped by a very stunning wide brimmed hat...As far as I can recall during True's regime every Dominion Day was treated to the sight of True in another special outfit."

The good weather enjoyed by Dominion Day Parade became part of the True Davidson myth in East York. Jack Christie remembered that "There has never been enough rain to get in the way of the event but...the year after True died he went down to the park where the parade was assembling and it was raining and it looked like it was going to get worse. One of the women said something like, "It looks like we're going to be rained out. This never happened when True was here," and he replied, "True is closer to the controls now than she ever was and

I'm not worried," and almost immediately the rain stopped and the sun came out.[3]

The East York Dominion Day (now Canada Day) parade and the festivities at Cedarvale Park (now Stan Wadlow Park), which began with True, did not end with her. The July 1 celebrations have been continued by a volunteer committee both up to and even after the municipality was amalgamated with Toronto in 1998. True appointed Les Anthony to chair the committee and he continued in that role for many years with the help, support, and able assistance of Roly Sheaves, Mel Graham, Norm Clarke, Christopher Salmond, Wilf Tanner, and Horst Kummer, who ultimately succeeded Les as committee chair when he finally stepped down.[4] The Canada Day committee, which to Les Anthony was always the Dominion Day committee, has been carried on after amalgamation by many others, including Christopher Salmond, Don Duvall, Murray Smith, Shamsh Kara, and Shannon Timms-Ugochukwu. The continued existence of the Canada Day committee provides evidence that in spite of amalgamation, East York continues to exist.

"In addition to chairing the Works Committee during her first term on Council, True served on all but two of the municipality's regular committees, was chair of the Finance Committee and also of the Special Committees responsible for studying uses of Township lands and planning extensions to the Municipal Building. In 1960, she decided to run for reeve at the urging of the president of the Ratepayer's Federation of East York 'because it was felt that the previous mayor had acted unilaterally and that he had to be replaced. He said to me, you are the only one who can do it. I thought this was probably true because I was the best known. So I ran.' Her campaign literature stated that 'I am offering myself for the reeveship because I have been convinced by my own observations and by the arguments of my fellow citizens, including officers of almost all Ratepayer groups, that there must be a change.' Jack Christie was a member of a group opposed to the Rexleigh Apartments which Reeve Allen supported. He remembered that some of his group thought that Allen was in the pocket of the developers because he was close friends with some of the men who worked for it. 'Feelings were so strong that one of

3. Darke, Eleanor, *Call Me True, A Biography of True Davidson*, Dundurn Press, 1997, 7
4. Interview with Roly Sheaves, January 19, 2017

the members of the residents' association followed Allen downtown after a Council meeting one time to the Lord Simcoe Hotel bar where he met representatives of the development company.' He urged the ratepayers to 'support True because he thought that she shared their philosophy and because he thought that she had the best chance of winning.' He said that, when she was in hospital shortly before her death, she introduced him to someone 'as the person who got me elected as reeve the first time.'

"Charlotte Maher remembered True telling her that the campaign 'was really hard-fought' and nasty because 'scandal is unusual in municipal government in Metro. Councils may not have been smart but they have been pretty pure. But that was rough, and tough going.' Her printed material did not address the development controversy directly although they made a point of noting that she had 'no customers or clients but you to please' and that she stood for 'loyal adherence to Council decisions' and 'high standards for redevelopment.'

"The hottest issue of the campaign was the Reeve's development policy for the Township. True later wrote that 'Jack Allen...was a brisk young landscape gardener, full of ambition and drive, for himself and his township. He seemed to see himself as a junior Fred Gardiner, developing East York as Fred was developing Metro, riding down all opposition with a jolly smile.' He and his planning consultant 'an apartment architect named Sulio Venchiarutti...saw East York's future as one great apartment city, spreading from an arterial road in Taylor Creek valley, up both sides of the ravine.' Allen pushed his plan through the Planning Committee, then Council turned it down, but couldn't muster the two-thirds vote to amend it. True noted that 'Planning was at an impasse,' and later wrote, 'Well do I remember the shocked glances which Mr. Blair, Mr. Brigham and I exchanged in the offices of Mr. Venchiarutti when we visited him soon after our election to see his plan. It showed a road through the valley (infamous in history as the Cosburn Avenue extension) with apartments lining both sides. In fact, there were apartments everywhere in the township.'

"Willis Blair, Roy Brigham and she were 'swept into council' in 1958 and 'we got a new planning board. We got a planning commissioner of our own. We started on a plan which would represent the real desires of East York. And we fought a valiant, if largely unsuccessful, rear-guard defence of a freezing bylaw designed to prevent premature and undesirable development.' She described them as being 'as green as the grass and trees we were trying to save.' They thought the ravines, at least, were safe because they would be protected by the Conservation Authority, but didn't know that Metro already had changed the route of the Bayview extension partly to 'open up an undeveloped area' in East York's section of the Don Valley. 'We saw the owners uprooting trees and changing contours, but Jack (Allen) assured us that he had spoken to them and that their operations had been necessitated by the road –building. After all, we had no suspicion that the reeve, disregarding our pledges to neighbours (in Leaside) had secured approvals from Metro, and that a reluctant building inspector had granted a permit for an apartment building, to be the first of a whole herd of 'white elephants,' on this choice bit of (valley land.)' The builders began construction immediately. 'We advised them that the permit had been improperly issued. They put on extra shifts and worked under truck headlights. We advised them that they had not complied with our by-laws regarding unserviced properties, and that we would now refuse them services. And we did. And we stuck to it. That's why I call the famous 'white elephant' on Bayview a monument to a council that wouldn't be coerced or cajoled.'

"She said that it was 'also a monument to Metro's greed for assessment' and that they had tried to mislead her when she asked about the Bayview extension and expropriation plans for the property. 'It was a disillusioning experience...there's still a bad taste in my mouth when I remember.'

"Although no one was ever charged in regards to these events, Doris Tucker well remembered the day when the people from the Department of Municipal Affairs came up and interviewed the building inspector. He called and said, 'They want to talk to me about the passing of the permit for that building.' Jack Allen, you see, had sort of pushed that thing. He was a bit of a bully if he wanted to get his own way. He talked big and I guess he had to prove himself down at Metro.' The person from Municipal Affairs asked Doris to attend the interview, so 'he came down...and asked questions and I said to him before (the building inspector) came in, 'This man's a very nervous man but he's one of the most honest men we have. Whatever he says will be the truth. Whatever he did was on the very best intentions.' So on that basis we started and he was there quite a while. I'll never forget that. Poor old Freddy Wild [the building Inspector.] I'll bet he was sick. You know when you're honest and you're trying to do a job and you know your job and other people are trying to push you around, why it's terribly disheartening.'

"True defeated Allen handily, receiving 5,065 votes to his 3,458 largely as the result of the highest voter turnout (40%) in the township's history to that time. True told reporters that it had been a hard fight 'but I couldn't be more touched by the confidence of the people in me.' Allen did not appear at the township offices, never conceded the election and was obviously disappointed at the outcome. He was quoted as saying, 'I find it's unpopular to do the right thing. I'm glad to get out. It will be a relief to get back to my family and job after so many years.'

"True never forgot this struggle, asking years later, 'What are we to do with developers who destroy green-belt land and then demand alternative zoning?' and noting that 'In planning, it often seems municipalities have responsibility without power and nothing brings discredit to a law faster than inability to enforce it.'

"From this campaign she gained a reputation as a fighter for residential neighbourhoods, but Willis Blair remembered that she never expressed a clear definition of what made a development suitable. 'She knew some of the old row houses in East York just had to be torn down...if she felt the developers were up-front about it and the community didn't object too much she'd allow it' although 'she was big on making the developer set up a little parkette or something. There are a lot of those little parkettes around now (because of True.)' In effect, she wasn't opposed to development, she just wanted it to be orderly and acceptable to the community. As her honorary doctorate from York University stated, 'She imparted her own intense concern with building and sustaining an environment congenial to the sustenance and growth of its every individual member.'

"As always, it is her poetry that best shows the sort of community that, emotionally, she most valued. She wrote the following poem for her 1964 Christmas card.

Between the factories of Toronto and Leaside,
North York's and Scarborough's looming towers
East York has grown like an old-fashioned village
Where friendships flourish and children and flowers.
East York is full of neat little houses

On modest pieces of well-kept land
With neighbour to offer across the fences
A piece of their minds or a helping hand. [5]

"When True was first elected as reeve, she said she would "sit and learn and do the best I can" on Metro Council. Soon, however, she became known to the rest of Metro as a colourful character from the pocket municipality, but the people of East York identified her as their voice on Metro Council.

"The *Toronto Star* described her as dauntless, 'a forceful voice in Metro Toronto politics, out-spoken, aggressive, exasperating to her colleagues, and winner of many a council debate as often by quick wit as pure logic.' Jack Christie said that while he didn't have much to do with Metro Council, he felt that 'she was effective and she couldn't have gotten all she did for East York there if she hadn't been capable or had alienated members of Metro Council or its bureaucracy.' The *Toronto Star* wrote of her that 'despite her age…she is one of the keenest participants on the moribund Metro Council.'" [6]

While Metro Council had been working well as far as East York was concerned, in 1964, the premier of Ontario, John Roberts, established a Royal Commission headed by Carl Goldenberg to review the workings of the Metro system of government ten years after it had been created. This fulfilled the promise of his predecessor, Premier Leslie Frost, to have a ten-year review.[7]

"Before the commission's public hearings got underway, the City of Toronto Council, likely realizing that the combined population of the suburbs would soon outstrip that of the city, renewed its application to the Ontario Municipal Board for total amalgamation. The Ontario government responded quickly, however, suspending the powers of the OMB to hear the city's application prior to receiving Mr. Goldenberg's study and recommendations."[8]

True fought total amalgamation with all her heart and soul on behalf of the township and always remained opposed to future amalgamations,

---

5. Darke, Eleanor, *Call Me True, A Biography of True Davidson*, Dundurn Press, 1997, 77

6. Darke, Eleanor, *Call Me True, A Biography of True Davidson*, Dundurn Press, 1997, 86

7. Redway, Alan, *Governing Toronto: Bringing back the city that worked*, Friesen Press, 2014, 61

8. Redway, Alan, *Governing Toronto: Bringing back the city that worked*, Friesen Press, 2014, 61

stating firmly that she was "against total amalgamation of the city and the five boroughs because politicians can't get close enough to the people in such a system."[9]

In the result, the thirteen Metro municipalities were reduced to six in 1967, but East York survived the review and was merged with Leaside to form the Borough of East York, one of the now-six municipalities of Metro Toronto.

Canada's Centennial year was also in 1967.

East York's largest celebration during that Centennial year was the official opening of the Todmorden Mills Museum on Pottery Road in the Don Valley. It is likely that Charles Sauriol was responsible for getting True interested in this site. He had written about its history on several occasions in his newsletter, *The Cardinal*, during the early 1960s as part of his campaign to educate people about the environmental and historical significance of the Don Valley. If so, True proved to be one of his most productive converts-throwing all of her extraordinary energy, enthusiasm, and position into the preservation of the remaining historic structures on the site and, later, into the restoration of the valley's seriously damaged environment.

In 1967, the Todmorden site consisted of four of the original structures of the old mill village of Todmorden: a frame house attributed to Parshall Terry, a mud-brick and board-and-batten house attributed to William Helliwell, the Taylor/Davies paper mill and the shell of part of the Helliwell brewery. The train station was moved to the site several years later.[10]

Prior to its merger with East York, the Town of Leaside had finalized plans for its own Centennial project, the Senior Citizens Drop-in Centre in Trace Manes Park, so the new Borough of East York had two Centennial projects in 1967.[11]

Anticipating the possible disappearance of East York by amalgamation, "True founded the East York Foundation. The foundation was established to serve as a non-governmental guardian of many of the borough's treasures and as a fund-raising agency providing for

---

9. Darke, Eleanor, *Call Me True, A Biography of True Davidson*, Dundurn Press, 1997, 90

10. Darke, Eleanor, *Call Me True, A Biography of True Davidson*, Dundurn Press, 1997, 107

11. Darke, Eleanor, *Call Me True, A Biography of True Davidson*, Dundurn Press, 1997, 117

cultural and recreational enrichment in fields that could not be covered by community taxation. Over the years, the East York Foundation has achieved many of True's dreams for the Borough, raising the funds for arts and cultural activities that, increasingly, have been unavailable from government sources. By providing a means of channelling bequest and other donations from individuals back into the community, the foundation successfully raised much of the money needed to renovate that paper mill at Todmorden into an art gallery and community theatre, collected a sizeable collection of art by local artists including several works by members of the Group of Seven; provided funds to restore and exhibit some of the Borough's greatest treasures, and continue to provide financial assistance to publishers producing books about the community; as well as supporting numerous other community projects."[12]

Ed Barnett chaired the foundation for many years followed by Ray White when Ed stepped down.[13] With January 1, 1998, fast approaching, the Borough of East York Council passed the following resolution confirmed by its closing by-law: "That in the event of an amalgamation that Council hereby approves the transfer in ownership, to the East York Foundation, the artistic, cultural, and historical articles owned by the Corporation of the Borough of East York."[14]

"True always believed that a city was made more by the activities of its citizens than by its bricks and mortar. She took great pride in the Borough's libraries, its winning high school football team The Goliaths, its honour roll of Ontario Scholars, and 'the talented young people who performed at the Sunday afternoon Musicales.' She praised the work of the East Side Players, the Don Valley Art Club and 'Mrs. MacDonald's theatre group at the Collegiate.'"[15]

"Alan Redway remembered how difficult it was to say 'No' to True when she wanted something to happen. Shortly after the amalgamation of East York and Leaside, she decided that the new municipality needed a new chain of office for the mayor and began to approach all the service clubs in the community to contribute towards its purchase. Alan Redway

12. Darke, Eleanor, *Call Me True, A Biography of True Davidson*, Dundurn Press, 1997, 118
13. Interview with Raymond White, January 26, 2017
14. East York Council minutes, December 16, 1996
15. Darke, Eleanor, *Call Me True, A Biography of True Davidson*, Dundurn Press, 1997, 117

was the president of the Leaside Lions Club at the time and remembered her phoning one day with this request. He declined, saying that the club really didn't have enough money to help out. 'But True was never one to take no for an answer and she kept calling and pushing and eventually we found the money somehow.'"[16]

True retired as mayor of East York at the end of 1972 and passed away September 18, 1978. Her home on Woodmount Avenue at the corner of Mortimer still stands, unmarked and privately owned.[17]

As the days remaining for East York's existence as an independent municipality dwindled away in the face of the Provincially imposed amalgamation into the new Toronto megacity, Councillor Norm Crone approached Mayor Michael Prue to suggest that True Davidson be honoured at the final council meeting. Prue encouraged the idea and, at the October 7 council meeting, Councillor Crone's original motion to name the council chambers in honour of True was passed unanimously.

On November 17, 1997, the East York Council Chamber was designated the True Davidson Council Chamber. Her formal portrait, painted by A. Good in 1971, was hung inside the chamber to remind all of her many contributions to East York. The mayor's chain of office presented to her by the service clubs of East York (the Lions, Kinsmen, Kiwanis, and Rotary clubs) will remain in East York in the care of another of her creations, the East York Foundation.[18]

During True Davidson's time as reeve of the township, East York was spared from total amalgamation once again, this time by its merger with the Town of Leaside to create the Borough of East York. The story of that merger is next.

---

16. Darke, Eleanor, *Call Me True, A Biography of True Davidson*, Dundurn Press, 1997, 117
17. Redway, Alan, *East York Chronicle*, 2016, 3
18. East York Council minutes, Final meeting, 1997

True Davidson
(Source: Leaside East York)

Township of East York Council 1963-64
(Source: East York Foundation)

Todmorden Master Plan
(Source: East York Foundation)

True Davidson 1966
(Source: East York Foundation)

True Davidson opening Todmorden Mills
(Source: East York Foundation)

Reg Martin, President of EY Kiwanis, presenting
Chain of Office to Mayor True Davidson
(Source: East York Foundation)

True Davidson and Willis Blair at first Centennial Ball
(Source: East York Foundation)

True Davidson House Woodmount Ave corner of Lumsden
(Source: google.ca)

– Chapter 11 –

THE MERGER

True Davidson's greatest battle during her first two terms as reeve was waged against the Goldenberg Commission's plans for amalgamation.[1]

In 1962, Ontario Premier John Robarts appointed Carl Goldenberg, Q.C., to head a Royal Commission to review the Municipality of Metropolitan Toronto, created by the Province ten years earlier. East York was one of the thirteen municipalities making up Metropolitan Toronto at that time. Before the commission hearings got underway, the City of Toronto, one of the other thirteen municipalities, applied to the Ontario Municipal Board for the total amalgamation of all thirteen. The OMB adjourned the city's application until the Goldenberg Commission had reported. [2]

Three years later, Goldenberg's report recommended that the thirteen Metro municipalities be reduced to four. Both East York and Leaside were to be eliminated and merged with the city of Toronto. This caused True to fight back "with tigerish tenacity." [3]

---

1. Darke, Eleanor, *Call Me True, A Biography of True Davidson*, Dundurn Press, 1997, 90
2. Redway, Alan, *Governing Toronto: Bringing back the city that worked*, Friesen Press, 2014
3. Darke, Eleanor, *Call Me True, A Biography of True Davidson*, Dundurn Press, 1997, 90

Doris Tucker, the township clerk, said, "True really fought because she really thought East York was going to be swallowed up." Doris remembered when True had all the senior township staff go over to talk to Carl Goldenberg one Saturday morning. "She bullied him into meeting us. And we all had to talk about what we did in East York and give him a good picture of East York so he would know that we were a good viable municipality and as she said, '100,000 population isn't to be sneezed at. That's a better type of population than a great big one and if they put us in with some of the others it wouldn't be nearly as well run.'" [4]

Davidson told the commission, "East York has within it a rare vitality—its people wish to survive as a group. This is not because of any especially favourable financial position, for the township enjoys none—East York is small enough to know what services and amenities its people want and need, and large enough to supply them. More than seven hundred people are engaged in some sort of voluntary work with or for the township and there is a remarkable sense of fellowship... There is a tremendous community pride, which gives residents a sense of security and of significance." [5]

Leaside, soon to be merged with the township, had something to say as well. Its mayor, Beth Nealon, told the commissioner, "Metropolitan Toronto's greatest asset, its provision for flexible self-determination, would preserve desirable local autonomy and avoid increased burdens of costs red tape and as well the inevitable inefficiency that goes with excessive centralization." [6]

Of course, the Goldenberg Report satisfied none of the thirteen municipalities, but since it was clear that the final decision would be up to the provincial government, the suburban municipalities continued their efforts to try to influence that decision. Township Aldermen Willis Blair, Norman Maughan, and Jim McConaghy added their voices to that of Reeve True Davidson in urging that East York survive. None of the input of the suburban municipalities nor the concerns of his Progressive Conservative MPPs representing Metro constituencies escaped the premier as he considered the government's response to the Goldenberg.

---

4. Redway, Alan, *Governing Toronto: Bringing back the city that worked*, Friesen Press, 2014, 63
5. Redway, Alan, *Governing Toronto: Bringing back the city that worked*, Friesen Press, 2014, 63
6. Redway, Alan, *Governing Toronto: Bringing back the city that worked*, Friesen Press, 2014, 64

When the Progressive Conservative Metro MPPs either asked to meet with suburban councils, or were invited to do so in order to discuss the Goldenberg Report, the councillors considered this as their opportunity to give their local MPP marching orders to oppose the Goldenberg recommendations. For example, in September at a packed public meeting held in Leaside High School, Hollis Beckett, Q.C., MPP for York East, told five hundred residents that he opposed total amalgamation as well as the Goldenberg four-city plan. However, he recommended a six-borough plan in which Leaside would merge with the township of East York to create an East Toronto borough. He pointed out that under the Goldenberg plan, Leaside would become part of the City of Toronto and thus have no direct representation on Metro Council. However, the rowdy meeting sent Mr. Beckett on his way after unanimously passing the following resolution:

"That Mr. Hollis Beckett Q.C. MPP York East be requested to oppose amalgamation of any form when the report of the Royal Commission is considered in committee and when presented in the legislature."

Mr. Beckett replied to Leaside Council, in a letter dated November 15, 1965, advising that he would do everything in his power to carry out the resolution passed at the public meeting opposing any kind of amalgamation.

Former Leaside Councillor Keith Stainton told me that while Leaside Council clearly preferred the status quo, his personal fallback position was a merger with East York rather than the City of Toronto. He argued that as a former member of the Leaside Board of Education, he considered the Leaside education system was more closely aligned to that of East York than to that of the City of Toronto.

In the months that followed the release of the Goldenberg Report, the Metro area Progressive Conservative MPPs and cabinet ministers reviewed and debated every detail in the report. Finally, just before Christmas 1965, inister of Municipal Affairs Wilf Spooner presented the recommendations of the PC caucus to the premier. These were fundamentally different from the Goldenberg recommendations in that Metro would be a six- not a four-borough city; East York and York would continue to exist.

The premier then wasted no time in making the Ontario Government's position clear. On January 10, 1966, he delivered a policy statement in the legislature, the forerunner of the new Municipality of Metropolitan Toronto Act, Bill 81. During its introduction in the assembly, the premier said, "The bill cannot be expected to please all of the people of Metro Toronto but is in the best interests of all." Rather than total amalgamation, the metropolitan system of government, which had been endorsed by Commissioner Goldenberg, was to continue as a two-level federated system but consolidated into a smaller number of local municipalities.

The City of Toronto would be made up of the existing city together with Forest Hill and Swansea. The Borough of Etobicoke would consist of the former township of Etobicoke plus Long Branch, New Toronto, and Mimico. The Borough of York would be made up of the former Township of York plus Weston. The Borough of East York would consist of the former township of East York together with Leaside. The Townships of North York and Scarborough would each remain as-is but become boroughs rather than townships. The new Metro Council was to have thirty-two members of elected local councils, plus a chairman to be elected by the members of Metro Council. The membership was to be made up as follows:

City of Toronto	12
Borough of North York	6
Borough of Scarborough	5
Borough of Etobicoke	4
Borough of York	3
Borough of East York	2
Chairman	1

Conventional wisdom in East York credits True Davidson with convincing Goldenberg to recommend six rather than four boroughs. However, as we have seen, Goldenberg actually recommended four boroughs, not six. The same day that Premier Robarts announced the plan for a six-borough Metro, the Provincial Liberal Leader Andrew Thompson accused Hollis Beckett, the PC MPP for York East, of exercising undue influence on the premier. He said, "The creation of East York owes more to the opportunism and the persuasive voice of Mr. Beckett than it does to the careful considerations of Dr. Goldenberg. The local municipalities make absolutely no sense. By no stretch of the imagination-except perhaps in the mind of Hollis Beckett, is East York and Leaside a community in any sense of the word." After the Goldenberg report was released, Beckett had proposed a six-borough Metro. At the time, he claimed his plan was favoured by a majority of the twenty-six MPPs on a special committee appointed to rule on the form of government for Metro, which was made up of seventeen PCs, four Liberals, and five of the NDP. "They don't care much for Goldenberg's proposals," Beckett said at the time.

Former Toronto Mayor David Crombie, who teaches a course on the history of Toronto, believes that York East MPP Hollis Beckett was the key to saving East York by the merger with Leaside. Then, Crombie says, in order not to show a preference for East York, the PC caucus committee recommended six rather than five boroughs by merging Weston with York Township. Darcy McKeough, a former Ontario Minister of Municipal Affairs, wrote me to say, "It was really the Tory caucus MPPs who were in favour of doing nothing. They were a large group (not many opposition MPPs). They got along well with the borough mayors and councils who vociferously did not want to be amalgamated with the big spending, erratic, City of Toronto Council. Robarts didn't feel strongly about amalgamations and didn't feel strongly enough to take on Toronto caucus." While the Beckett plan and the Robarts plan had many similarities, they differed with respect to the borough boundaries. The Beckett plan carved up the City of Toronto and the Township of North York arbitrarily to increase the population of York and East York. The Robarts plan respected the existing local boundaries, as had the original Frost plan for Metropolitan Toronto. [7]

When Premier Robarts said, "The bill cannot be expected to please all of the people of Metro Toronto," he knew what he was talking about. Less than two weeks after the premier's statement in the legislature, the *Toronto Star* declared:

> *"Local Councils have no place in New Metro.*
> *The Star acknowledges a certain merit in local government—but only so long as it performs a useful function. And in the case of boroughs proposed by Premier Robarts, we mention that they do not serve a useful purpose and are in fact, costly window dressing for a principle that no longer has any validity in Metro Toronto.*

---

7. Redway, Alan, *Governing Toronto: Bringing back the city that worked*, Friesen Press, 2014, 69–82

"If the responsibilities of borough councils were assumed by departments of central Metro government, taxpayers would have the same opportunity to meet with responsible civic officials as they have now.

"It appears more logical to assume that Premier Robarts has bowed to pressure from local politicians anxious to retain their jobs, even with meagre authority, at the expense of logical, cohesive and effective government over the entire Metro community" shades of the megacity to come."

The *Globe and Mail* had this to say:

"Government Out of Touch.

We believe that the people of Metro Toronto care little for municipal boundary lines which run invisibly down the middle of some streets, in spite of the bugle call ballyhoo of their elected representatives. They are aware, rather, of belonging to Greater Toronto; sleeping in one part and working in another, perhaps but living in the whole of it."

However, according to section 92(8) of the British North Act, 1867, now the Canadian Constitution Act 1982, municipalities are the creatures of the provinces and like it or not the Province of Ontario had spoken. Premier Robarts had decided where he wanted Metro to go.[8] The decision had been made. Now the work began to make the merger a reality.

Doris Tucker remembers that it took quite "a little time for everyone to adjust" to the new situation. The two councils met and discussed how things were to work and True "spoke to the staff and said it would be nice if we could absorb those people up there. So for a whole year, I never took on staff. I needed help but I think about three people left so we were able to take everybody" from the Leaside Clerk's Department. "I was appointed municipal clerk and the late Fred Cook, the former clerk of Leaside, was named deputy clerk. As a matter of fact, the staffs of both municipalities were entirely integrated and all had to be appointed as members of the newly formed borough staff."[9]

_____

8. Redway, Alan, *Governing Toronto: Bringing back the city that worked*, Friesen Press, 2014, 82

9. Darke, Eleanor, *Call Me True, A Biography of True Davidson*, Dundurn Press, 1997, 93

Now that they were all working in the same municipal building on Coxwell Avenue, the merger of the former town's inside workers with those of the former township produced a few tensions. Whereas those same problems did not exist with the outside workers since they continued to work in the same areas of the new borough as they had before the merger. Perhaps integration of the outside workers was assisted that year by the Metro garbage strike during which both the Bermondsey Road garbage transfer station and the Beare Road landfill site in Scarborough were closed and picketed by Metro Union employees. That forced the new Borough of East York to temporarily lay off fifty of their recently merged outside workers. Now all were in the same boat.[10]

Robarts Goldenberg
(Source: John Gilles Globe and Mail June 15 1965)

---

10. Interview with Jim Lister, October 19, 2015

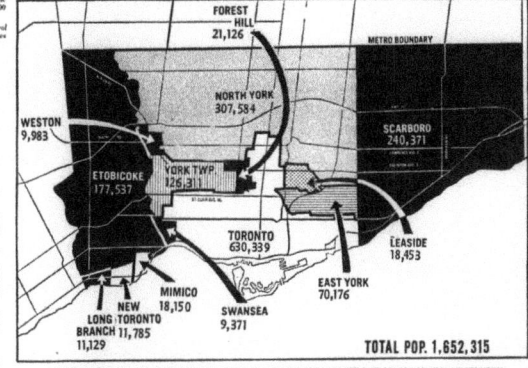

Master Plan Jun 17 1965A

(Source: Tor Star Jun 17 1965)

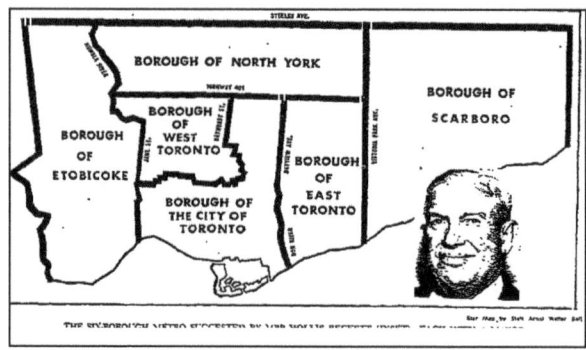

Hollis Beckett's 6 Borough Plan
(Source: Tor Star Aug 28 1965)

Leaside Crest
(Source: East York Foundation)

Leaside Centennial Project
(Source: Toronto.ca)

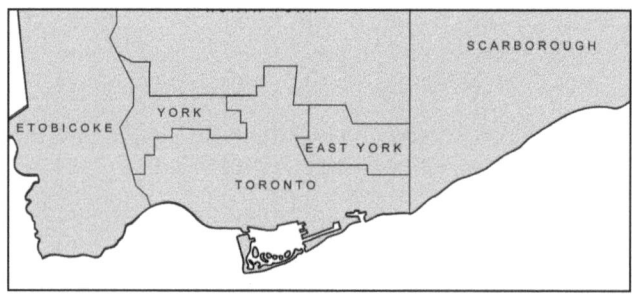

Metro Toronto in 1967
(Source: Valentine De Landro)

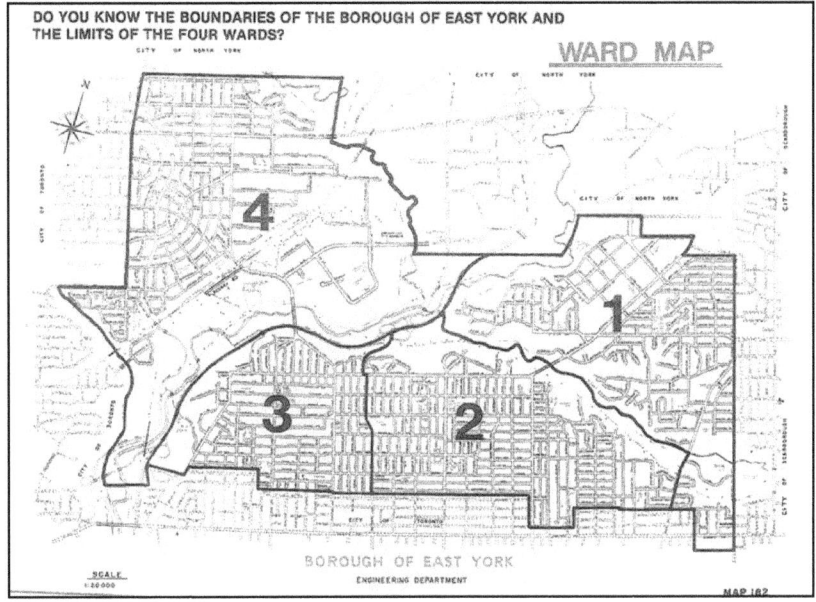

EY Boroughs Map 1990
(Source: East York Foundation)

Borough of East York Crest
(Source: East York Foundation)

"The 1966 election campaign for the new borough did little to improve relations. True Davidson was certainly not the sort of politician to which Leasiders were accustomed! Her main competitors were Royden Brigham and the former Leaside Mayor, Beth Nealson, and the campaign was described by one Toronto newspaper as a "bombastic, free-wheeling affair." With complete confidence in herself, True sent "an open letter to the people of Leaside" which she designed to present her "credentials where I am less well known." This sort of dignified campaigning didn't last long. True was soon quoted as having said, "I'm no wishy-washy, sissy little sweetheart" with the implication that Beth Nealson was, and as calling Brigham, "a defenseless little creature." He reportedly said that he has claws, but vowed "to remain a gentleman forever." True told a ratepayer's group that "if you want someone beautiful and elegant, or glamourous, I'm not that." Voter interviews from the time overwhelmingly disapproved of these personality clashes with comments like "The hurling of abuse and insults during campaigns is most degrading" and candidates can clash by their fiery personality, but it should not descend to unmannerly abuse and insults. This is not businesslike, and it really insults the voter." One voter, however, acknowledged that "it does put excitement into the meetings. After all, candidates are in there fighting to win...and they can't always be calm and polite."

"True finished the campaign in hospital recovering from a heart attack, but won an easy victory at the polls. Jack Christie remembered that she was pleased to have been retained as mayor "not really exultant though – just satisfied," and that she just "seemed to regard this as another challenge," the problem of how to handle the bad feelings that resulted from the merger. He said that "she wanted to keep Leaside as much like it was as possible. She made no attempt to absorb it – just to add it on."

"Faced with the challenge of merging two proud municipalities into one, True used the public celebrations associated with Canada's Centennial to create opportunities for individuals and groups from each area to work together. Doris Tucker remembered how many activities were planned to celebrate Canada's Centennial year and "also the birth of a new municipality...We started off with a New Year's Eve service in the Council Chambers and later in the month a Centennial Ball was held...at the Inn on the Park. Everyone attending was encouraged to wear period costumes. Many did, both men and women. It was a beautiful sight to see the women in lovely silk and satin bouffant gowns swirling around the dance floor on the arms of the men in their elegant period costumes. Of course, the belle of the ball was True Davidson, in a gorgeous rose-pink gown, trimmed with a Grecian key design in purple around the bouffant skirt...True wore the same gown throughout the year at many other Centennial celebrations."[11]

Nice try, but it took some time for the residents of the former township and the former town to feel comfortable with each other. The Leaside Bridge, which opened in 1927, was intended to provide a connection and bonding link between the two municipalities but instead it became a psychological barrier between them. The decision by the OMB to award Thorncliffe to Leaside rather than East York only made matters worse. Many East Yorkers and many Leasiders thought that those on the other side of the bridge were somehow different from themselves. [12]

This is illustrated by the following passage in Eleanor Darke's book, *Call Me True*:

Leaside had fought fully as hard to preserve its autonomy and many of its residents were angered by the decision to merge it with East York. The town benefited from a strong industrial tax base and Leaside residents enjoyed the resultant services and low residential taxes and feared high taxes and lower services as "their" revenues were "sucked up" by East York. Doris Tucker felt that some Leaside residents believed that being part of East York would lower their social status. "A lot of them had lived in East York and when they got a bit more money they moved up to Leaside. They felt they were a little better off. We were the south side of the tracks and they were the north side of the tracks."[13]

The truth of course was quite the opposite. These were misconceptions. East Yorkers and Leasiders have more in common than their imagined differences. The two municipalities were merged in 1967 to form the Borough of East York. I was elected to the Borough Council in 1972 and served ten years, six of them as mayor of the borough. It was immediately evident to me how similar the two communities really were whether they realized it or not. Perhaps they actually realized it

---

11. Darke, Eleanor, *Call Me True, A Biography of True Davidson*, Dundurn Press, 1997, 105
12. Redway, Alan, *East York Chronicle*, April 2016, 3
13. Darke, Eleanor, *Call Me True, A Biography of True Davidson*, Dundurn Press, 1997, 93

but were not prepared to admit they had been wrong. The people of the former Township and the former Town both had been and continue to be, very watchful of the way in which their council spent their hard-earned property tax dollars. All wanted excellent local services but at the least possible cost. People from every part of the borough, whether they had to cross the Leaside Bridge or come from the Danforth and Dawes Road or cross the Woodbine Bridge to do so, were always at council and committee meetings to hold our feet to the fire. No matter where they lived in the borough, residents insisted that their council maintain the physical character of their own neighbourhoods and they would come in force to see that Council got their message and looked after their interest. Differences between the people of East York and Leaside, I could never see any and I still can't.[14]

Beth Nealson front of Leaside Town Hall
(Source: East York Foundation)

14. Redway, Alan, *East York Chronicle*, April 2016, 3

Beth Nealson
Leaside Mayor
(Source: East York Foundation)

Royden R Brigham 1959-60
(Source: East York Foundation)

True Davidson 1959-60
(Source: Get Stock)

Thorncliffe Race Track
(Source: East York Foundation)

Vern Page and Dave Jagger 1st EY Aldermen from Leaside
(Source: East York Foundation)

– Chapter 12 –

THE TIMES THEY ARE A CHANGING

The flowers may change but the Garden of Eden continues to bloom.

New East Yorkers

For years, the borough maintained a stable population made up of people with origins mostly in the British Isles, with little turnover. But following World War II, the population started to change. Newcomers from countries all over the world were settling in East York. Initially, Italian and Greek Canadians arrived in large numbers. Some came for economic opportunities, while others came to escape wars and persecution. All came for a better life. By 1980, according to the borough's director of education, Dick Dodds, there were seventy-three different languages and dialects spoken by students at Overlea Secondary School (now Marc Garneau Collegiate).

Each newcomer had their own story. A perfect example was the Janikas family, who came from Greece. The family name was actually Giannikas but it was anglicized, as were many names in those days. George Giannikas grew up in a poor farm family in a country ravaged first by the German army occupation and then by civil war. He was an orphan at the age of thirteen. After completing his compulsory military service, he joined the police force but had to leave when he married Maria, as the Greek police force did not allow their policemen to be married. So, George and Maria immigrated to Canada with financial help from the villagers in the community where they lived. When they arrived, neither George, with a grade-six Greek education, nor Maria, with a grade-two education, spoke English. Their son John tells the story from there.

Our father and mother, George and Maria Janikas, immigrated to Canada on January 22, 1958. At that time, my eldest sister Bassie was 1½ years old and my mom was six months pregnant with my second eldest sister, Diane, who was eventually born in Toronto. My sister Tonie and I were also born in Toronto, Canada.

Our parents' decision to leave Greece was very difficult. Our mother had an uncle and some cousins here and they were going to sponsor our family. Canada was seen as a land of great opportunity. Our parents were looking for a better future for us. My sister Bassie and I often wonder now, how difficult it was for them to make that decision. To leave the comforting surroundings and families of your native home and to come to a country where you do not speak the language, do not know the culture and with very little money. But they did it and we thank God every day for our blessings to have been raised in Canada.

Our family settled in the Cabbagetown area of Toronto. We rented for a few years until we could afford to buy our own home. Our first house was a row house on Geneva Avenue. I remember as a little three-year-old how my dad would be working three jobs. He would come home, sleep for an hour or so and off to another job. Our mother stayed home to raise the four kids. After our parents became Canadian citizens, they themselves started to sponsor many other family members from Greece to settle into Toronto. I always remember our house was like a transition point for many family members. They would stay with us until they found a job and got on their feet. Our parents were very respectful, very religious, very loyal citizens and they instilled that in all of us.

We moved to East York on Canada Day and Canada's hundredth birthday, July 1, 1967. Our mother wanted a detached home, with a back yard, close to schools and just a little more space. It seems that the real estate agent that sold our home on Geneva Avenue knew exactly what our mother was looking for. He showed the house in East York, explaining to our parents all that this area had to offer. Schools were everywhere, hospital down the street, TTC bus stops just steps away, the East York Civic Centre a few blocks away and the Danforth a short distance away as well. It was as close to utopia for us as you can imagine. Our parents even found new employment in East York. Later my sister Bassie worked in a local hair salon, my sister Diane worked at a local linen store and my sister Tonie and I ran a paper route for several years. East York was like the centre of the universe for us in many ways until today—it is still the same for me. There was something magical about East York. We had aunts, uncles, cousins, and friends that moved to East York as well, as everyone it seems realized what a gem of a place this was. To this day, there are a lot of friends and acquaintances from high school that continue to live in East York today with their families. Everything was so close and personal. We had community centre, parks, police presence, corner stores, great neighbours and local councillors and a local mayor. If you had an issue, you can walk, just walk right over to the Civic Centre and talk to someone.

When I was going to East York Collegiate and had basketball practice in the early mornings, I remember running into our then-mayor, Alan Redway. This was 6:30 in the morning and it was in the East York Civic Centre parking lot. It was something special to talk to our mayor on several occasions throughout my high school days in that parking lot. I used to say to myself, *Wow, the mayor took time out of his busy and long day for a chat.* That is where sense of community and culture of our Borough of East York comes from. It starts at the top and once citizens see you care, then the whole community takes on that personality of respect, common courtesy, friendliness, and just good old family values. I think that is the best way to describe East York. It was a great place to live, to shop, to work and to raise a family. It had that old town charm that you do not see in too many places now. We still have a family tradition of seeing the East York Canada Parade from the corner of Coxwell and Mortimer and then having a fun family day at Stan Wadlow Park. We were truly blessed in East York. We had great leaders of the community, we had great school teachers, and we had great family values all around us.

I remember in the nineties when talk started about having a mega city. I don't know where that whole mind set of bigger is better comes from. Where centralized power and centralized decision-making trumps local community needs. Probably power and centralized decision-making trumps local community needs. Probably from our U.S. neighbours and probably from people with big egos that want to leave their mark on the city. East York was the smallest of the boroughs when Mega City was implemented and the one that was most prone to getting a lot of their services cut and lose the most. You would hear the jokes that we were "Least York." Really bothered me to say the least. Kudos to the people that tried to fight the amalgamation. The smaller borough system was way more effective in governing the city. Local issues, need local leaders, to attend to local needs. What was important for the people of East York may not be what was important to the citizens of Scarborough, or York, or Etobicoke. Or for sure not important to the GTA areas like Halton Region, York Region or Peel Region. You see this in so many companies as well where they try and centralize everything thinking that expenses would be reduced by having one central home base. What happens in most cases is the opposite. There is great division created, expenses DO NOT go down and the decision process is stalled to a snail's pace. It just does not work. It becomes very fractured. I go back to my earlier point of having direct access to our local councillors and mayor. If I had a problem, I would go to our civic centre at our council meetings and ask questions at the open forum directly to our mayor and councillors. It may not have been approved, but you know, at least someone was there to listen to you and give you your time to express your concerns. In person. Not by e-mail or some 311 phone call.

I keep hearing that for Toronto to become a world-class this or a world-class that, it needs to do this and or it needs to do that. I think for Toronto to become anything, it needs to de-amalgamate, bring back smaller forms of government in the old borough system, take care of local concerns for the local citizens and bring back a truly caring society that does not marginalize people. East York had at one time the second highest per capita senior citizens next to Victoria B.C. Seniors require special care that a mega city cannot support. East York is home to Thorncliffe Park and to the Dawes Road area. Again, transitional areas of new immigrants that have very different needs from the citizens of Leaside for example. The list goes on.

I still live in East York with my wife. My brother in-law and my niece live in East York as well. It has been forty-eight years of growing up and living in East York and I do not think I will ever move from here. I absolutely love walking in the neighbourhood and meeting people and just saying "hello." But the neighbourhood is changing rapidly. Large retail box formats are coming and so are more condo developments. It seems that with big government to support the mega city we need large revenue streams. So city planners are approving not what is right for the city but what is necessary as a revenue generating tool.[1]

The Janikas family story is only one of the thousands of stories of the new comers to East York from all over the world.

With so many people coming to Canada from different countries, the Canadian government adopted a multicultural policy administered by the Canadian Multicultural Council. At the suggestion of a well-known Jamaican Canadian East Yorker, Bromley Armstrong, Mayor Alan Redway established the East York Mayor's Multicultural Advisory Committee. It was the first municipal committee of its kind in Canada at the time. Other municipalities followed suit with names such as the Race Relations Committee, Ethnic Cultural Council, and Human Rights Committee.

The East York Committee was originally and for many years chaired by Shamsh Kara, an Ismaili Muslim who had come to Canada with his wife Yasmin to escape persecution in Tanzania from Idi Amin. They arrived from Africa in the middle of winter to a foot of snow with only light summer clothing. The Karas immediately rented an apartment on Stag Hill, later moving to Thorncliffe Park. Shamsh got a job within a few days and Yasmin did as well.

Sebastiano DiLorenzo represented the East York Italian Canadian community on the committee. He and his family immigrated from Pachino in Sicily. He used to say that when he left, there were 10,000 people in Pachino. Now he said there are 10,000 people from Pachino in East York and there are still 10,000 people in Pachino.

Other original committee members represented East York Canadians from a variety of other origins including George Vasilopoulos, Greece; Marg Lewsey, Barbados; Ping Kwan, China; Indu Grover, South Asia; Mae Ogaki, Japan; Millie Castro, the Philippines; Ruth Goldhar, Jewish; Jane Gibson, Board of Education; and Jim Buller, First Nations.

---

1. Interview with John Janikas, January 23, 2016

The committee organized an annual East York Day to illustrate the enormous talents that the newcomers brought to the community. Almost 2,000 people jammed St. Clement of Ohrid Church Hall on the first East York Day. Another annual event organized by the committee was the Sunrise Citizenship Court, held in the Council Chambers each Canada Day, when a great number are sworn in as new Canadian citizens by a Citizen Court judge flanked by a RCMP officer in scarlet tunic. But just as in years gone by, celebrations of St. Patrick's Day on March 17 and the anniversary of the Battle of the Boyne in Ireland on July 12 were controversial. As well, some of the newcomers brought with them old controversies. Together with East York Council, the Multicultural Committee played an important part in keeping the borough on an even keel when those controversies boiled over from time to time. These could include problems caused by traffic problems on Orthodox Good Friday in Thorncliffe Park or by the parking and litter problems on the Donlands commercial strip, which sparked an investigation by the Ontario Human Rights Commissioner Dr. Bhausaheb Ubale.[2]

In 1989, the Mayors Multicultural Committee was renamed the East York Multicultural and Race Relations Committee. In 1995, it was renamed again as the East York's Mayor's Committee on Race Relations. Shamsh Kara was succeeded as chair by Mahir Ghosh, an East Yorker with origins in Pakistan. In spite of amalgamation, the committee still exists, continuing the annual Canada Day Citizenship Courts under the name of the East York Race Relations and Multicultural Institute.

The newcomers also encouraged Council to twin the borough with communities in their former homelands. Mayor True Davidson twinned East York with the earthquake-devastated city of Skopje, then in Macedonia, Yugoslavia. Tripolos in Greece twinned with East York at the urging of Councillor George Vasilopoulos (a long-time member of the Multicultural Committee), former Councillor Steve Mastoras, and Councillor John Antonopoulos. On the eve of the borough's absorption by the megacity of Toronto, the Hellenes Grounds were established at the southwest corner of Cosburn Park near the S. Walter Stewart Library, where a memorial monument for the Hellenes was erected flanked by the Greek flag and the Canadian flag. Under an agreement with East York

2. Redway, Alan, Recollections, 1976–1982

Council, the Hellenes Grounds and monument were paid for and are to be maintained by the Greek Pontian Brotherhood.[3]

The Janikas Family #1 (L to R) John, Diane, Maria, George, Bassie and Tonie
(Source: John Janikas)

The Janikas Family #2 (L to R) George, Maria, John, Bassie, Diane, Tonie
(Source: John Janikas)

Yasmin (L) Parveen (M) Shamsh (R) Kara
(Source: Shamsh Kara)

3. East York Council minutes, November 1997

Multicultural Committee 1982
(Source: East York Foundation)

Sebastiano DiLorenzo (L) EY Day Vertis Club Italian Group 1978
(Source: Sebastiano DiLorenzo)

Bhausaheb Ubale
(Source: wikipedia.org)

EY Day (LF) Pauline McGibbon (RF) Mayor Alan Redway
(LR) Louise Redway (RR) Mr. McGibbon
(Source: Alan Redway)

Seniors

In 1980, 22% of East Yorkers were over sixty years of age, as compared with 14% of Metro Toronto as a whole, while 16% were over sixty-five, compared with 10% of the Metro population.[4] As the long-time borough residents aged, there was a pressing need for seniors housing in the community to accommodate those wanting to downsize and those with mobility issues. The Ina Grafton Gage Home (formerly the Taylor home called Fernwood) at the corner of Broadview and O'Connor Drive, which housed 110 senior women, had been doing the job for years, but clearly more was needed. [5]

First came East York Acres at 9 Haldon Avenue, built in 1962 by the Metropolitan Toronto Housing Company Limited on land donated by the township, financed by Central Mortgage and Housing Corporation under a National Housing Act limited-dividend loan and a provincial government grant. Its two hundred suites came in under budget, something unheard of today.[6]

Ten years later, True Davidson Acres Home for the Aged, accommodating 280 residents, was opened on Dawes Road.[7] Then in the 1980s, a number of new seniors' residences were opened, including Blair Court at 226 Donlands with 254 suites; The Overlea on Thorncliffe Park Drive with 219 suites; The Finnish Canadian Seniors Centre, Suomi Koti, on Eglinton near Laird Drive with 88 suites; Canadian Macedonian Place on O'Connor Drive with 93 suites; and St. Clair O'Connor Community (SCOC) with 128 apartments and 25 beds for long-term care.[8] These were followed in the early 1990s with three more church-sponsored residences: a United Church project, Chapel Court, at 16 Thorncliffe Park Drive with 109 suites; Canadian Martyrs Catholic Church project, Kendrick's Court, at Woodbine and Plains Road with 63 suites; and a project of Westminster Presbyterian Church on Floyd Avenue, Westminster Court, with 42 suites. All were financed at least in part with CMHC mortgages and rent subsidies.[9]

---

4. The *East Yorker*, 1980

5. The *East Yorker* 1980

6. McMahon, Michael, The Metropolitan Toronto Housing Company, 1990, 47

7. The *East Yorker*, 1972

8. The *East Yorker*, 1982

9. Alan Redway, Recollections, 1984–1993

Later in the 1990s, a senior citizens condominium was built privately at 955 Millwood Road. Two private seniors' residences were built, one at 921 Millwood Road. The other, Leisure World on O'Connor, was opened on O'Connor Drive near Sunrise Avenue. Finally, a seniors' life lease building, Stay At Home in Leaside, was constructed at 1387 Bayview Avenue.[10]

East York Acres
(Source: East York Foundation)

Canadian Macedonia Place
(Source: google.ca)

10. Redway, Recollections, 1993–2010

St Clair O'Connor
(Source: coc.ca)

The Physically and Mentally Challenged

For some East Yorkers at least, there was another consequence of aging. What shall become of their physically or mentally challenged adult children living with them at home?

For almost thirty years, the "Happy Gang," as they were known, organized by great East York volunteers Rita Boshier and Sharon Hagle, with the help of many other volunteers, provided a social outlet for many of the borough's challenged adults and a break for their parents by organizing dinners, dances, bowling, and swimming parties on Saturday afternoons and evenings. But while this gave the parents a break from the constant care of their adult children, it did not provide an answer for the question of what would happen to them when the parents could no longer care for themselves.[11]

An answer for some, at least, was the proposal in 1973 to build a four-pod supervised residence for their care at the corner of Sibley Avenue and Dentonia Park Avenue, but this meant building what some saw as an institution in a residential neighbourhood. The proposal was controversial and split the community. In the end, however, with strong support by local social activists such as Cecilia Murphy, Council approved the project.[12]

---

11. Redway, Recollections, 1977–1982
12. Redway, Recollections, 1973–1976

Cecilia Murphy
(Source: Verna King)

Working Mothers' Children

In her inaugural address to Council in 1970, Mayor True Davidson said, "The winds of change are affecting...the demand for special community services. How can we meet the needs?"[13]

Before World War II, almost all East York mothers were exclusively stay-at-home homemakers. The war changed all that and the feminist movement brought even greater change. Now, married women with children were working outside the home (whether they needed to or just wanted to) and needed day care for their children, all-day care for pre-schoolers, or after-school hours for older children. Commercial day-care centres started to open in residential neighbourhoods and controversy followed quickly

In the 1970s, a commercial day-care centre was established in a detached house located at 100 McRae Drive. Immediately, the neighbours raised concerns about the traffic caused by parents dropping off and picking up their children, but more especially because it was a business operating in a residential neighbourhood. It turned out, however, that 100 McRae had been owned for many years by a plumber, so when the Leaside zoning by-law was passed, the house had been zoned commercial to accommodate that long-established business.[14]

---

13. East York Council minutes, January 1970
14. Redway, Alan, Recollections, 1973–1982

Demand for day care continued to increase. Mrs. Veronica Roynon, the owner of Leaside Day Care at 100 McRae Drive needed more space, so she purchased a large home at 73 Fleming Crescent overlooking Talbot Park. This was clearly in a residential not a commercial zone. However, the Leaside zoning by-law passed prior to the merger with the Township of East York allowed day nurseries in residential zones. In spite of that, the residents of Fleming Crescent took up a petition signed by 760 people and supported by the Leaside Property Owners Association asking Council to amend the zoning by-law to delete day nurseries as a permitted use in residential zones. Council agreed to do so but the Ontario Municipal Board (OMB), and subsequently the Ontario provincial cabinet, refused to approve that amendment. In the meantime, while the appeals were pending, the neighbours and Mrs. Roynon agreed on a limit of the number of children to be cared for at 73 Fleming.

Ultimately, East York Council passed a new by-law prohibiting day nurseries in R1 and R2 zones but allowing them in all other residential zones, as well as in churches and schools. Subsequently, the East York Board of Education set aside two rooms in Bennington Heights School for day nurseries. Shortly after that, Mrs. Roynon sold 73 Fleming Crescent and moved her day care centre to the school. It was a satisfactory solution for all parties.[15]

Group Homes

Another product of changing times in East York was the group home. The Ontario Government was encouraging municipalities to amend their zoning by-law to allow group homes of three to ten persons, exclusive of staff, to locate in residential neighbourhoods to facilitate the provincial policy to move the physically and mentally challenged, the mentally ill, ex-offenders, individuals undergoing rehabilitation from alcoholism or drug abuse, children in the care of the Children's Aid Societies, and children suffering from emotional or psychiatric disorders, in order to get them out of institutions and into the community.

In 1966, the Rev. Gordon King, the minister at St. Luke's Anglican Church at Cosburn and Coxwell Avenues, asked Council to provide a

---

15. East York Council minutes, May 1976

site where the Anglican Church, the East York Rotary Club, and others sponsored by the Ontario government could erect a halfway house in the vicinity of Oak Park Avenue and Everett Crescent. After identifying a possible location, the Rev. King, at the request of Council, canvassed the surrounding neighbourhood, delivering 75–80 letters in an area approximately 750 feet from the site, notifying the neighbourhood of two meetings he was holding at the East York Memorial Arena to explain the project and providing his personal telephone number for individual interviews.[16]

Speaking in his capacity as president of the East York Federation of Ratepayer Associations, Ed Shaw asked that a decision be delayed until ratepayer organizations in the area had an opportunity to discuss the proposal. The next year, Council approved the proposal of the Rev. King, amended the zoning by-law, and ultimately conveyed the property to Yorklea Children's Lodges for use as a halfway house.[17]

The township had expropriated the Goulding Estate property with its magnificent Tudor-style house at 305 Dawes Road in 1965. The house, which stands in a park-like setting, was ideal for another group home. Six years later, it was leased to the Corrigan Boy's Residence operated by the Children's Aid Society.

Shortly after that, another home for eight children with developmental difficulties was established at 88 Dentonia Park Avenue, and Yorklea Children's Lodges opened two more homes accommodating six children each at 49 and 51 Chapman Avenue.

By 1978, when an application was made to establish a group home for children at 25 Eastdale Avenue, the time had come for the borough to develop a formal policy setting criteria for the approval of group homes in residential areas, rather than just approving them on an ad hoc basis. The East York Planning Board held a public meeting on the issue and Metro Toronto Council developed its own policy as well. Some residents, such as Vi Thompson and Marg Reilly, supported the zoning for group homes, but other residents did not. Mrs. M. Maxwell of 20 Rivercourt Boulevard expressed the strong feelings of those who did not in her letter to Council:

---

16. East York Council minutes, July 1966
17. East York Council minutes, May 1967

"We wish to bring your attention to a petition sent to Mayor Redway by residents of the Rivercourt R-1 area who are opposed to rezoning that would permit Group Homes to be located in all East York residential districts. A copy of the petition is enclosed.

"We wish particularly to stress that we are not opposed to the concept of returning to the community, people who are institutionalized for the reasons described in the *East Yorker*. We do, however, believe that the municipality would get a more positive response from the community if it took a different approach to the re-zoning project.

"As we see it, the whole purpose of residential zoning is to make it possible for neighbourhoods to establish and maintain a distinctive character, to ensure their continuity and to protect the homeowners" investments. This purpose is destroyed at one stroke when re-zoning is made to apply to all residential areas, leaving homeowners throughout the Borough uncertain as to what the future may hold for their respective neighbourhoods. This is a totally unfair approach.

"We consider it possible that re-zoning for the purpose described by the Mayor might be suitable for specific areas, but we strongly object to a blanket proposal by which such Homes could be located at the municipality's discretion anywhere at all in East York. In other words, if the borough were to come forward with proposals for specific properties in specific neighbourhoods, residents would then be able to assess the probable effects of re-zoning, which in some cases might actually enhance the neighbourhood, but in others, damage it irreparably.

"These points are in addition to those raised in the enclosed petition. We earnestly wish to have the opportunity of discussing them, and all other aspects of the re-zoning proposal, in a special meeting at the earliest possible date, and hope we can count on your support for such a meeting."

Petition from Area Residents of Rivercourt Boulevard:

"We the undersigned Residents in the Rivercourt R.1 area oppose re-zoning of all East York Residential districts to allow group homes in said districts.

"We are against profit-making individuals acquiring real estate solely for the purpose of making money under the guise of helping the unfortunate people describe in the June 1980 *East Yorker* under the heading 'Mayor Redway Says' namely, the mentally ill; the physically and mentally handicapped; ex-offenders; individual undergoing rehabilitation from drug abuse or alcoholism; children in the care of the Children's Aid Societies; children who are wards of the court, and children suffering emotional or psychiatric disorders out of Institutions into the community. This, in our opinion, is the government's authority and it is trying to shift its responsibility.

"We have always been willing to pay our share through our taxes to help with the care of these unfortunate people, but resent paying out money to outsiders who own and run these homes to enrich their financial position. As an example, one has only to visit some of the privately-owned nursing homes, where most of the patients are subsidized by our taxes, to find out what sort of care we are paying for. Shocking beyond belief! We feel as taxpayers in East York we should have guarantees that the residents of the group homes (if they are allowed) have the proper care and living conditions, are well and often inspected to make sure they are not allowed to deteriorate into the state of nursing homes mentioned.

"We would appreciate the following questions answered in the next *East Yorker* before any decision of re-zoning and group homes is made:

Does the Ontario Government or East York license the home?
Who inspects the home? How often?
Would residents be permanent or temporary?
How many residents to a bedroom?
How many bathrooms for ten residents?
How many safety precautions? (Fire escapes, smoke detectors)
Will property be adequately fenced?
If the group home becomes incompatible with the neighbours, is it closed? Or will it be 'Once a group home always a group home'?

"We hope our Mayor, Council and Planning Board will give the ratepayers of East York more consideration than the business interests attempting to open group homes in our community.

"We would also like to have on record (if group homes are allowed) the following:

Any area where group homes are anticipated the residents must be consulted well in advance before the homes become a fact.

If nothing can be done about the situation, they will at least have a chance to sell their home (if they desire) for a proper price before the 'Block Busting' (as it is called by many) down-grades our quiet peaceful community where we all live in harmony.

"Thank you for your attention." [18]

While Council was wrestling with the issue and attempting to formulate an East York policy, the Corrigan Boy's Residence on the Goulding Estate at 305 Dawes Road (formerly a Children's Aid foster home) wanted to convert to a group home. Salvation Army's Broadview Village at 1132 Broadview Avenue did as well because in both cases, some of their residents had reached twenty-one years of age and could no longer be considered as children.[19]

Pending a policy decision, none of the applications were approved. After Metro Toronto adopted a group home policy as part of its Official Plan, Mayor David Johnson met with the Hon. Margaret Birch, Ontario Cabinet Minister for Social Development, and shortly thereafter, the borough enacted a group home by-law in conformity to the Metro Toronto Official Plan.[20] In 1992, East York had thirteen group homes. (See Schedule C[21])

Goulding Estate
(Source: East York Foundation)

18. East York Council minutes, June 1978
19. East York Council minutes, February 1982
20. East York Council minutes, August 1992
21. East York Council minutes, August 1992

Touchstone Youth Centre

Neighbourhood concerns with group homes came to a head in 1989 when Touchstone Youth Centres applied for changes in the Official Plan and zoning by-law to permit the conversion of 1076 Pape Avenue as a youth centre to accommodate twenty-three youths aged sixteen to twenty on a short-term basis, during which time they would receive counselling.

The building had been purchased eleven years earlier by the Metropolitan Toronto Community Services Department and used for the past ten years as an area social welfare office. At that time, the office had a daytime staff of forty-eight and averaged ninety-four clients coming and going each day.

The Touchstone application was strongly opposed by the neighbours. Led by the president of the Ward Three Ratepayers Association, Ruth Fraser, together with the East Aldwych Committee and Russell English, they pointed out that the property was zoned residential and expressed concerns about the character of the young people, the numbers to be accommodated, and the program staff. In response, the Touchstone spokesperson advised that while priority was to be given to East York homeless youth requiring assistance, that it had a policy of excluding those demonstrating violent behaviour, drug or alcohol problems, and those with psychiatric or suicidal tendencies. As well, Touchstone had a curfew of ten p.m. through the week and eleven p.m. on Fridays and Saturdays for its clients.

A public meeting to hear all of those interested was arranged and held at William Burgess Public School, virtually right across the road from the site in question. It was a heated meeting to say the least and went on until well after midnight. In the end, however, over the objections of the Ward Councillors Steve Mastoras and Helen Kennedy, Council approved the application on a 7–2 vote in favour.[22]

---

22. East York Council minutes, September 1989

Touchstone
(Source: google.ca)

A Redevelopment Area

Dating back to 1965, the words "redevelopment area" have struck fear into the hearts of East Yorkers. This is because amendments to the National Housing Act that year made financing available to municipalities, if so requested, to assist them in the rehabilitation of older areas of their community. At the time, Councillors Cheeseman and McConaghy pointed out the designation of one area by any name as different from other areas puts a stigma on it, discouraging normal investment and creating feelings of insecurity among the in the inhabitants.[23]

The words "redevelopment area" came back to haunt East York in 1980 when the Ontario government offered the borough a $1,350,000 Community Services Contribution Program grant if Council would only designate the area between Dawes Road and Woodbine Avenue south of Lumsden Avenue to our boundary with Toronto as a "redevelopment area." That money was awfully tempting and sorely needed for sewers, roads, and sidewalks, as well as parks and recreation facilities in that area. Understandably, the southeast community, led by Ed Shaw, president of the East York Federation of Ratepayers, rebelled strongly against their homes being designated as such. On the other hand, Dave Cummins, a teacher at Gledhill Public School and chairman of the Gledhill School-

---

23. East York Council minutes, February 1965

Community Association Site Development Committee, along with five others, requested approval of the designation on behalf of the Gledhill, as well as the Oak Park and Secord neighbourhoods.

This required serious negotiation. In my capacity as mayor, I met repeatedly with the opposing parties. At Gledhill School, when I sat across the desk from the principal in his office, he pointed out to me that my chair was in East York while his was in the city of Toronto. The Toronto Board of Education, he told me, was prepared to spend money for both the school gymnasium located in the city and improvements to the school yard, which was located in East York. The East York Board of Education was also prepared to contribute to a community centre at Secord School, if Council would also assist financially by designating the south-east community a "redevelopment area."

As expected, Ed Shaw was adamant. In the words of the old union song, "We shall not be moved." He came across loud and clear. Ed Shaw had always been a strong supporter of mine but he made it clear that the past meant nothing in this case. Fortunately, it then came to me that since all we wanted to do was to fix the sewers, roads, sidewalks, and recreation facilities, "How would it be, Ed, if we only designated those items as a redevelopment area?" In the end, Ed Shaw agreed, but now I had to convince Council and the Province of this change of direction.

Fortunately, Council agreed, and with the great assistance of our members of the Ontario legislature, Dr. Bob Elgie and Dennis Timbrell, the Ontario government also agreed to let us designate only publicly-owned property — the roads, sidewalks, and school yards — as the redevelopment area. Most of the funds were spent on improving sewers, roads, and sidewalks, but because the terms of the grant required us to spend 40% on parks and recreation facilities, funds were allocated for a multi-purpose room at Secord School and improvements to the playground at Gledhill School. All of the cost of operating the Gledhill facility was paid for by the Toronto Board of Education, but it was built on the East York part of the school property. The East York Recreation Department had the exclusive right to issue permits for its use after school hours.[24]

---

24. Redway, Alan, Recollections, 1981–1982

| Ed Shaw | Secord Community Centre |
| *(Source: google.ca)* | *(Source: google.ca)* |

Family Housing Geared To Income

The late professor Albert Rose of the University of Toronto calculated that 20% of all Canadians will never be able to afford to buy a home and will require ongoing assistance for their housing needs.[25] East York has its share of seniors and families in that situation. Rent-geared-to-income for seniors housing is usually welcomed by its neighbours but not so with rent-geared-to-income for family housing. There are three rent-geared-to-income buildings for families in East York. 444 Lumsden Avenue, with 293 suites, originally an Ontario Housing Corporation building (now Toronto Community Housing Corporation) was the first to be constructed in East York and met with no neighbourhood resistance. Neither did the second, which was erected in 1997 on the site of the former Woodbine United Church at 704 Mortimer Avenue at Woodbine Avenue by the Toronto United Church Council's Community Homes. That building, with twenty-nine suites and fifty-nine tenants—including children—is leased to and managed by the Fred Victor Centre.[26]

However, the third building, the St. Vincent de Paul Family Homes at 10-12 Gower Street, did raise a great deal of neighborhood concern and

25. Rose, Albert, Canadian Housing Policies, 1935–1980, Butterworth and Company (Canada) Limited, 1980, 195

26. United Church of Canada Archives, Woodbine United Church

opposition when the proposal was made to build 164 family suites; 75% rent geared to income and 25% market rent[27] on land formerly the site of the Sobara grocery store.[28] East York Council held a meeting with the neighbours to consider the proposal at the nearby George Webster Public School. The gym at the school, where the meeting was held, was packed, standing room only. In spite of the heated tone of the meeting and the fact that the two ward councillors—Case Ootes and Michael Prue—both voted against it, the project was approved.[29] Speaking in 1994 after Gower Park Place was completed, Nick Volk, Vice President of St Vincent de Paul Family Homes, said, "The neighbourhood was split between having the project as proposed and having a community centre, so we gave them both." [30]

St Vincent DePaul 14 Gower
(Source: google.ca)

Yes, the times most definitely had changed.

---

27. Interview with Case Ootes, February 1, 2017
28. Interview with Lyn Ridout, August 17, 2016
29. Interview with Case Ootes, February 1, 2017
30. Gower Park Place website

Schedule C

East York Group Homes

Address	Type	Capacity
49 Chapman Avenue	Boarding Home for Children	6
51 Chapman Avenue	Boarding Home for Children	6
99 Chisholm Avenue	Functionally Disabled Children	6
276 Chisholm Avenue	Children with Mental Retardation	7
88 Dentonia Park Avenue	Children with Development Difficulties	8
25 Eastdale Avenue	Emotionally Disturbed Children	4
1091 Woodbine Avenue	Children with Mental Retardation	6
325 Mortimer Avenue	Adults with Mental Retardation	4
305 Dawes Road	Boys Residence (4 houses with 6)	24
33 George Webster Road		

Residential Care Facilities

1102 Broadview Avenue
1132 Broadview Avenue
67 Everett Crescent
65 Sibley Avenue

NOTE: Distancing factor contained within Group Home By-Law applies between group homes, and group homes and residential care facilities

– Chapter 13 –

PARKS AND RECREATION

One of those changes was municipal recreation. Before World War II, there was no organized recreation in the township, as we know it today. There was no television to watch, no devices for video games, nor cellphones for texting. East Yorkers had to entertain themselves.

"One main activity was swimming. There were about six swimming holes dammed up in Taylor's Creek. At the top of Chisholm there was a dam creating the "girls" swimming hole. By Dawes Road there was a swimming hole called the "Big Boys' Swimming Hole." Here, the boys went skinny-dipping on the first warm day of spring. The truant officers would go down to the swimming hole at about recess time and haul between twenty and forty kids back to school. One person in the community remembers these times. 'The girls would run like blazes when the boys came out of the water and started running. The girls would try to get their peeks, you know.' Anyone who would not go swimming before May 24 was a 'chicken'. At the north end of Westlake and also Eastdale, there was a swamp which the kids would dam up in the summer with whatever they could find: sods, corrugated iron, and the like. It would become about eight feet in depth and it washed out the next spring. On Dawes Road just back of where True Davidson Acres is now, was the frog pond. Kids used to catch many frogs here. If you go up there now, you can still find bull rushes and other signs that the pond existed.

"In the winter, there were many places to skate and sleigh. The kids skated on a pond where Dentonia Park is now. People also skated on Massey's pond an on a rink beside Hope Church at Chisholm. Some winters they hooked all the garden hoses together and flooded a corner of Massey's field at the north-east corner of Coleman Ave. and Dawes Rd. to make a skating rink. There was a rink in Secord School yard. The girls skated there and the boys played hockey. The kids sleighed from one yard to another. When the snow got deep, they would drive a dog and sleigh. The children tobogganed behind Chisholm into the Taylor Creek Valley. They went sleigh-riding down the hills in the ravine between Eastdale and Barrington. When Crescent School was in operation, the children tobogganed down the hills on the southern part of the property. They gave the hills different names such as Little Dipper, Big Dipper, Sugar Bowl and Milk Jug. It was possible to drive a car into these hills as a road let to them through Dentonia Park (see map) kids often played among these hills, and teenagers used them as a 'Lover's Lane.'"[1]

Don Wadlow tells the story of those early days as well.

Being an Old Country settlement, soccer was predominant in the early 1920s, where it is said that shopkeepers closed their stores to follow the football team. In 1924, twelve people gathered together to form a horticulture group, which today boasts a membership of 160.

With the influence of present day, Councillor Norm McKay a number of interested lawn bowlers met in 1929 and in 1930 on the 24th day of May, complete with parade and brass band, the Cosburn Park Bowling was initiated. For two years, a club of men playing under the name of the Secord Club was in operation but later joined in to strengthen the membership of the Cosburn Club.

Children's programmes date back to the early thirties when the Burgess Ratepayers promoted a decorated doll carriage and bicycle parade, which set out from Don Mills Methodist Church, now Don Mills United, down Pape Avenue to Hartman Jones Public School where the judging took place.

---

1. Fagan, Lu Ann, *The Secord Arena*, East York Board of Education, 1974, 34

Softball played a prominent role in the middle twenties for the men and ladies' softball got its start as early as 1928 when the George Hare Trophy was competed for by such teams as McGregors, Owegos, and Danforth Park. This league operated until 1933 when all the East Yorkers moved into the Sunnyside Ladies League.

In the early thirties, Secord Community Centre in Secord Public School proved the leadership of the late George Webster, where an athletic programme of soccer, softball, and swimming was provided. Under the late Johnny Walker, such outstanding swimmers such as George Young and Pirie were trained in Secord Tank.

Many a person made use of the natural parkland of Taylor's Bush, now known as Woodbine Park, when car travel was not extensive. As early as 1920, a refreshment stand was erected by the late John Hollinger to cater to the many picnic parties. As time went by, this area was the focus point of big-time wrestling which was held in conjunction with the big picnics and it is said that it was nothing at all to see 10,000 people enjoying the beauty of the countryside. Out of this recreation, through the generosity of Mr. Hollinger offering rides to the Danforth to people on rainy days, a big transportation company, namely the Hollinger Bus Lines, was put into service.[2]

In 1926, the Township Council appointed John Hollinger (who had his refreshment stand where the Trillium Apartment building is today) as a special constable to keep order Woodbine Park. On one occasion, Hollinger arrested George William Scott, who subsequently sued John for false arrest and imprisonment. While the Council agreed to defend him, the minutes do not record who won.[3] The wrestling matches at the picnics feature East York's own Billy Potts, who grew up on Rosevear Avenue. Potts later gained fame all over North America wrestling under the name of Whipper Billy Watson.

While it was more entertainment than recreation, the circus was popular in the early days. As a boy growing up, George English remembers a circus complete with elephants performing in the vacant fields on Woodville west of Pape Avenue.[4] In 1931, Branch 22 of the

---

2. Wadlow, Don, *The History of Recreation in East York*, Self–Published, 1961, 1
3. East York Council minutes, November 1926
4. Interview with George English, December 29, 2015

Legion sponsored a circus that performed on the then vacant land north of Sammon Avenue, west of Woodmount Avenue.[5] Ringling Brothers and Barnum and Bailey circus performed for two days on the Woodbine Golf Course just before the property was sold to Farlinger Developments in 1950,[6] and two years later, the East York Police Association sponsored a three-ring circus held in the East York Memorial Arena.[7]

Don Wadlow takes up the story again. "Leading up to 1945, the Teachers' Playground was organized and operated at the different school grounds throughout the summer. Winter sports were mostly carried on in the Woodbine Golf Course, where the rolling hills and valleys offered thrills for skiing and tobogganing as well as the summer enjoyment of a pleasant game of golf."[8]

Woodbine Park Slide
(Source: East York Foundation)

Whipper Billy Watson (Bill Potts) (L) Reeve Jack Warren (R)
(Source: East York Foundation)

Cosburn Park Lawn Bowling Club
(Source: Cosburn Lawn Bowling)

_____

5. Faulkner, Len, *Early Days of Branch 22,* Self–Published, 3
6. Dolbey, Michael, *A History of Woodbine Gardens,* Self–published. 2015
7. East York Police Association Souvenir Program, 1954
8. Wadlow, Don, *The History of recreation in East York,* Self–Published, 1961

The Physical Fitness Act

All that changed after the war. In 1945, the Ontario Legislature passed the Physical Fitness Act, which allocated money to the municipalities to create community recreation programs. Shortly thereafter, East York established a Community Centres Committee, which then hired Stan Wadlow as the director of recreation. Since there was no space available in the municipal offices, he worked out of his home at 241 Queensdale Avenue until the Board of Education found him a room in R.H. McGregor School.

When Stan was hired, there were only four parks in the township. He describes the situation:

Todmorden Park was in the valley at the bottom of Don Mills Rd.; Dieppe Park, an old farm, was located between Linsmore Cr. and Greenwood Ave. at Cosburn Ave. This park was partially developed with a softball diamond and bleachers in the northeast corner. Unfortunately, this area had lost much of its top soil and the clay that was left became a soggy mess every time it rained. Cedarvale Park was filled-in ravine land that ran along Cosburn Ave. between Cedarvale Ave. and Oak Park Ave. The plans for this park called for the laying of topsoil, grading and the demolition of two old houses on the park boundaries. Topham Park was the fourth. It had been a market garden and was now set aside by Council as a park. It was undeveloped at this time.

The remaining facilities included Cosburn Park and East York Collegiate. Cosburn Park, at Durant Ave. and Cosburn Ave., was home to the Cosburn Park Lawn Bowling Club. Behind the bowling area were three cinder tennis courts. The board offered me the use of East York Collegiate. Council eventually built a stadium beside the school, but in 1946, it was nothing more than sand dunes. This was the extent of recreational park facilities outside of the school playgrounds.

Anxious to roll programmes, I asked Les Hanly and Horace Harmer to assist me in setting up the East York Softball Association. We drew up a constitution, then set about organizing teams for boys and girls in various age groups. We also had plans for a major league.

Softball became a popular programme and to accommodate the growing interest the Township cooperated with the Community Centres Committee in the construction of a softball backstop on the field at East

York Collegiate. This helped relieve the crowded conditions at Dieppe Park, but it wasn't enough. We applied to the City of Toronto for permission to use the northeast diamond at Dentonia Park every Tuesday and Thursday; as well, we asked the City Board of Education for permission to use Earl Kitchener Grounds from 7 to 9 p.m. on weekdays and on Saturday afternoons. With these permits, we were able to accommodate an expanding softball program.

My interest in soccer prompted me to set up a soccer programme. With the assistance of Bert Lipsham, Ron Gibson, Dick Callacher, and Bill Wilson we formed a senior team. East York United, and joined the National Soccer League. At the same time, we set up a juvenile team, the Owegos, and entered it in the Juvenile League. Dieppe Park would be used as their home field so with the help of the Works Department, under Len Swain, goals were put up, change rooms put in, and the field was marked out.[9]

East York Soccer Club

Although both Stan and Don Wadlow refer to soccer in the early days, it was not until 1977 that Bob Dale, later a borough councillor, and Dragan Zagar founded the East York Minor Soccer League for boys and girls from four to eighteen years of age. About 1500 boys and 900 girls participate each season in three levels, house league, rep, and competitive. Some years there were men's and women's teams as well. They played at various venues in East York and south of the Danforth.[10] According to long-time East York Recreation Department Assistant, Kevin Chisholm, indoor soccer began in 1975, resulting in about 800 fewer boys playing hockey that year.[11] A number of East York players went on to professional soccer careers, including Theo Zagar for Canada, Hossein Khamsei and Manuel Aparicio with Spain, Abdallah Elchanti with Sweden, and Luca Stavrou with Cypress. Soccer has continued to grow and thrive in East York through the efforts and dedication of Dragan Zagar, Ed McConnell, Miguel de Sousa, Kim de Sousa, and Karen Sommerville.[12]

---

9. Wadlow, Stan, *East York Recreation, The Early Years,* Centennial College Press, 1982, 2
10. Interview with Karen Sommerville, June 29, 2017
11. Interview with Kevin Chisholm, April 28, 2017
12. Interview with Karen Sommerville, June 29, 2017

Stan Wadlow goes on:

That spring I contacted Irene and Bert Pezzack about the formation of a tennis club at Cosburn Park. The tennis programme drew considerable interest and with the help of volunteers, we watered, rolled, and marked the tree courts every day.

The Teachers' Playground Association continued to operate their summer playground programme after I joined the township. This group was set up during the war and they received financial assistance from the township and the Board of Education. Their programme involved many children from the various school areas for a period of six weeks during July and August.

I was able to organize a summer "Learn to Swim" programme under the capable direction of Mrs. Finley and William Gibson. This programme operated for a period of seven weeks at Danforth Park and Secord Public Schools. Over 300 children registered that first summer.[13]

The swimming programme at Danforth Park (now D.A. Morrison Middle School) continued with Gert Hart keeping tabs for the Recreation Department for many years. The swimming pool at Secord School closed but the Secord Community Centre was rehabilitated in the 1980s.

"During 1946-47, Stan Wadlow went on to organize summer playgrounds at Hartman Jones, (now Westwood Middle School), William Burgess, R.H. McGregor, Secord, Danforth Park (now D.L. Morrison), and Plains Road (now Diefenbaker) schools, swimming classes at the Danforth Park and Secord swimming pools, a softball league at Dieppe Park, a hard ball team, two soccer teams, public school inter-school soccer, a volley ball league, the Cosburn Horseshoe Club, a bowling league, a badminton club, a cribbage league, and a golf school. In addition, he spearheaded the development of the Secord-Dawes Road Community Centre and physical improvements to Dieppe Park, Cosburn Park, and Cedarvale Park."[14]

---

13. Wadlow, Stan, *East York Recreation, The Early Years*, Centennial College Press, 1982, 3
14. Wadlow, Stan, *East York Recreation, The Early Years*, Centennial College Press, 1982, 4

Gert Hart
(Source: Doreen Hart)

Next on Stan's agenda was hockey.

East York Hockey Association

"During the month of September 1944, at the request of Roy Turner, a meeting was arranged by a Committee of Council, which had been appointed to deal with financial assistance to athletic organizations. At this meeting, held at East York Collegiate, Council arranged to build two hockey cushions, along with a pleasure rink in Dieppe Park. Council arranged to flood the rinks and to build two shacks with stoves that would serve as change rooms. In January of 1945, hockey games were set up for boys in the Bantam and Midget age groups.

"After my arrival home from my duties with the Navy in December 1945, I was contacted by Roy Turner and asked to attend a meeting of the East York Hockey League. The meeting was to be held in Watts' family apartment, above the Watts' Butcher Shop at Woodbine and Queensdale Aves. The League organization, Roy Turner and Alvin Watts, Ted Stedman, George Gourlie, and Bob Thomas, asked me to join them and assist in the organization of the forthcoming 1945-46 season.

"Knowing of my impending appointment as director of recreation I discussed the plans whereby this group would function as an association and how it would work within the overall recreation programme. On that night, we formed the East York Hockey Association. A constitution was later drawn up and adopted after my appointment.

"In the 1945-46 season, we operated sponsored teams in the Minor Bantam, Bantam, Midget, and Juvenile divisions. The programme involved some 250 boys that year. At a meeting when plans for the next season were discussed, I felt we could expand the programme if we could line up sponsors for the teams. I approached the Kiwanis Club of East York and got them to agree to sponsor six teams in a Pee Wee league. This league would be called the 'Little N.H.L.' and the teams would be named after the six major league teams. The other big sponsors that year were the East York Fire Department and Whipper Watson's Whipper Pack. The outdoor ice rinks were becoming busy places. The Pee Wees played every Saturday morning while the other teams played during the week, if the weather was good.

"The winter of 1946-47 brought numerous power shortages so the township purchased a large generator to provide lights for the two hockey cushions and the skating rink. The Township did everything they could to make our season a success.

"The changing facilities consisted of two large shacks heated by coal stoves. To help the executives of the league weather the zero and sub-zero temperatures a small plywood shelter was set up between the two cushions. To help the referees, we painted the blue and centre lines on the side of the rinks. Later these lines were painted on the ice. This worked fine until a warm spell came along and melted the ice.

"Ironically, it was warm weather and cold weather that made up the biggest obstacle to those running a hockey schedule on outdoor surfaces. One season we had to complete our finals in the Danforth Park School Gymnasium playing floor hockey. While battling these conditions, I was continually pushing for an artificial ice surface. I rallied members of the Association and we finally talked it over with Arthur Dyson, who was chairman of the Boys and Girls Committee for the East York Kiwanis. With the support of the Association and the Kiwanis Club we were able to convince the Council of the need for an indoor ice surface. By 1949 the 'Build the Arena' campaign was on the tracks."[15]

During the summer of 1947, in addition to the school playgrounds, an effort was made to provide young people with an organized opportunity to enjoy the outdoors as they had done on their own before the war.

---

15. Wadlow, Stan, *East York Recreation, The Early Years*, Centennial College Press, 1982, 13

"The Don Valley attracted many youngsters during the warm weather and since it was right on our doorstep we chose Todmorden Park as a rendezvous point for daily hikes. Here the young people met Dr. Beare of the collegiate staff and a man who was fully qualified to interpret nature's secrets. The response to his efforts was tremendous. His programme to encourage the use of the Don Valley as a playground was a success." [16]

Stan Wadlow
(Source: East York Foundation)

Willis Blair (L) Stan Wadlow (C) Art Dyson (R)
(Source: Norm Dyson)

East York Track

"The summer of 1947 also saw the formation of the East York Track Club. The club was coached by Fred Foot, a graduate of East York Collegiate who had returned from war service. He was a former track star who gave a great deal of his time to the development of his sport." In the early part of 1962 the East York Track Club, in cooperation with the Township of East York was granted their request to host the British Empire Trials for the second time. The event would be held at the Memorial Stadium at the beginning of August. A committee was formed to organize the big event.

"We approached this event in the same way we handled it the first time. The community was asked to open up their homes to the visiting athletes and once again, the response was tremendous.

———

16. Wadlow, Stan, *East York Recreation, The Early Years*, Centennial College Press, 1982, 15

"The success of the meet was due to the involvement of the community committee members, officials, and homeowners who were delighted to play a part. To this day people say to me how pleased they were to house one of the competitors. Introducing the people to the competitors in this way went a long way to raising interest in track and field. Many people became fervent supporters of the sport.

"The names of the competitors read like a who's who of Canadian sports: Bruce Kidd, Bill Crothers, Harry Jerome, Lynn Eves, George Shepard, and Abbie Hoffman. Fred Foot developed and trained Bruce Kidd and Bill Crothers, who set record times in the two mile and 1000 yard respectively in 1963 at the international track meet at Los Angeles, California."[17]

Bruce Kidd 1960
(Source: East York Foundation)

Bill Caruthers (L)
(Source: East York Foundation)

17. Wadlow, Stan, *East York Recreation, The Early Years*, Centennial College Press, 1982, 15

Stan Wadlow continues:

"In the fall and winter of 1947-48, Harry Hull, a teacher at East York Collegiate, began to give his energies over to a gymnastic programme. Classes were held at the Collegiate every Wednesday night. Some forty boys enrolled in his course that first year."[18]

Three collegiate teachers, Hager Hull and Miller, coached the great EYCI Goliath football teams.[19] "High school football was a popular attraction at the new stadium. On Friday nights, the place was packed with collegians and their parents. The East York Band and Majorettes provided half-time entertainment and the games were always exciting. It was a sad day when the collegiate decided to play their games during the school hours. I always believed that the night games generated great community spirit."[20]

In 1981, former East York Collegiate Goliaths quarterback Nelson Martin Jr. was named the most valuable player in the Grey Cup game won by his team the British Columbia Lions. Nelson, who told me he didn't know what it was like to lose while playing for the Goliaths, broke his neck while playing football at Simon Fraser University. Although warned he would risk his life if he ever played football again, he disregarded the warning and went on to star in the Canadian Football League.[21]

Merkle Hager, Harry Hull, Bruce Miller coaches of EYCI Goliaths
(Source: schoolweb.tdsb.on.ca)

---

18. Wadlow, Stan, *East York Recreation, The Early Years*, Centennial College Press, 1982, 15
19. Norman Dyson, Interview, February 15, 2012
20. Wadlow, Stan, *East York Recreation, The Early Years*, Centennial College Press, 1982, 17
21. Redway, Alan, Recollections, 1981–1995

Nelson Martin Jr.
(Source: Canadian Football League as the defensive coordinator of the Winnipeg Blue Bombers, Toronto Wild Cats)

Kiwanis Swimming Pool

"The opening of the Kiwanis Swimming Pool in Cedarvale Park, on June 19, 1948, was a dream come true for the members of the Kiwanis Club. Along with the pool, there were dressing rooms, showers and washrooms. There was a sanded area around the pool for those who wanted to sunbathe.

"The facility was built at a cost of $85,000. The Kiwanis Club contributed $25,000 while the Township paid the balance.

"The official opening was attended by dignitaries from Council, the Government of Ontario and the East York Kiwanis Club. Brigadier Milton Martin officially opened the pool. After the ceremonies an exhibition was put on by members of the Gus Ryders Club for the large crowd.

"The pool was a popular place to be during the hot summer days; attendance was running at a peak until other municipalities around us built their own pools. The Scarborough Lions Pool on Birchmount Ave. was the next one completed. As these pools were built, the numbers began to thin out at our pool. When it was built the Kiwanis pool was the only outdoor pool east of the Mineral Baths on Bloor St., near High Park." [22]

---

22. Wadlow, Stan, *East York Recreation, The Early Years*, Centennial College Press, 1982, 19

Kiwanis EY Memorial Pool 1959-60
(Source: East York Foundation)

Rifle and Revolver Club

"A Rifle and Revolver Club was another addition to that winter's programme list. A rifle range was built in the basement of the Collegiate, and under the guidance of Mr. Byford, a local resident and Dominion of Canada Marksman, interest was sparked. The club generated interest in revolver shooting. Art Barney, a former member of the Toronto Revolver Club gathered interested people into a group and formed the East York Revolver Club. The two groups shared the same facility on alternate night, however the Revolver Club's growing popularity put too much of a strain on the Collegiate range. The club began to look around for their own building. The Revolver Club and the Toronto Revolver Club pooled their resources to purchase a piece of property on Gower Ave."[23]

In 1978, Commonwealth Games were held in Edmonton, Desmond and Patrick Vamplew of Alder Road won a gold and bronze medal respectively in the full-bore rifle event.[24]

By the end of 1949, the Recreation Department had seen tremendous development in its programmes. We offered a wide variety of activities to the people of East York and we were still trying to improve our programmes. We had everything from archery to golf, from a Soap Box Derby to touch rugby."[25]

---

23. Wadlow, Stan, *East York Recreation, The Early Years*, Centennial College Press, 1982, 22
24. East York Council minutes, June 1978
25. Wadlow, Stan, *East York Recreation, The Early Years*, Centennial College Press, 1982, 23

"Build the Arena" Campaign

"While all of this was going on, I was still working on garnering support for an indoor ice rink. Our "Build the Arena" campaign was started in 1949 and in 1950, Ted Steadman was hired as manager of the fund raising campaign.

"In the growing years of 1948–50, the East York Hockey Association continued to thrive and the demand for an artificial ice surface became paramount in the minds of the association executive. I felt that if something wasn't done soon we would lose the volunteers who were so important to our hockey programme. I contacted Arthur Dyson of the Kiwanis Club and together we set up a case for the arena. Our presentation to Council was accepted and they called tenders. N.O. Hipel Co. Ltd.'s tender was accepted. Hipel's tender was a complete package for an ice surface with other necessary facilities. The arena was financed by the issuance of a $200,000 debenture.

"When it was completed, the arena had an 80 by 185 ft. ice surface and seating capacity for 1,667 people and room for 1,800 more to stand. It was named the East York Memorial Arena after those who had died in the two World Wars."[26]

East York Memorial Arena

"East York Memorial Arena held its Grand Opening on Wednesday, October 10, 1951. To the sports-loving public of East York, this day was a dream come true.

"When the arena opened, the East York Hockey Association was able to use all of the Saturday morning ice time. We played thirty-minute games in Atom, Minor Pee Wee, Pee Wee, and Minor Bantam leagues. During the week our Bantams, Minor Midgets, and Juveniles would play in the evenings.

"I have fond memories of those Saturday mornings. I never missed a whistle as I shuffled teams on and off the ice at their scheduled times. It was necessary to follow a strict system because artificial ice was too

---

26. Wadlow, Stan, *East York Recreation, The Early Years*, Centennial College Press, 1982, 23

valuable to waste. Another Recreation Department organization that was soon to take advantage of the indoor ice was the East York Skating Club.

"In the early 1950s, we started a Christmas Jamboree as a fund raising event for the East York Hockey Association. It began as a series of home and away games with teams from Simcoe. These were fun days for players and as for the parents we were a noisy group of supporters, win or lose.

"Over the years, we began exchanging games with teams from Peterborough and Brampton. Playing games in different towns and cities evolved into a tournament where teams from four communities were invited to East York for a one-day series of games. From their experience came the next step of selecting teams from our house leagues and making the tournament bigger. The Jamboree had done much to generate hockey enthusiasm in the community and it helps the Association raise money for its hockey programme."[27]

East York Lyndhursts Represent Canada in the 1954 World Hockey Tournament

In 1954, the East York Lyndhurst's Senior B team (players shown in Schedule "D") was selected to represent Canada in the World Hockey Tournament in Stockholm, Sweden. George Sayliss who grew up on Rumsey Road opposite Trace Manes Park, was a forward on that team. He told me that prior to the Russian game, Lyndhurst trounced Norway, Sweden, Finland, Czechoslovakia, Switzerland, and Germany, outscoring their combined opponents 57-5. In contrast, Russia beat the same opponents with a combined score of 30-8. The Canada-Russia final was played on outdoor natural ice in a snow storm before 17,000 fans. The Moscow Dynamos Soviet army team relied on the speed and finesse, while East York, playing the usual Canadian physical style, drew a great many penalties from the European referees. When Russia won that game 7-2, a collective groan went up across Canada. Years later of course, even Canadian teams with NHL players have suffered losses at the hands of the Russians. George Sayliss' Lyndhurst sweater and memorabilia from the

---

27. Wadlow, Stan, *East York Recreation, The Early Years*, Centennial College Press, 1982, 27

1954 Canada-Russia game have an honoured place in the Peterborough Hall of Fame where he moved after leaving East York. [28]

Stan Wadlow continues the story of the East York Hockey Association.

In the 1953-54 season, the association received permission from the National Hockey League to name a trophy the "Little Stanley Cup." It was donated by S. Walter Stewart to the champions in the Pee Wee divisions. Our trophy was the only authorized replica of the Stanley Cup.

In 1954-55, an idea of Roy Turner and Ernie Head became the first hockey school in Toronto. The school was set up for five, six, and seven-year-old boys on Saturday mornings. Here the youngsters were taught the basics of skating, passing and shooting by knowledgeable instructors.

In the 1956-57 season, the association president, Les Hanly, introduced the President's Dinner. It was an occasion to honour those who had spent their hours in volunteer service to the community's youth.

The association was also looking at ways to improve its game. They started a referee's clinic and soon they were developing talented referees along with talented hockey players.

I was in Montreal in the early 1960s and saw that they had made helmets mandatory in their hockey programme. I mentioned this to other members of the East York Association and we became the first association in Ontario to enforce a helmet rule.

During the 1962-63 season, after a few meetings with the associations in neighbouring Leaside, Don Mills, Wexford, and Scarborough, the East Metro Hockey League was set up. The spark plugs in this idea were Ernie Head, Les Hanly, Herb Brown, and Ernie Fish.

In 1967, the Borough of East York, under the Metropolitan Government Official Plan, joined the Township of East York and the Town of Leaside. To bring the two communities together, I instituted Borough Championships.

The years continued to pass along and the association continued its work within the community. We set up the Bulldog Hockey Tournament in 1974 as part of the old Township's fiftieth anniversary. We raised money for East General Hospital in 1975 and in 1977, we helped raise money towards the cost of renovating East York Memorial Arena. The

---

28. Redway, Alan, Leaside Life, Ruth G. Publishing Inc, April 2013, 27

happy hours and camaraderie I spent in the East York Hockey Association will never be forgotten.[29]

Over the years that followed, other key members of the EYHA included Ron Sibbick, Roy Turner, Bob Campbell, Herb Smith, Fred Backman, Bob Paterson, Tom McMaster, and Ed Svelnis.[30]

Norm Gray EY Lyndhurst
(Source: East York Fire Dept)

Stan Wadlow recalls the development of:

CEDARVALE PARK

Renamed October 29, 1979 as STAN WADLOW PARK and RECREATION COMPLEX

"My memory of this area dates back to 1919 when a friend of the family decided to build a frame home north of Lumsden Ave and Meagher Ave. (now Oak Park Ave.) in an open field now called Everett Crescent. This home was built in a cluster with three others. Apart from these homes was one little bungalow, lived in and owned by the Screaton family. This home still stands on what later became Cosburn Ave. The well on the Screaton property was the only water supply for those settling this area.

---

29. Wadlow, Stan, *East York Recreation, The Early Years*, Centennial College Press, 1982, 28
30. Interview with Kevin Chisholm, April 28, 2017

At this time, ravines surrounded the highlands and ran south ending at Lumsden Ave. Many of these ravines were eventually filled in with garbage and topsoil so as to open up the area. What became Cedarvale Park was ravine land where raspberries and mushrooms grew. Up though the 1930s we would pick mushrooms in this area and in the trunk ravine on which the East York Sports Centre was built in later years.

The only building on this land in 1946 was the home of Alex Main. It was located at the corner of Cedarvale Ave. and Cosburn Ave. Farther north was what had been a farm house and later a dairy; while on Cosburn Ave. was a small frame home. All of these homes were expropriated and demolished to make way for the complete development of the site. By 1946, top fill was required for the main area of the park. From 1946 to 1948, top fill was brought in and graded until a satisfactory grade had been established. A berm was created along the Haldon Ave. side to prevent washouts on the slopes.

In 1946, the postal authorities decided to close down various portable post offices. One of these was located on O'Connor Dr. near the industrial area. We approached the authorities and were able to obtain it providing we removed it. Council decided to build a cement black basement and equip it with showers. When this was completed, the building was moved by the township forces and placed on the new foundation behind the Kiwanis swimming pool in Cedarvale Park. It was large enough to accommodate two large dressing rooms and a large storage space. A stove was installed to heat the building during the cool fall evenings and for winter skating.

With Council's permission, I was able to install two backstops. The one for junior ball was built by Len Swain's Township forces and placed in the north area. The other was tendered and built adjacent to Cosburn Ave. on the southwest corner. Later Council granted my request to have the junior diamond floodlighted. On August 24, 1959, we officially pressed the switch for night ball. Those present representing Council were Jack Allen, Reeve, who threw the first ball; at the catcher's position was Roy Brigham, Councillor, and Vic Dobson, East York Baseball Association. Through the years, this has proven to be a wonderful addition to the baseball programme in Cedarvale Park.

Three weeks after the opening of night ball, the East York Baseball Association presented me with a shield depicting the lights and displaying the first ball pitched. Inscribed on it were the signatures of Jack R. Allen, Roy Brigham, and Vic Dobson. It read "E.Y.B.A. The first one under the lights at Cedarvale – Thanks, Stan!" [31]

East York Memorial Arena
(Source: Toronto.cadataparkfacilitycomplex)

Little Stanley Cup
(Source: Inside Toronto)

East York Baseball Association

Stan Wadlow referred to pressing the switch on August 24, 1959, for the first night game at Cedarvale Park (now Stan Wadlow Park) but the EYBA was actually founded in 1952 by my mother's first cousin, Norm Bryan. It has been growing and thriving ever since with the efforts and leadership of Marie Rose, Dave Hocking, Bob Nelson, Murray Marshall, Rick Johnston, Greg Hamilton, Harry McAloney, Tom Adams, Jeff

31. Wadlow, Stan, *East York Recreation, The Early Years*, Centennial College Press, 1982, 33

O'Brien, Alfie Payne, Rob and Rich Butler, Mike Holmes, and Andrew Green.

Jim Vipond, the late sports editor of the *Globe and Mail* and an East Yorker, said, "It's better for kids to steal a base than to steal a purse." The EYBA provides kids ages six to eighteen with just that opportunity to steal a base. Association Tyke, Bantam, Minor Midget, Midget, Juvenile, and Senior teams have won local, provincial, and Canadian championships. Individual players have starred as amateurs and professionals. Rick Johnston played for Canada in the 1988 Olympics. Greg Hamilton is the main man at Baseball Canada in Ottawa. Alan Butler, no relation to Rob and Rich, played for the Blue Jays Class A farm team. Of course, Rob and Rich Butler both played Major League ball with the Toronto Blue Jays. Rich played on the Jay's 1993 World Series Championship team.[32]

Norm Bryan	Rich Butler	Rob Butler
(Source: dignitymemorial.com)	*(Source: torontopubliclibrary.ca)*	*(Source: google.ca)*

Stan takes up his story again.

"Five years later, Council decided to design, landscape, and sod the area replacing the dressing accommodations with a more modern building. Under the same roof would be a large multi-use room, which could be divided with folding doors. In addition, there would be a snack bar, cloak rooms, toilets, a furnace room, and a storage room. The building was designed and built to serve the needs of many community activities. Jerome Markson, architect, was selected to design the building. He eventually received a Canadian architectural award for his design.

---

32. Interview with Andrew Green and Mike Holmes, June 29, 2017

With practically all work completed, the park was a beauty to behold. On Thursday, November 11, at 3 p.m., in the presence of assembled guests, the clubhouse was officially opened. In attendance were the Cedarvale Senior Citizens Club, other recreational organization representative, Reeve True Davidson, Councillors Willis Blair, Roy Brigham, Howard Chandler, Norman Cheeseman, Norman Maughan, and Jim McConaghy; officials Des Corcoran Commissioner of Parks and Recreation, Stan Wadlow, Deputy, Doris Tucker Clerk, Duncan Little Treasurer, and Ernie Heyes Director of Recreation; honoured guests Steven Otto M.P., Jerome Markson architect, and Droge Construction Ltd. Contractors, Reeve True Davidson spoke on behalf of Council followed by Jim McConaghy Chairman of the Parks and Recreation Committee, Steve Otto, recently elected M.P. representing East York, was introduced by Reeve True Davidson. After his remarks, we assembled around the plaque in the hall for the official ceremony conducted by Steve Otto, M.P.

In the following year, these additions were made: four baseball screens, plank seating for the bleacher section, four score boards, hose and sprinklers, drinking fountains, storage space, and a catering facility. In 1969, two baseball courts were installed in Cedarvale Park. These were donated by Verne Hislop and his family in loving memory of his son.

Cedarvale Park, now renamed Stan Wadlow Park and Recreation Complex, is now the largest in the municipality. It provides an ideal place for large crowds to gather for Dominion Day, baseball games, and picnics. It is the only park large enough for a fireworks display. Located beside the Haldon Ave. Senior Citizens Home, it presents a beautiful view from their front windows, and provides them with the use of a putting green, horse shoe pitch, and shuffleboard courts."[33]

Stan Wadlow Club House
(Source: toronto.ca)

———

33. Wadlow, Stan. *East York Recreation, The Early Years*, Centennial College Press, 1982, 34

In 1978, following the collapse of the Listowel, Ontario, arena roof, resulting in the death of a number of midget hockey players who were in the rink at that time, East York Council obtained a report indicating that there were structural deficits in the roof of the East York Memorial Arena. The bearing capacity did not meet the requirements of the National Building Code. Although the report recommended the arena be closed, the Ontario Ministry of Labour granted permission for the arena to remain open subject to strict monitoring conditions while the roof structure was being replaced at a cost of $300,000.

A fund-raising committee to "Save the Arena" headed by Stan Wadlow, the former Parks and Recreation director and former alderman, succeeded in obtaining $88,000 in tax receiptable private donations made through the East York Foundation. That, together with grants from Wintario and under the Ontario government's Community Recreation Centres Act, paid for the new roof without the addition of one cent to the property tax bill. A great example of East Yorkers working together for the greater community.[34]

Senior Citizen's Clubs

"On a Tuesday in April 1950, in the East York Y.M.C.A. at Coxwell and Cosburn, the Senior Citizens Organization was founded. Their meetings, every Tuesday, became a day of sunshine and old song in East York. It may have been raining or snowing outside, but for more than three hundred seniors, it was a warm day of companionship, filled with hope and happiness. I saw that this club made a vital contribution towards giving the old folks an interest in life. 'A blizzard wouldn't stop these people from coming out to the meetings,' said my wife, Lilian, who was one of the volunteers who helped in the serving of refreshments. Other volunteers were Mrs. Percy Busten, Mrs. Jack Heaton, Mrs. Harry Simpson, Mrs. Peggy Ross, Mrs. Gladys Bustin, Lottie Spencer, and Nellie Ridout.

"The club grew to a capacity membership of 370 very quickly, and a waiting list of potential members grew longer. To help cope with the demand, a branch was opened in March 1952 at St. Andrews and

---

34. East York Council minutes, January 1978

St. Luke's Anglican Church. The Rector, Herb Snell, opened up his church facilities to the seniors every Thursday. In a short time, as with the Coxwell branch, the club was full. In some cases people would attend the Coxwell meetings on Tuesday and the St. Luke's meetings on Thursday. The interest in the Senior Citizens Clubs mushroomed, creating a constant demand for facilities throughout the Township. Clubs were opened at Cosburn United Church in 1959, Topham Park Community Centre in 1960, Cedarvale Club in 1962, All Hallow Anglican Church in 1964, Woodbine United church in 1965, and Harmony Hall in 1968.

"With all of these clubs, it was necessary to set up a Central Committee to coordinate activities. The committee was made up of members from each club. A membership fee was charged and the money was used to subsidize members who used private facilities when they were with the club and it was also used to underwrite the annual picnic.

"When I retired in 1971, membership in the Senior Citizen Clubs had gone over the eight hundred mark. The success of these clubs has shown that while the seniors have retired from the working world, they have not retired from life."[35]

The Handicapped

"In the spring of 1951, I saw a need for a recreational programme that would involve handicapped people. We set up a swim programme on Saturday mornings at Danforth Park School for those afflicted with cerebral palsy and polio. This programme was one of the most soul-satisfying experiences of my life. There were many volunteers for this programme. Pop McGrath, a man in his seventies and a former masseur, helped out every week."[36] Later, another programme for the disabled called Stroke Breakers was initiated by Harold Cooper, an East York firefighter prior to suffering a debilitating stroke himself. Harold and his wife held monthly meetings at Stan Wadlow Clubhouse for the group, which grew to substantial numbers.

---

35. Wadlow, Stan, *East York Recreation, The Early Years*, Centennial College Press, 1982, 24
36. Wadlow, Stan, *East York Recreation, The Early Years*, Centennial College Press, 1982, 26

Harold Cooper, EY Stroke Breakers
(Source: East York Fire Dept)

The Barbershoppers

"One day in the spring of 1950, while sitting in my office, a knock on the door ushered in Herb and Art Moores. The two of them had a passion for Barbershop singing and they thought an East York Chapter would be popular.

"My policy, due to the fact that I had to use many volunteers, was to challenge anyone who came in with an idea to be the first president and it always seemed to work. I was able to assist the new organization in getting facilities.

"I will never forget the first time I went down to see how the new group was making out. I arrived at approximately 9 p.m. to find groups of men and boys singing different songs in four-part harmony. The whole group singing the national anthem still rings in my ears. After the meeting broke up, I watched groups of people going off into the night still singing. Their enthusiasm rubbed off on me and I became a great supporter of the Barbershoppers. Through the years, this organization has travelled far and wide. They won many awards in local competitions and they did well in international competitions. Their achievements took them to Britain and Europe. They were goodwill ambassadors from East York, spreading the gospel of Barbershopping wherever they went.

"The success of the Barbershop Chapter led them to look for their own facility. The school where they rehearsed was not available after 10:30 p.m. and many of the members wanted to stay beyond that time. They eventually found a place at Gerrard and Jones Ave. They stayed there for many years, but despite moving out of East York, they continued to participate in many of our special events.

"I was honoured one night when they invited me to visit them in their new home. Arriving there, I found I was the audience. I was told to sit down and make myself comfortable. They sang, in beautiful harmony, many of my favourite old songs. The night will linger long in my memory.

"In 1967, the Barbershoppers decided to move back to East York. In a driving rain on Centennial Day, Mayor True Davidson turned the sod on the site of Harmony Hall. George Shields and his Committee had approached the Borough Council for a lease on the property at the corner of Gower and Cedarcrest Aves. When permission came from the borough the members built their own home. On May 11, 1968, we attended the official opening of Harmony Hall and Senior Citizens Centennial Centre. The hall was packed and the chorus entertained. I was proud to stand up and praise the tenacity of those who had worked towards this goal." [37]

The Skating Club

"When Memorial Arena opened we were looking for a programme to complement our Tap and Ballet programme. We now had ice time, so we set up the East York Skating Club. This was the first recreational skating club in Canada. Up to now, figure skating was organized by private clubs and the sport was beyond the reach of the average working man or woman. Memberships were set at $10 a year and lessons and patches were available at a reasonable rate.

"Under the capable professional direction of Miss Kay Amys, we had eighty-five children in our first season. Kay worked hard that winter and she produced some fine skaters, including Jeannie Sanders, who later became the Canadian Ladies Junior Champion. At the end of the season the first of what was to become an annual affair, Ice Revue, was presented. The show featured all of the skaters in the various roles. Guest soloists included Marlene Smith of the Toronto Skating Club, who was the current Ladies Senior Champion in Canada.

"In the spring of that year, we made an application to the Canadian Figure Skating Association for our junior membership. I appeared

---

37. Wadlow, Stan, *East York Recreation, The Early Years*, Centennial College Press, 1982, 25

before their annual meeting, armed with our constitution and the names on our executive. We wanted to join the C.F.S.A. so that our skaters would be eligible for competitions and for our test results to be recognized. Our acceptance helped boost the club membership in the next few years.

"We had a new professional in our second year, June Anderson. She has continued to work with skaters to this day. Under her direction, the membership increased to three hundred and we needed another professional to relieve Jane. That professional was Ellen Burka. One of Ellen Burka's students was her young daughter, Petra, who would eventually win a world championship.

"For the rest of our skaters the annual Ice Revue was the highlight of the year. Over the years, our productions included *Snow White*, *Peter Pan*, *Aladdin and His Wonderful Lamp*, *Sleeping Beauty*, *Pinocchio*, *Robin Hood*, *Hello Toronto*, *Fantasy of the Winds*, *World of Music on Ice*, and *Dance International*.

"For years, Mrs. Reg Jakeman was in charge of the costume design for the Ice Revue. The beauty of the whole affair was that it became a family affair as parents worked behind the scenes and sometimes skated, while the children enjoyed themselves.

"The Canadian Figure Skating Association, being a recreation organization, was interested in how we operated our club; especially the way we got the most out of one ice surface. The association president visited me on his way back from their annual meeting and he expressed admiration for our organization. As the years passed I received many telephone calls from other recreation people who were looking to set up a programme that was similar to our success story." [38]

In 1981, East York's Kay Thompson of Leroy Avenue won the gold medal at the Moscow International Figure Skating competition.[39] During the years that followed, key members of the East York Skating Club included Anne Paterson, Norma Nairn, Ed Britton, Mike Babineau, June Barrington, and instructors such as Donald Jackson, Sandy Villiers Johnson, and Betty Hicks. [40]

---

38. Wadlow, Stan, *East York Recreation, The Early Years*, Centennial College Press, 1982, 28
39. East York Council minutes, June 1981
40. Interview with Kevin Chisholm, April 28, 2017

Curling

"East York Memorial Arena opened its doors for curling in October of 1960. It was the first time in over ten years that curlers and hockey players were going to share the same ice.

"However, the year before this happened I was in Simcoe for the Christmas Jamboree and I saw an arena that had an ice surface designed for both sports. The thought struck me that if we were able to introduce a curling programme we could attract a great many adults. The Arena Board of Management liked the idea but I had many problems in front of me. Special ice markings were needed, hacks had to be screwed into the ice, rocks had to be bought and then kept frozen, special watering equipment was needed, and I didn't know where to start. Money had to come out of the 1960 budget if we were going to begin the programme in the 1961 winter season.

"An order was placed with a local agent for the rocks and I proceeded to order the necessary equipment needed to refrigerate the storage room. A plan was designed with all the ice markings and measurements to provide five sheets of ice. In September, we were ready to paint in all the lines we would need for hockey and curling. To secure the hacks to the ice we used perforated steel plates attached to the hacks. When the plate was heated, it would bury itself in the ice and the hack would be secure.

"I sought out the advice of Ted Beckman, who had many years of curling experience. He explained the rules, made sure the ice was properly marked and he showed my son Don and me how to play the game. In the few weeks, prior to our official opening the two of us became quite knowledgeable and as time passed we spread our knowledge and skill around.

"In a very short time after we opened our doors, we had enrolled 80 men and women. As others registered, we used them as spares to fill in for absentees. Fees were set at $35 for men, $30 for women, and $60 for husband and wife.

"The first sessions were set up as learning classes. After a bit of practice we were ready to start our Mixed Curling League.

"That same season we started an inter-church league for teen-agers. One group played on Tuesdays between 4:00 and 5:30 p.m. and another group played between 5:30 and 7 p.m.

"In the next year's programme, we included a Housewives League. By 1963, curling had established itself in the community, creating the need for a facility of its own. A brief, prepared under the leadership of club President Jake Manley, was presented to Council in October 1963. Speaking on behalf of the club, Jake described the building that the club was looking for; one with six sheets of ice and the facilities necessary to give the club a social atmosphere. He provided information on the club's present membership, its, operating expenses and an estimated cost of the new facility.

"Council was asked to build and operate the curling rink, but in order to have it ready for October 1964, the construction should begin no later than May of the same year.

"Council said they would look into the proposal and the wheels of bureaucracy started to turn. The property on the south-west corner of Gledhill and Virginia Aves. was re-zoned for park and recreational purposes and a proposed budget was shown to council members.

"Tenders were opened on June 1, 1964. Construction proceeded through the summer and an official opening was planned for January 30, 1965.

"The rink has served the community well throughout the years. It has engendered a community spirit among its users. It is used by young and old and given both the chance to meet on common ground. The rink has hosted the World Junior Curling Championships, the '74 British Consul Playdowns, and many local champions." [41]

East York hosted the first International Junior Curling Championships in 1973, thanks to the personal efforts of Mayor Willis Blair.

After the merger of the township and the town, the new borough had two municipally-owned curling rinks, the Leaside Curling Rink and the East York Sports Centre and two curling clubs, Leaside and East York. In order to administer the facilities and the clubs, the Borough established the East York Curling Rinks Board. Although members of council sat on this board as well, key curlers on the board included Herb Falconer, Charlie Bryan, Gord Cook, Ted Hall, Jake Manley, Fred Knight, Bob Kennedy, Jack Eilbeck, and Dr. Bob Murray.[42]

---

41. Wadlow, Stan, *East York Recreation, The Early Years*, Centennial College Press, 1982, 30
42. The *East Yorker*

East York Curling Club
(Source: toronto.ca)

Leaside Curling Club
(Source: yorkregion.com)

East York Community Centre, Pape Avenue Branch

"On Thursday, October 12, 1961, the East York Community Centre, Pape Avenue Branch, was officially opened by the Lieutenant-Governor of Ontario, Lt. Col. J. Keiller Mackay.

"The construction of the centre was undertaken after a public survey and meetings with the interested community groups. Spearheading the drive for the centre, along with myself, was Councillor Roy Brigham. The survey showed a great need within the community for a new recreational facility because the residential development on Cosburn Ave. would put a strain on the existing facilities.

"The East York Community Centre was designed by Pentland and Baker and built on land that was owned by the township. It has proven to be a valuable and efficient building.

"The north end has a large double gymnasium that can be divided into two standard-size gymnasium surfaces. There is a large stage area and a balcony at the other end for extra seating capacity. The gym floor was marked for badminton, basketball, and volleyball. The west side of the building had a games area, which could be used for many activities. Its versatility makes it a valuable space. The centre core of the two-storey building contains the administrative offices and dressing rooms. In the years to come, this area was renovated and extra office space was built on to the existing structure.

"The south end of the building had a swimming pool, equipment room, bleachers, and a staff area. We were very fortunate to obtain the services of Ernst Vierkoetter as our swimming supervisor. He was a well-known long distance swimmer who had bested many of the world's best. When he raced, he was known as the "Black Shark." Under his leadership, the swimming programme attracted many people. He developed many good swimmers over the years." [43]

Later the swimming programme continued to develop many more good swimmers under the direction of Marie Railey.[44]

East York Community Centre Site
(Source: East York Foundation)

43. Interview with Bill Alexander, January 4, 2017
44. Wadlow, Stan, *East York Recreation, The Early Years*, Centennial College Press, 1982, 29

East York Community Centre
(Source: adoborepublic.net)

Topham Park and Sunshine Valley

"At the conclusion of World War II, East York planned to provide an area for homes and a park for returning veterans. We named this community Sunshine Valley, and it lives in the minds of those who served during the war years and came back to settle in this area.

"Sunshine Valley in 1946 was a graded tract of land bounded by St. Clair Ave. E., O'Connor Dr., and Victoria Park Ave. These streets were dirt roads prior to the war, and where St. Clair Junior High School (Gordon Brown Middle School) is now located, the clay-surfaced road dipped into a valley. When it rained, many cars could not make it to the top of the hill. During the war, victory gardens were located here.

"The park created was named after Frederick George Topham, a World War II recipient of the Victoria Cross. Topham Park gradually developed and now includes a children's playground, two softball backstops, a football field, and two tennis courts.

"The tenacity and drive of the men and women of Sunshine Valley to provide the comforts and amenities of life was a pleasure to behold. They were instrumental in obtaining a Toronto Transportation Commission frame building for a clubhouse, and transporting it from Eglinton Ave. and Yonge St. to the park.

"With this facility, we were able to have a community centre for meetings. The building was divided into a large assembly hall, a kitchen, washrooms, etc. The Township assisted by installing a furnace and radiators in the building. In the fall and winter months, movies, crafts, and many other programmes were introduced. It was at this building that Rev. Lennox pioneered the Anglican Church, St. Columbia. They met here every Sunday until enough money was raised to build a church.

"On May 17, 1960, The Topham Park Sports Building was officially opened by Reeve Jack R. Allen. Members of Council, the Board of Education, and the Recreation Council were in attendance. We pride ourselves in this fine facility with its large meeting rooms to meet the needs of all interests. Topham Park has played an important part in the lives of the youth and senior citizens of the community." [45]

Topham Park became a busy sports centre with boys and girls softball, men's and women's soft ball leagues, T-ball, slow pitch, and a tennis club. John and Liz Shelton played a large part in developing the men's ball programs as well as the snack bar at the park. [46] The ball diamond has been named for John. Betty Hicks started women's ball and together with Gladys Ovenell played a large part in the Topham Park Tennis Club. [47]

Topham Park Club House
(Source: torontoneighbourhoods.net)

45. Ken Chisholm, Interview, April 38, 2017, Mary Ellen Trimble, Interview, May 23, 2017 and Betty Hicks, Interview, May 23, 2017
46. Wadlow, Stan. *East York Recreation, The Early Years*, Centennial College Press, 1982, 31
47. Interview with Elizabeth Shelton, September 16, 2016

John Shelton Baseball Diamond
(Source: google.ca)

Webster Park

"George Webster Park, located on the former site of the Halsey Chapman Brick Works, was named after the late George Webster, a member of the East York Board of Education. He served as a chairman during his many years of service on the board and was honoured by the Teacher's Federation of Ontario with the presentation of the 'Lamp of Learning.' This amiable, energetic Scotsman was an avid recreationist during those years. He was the founding chairman of the East York Recreation Council.

"The park and school named in his honour are located in the central part of the community on Chapman Ave. This area was chosen for the parkland to meet the needs of rapidly increasing new housing developments and high rise apartments to the south and east of Dawes Rd. north of the Massey Estate." [48]

Donora Park

"Donora Park, located on the south side of Donora Ave. between Dawes Rd. and Victoria Park Ave., was a former trunk of valley land

---

48. Interview with Betty Hicks, May 23, 2017

feeding into the Massey Estate. It was chosen to provide facilities for the area wedged between two busy streets which were hazardous for children to cross.

"The valley area was partially filled and graded to provide sledding, tobogganing and junior skiing during the winter months. In the summer, this area is a lush green and provides a walk way thorough the Massey Estate to the Metropolitan park area below.

"The flat land at the street level was graded, sodded, and equipped with swings, climbers, teeters, and benches. At the back of this area is a large open space for pick-up games." [49]

Bennington Heights Park Facilities

"On January 24, 1966, the council approved the Parks and Recreation Committee's recommendation to develop a large central park area for use by the entire northwest community of the township. The parks and recreation commissioner and the planning commissioner submitted the following report:

'At present the northwest community is reasonably well served with parklands, but these are generally small and dispersed. There are few neighbourhood parks of a size adequate to provide for a variety of sports and recreation; although there is a swimming pool, an arena, and a curling rink nearby in Leaside.

"'It is desirable that school grounds and parks be located adjacent to each other whenever possible. The Bennington Heights School and the small adjoined public park could provide the nucleus for a desirable park development along with the piece of Township land adjoining the turning circle on Heath St. Around these facilities are tracts of unused and semi-derelict land such as the former roadbed of old Pottery Rd.

"'Those lands are not owned by East York. Therefore, it is suggested that in order to forestall any other development of them they should be acquired from Metro and designated as public open space to be consolidated with the existing park and school grounds. Such action could create a school park complex of over thirteen acres. A public open

---

49. Wadlow, Stan, *East York Recreation, The Early Years*, Centennial College Press, 1982, 36

space of this size, with the varied topography, existing trees, and fine view over the city could be an attractive facility for the area.'

"The committee discussed the report and agreed in principle that such park facilities should be provided in conjunction with school properties. The Board of Education should be consulted on this matter.

"Since that time, Bennington Heights Park has developed into a multi-use recreation complex with a clubhouse, children's playground, tennis courts, and softball diamond. It has grown as the needs of the surrounding community have grown." [50]

Dentonia Park

"Dentonia Park, named after Denton Massey, is located north of Dentonia Park Ave. between Dawes Rd., and Victoria Park Ave. The Massey family acquired these bush lands in the late 1800s and built their home on the site where in later years Crescent School was located. This school was demolished during the development of Crescent Town. Due to a long-standing disagreement with the East York Council, the land designated by the Masseys as parkland and located on the boundaries of East York was given to the City of Toronto.

"In the ensuing years, the City of Toronto equipped the park with a parks building, softball area with bleachers and floodlights, a football field, picnic and playground areas, and tennis and lawn bowling courts. It was serviced by the City Parks Department for many years. East York had little use of the area. However, the growing population of the area and the development of Crescent Town necessitated negotiating with the City of Toronto to rent the park. It was agreed that the City of Toronto would rent this park to East York for one dollar a year for a period of twenty-five years, open for renegotiation.

"On July 9, 1964, the Board of Control, City of Toronto, had before it East York's recommendation for consideration of the acquisition or rental of Dentonia Park. This matter was deferred until the report was released from the Goldenburg Royal Commission.

---

50. Wadlow, Stan, *East York Recreation, The Early Years*, Centennial College Press, 1982, 36

"On March 22, 1966, East York's commissioner and deputy commissioner met with Mr. I.B. Forrest, commissioner of Parks and Recreation for the City of Toronto, to discuss the City of Toronto's position and recommendation.

"We were advised that the City of Toronto had purchased the property in 1922 for $130,000. The city would give favourable consideration to leasing the athletic field together with the tennis courts and bowling green for one dollar per year. They may also consider selling the property based on revaluation. The City of Toronto has a similar agreement with the Township of York for Humber View Park.

"It should be noted that the bowling green and tennis courts are operated by organized clubs. The City of Toronto assumes certain maintenance and lighting costs amounting to approximately $1,500 per year. The maintenance of the tennis courts and bowling green requires the services of three men during the operating season.

"The question of taxes on this property was raised. While this might be considered by the solicitor along with other matters, it did appear that the property may be exempt according to Section 265 of the Metropolitan Toronto Act. The committee directed this matter to be held over for further consideration and requested the commissioner to submit a detailed report of the facilities available in the park and the approximate operating costs.

"On June 6, 1966, Council approved the leasing of Dentonia Park from the City of Toronto with a request for a term of at least twenty-five years with the right of first refusal if the City should decide to sell. In October, 1969, the Health, Safety, Public Relations, and Property Committee recommended that the revised draft lease for Dentonia Park be referred to the solicitor and Parks and Recreation Commissioner for further study and revision concerning repair, obligations, water service, recognition and compensation by the City for improvements made by the Township. They were also to explore the possibility of extending the terms of the lease to ninety-nine years. This recommendation was accepted without amendment by Council on October 29, 1969.

"On April 6, 1967, the Parks and Recreation Committee recommended approval of the purchase of equipment located in Dentonia Park for the sum of $2,437. This purchase included picnic tables, park benches, slides, teeters, and other playground equipment.

"In December of 1972, eight years after its initial inception, the final lease for Dentonia Park was signed by both Councils. The residents of

Crescent Town and the surrounding area are now assured of the continued use of this fine facility."[51]

McLean/Goulding Properties

"The McLean and Goulding properties, located within the former Massey Estate and situated north of the creek on the norther slope of the Don Valley between Dawes Rd. and Victoria Park Ave., were expropriated and purchase by the East York Municipal Council in 1964.

"It was necessary that the council take the action as high rise developments were gradually devouring all these beautiful locations, and creating deficiencies in open space parks for the residents in the area. The forthcoming development of the Crescent Town high-rise complex required the acquisition of these properties to meet the needs of the increasing population. Later, this property was purchased by the Metropolitan Toronto Council to be serviced and held in perpetuity." [52]

Gamble Park

"The area around Cosburn Ave. between Broadview and Donlands has a high density of single family dwellings located along streets with no central cross streets connecting them. This situation became a problem in 1964 when Council decided to change the zoning on Cosburn Ave. to permit high rise apartment construction. To solve this dilemma, it was decided to locate a children's playground and park complex on the north side of Gamble Ave. halfway between Donlands and Pape Aves.

"To accommodate the growing population in the area, it was necessary to expropriate enough property between Cosburn and Gamble to create a throughway to the park. This throughway was named Todmorden Lane after the original town, Todmorden.

"A small church and a number of small houses located on the park site were demolished. The area was then graded, sodded, and equipped with a wading pool, swings, climbers, and teeters. This park also has a shaded, passive area with a number of benches. It has been a welcome addition to the surrounding community." [53]

---

51. Wadlow, Stan, *East York Recreation, The Early Years*, Centennial College Press, 1982, 37
52. Wadlow, Stan, *East York Recreation, The Early Years*, Centennial College Press, 1982, 37
53. Wadlow, Stan, *East York Recreation, The Early Years*, Centennial College Press, 1982, 39

Leaside

When the Town of Leaside merged with the Township of East York in 1967, it already had a well-developed recreation program. The town had also taken advantage of the 1946 Ontario Physical Fitness Act by hiring former Toronto Maple goalie Phil Stern as sports director followed shortly thereafter by the appointment of Ron Hanegan and still later, Bob Davidson as its recreation director. Twenty years later in 1967, when it entered the Borough of East York, Leaside had five parks: Trace Manes, Howard Talbot, Sandy Bruce, R.V. Burgess, and Leaside Park. It also had the Leaside Memorial Community Gardens, a curling rink, its own lawn bowling club at Talbot Park, a tennis club at Trace Manes Park, aquatic club at the Leaside Memorial Community Gardens swimming pool, a hockey association, and skating club at Leaside Memorial Community Gardens. There was the Baseball Association at Talbot Park, Atom Baseball Association at Trace Manes Park, not to mention the Leaside Garden Club, the Business and Professional Women's Club, the Leaside Debating Club, and the Leaside-East York University Women's Club.[54]

In 1975, the Leaside Lions Club initiated and contributed financially to the construction of addition tennis courts in Rolph Road and Northlea schoolyards. A year later, the Leaside Lions purchased new playground equipment for Trace Manes Park.[55]

Leaside Lawn Bowling Club
(Source: East York Foundation)

---

54. Pitfield, Jane, *Leaside*, National Heritage Books, 1999, 168–183
55. East York Council minutes, September 1976

Leaside Baseball Association

The Leaside Baseball Association (LBA) was established in 1946 by Phil Stein, together with the help of the then-mayor and reeve of Leaside. It continued to grow and thrive at Talbot Park through the efforts of a great many volunteer coaches including Ron Roncetti, Roger Neilson, Ron Dominico, Carmen Bush, Leith Hibbert, and Wes Taylor.

When the town and township merged, there were three hundred players overall in the LBA ranging from age eight to over twenty-one playing in some seventeen different age groups from House League to Seniors. That number has risen since to over 1100 players. The Leaside Leafs senior team, which was started the year of the borough merger, has won nineteen league championships and eleven Ontario titles. The team won the provincial championship in 1971 and 1977 as well as eight GTA Junior titles since 1967. In 1992, the Midgets won the bronze medal at the national championships.

Several LBA players have gone on to college or professional baseball careers, including Tim Appleford, Cec Kozlowski, Ron Dominico, Jim Stevenson, Davey Wallace, Drew Taylor, Pat Nailer, Mike Dryden, and Ben Krantz. Of course, Dr. Ron Taylor, Drew Taylor's father, pitched for two World Series winners, the St. Louis Cardinals and the New York Mets. He is the shining example of a graduate of the LBA who went on to a great career in professional baseball. While playing professional ball Ron Taylor gained an engineering degree from the University of Toronto. After an outstanding career as a pitcher in the major leagues, he obtained a medical degree and practiced sports medicine for many years with the Toronto Blue Jays.

The key to the LBA's success has been and continues to be its long-time President Howard Birnie, with the assistance of dedicated volunteers, including Rob Atkinson, Charlie Wilkens, and Colin MacDougall, as well as coaches such as Ric Fleury, Joe Irvine, Steve Grant, Bill Ferryman, Jim Grant, Mel Antflyck, Greg Brandes, Sean McCann, Greg Thomson, and Kevin Bly. [56]

---

56. Interview with Howard Birnie, September 24, 2017

Howie Birnie   Ron Taylor
(Source:Howie Birnie)   *(Source: google images)*

Leaside Atom Baseball Association

The Leaside Atom Baseball Association (LABA), which plays its games at Trace Manes Park, was established in 1952 for boys 10-11 years of age. The game of baseball has become so popular that the LABA has been overwhelmed by applicants far exceeding the number that it can accommodate. The key to the association's early success was President Norm Ahier, now succeeded as president by his son Charlie Ahier, and ably assisted over the years by Gord Scott, Pete Dudley, and Ken Anderson, among others.[57]

Leaside Hockey

Over the years, many graduates of the Leaside Hockey Association have gone on to star in the National Hockey League, including Peter Mahovlich with Montreal Canadians, Jack Caffrey with Boston Bruins, Terry Caffrey with Chicago Black Hawks, Brad Selwood with the Toronto Maple Leafs, Dave Gardiner with Montreal Canadians, Paul Gardiner with the Pittsburgh Penguins, Mike McEwan with the New York Islanders, Tom Edur with the Colorado Rockies, and Bill Stewart with the Toronto Maple Leafs. All their sweaters are hung in the Leaside Memorial Community Gardens.[58]

---

57. Interview with Pete Dudley, September 17, 2017
58. Members of Leaside Sports Hall of Fame, sweaters hung at Leaside Memorial Community Gardens

One Leaside hockey player who never did make it to the NHL was the future prime minister of Canada, Stephen Harper, who grew up on Bessborough Drive and attended Northlea School in the Borough of East York. He played hockey for a Leaside Lions team at Leaside Memorial Community Gardens.[59]

Prime Minister Stephen Harper
(Source: Leaside Life online)

Leaside Lions Hockey Team Where is Harper?
(Source: Leaside Life online)

---

59. Thornton, Chuck, Interview

Leaside Skating Club

The club was founded in 1952 by Dr. Sidney Soanes. Over the years, other key volunteers have included Kathleen Mackenzie, Vesla Graham, Shelly Grossman, Marnie Phoenix, Patrick Devine, Liz French, Bridgit Child, Tanya Schmid, and Shaolin O'Neill. Since the Borough of East York was created in 1967, the club has flourished. The skaters range in age from three to eighteen, with approximately eighty participating in the program each year. Leaside skater Tracy Waiman went on to an exceptional career as a professional.[60]

In 1981, Sean O'Sullivan of Donlea Drive won the gold medal in the Light Middleweight Division at the World Cup Boxing Championships. [61]

Jenner Jean Marie Community Centre

Sod was turned by Mayor Davidson on October 31, 1970, for this combination library, daycare, and recreation building at 44-50 Thorncliffe Park Drive on land donated by the Goldlist Construction Co.

The two-storey structure houses the library on the main floor and facilities for day-care and recreation activities on the lower floor. In the evening, the facility is freed for recreation use. It is under the jurisdiction of the Parks and Recreation Department.[62]

In 1995, after extensive renovations, the facility was named the Jenner Jean-Marie Community centre in honour of the late East York Councillor who had passed away suddenly a few months earlier while serving in office.[63]

In 1978, the East York Memorial Arena required a new roof because an engineering report required by the province revealed that the bearing capacity of the original 1951 roof did not meet National Building Code requirements. Another such report in 1978 indicated that the Leaside Memorial Community Gardens roof had the same problem. In this case as well, the Ministry of Labour allowed the gardens to remain open again

---

60 Kathleen MacKenzie
61. Redway, Alan, Recollections, 1977–1982
62. Wadlow, Stan, *East York Recreation, The Early Years*, Centennial College Press, 1982, 90
63. East York Council minutes, March 1995

with strict monitoring, but this time it came with a deadline, which if not met, would require the gardens to shut its doors completely until the new roof structure was installed for an estimated price of $320,000.[64]

Once again, the community rallied to support the "Save the Gardens" fundraising committee, led by former Alderman Edna Beange and Rick Gossling. Funds raised privately through donations to the East York Foundation, together with Wintario and Community Recreation Centres Act grants, paid for the new gardens roof without any contribution from the property tax payers. It was another example of the community spirit of the people of the Borough of East York. [65]

Leaside Memorial Community Gardens
(Source: East York Foundation)

Edna Beange
(Source: leasidelifenews.com)

Winter Carnivals

For several years in the 1970s and 1980s, so long as the weather would co-operate, the Parks and Recreation Department not only maintained outdoor natural ice rinks in many of the parks, but also held winter carnivals during a three-week window each year. These came complete with a hay wagon borrowed from Centre Island and horses from Lionel Purcell's Pony Farm at each of Dentonia Park, George Webster

---

64. East York Council minutes, January 1978
65. East York Council minutes, January 1978

School, Dieppe Park, Stan Wadlow Park, Westwood Middle School, Thorncliffe Park, Trace Manes Park, Bennington Park, and Taylor Creek Park.[66] Unfortunately, the lack of freezing temperatures was always a problem and by mid-February, the sun was too high in the sky to hold natural ice.[67]

Borough of East York Parks

Park Name	Historical Significance of Park Name
Bennington Heights Park	Park named after Bennington Heights community and street. The street was named after Evelyn Bennington, wife of Tom Weatherhead, owner of the first house on Bennington Heights Drive. He served as a solicitor for the East York Board of Education for 30-40 years.
R.V. Burgess Park	Named in honour of R.V. Burgess, who served as town clerk for the Town of Leaside.
Eastdale Parkette	Named after Eastdale Avenue.
Leaside Park	Named after the community of Leaside, which received its name after the octagonal house built by William Lea in the period 1851-1854.
Nesbitt Park	Named after Nesbitt Drive.
Trace Manes Park	Initially named Millwood Park. Renamed on 17 March 1958 to Trace Manes Park, in recognition of Mr. C. Trace Manes for his conspicuous and outstanding service to the Town of Leaside as a member of Town Council in various capacities and as mayor.
Treasure Island Park	Park was constructed in the 1960s as a result of open space having been made available in the development of the parcel of land previously owned by Robert Mac-Gregor.
Aldwych Park	Named after Aldwych Avenue.
Arthur Dyson Park	Named in honour of Arthur Dyson, who volunteered considerable time to organizing sports teams and leagues and to coaching sports teams. He also participated in the Board for East York Arena, and as president of the Kiwanis Club, was instrumental in the construction of Cedarvale Pool, which is now named the Kiwanis Pool.

---

66. Interview with Kevin Chisholm, April 28, 2017
67. Redway, Alan, Recollections, 1977–1982

Binswood Parkette	Named after Binswood Avenue.
Sandy Bruce Park	Named in honour of Sandy Bruce, the first Leaside police chief.
Cullen Bryant Park	Named in honour of E. Cullen Bryant, a prominent doctor of East Toronto General Hospital who lived in the area and gained recognition for his participation in community organizations.
Dentonia Park	Dentonia Park was established in the 1890s by Walter Massey of the Massey Ferguson Company as an experimental dairy farm. Walter named the farm after his wife, whose maiden surname was Denton.
Dieppe Park	Dedicated to the soldiers who fought in the Dieppe raid of WWII.
Donora Park	Named after Donora Drive.
Evergreen Playground	Named after the Evergreen Gardens.
East York Tennis and Lawn Bowling	Named after the tennis and lawn bowling club.
Father Caulfield Park	Named after the first pastor of the original St. Anselm Church, which was constructed in 1938.
Four Oaks Park	Named after the farm that had been owned by John Taylor, who named it "Four Oaks" because of the four prominent oaks on his property. The street was also named after the farm because the only entrance to the street when it was first opened was through the farm.
Gamble Park	Named after Gamble Avenue.
Gledhill Park	Named after Gledhill Avenue.
George Webster Park	Named in honour of George Webster, who served as chair for the East York Board of Education and made significant contributions to his community.
Hillside Park	Named after Hillside Drive.
Kiwanis Parkette	Named in honour of the Kiwanis Club.
Livingstone Park	Originally named Woodville Park. Park was renamed in honour of John A. Livingstone, who played a significant role in the Rate Payers Association and made significant contributions to his community.
Mallory Green	Named after Mallory Crescent.
Maryland Park	Named after Maryland Boulevard.
Memorial Gardens	Named in honour of the fallen soldiers of World Wars I and II and the Korean War.

Stan Wadlow Park	Named in honour of Stan Wadlow, who was the founder and first commissioner of the East York Parks and Recreation Department, and was also a council member.
Talbot Park	Named in honour of Howard Talbot, who was the mayor of the Town of Leaside from 1938-1947.
Todmorden Mills Park	Named after the various mills in the village of Todmorden, which was established in 1850.
Topham Park	Named in honour of World War II hero, Frederick Topham, who was decorated with the Victoria Cross and was a local resident."[68]

Schedule "D"

The 1954 East York Lyndhurst Senior B Team Members

Head Coach - Greg Currie	Captain - Tom Campbell
Benny Chapman	Earl Clements
Don Couch	Harold Fiskari
Norm Gray	Moe Garland
Tom Jamieson	Larry Kearns
Bob Kennedy	Gavin Lindsay
Don Preston	John Petro
Russ Robertson	George Sayliss
John Scott	Bill Shill
Vic Sluce	Reg Spragge
Dan Windley	Eric Unper [69]

Don Wadlow (R) and Recreation staff
(Source: Alan Redway)

---

68. East York Council minutes, June 1983
69. Interview with George Sayliss, May 15, 2013

– Chapter 14 –

PLACES OF WORSHIP

A cornerstone of most East Yorkers' lives has been their place of worship.

In the early days of both the Township of East York and the Town of Leaside, churches were not only places of worship but centres of community social life and recreation as well. Churches were fully attended and there were many entertaining events such as socials, garden parties, dances, and picnics for the whole family. Sports for boys were sponsored by the church. Women would have quilting bees and auction sales. But as time went on, while social events were still held by the churches, they lost much of their influence in the community, as there were other things for people to do.[1]

1832—Don Mills United Church

The first church in what was later to become the Township of East York was Don Mills United at 126 O'Connor Drive, named as such because O'Connor Drive was formerly called Don Mills Road. There are

---

1. Fagan, Lu Ann, *The Secord Area*, East York Board of Education, 1974, 74

indications that there was a church on the site as early as 1832. The first recorded reference of the church was in 1851 when land was granted by one Samuel Sinclair, yeoman, for the sum of five shillings in trust forever as a site for a Methodist Chapel. The Sinclair gravestone still stands in the church's cemetery, which dates back to 1841. The earliest church was a frame one (date unknown); however, in 1829 a preacher was sent from England and in his diary he wrote: "I have preached sixteen times, ridden fifty miles, walked seventy." Among the places where he preached, he listed Don Mills. In 1859, the frame building was replaced with a new brick church, and in 1860 a new deed was granted to the church by the three Taylor brothers—John, Thomas, and George (paper-mill owners)—whose families were closely associated with the work of the church. In 1910, the church was enlarged and in 1933, the present Sunday school building was erected, standing where, in the early days, the driving shed for the congregation's horses and buggies stood.[2]

1890—St. Cuthbert's Anglican Church

The first church in the Town of Leaside was St. Cuthbert's Anglican Church at 1399 Bayview Avenue. William Lea donated the land on which a small frame building was erected in 1890 then known as the Leaside Mission. In 1908, the name was changed to St. Cuthbert's and a new church building opened in 1914. In 1922, the present church building was constructed and the parish hall, Lamb Hall (named for the first Rector Canon P. Morland Lamb), was added in 1951.[3]

In the years that followed, many other places of worship were established in what would become the Borough of East York.

Other Anglican Churches

1906—St. Luke's, 904 Coxwell Avenue

The present St. Luke's was created in 1971 by the amalgamation of two Anglican parishes, St. Luke and the Church of the Comforter, under the direction of the Rev. Kenneth Maxted. However, its East York origins trace back to June 11, 1906, with the building of St. Andrew's Anglican Church at the north-east corner of Pape and Cosburn Avenue under the

---

2. Bustin, Percy, List of Churches, Borough of East York, Clerk's Department, 1993, the Don Mills
   United Church history, S. Walter Stewart Library, Self–Published, 22
3. Pitfield, Jane, *Leaside,* National Heritage Books, 1999, 101

direction of the Rev. Frank Vipond. That church building was started and completed on the same day. McDonald's restaurant stands on that site today. The original St. Luke's had been established in 1870 on Bay Street in downtown Toronto, but after business invaded the area, it moved to 170 Westwood Avenue in East York, a site purchased from the Davie Estate. In 1936, St. Luke amalgamated with St. Andrew's becoming known for a short period as St. Andrew's and St. Luke. The Church of the Comforter, which was originally built on clergy reserve land, opened in 1926 on the north side of Cosburn Avenue east of the collegiate. In 1954, a new building was erected at 904 Coxwell Avenue at the north-west corner of Cosburn. That became the home of St. Luke's after it amalgamated with the Comforter. The former St. Luke's Church at 170 Westwood Avenue was sold to the East Toronto Seventh Day Adventists.[4]

1912—Church of the Resurrection, 1100 Woodbine Avenue
As a mission of St. John's Norway Church, the Church of the Resurrection was originally known as North Norway Mission. The first service was held in a large tent (donated by Joseph B. Harris, a Baptist), pitched on the north-east corner of Danforth and Woodbine Avenues, later the site of the Prince of Wales Theatre, and still later, the site of a Dominion Store, now a ValuMart supermarket. The tent was replaced by a frame building erected by volunteer labour and then by a new brick church on its present site at Woodbine and Milverton, which opened in 1922. In 1927, the old frame church of Rogers Memorial Presbyterian Church was moved to the rear of the Resurrection and bricked to provide a parish hall.[5]

1947—St. Augustine of Canterbury, 1847 Bayview Avenue
St. Augustine's was established as a mission of St. Cuthbert's Anglican Church. The church site on Bayview Avenue was an apple orchard when it was purchased on D-Day, June 6, 1944. Prior to the completion of the present church building in 1957, the parishioners met in private homes, the basement corridor of Northlea Public School and the church basement itself.[6]

---

4. Bustin, Percy, List of Churches, Borough of East York, Clerk's Department, 1993; Anglican Church Archives; Crone, Norman, email August 20, 2016
5. Anglican Church Archives
6. Pitfield, Jane, *Leaside,* National Heritage Books, 1999, 110

1948—St. Columba and All Hallow's Anglican Church, 2723 St. Clair Avenue East

The present site of the church was purchased in 1946, however, the first service was held in 1948 in the community hall erected by the Sunshine Valley Community Association in Topham Park. Three congregations met there. The Roman Catholics, who owned the organ, met at 9 a.m. The Anglicans, who owned the chairs and the altar, met at 11 a.m. The Presbyterians, who owned the pulpit, met there at 7 p.m. The building on its present site was completed in 1954 following a fundraising campaign chaired by Whipper Billy Watson, the well-known professional wrestler. In 1956, after a gas explosion demolished a home in Parkview Hills, the members of the congregation raised close to $7,000 to help the family. Two years later, the church purchased the parking lot from the township, which had been holding the land for a public library site. Years later, when the church needed a new roof, it was shingled by a group of men and women that included Pat Ootes, the wife of Case Ootes, who was later to be an East York Councillor.

The original All Hallows Anglican Church started as a mission, established in 1913 and located in a portable in Secord School yard. It later moved to 363 Main Street before moving north to Main Street and Doncaster Avenue. All Hallows Church, which was one of only two High Anglican churches in Toronto and suburbs at the time, merged with the Church of St. Columba's in 1990.[7]

Armenian
Armenian Catholic Community, 46 Yardley Avenue [8]

Associated Gospel
Dawes Road Gospel Church, 383 Dawes Road [9]
Pape Avenue Gospel Hall, 871 Pape Avenue [10]

---

7. St. Columba and All Hallow's Church history, S. Walter Stewart Library, Hough D.E., Some of my Memories of East York, 6
8. Borough of East York, Clerk's Department, 1993
9. Borough of East York, Clerk's Department, 1993
10. Borough of East York, Clerk's Department, 1993

Baptist

1918—Bethany Baptist Church, 1041 Pape Avenue

Originally, the members met in a home on Gowan Avenue, but in 1921, the congregation walked to the new building located at the south-east corner of Pape and Bee Street (now Cosburn Avenue) singing "Onward Christian Soldiers." In 1922, the church changed its name from Todmorden Baptist Church to Bethany Baptist.[11]

1920—Woodbine Heights Baptist Church, 1171 Woodbine Avenue

A modest building was erected on the present church site at the north-east corner of Woodbine and Sammon Avenues in 1920, although the first meeting was held in Mr. Madell's store at Woodbine and Dunkirk Avenues. That year, the church paid $7.00 to have a team of horses haul a tank wagon of water to the church so that a baptismal service could be held. The church has survived in spite of a split in the congregation in 1921 and the treasurer running off with the building fund halfway through the project. Recently, it has housed a food bank and a pre-school drop-in centre. [12]

East York Church of God, 63 Barker Avenue [13]

Bible Chapels

1950—Leaside, 826 Eglinton Avenue East

Organized by members of the Plymouth Brethren faith, it was originally intended to be located at Eglinton and Rumsey Road but Leaside Council felt it would be too close to Leaside Presbyterian Church, so it relocated to Eglinton near Laird Drive.[14]

Christadelphians

Christadelphians, 975 Cosburn Avenue[15]

---

11. Bethany Baptist Church History, S. Walter Stewart Library
12. Woodbine Heights Baptist Church History: Rev. Barbara Bishop, 1997 and Rev. Bob Patison with email August 22, 1916
13. Borough of East York, Clerk's Department, 1993
14. Pitfield, Jane, *Leaside,* National Heritage Books, 1999, 114
15. Borough of East York, Clerk's Department, 1993

Church of the Nazarene

1938 — Church of the Nazarene, 363 Main Street

Church of the Nazarene located at 363 Main Street, formerly the site of All Hallows Anglican Church. [16]

Evangelistic

Toronto Ling-Liang, 186 Floyd Avenue[17]

Gospel

Greenwood Chapel, 949 Greenwood Avenue[18]

Faith Gospel Chapel (Brethren Assemblies), 1266 Victoria Park Avenue[19]

Jehovah's Witness

Kingdom Hall

Donlands Lands Congregation, 172 Donlands Avenue[20]

Kingdom Hall

Glencrest Congregation and Treverton Park Congregation, 64 Tiago Avenue[21]

Mennonite

Toronto Chinese Mennonite Church, 1038 Woodbine Avenue[22]

Greek Orthodox

1967 — St. Demetrios, 30 Thorncliffe Park Drive[23]

1985 — Metamorphosis, 40 Donlands Avenue

Formerly, this building was Donlands United Church. It was erected in

---

16. Bustin, Percy, List of Churches, Borough of East York, Clerk's Department, 1993

17. Borough of East York, Clerk's Department, 1993

18. Borough of East York, Clerk's Department, 1993

19. Borough of East York, Clerk's Department, 1993

20. Borough of East York, Clerk's Department, 1993

21. Borough of East York, Clerk's Department, 1993

22. Borough of East York, Clerk's Department, 1993

23. Rocca, Basillios, Secretary to the Metropolitan of the Greek Orthodox Church, Interview, June 15, 2017

1918 as Donlands Methodist Church, which after the church union in 1922, became Donlands United. During the Great Depression, the attendance was so large that Sunday night services were held in the auditorium of Danforth Technical School.[24]

1997 — St. John the Theologian, 86 Overlea Boulevard[25]

Greek Orthodox Old Calendar Church
Church of St. Raphael, 230 Glebemount Avenue[26]
St. Kosmos Aliholos, 2815 St. Clair Avenue East[27]

Macedonian Orthodox

1965 — St. Clement of Ohrid Macedonian Orthodox Cathedral, 76 Overlea Boulevard
The church building was opened in 1965. It is the spiritual matriarch to 25 Macedonian Orthodox Churches in North America.[28]

Presbyterian

1921 — Westminster Presbyterian Church, 152 Floyd Avenue
Originally established in 1921 as Todmorden Presbyterian Church (a mission church of Riverdale Presbyterian Church), its congregation met in a room at the rear of the Bank of Nova Scotia building at Pape and Gowan and then in a frame church on 154 Floyd. The new brick and stone building was opened in 1936. In 1993, the church built a seniors' housing complex called Westminster Court next door on church property.[29]

---

24. Rocca, Basillios, Secretary to the Metropolitan of the Greek Orthodox Church, Interview, June 15, 2017
25. Rocca, Basillios, Secretary to the Metropolitan of the Greek Orthodox Church, Interview, June 15, 2017
26. Rocca, Basillios, Secretary to the Metropolitan of the Greek Orthodox Church, Interview, June 15, 2017
27. Rocca, Basillios, Secretary to the Metropolitan of the Greek Orthodox Church, Interview, June 15, 2017
28. Borough of East York, Clerk's Department, 1993, Gadjovich, Sam, interview
29. Self, Leonard Rev., *History of Westminster, 1921–1991*, S. Walter Stewart Library, Self–Published

1923—St. James Presbyterian Church, Dawes Road

This was formerly located on the west side of Dawes Road north of
Secord Avenue, with a congregation made up of Presbyterians who
refused to unite with the Methodists at the time of church union in 1922.
Originally called MacPherson Presbyterian Church and located in the old
Legion building at the south-east corner of Dawes and Coleman Avenue,
it relocated in the 1930s and changed its name to St. James Presbyterian
in 1939. Some members left the church to establish Danforth Presbyterian
but later rejoined St. James at the end of the 1940s.[30]

1930—Rogers Memorial Presbyterian Church, 1038 Woodbine Avenue

It stands on the boundary of East York and Toronto. A popular saying is
that city folk enter by the back door, which is in the city, and East Yorkers
by the front door, which is in East York. The original church was built on
Cedarvale Avenue in 1910.[31]

1942—Leaside Presbyterian Church, 670 Eglinton Avenue East

Originally, the congregation held their services in the Bayview Theatre
(now Shoppers Drug Mart) and later in Bessborough Public School. The
present church site was purchased in 1944 and the present church itself
constructed in 1945.[32]

1956—Westview Presbyterian Church, 233 Westview Boulevard[33]
Faith Presbyterian Community Church, 140 Dawes Road[34]

Roman Catholic

1928—Holy Cross Roman Catholic Church, 291 Cosburn Avenue

Named by its first pastor, Father Robert Miller, the property was purchased
and both an original school and church were all built the same year,

---

30. Bustin, Percy, List of Churches, Borough of East York, Clerk's Department, 1993
31. Davidson, True, *The Golden Years of East York*, Centennial College Press, Toronto, 1976, 54
32. Bustin, Percy, List of Churches, Borough of East York, Clerk's Department, 1993
33. Pitfield, Jane, *Leaside,* National Heritage Books, 1999, 107
34. Borough of East York, Clerk's Department, 1993

1928. The present church was erected on the same site in 1948. Cardinal Aloysius Ambrozic served as its third pastor.[35]

1932—St. Anselm's Roman Catholic Church, 1 MacNaughton Road
Originally, the church was located in a leased store front at 609 Bayview Avenue (now 1609 Bayview Avenue), although the diocese had purchased the site on Millwood Road between Bessborough Drive and MacNaughton in 1926. The first church built on that land was opened in 1941. While the present church building was being constructed in 1966, mass was held in Leaside High School.[36]

1949—Canadian Martyrs Roman Catholic Church, 522 Plains Road
Located on the northwest corner of Woodbine Avenue and Plains Road (formerly a part of the Segriffs' farm and across the road from the Hollinger Bus Lines yards and terminal now the Trillium Apartment), this church was constructed in 1968. The first pastor was Father Peter Hendriks. Hendriks Court senior residence, which opened in 1991 next door to the church, was named for Father Peter.[37]

Blessed Edith Stein Roman Catholic Church, 16 Thorncliffe Park Drive[38]

Salvation Army
Salvation Army, 107 Cedarvale Avenue[39]

Seventh Day Adventists

East Toronto Seventh Day Adventists, 170 Westwood Avenue
The building was erected in 1936 for St. Luke's Anglican Church and acquired by East Toronto when St. Luke's united with the Church of the Comforter at the corner of Coxwell and Cosburn Avenues in 1971.[40]

Japanese Seventh Day Adventists, 19 Mortimer Avenue[41]

---

35. Borough of East York, Clerk's Department, 1993
36. Holy Cross Parish, East York, Ontario, 1928 – 1988, S. Walter Stewart Library
37. Pitfield, Jane, *Leaside,* National Heritage Books, 1999, 108
38. Church of the Canadian Martyrs, Toronto, 1949–1999, S. Walter Stewart Library
39. Borough of East York, Clerk's Department, 1993
40. Borough of East York, Clerk's Department, 1993
41. Borough of East York, Clerk's Department, 1993 and Anglican Church Archives

United Church of Canada

1928—Dentonia Park United Church, 107 Dawes Road

Originally, this location and building was MacPherson Presbyterian Church, which began in 1906. But when the Presbyterian and the Methodist churches merged, MacPherson Presbyterian became MacPherson United. However, some members left the United Church to continue as Presbyterians forming their own church, St. James Presbyterian. In 1928, the remaining members of MacPherson United changed the name to Dentonia Park United in honour of Walter Massey's wife, Susan Denton Massey. The church has now amalgamated with Hope United.[42]

1928—Leaside United Church, 822 Millwood Road

The church site was purchased by the United Church in 1925 and a portable building was moved from Manor Road to the site. The present church was built and opened its doors in 1941 after holding services in the auditorium of Bessborough School while the new building was under construction.[43]

1933—Cosburn United Church, 1108 Greenwood Avenue

The church site, then part of R. H. (Bob) McGregor's market-garden property, was acquired from him in 1933. A portable building was moved to the site at that time. In those days, Greenwood Avenue ended at Mortimer. Father Larry Marcille, pastor of Blessed Sacrament Parish at Yonge and Lawrence, who grew up on Greenwood Avenue, remembers Cosburn United Church sitting in the middle of a farmer's field. With the exception of McGregor's barn, Smith's house and two houses on Cosburn near Linsmore, the land was vacant from Cadorna east to Coxwell, and from Mortimer north to what is now O'Connor Drive. New houses began to appear in 1940 when St. Hubert was opened. Greenwood was extended north from Mortimer to O'Connor in 1941. Reeve John Warren laid the cornerstone for a new church building that same year. It was completed and opened the following year. The Education Centre was added in 1960.[44]

1950—Northlea United Church, 125 Brentcliffe Road

Originally, services were held in Northlea School. Although the site was purchased in 1945, the Church building was not opened until 1954.[45]

---

42. Borough of East York, Clerk's Department, 1993
43. Bustin, Percy, List of Churches, Borough of East York, Clerk's Department, 1993
44. Pitfield, Jane, *Leaside,* National Heritage Books, 1999, 103
45. United Church Archives

1952—Presteign-Woodbine United Church, 16 Presteign Avenue

The site was donated to the United Church by sub-divider and builder William Pugh Sr., in 1952. The church opened two years later with a congregation of 516 from Parkview Hills, Topham, and Woodbine Heights. When Woodbine United Church closed, it merged with Presteign United. Woodbine, originally a mission of Hope Methodist called Gledhill Mission, was established in 1918 on the site of the present D.A. Morrison Middle School. It relocated in 1921 to the northwest corner of Woodbine and Mortimer (then called McMichael Avenue) as Woodbine Heights Methodist Church, renamed after church union in 1922 as Woodbine Avenue United Church. During the Great Depression in 1934, the church ladies handed out food parcels to a line of men and women stretching west back to Woodmount Avenue. An assisted family building was erected on the former Woodbine United Church site.[46]

1961—Chapel in the Park United Church, 16 Thorncliffe Park Drive [47]

Mosques

Masjid Darus Salaam, 4 Thorncliffe Park Drive [4]

Places of Worship outside East York attended by East York Residents

1974—St. Irene Chrysovalantou Greek Orthodox, 66 Gough Avenue
Bethel Baptist Church, 645 Millwood Road
St. Brigid's Roman Catholic Church, 300 Wolverleigh Avenue
923—St. Dunstan's Roman Catholic Church, 3150 Danforth Avenue
Our Lady of Fatima Roman Catholic Church, 3170 St. Clair Avenue East
1980—Jamat Kanas Ismaili Prayer Hall
Followers of His Highness the Aga Khan, 80 Overlea Boulevard
Kimbourne Park United Church, 200 Wolverleigh Avenue
1925—Hope United, 2550 Danforth Avenue[49]

---

46. Pitfield, Jane, *Leaside,* National Heritage Books, 1999, 112
47. United Church Archives and Wilkes, Fred, Rev. History of Woodbine United Church, S. Walter Stewart Library, Self–Published
48. United Church Archives
49. Kara, Shamsh, Rose, Vanessa, Interviews, October 20, 2017

Don Mills Church
(Source: East York Foundation)

Don Mills United Church
(Source: Margaret McRae)

St. Cuthbert's Church
(Source: South Bayview Bulldog website)

St Andrews 1906
(Source: Anglican Church Archives)

Bethany Baptist
(Source: bethanychurcheastyork.com)

St. Demetrios Orthodox Church
(Source: Wikipedia Commons website)

St. Clement of Ohrid Macedonian Orthodox Cathedral
(Source: Wikipedia website)

Westview Presbyterian Church
(Source: Wikipedia website)

Holy Cross Church
(Source: Wikipedia Commons website)

Leaside United 1928
(Source: East York Foundation)

Masjid Darus Salaam Mosque
(Source: masjids.ca)

– Chapter 15 –

SHOPPING

Shopping patterns have changed at least three times in East York. First there were the corner stores, then came the commercial shopping strip, and finally the shopping malls.

During early days in the township, East Yorkers shopped at the many corner and mid-block grocery and butcher shops. Lawrence Main, who grew up at 254 Glebemount Avenue at the corner of Holbourne Avenue, recalls:

Across from our home was a grocery store operated by Frank and Daisy Farn. There was just limited refrigeration in those days and no freezers. Ice in 25 or 50 lb. were delivered and dropped into the ice box every other day. Because of this shopping was done daily and Farn's grocery was a busy spot. They also ran up weekly and monthly bills to suit your financial situation. They also sold charcoal and kerosene for lamps and gave out bones for soup or your dog, of which there were plenty everyone had one.

One of his interesting stories of the day was about Frank Farn:

He was never without a cigarette hanging out of his mouth when he was grinding meat, the ashes would fall into the grinder, in fact the story went around that once he nipped off the end of his finger, but did not flinch and went on grinding the meat."

True or not, it certainly was typical of the times.

In these early days there was a fish and chip store on almost every street corner in the township. These stores sold fish and chips only and because of the large English, Irish and Scottish population, Friday night was their best night for sales. I remember our Aunt Marion Bowman use to come up from Chicago U.S.A. to visit with our mother and father and the first place she went was to the Fish and Chip store because she said the Americans have no idea how to cook them. I used to deliver for one of these stores at lunchtime. I left school and rode my bike to the store, made the deliveries and was back in time for school. Fish and chips were wrapped in white paper and then in newspaper, which of course would not be allowed today, but in those days, everything possible was recycled or burnt in the kitchen stove to heat the water.

Lawrence remembers the horse and wagon deliveries: "All of these wagons travelled the streets summer and winter whatever the weather. A couple who lived on Holborne Ave…Albert Croft and his wife—had a sign in front of their house reading 'drivers may water horses here.' This was a popular spot for the horses and a suitable pail was in the driveway under the tap… Another horse drawn wagon was what we called the rags and bones man. These drivers were usually full bearded men who would buy anything for 5 or 10 cents and this was a good source of getting rid of unwanted articles…Since our father grew everything from flowers to vegetables in our backyard he needed fertilizer. He had a large pail at the bottom of the garden. We would scoop up horse manure from the streets and place it in the pail, Father would mix water with it and this was our fertilizer for our garden." [1]

At that time, the Secord area had home delivery as well.

In those days, people had ice-boxes to keep their food cold. These were kept cold by huge blocks of ice, which were cut from Lake Simcoe. The ice-man delivered these with his two horses and his wagon. In the hot weather, the fifty-pound blocks would be a lot smaller than when they were cut. The heat melted them very quickly. In the hot summer, the ice-man

---

1. Main, Lawrence, *Growing Up in the Old Township of East York*, Self–published, 2013, 3

came every day. There was also a small ice-hut beside the store, which is Hutone Cleaners now. People could go and get their ice from there.

There were other deliveries, too, all by horse and wagon. Bread was delivered, probably from Brandon's Bakery. Coal was delivered for furnaces and stoves from the coal yards along Danforth. A uniformed mailman delivered the mail in the area every day including Saturdays and Christmas. In those days, a stamp for local mail cost 2 cents. Eaton's had regular delivery of their goods.

Many people in the area still had cows. They sold milk directly from the barns. One man tells us that every day he would go to the top of Chisholm to get his milk. The place was like a dairy farm. He would take gallon jugs there and fill them. There were also milk deliveries in the area of City Dairy, Acme Farmer's Dairy, and Rice's Dairy. The deliveries were done by horse and wagon. They would deliver early in the morning. The driver had a lantern in the wagon to light up the inside. In the winter, they used milk sleighs, which were like wagons with their top half cut off. The milkman brought around butter, eggs, and cheese as well as milk.

Farmers used to come around to the house and sell their fruits and vegetables off a wagon. Women bought raspberries and strawberries by the crate, then preserved them or "put them down." This meant that the fruit was jarred in syrup. There were very few canned goods sold and no frozen food. The preserves were stored in the basement. Some fruit was dried and stored in the attic, then soaked in water when they wanted to use it. In the cool basement, the family was able to store applesauce, apple butter, and sausages. Bags of potatoes were kept in the coolest corner; carrots and parsnips in the sand. Spices were used to preserve the meat.[2]

Joyce Crook, who grew up on Dilworth Crescent and later on Carlaw Avenue in the 1930s, remembers the fish wagon with a weigh scale selling fresh trout, salmon, and white fish.[3]

Former East York Councillor Norm Crone recalls:

When I first remember living in EY (late forties and early fifties), there were lots of corner stores in the residential areas—I guess it was

---

2. Fagan, Lu Ann, *The Secord Area*, East York Board of Education, 1974, 48
3. Interview with Joyce Crook, November 12, 2015

based on a British model. For example, there was a little grocery one block along Virginia from where I grew up. It was on the north-east corner of Virginia and Binswood. It was pretty typical of the little corner stores in EY—some groceries, tobacco, candy—that operated here and there in residential areas (they predated the first EY zoning by-laws 1959).

At the north-east corner of Woodmount and Dunkirk, there was a little "tobacconist" store run by a very elderly British lady—Miss Tomasen. Around the corner, attached to the back of her store, there was a shoe repairman—Mr. Mobby. He was an elderly British gentleman. His shop was narrow and dark, and there were lots of big sewing machines and the place smelled strongly of the leather glue and polishes that he used. All the shoes having been repaired, or waiting for repair, were tied together and kept in numbered pigeonholes, awaiting pickup by the customers.

Shelton's had a Fish and Chip Shop at Woodmount and Mortimer. There were other fish and chip shops dotted around the community— Cosburn and Linsmore, Coxwell and Plains, and Gledhill just south of Lumsden. Everyone had their favourites—Duckworth's (on Danforth), Parkview, Gledhill, etc.[4]

Ketts Grocery
(Source: East York Foundation)

---

4. Crone, Norm, emails, August 16, November 28, 2016

This letter to the editor of the *Toronto Star* in the early 1980s expressed local residents' warm feelings about their corner stores.

Letter to the Toronto Star

Our local "corner store" has been in business for decades. It was originally established by the father but for many, many years has been operated by a son—W.C. McCalden. This is also the name of the business, located at 70 Doncaster Avenue, East York.

Mr. Will McCalden, and his wife Isabel, are retiring at the end of June and are going to be missed by all of the residents in the area. This has been a real community store in which neighbours stop to chat and pass the time with Will and Isabel as well as other neighbours, whom we often do not see except in the store. The latest news is passed around during our little visits, whether it be about the local school, business in general, or the latest births, weddings, illnesses, deaths, etc. A lot of us have had credit with McCalden's for years and years, more of a convenience than out of necessity. Most of us buy whatever Will sells since his prices are either on par or lower generally than local supermarkets—"low overhead," Will says.

McCalden's have been sounding boards, crying towels, friends, good neighbours to so many of us for so many years, that I feel some honourable mention should be made of them in your publication, so that other people who have since left the area may be aware of their good fortune in retiring while still in good health and after so many excellent years of service to the community.[5]

Lawrence Main's father was not the only one growing his own vegetables. "In those days, everyone had a vegetable garden. People would pick up the manure that the horses left on the roads or would get it from the dairy, and use it for fertilizer. Most people also had rabbits or chickens in their backyards. One boy had to pick enough dandelions every day after school for his father's rabbits to eat. His father had one hundred rabbits so you can imagine how much he needed to get!" [6]

---

5. The *East Yorker*
6. Main, Lawrence, *Growing Up in the Old Township of East York*, Self–published, 2013, 4

"People on relief were allotted spaces about fifty feet square to grow vegetables, known as pogy plots and here they grew vegetables from seeds provided by the Township. These grew most family's needs over the winter. They were located between Cosburn and Plain's Road west of Woodbine." [7]

Besides the corner store, there were other stores well within walking distance, for some at least, on the Danforth, but it was another thing coming home with the groceries.

No fresh vegetables were available in wintertime and Mother used to shop for canned goods at Loblaws at Danforth and Woodbine Aves. Next door was Woolworths and Kresge's 5-10 and fifteen cent stores, which Mother and the children visited while Father would meet men friends at the Commadore hotel for a beer. On the Danforth on Saturday nights we would meet a Toronto police officer on patrol wearing his high pith helmet and he and Father would pass the time of day and these meetings gave me great respect for a policeman in those days. These Saturday nights were like social nights—the store stayed open a little later and you would meet your neighbours and stop to chat right on Danforth Ave. East Yorkers were a friendly bunch and knew each other very well. When it was time to go home, we would meet in a converted garage at the rear of a house on Woodbine behind the bank, operated by Hollinger Bus Lines as a waiting room. It had no heating but it was better than standing outside and it had long benches to sit on. The bus rumbled up Woodbine Ave to Holborne and we would lug our purchases the two blocks over to Glebemount.[8]

The fact that East Yorkers were shopping on the Danforth indicated that another shopping trend was taking place—the commercial shopping strip. Many of these developed on East York's main streets.

Broadview Avenue

Although Baters' store and post office at the corner of Broadview and what is now Bater Avenue sold anything and everything you might need or want, according to George England, who grew up on Woodville Avenue during the 1930s. Broadview Avenue has never been a major East

---

7. Fagan, Lu Ann, *The Secord Area*, East York Board of Education, 1974, 91
8. Main, Lawrence, *Growing up in the Old township of East York*, Self–published, 2013, 7

York shopping street. Jay Burford's grandfather had a store at the corner of Torrens Avenue. Hughie Reid's blacksmith shop was on Westwood Avenue and just off Broadview and the horse-drawn delivery wagons of Hastings Dairy occupied the site of the present Chester School. But there was no major grocery store on Broadview until Food City later. Sobeys located where the old Todmorden Hotel used to welcome its patrons before it was demolished. [9]

Pape Avenue

Pape Avenue was an entirely different story. It became a major strip shopping district.

Bob Ogden in his history of William Burgess School listed many of its stores and shops in the past decades.[10] Jack Bell, who had a barber shop on Pape for 52 years also has vivid memories of those stores and shops. Jack's wife told me he has a photographic memory.[11]

Picture yourself, in days gone by, walking from south to north on Pape.

East Side of Pape Avenue

South of Floyd Avenue:

The Cameo Theatre, where once upon a time, the owner opened the doors during the week for all of the William Burgess students to see the movie *Heidi* at the cost of two cents per child. Jack Bell recalls that this movie theatre had a sloped floor so the audience could see the screen no matter where they sat. According to local legend, mice would be running around your feet while you watched the movie. Later Loblaws acquired the site, leveled the floor, and got rid of the mice. TD Canada Trust is now located there.

North of Floyd and south of Gowan Avenue:

1007 East York Cycle and Sports. Bell remembers this as "Honest John Bikes."

1015 Laxton's Bakery was originally the Blue Bird Bakery, then the

---

9. Interview with George England, December 29, 2015 and Jay and Pat Burford, January 26, 2016

10. Ogden, Bob, *William Burgess School Then & Now 1914–1994*, East York Board of Education. 1994, Self–Published, 55–59

11. Interview with Jack Bell, August 16, 2016

Danish Bakery. According to Jack Bell this has been the site of a bakery for over 50 years.

North of Gowan, south of Cosburn:

1023 East York Pharmacy
1025 Sonley's Soda Fountain
1027 Reeve John Warren's Barber Shop and Star newspaper Outlet. Bill Lewis had his hair cut here by the Reeve. It was also the distribution centre for Toronto's daily newspapers at the time. Bill who had a large paper delivery route use to collect his suppy of the *Star* and the *Telegram* from Jack Warren's basement each day after his last class at William Burgess School. The customers paid 12 cents each week. The delivery boy received 4 cents per customer per week. However he received an extra 3 cents per customer for delivering the *Star Weekly* on Saturday.[12] Jack Bell rented the barber shop from John Warren in 1958. It worked well since the sign over the shop already read, "Jack's Barber Shop." It's now a restaurant.

On the south-east corner of Cosburn is Bethany Baptist Church built in 1928 with an addition in 1960, Jack Bell and his wife are still pillars of this church.

North of Cosburn, south of Gamble:
On the north-east corner of Cosburn was originally the site of St. Andrew's Anglican Church (now McDonald's). Jack Bell remembers it as the location of a Ford dealership and later a White Rose gas station before McDonald's.
Bramwell's Butcher Shop

North of Gamble, south of Torrens:
The two most familiar businesses in this block were located in houses that still stand today. At the corner of Pape and Torrens Avenues was the home of the dentist Dr. Reveler, and immediately south of him was Dr. Hargreaves, a family physician.

---

12. Interview with Bill Lewis, November 9, 2015

North of Torrens, south of O'Connor Drive:
Royal Canadian Legion (once called Vets' or Veterans' Hall) Todmorden Branch 10 (Pape and Woodville) .
West Side of Pape Avenue

North of Mortimer avenue and south of Gowan Avenue:
Dad's Cookies where when I was a little boy my parents would take me to buy a large bag of broken cookies for a few cents

North of Gowan, south of Cosburn Avenue:
On the north-west corner of Gowan The Bank of Nova Scotia is still there. Jack Bell recalls there was a Loblaws store immediately north of the bank that became an IGA store (Independent Grocers Association) when Loblaws moved across the street to the Cameo Theatre. It is now a Shoppers Drug Mart.
Azzarello's Fruit and Vegetables

A&P (Atlantic and Pacific grocery store), according to Jack Bell this was the very first A&P store ever.
Ledsham's Barber Shop

Curtis markets, later Hallam's Hardware Jack Bell recalls.

North of Cosburn, south of Gamble Avenue:
North-west corner of Cosburn was Crow's Cleaners, which Jack Bell says was the original Honest Ed's store and later a Bad Boy Appliance store before Crow's Cleaners located there.
Al Morgan's 12 Lane Bowling. Al Morgan later became an East York Hydro Commissioner
Bunt's Fish and Chips. If you stand in the small plaza where the Petro-Canada station is now located, you can see the name of this store on the north wall. According to Jack Bell, Bunt's sold chips for 5 cents and fish for 7 cents.

North of Gamble, south of Torrens Avenue:
Now a Dollar Store. Jack Bell says it was the site of the TD Bank before it moved to its present location where the Cameo Theatre use to be.

North of the Dollar store was a Dominion Store, now Food Basics

Immediately to the north, was a tobacco wholesale business, later a Metropolitan Toronto Social Service Centre before becoming a youth shelter called, "Touchstone."

O'Connor Drive east of Pape Avenue

158   Ted's Later known as Michael K's. Bernice Bunt would come all the way from her home on Victoria Park just north of the Danforth to Ted's in order to feast on his strawberry shortcake. [13]

Although this is not a complete listing of all businesses throughout the years, it is representative of the kind of services available to the people who lived in this part of East York, in years gone by.

As Don Hough recalled:

On Pape Avenue we had several stores—Jack Ledsham's (who gave me my first dutch-cut haircut) barbershop, Sonley's Drug Store, Bridson's grocery, Reg. Spencer's hardware, Jack Warren's (later on, reeve) barbershop, Azarello's fruit store, Croydon cleaners and Bramwell's butcher shop. One day, a friend of my brother, Doug, by the name of Shepherd, phoned Mr. Bramwell and asked him if he had any dripping. Mr. Bramwell replied that he had, and Shep told him to plug it. Of course, they forgot that the telephone operator, who placed the call, knew where it originated and told Mr. Bramwell that it was Gerrard 1334. My mother got an earful when she came home.[14]

Cameo Theatre Pape Avenue Cinema c 1934
(Source: Historic Toronto Website)

---

13. Strawberry shortcake with Bernice Bunt, 1977
14. Hough, D. S., *Some of My Memories of East York*, The East York Historical Society, 1992, 9

Donlands Avenue

Although Donlands had a more limited number of stores than did Pape, it was still popular for the nearby neighbours such as John Michailidis, who was raised on Cadorna Avenue. John has written of some of his memories of Donlands as he was growing up.

With two quarters tightly clasped in the fist of one hand and the torn cover flap of my dad's empty Rothmans cigarette pack clutched in the other, I would run like the wind the two short blocks down Plains Road before turning the corner onto the Donlands Avenue commercial area on my way to Ron's Smoke Shop.

A modest-size commercial strip of about twenty-five stores between Plains Road and O'Connor Drive, the Donlands commercial area in the late 1960s and early '70s, the time of my youth, served the shopping needs of East Yorkers.

Turning the corner at Plains Road, the first store you encountered was Donlands Credit Jewellers with its large display windows showing the newest styles of watches, rings, and vases. No matter how rushed you were, the window display grabbed your attention.

Many Mother's Day presents were purchased at Donlands Credit Jewellers, and the proprietor would gift wrap for free.

At the O'Connor Drive end was Tom's Shell Gas Station. Here Tom or another mechanic would inflate our footballs.

Toward the middle of the strip was the 840-seat Donlands Theatre with its grand marquee announcing the feature movie playing and the glass doors leading into a grand domed entrance with murals of Chinese mythical scenes on the walls and a ceramic floor with an inlaid Chinese symbol, perhaps representing prosperity.

The theatre opened in late 1948. The large letters B&F on the marquee stood for the Toronto-based theatre chain Bloom and Fine, which operated theatres from the 1920s to the 1970s.

John Candy, who lived a short walk from the theatre, no doubt got his love for movies at the Donlands Theatre. And no doubt, many first kisses were enjoyed in the back rows of the Donlands Theatre.

Chainway Variety was a favourite of my mother's. Chainway was a five and dime store similar to Woolworths or Kresge's, but on a smaller scale. Not much selection, but enough to satisfy most no-nonsense East Yorkers. It was a dimly lit store with most of its merchandise scattered haphazardly in large wooden boxes.

Saturday mornings, mother and I would walk the two blocks to the IGA Grocery store for our weekly grocery shopping. If our groceries amounted to three or more large paper bags, they were delivered in the IGA delivery van.

A favourite of my father was Bob's Men Wear. Donlands Shoe Repair and Skate Exchange was a favourite of mine. Every fall, I would take my old skates that I purchased there the season before to exchange for a larger size pair of used skates. I would be set to skate another winter at the Dieppe Park outdoor natural ice hockey pad.

Of all the shops on Donlands, Ron's Smoke Shop was the centre of our kids' world.

Ron Herman opened Ron's Smoke Shop in 1955. It served the community until the early 2000s. It was to Ron's I would race with my dad's torn flap of his Rothmans cigarette pack. I would hand Ron the torn flap and 50 cents. Dad couldn't be sure a ten-year old boy would remember the brand of cigarettes to ask for, thus the torn flap. Ron would hand me a fresh pack of Rothmans and sometimes he would point to the large jar of Double Bubble gum. I would grab a gum and race home.

Ron remembers John Candy buying sweets at his store before he became famous. Ron had his own movie fame. Part of the 1986 Ron Lowe movie *Youngblood* was filmed at the Donlands commercial area. Ron has a small part in the movie: he sells Lowe a book from Ron's Smoke Shop. [15]

Norm Crone (who served for many years on East York Council and grew up on Fairside Avenue just east of Coxwell in the 1950s and '60s), remembers the Loblaws store, now the Beer Store, on the south west corner of Donlands and O'Connor as well as the Dominion Store on the north east corner.[16]

Carl Wilcox, a resident of McClintock Towers seniors home just north of the Danforth on Pape, was born in the Wallace House on the north-west corner of Donlands and O'Connor. The Wallace House has had many different names but is still in business. The hotel was next door to Riverdale Memorial, where they made tombstones. Today, it's an apartment building.[17]

---

15. Michailidis, John, East York Mirror, October 16, 2015
16. Crone, Norm, emails, August 16-November 28, 2016
17. *Our Danforth: one hundred years of memories*, Lorne Miller & Associates, c. 2008, 75

John Michailidis
(Source: John Michailidis)

John Candy
(Source: East York Foundation)

Donlands theatre front Nov 1948
(Source: Inside Toronto)

Cosburn Avenue

Cathy Andrews remembers the commercial area on the north side of Cosburn Avenue between Linsmore Avenue and Derwyn Road in 1954 when she was growing up on Monarch Park Avenue. At that time the businesses located from 466- 488 Cosburn were:

466—Ladies and children's wear – Marjory Stevenson

468—Parkway Bar

470—Cowan's Bakery

472—Roy's Tobacco Shop—PO substation near Theo O'Connell barber

474—Parkview Fish & Chip

476—Golden Crest Donuts

478—Cleaners

480—Knox Radio & Electric

482—Jack Nelson Hardware

484—Allan's Groceries—Norm Crone remembers an A&P store here and later a Red & White store

488—Edward Allen Druggist[18] now Paul's Spaghetti House at the corner at Derwyn

Paul's Spaghetti
(Source: Google images)

Coxwell Avenue

Norm Crone has a clear and detailed memory of the Coxwell Avenue shopping strip when he was growing up in the 1950s and the 1960s:

On the south-east corner of Coxwell/Cosburn there was a building (still existing) that housed four small businesses. The corner location was anchored by Carry's Drug Store (W.E. Carry Rexall Drugs said the sign). After Mr. Carry died, the pharmacy was taken over by Mr. Ketcheson and his wife. They kept the "Carry" name for the store, and continued to run it for many years.

Attached to Carry's Drug Store, to the south, there was a small grocery store. For many years, the grocery was run by Al Sheffield and his wife, Wanda. For a time, it was called a Cloverfarm Store and for a time it was simply called Al Sheffield's Groceteria.

Around the corner, facing onto Cosburn, there were two small business locations. In the 1950s, a TV repairman worked out of this

---

18. Interview with Cathy Andrews, September 6, 2016

location for many years. It was the era of TVs with vacuum tubes—so house calls from the TV repairman were not infrequent. Later, this store became the premises of Tony Banwell Plumbing.

In the small space adjacent to the TV repairman, a small variety store operated in the fifties. I used to spend my weekly "allowance" there. Pop was sold in glass bottles from a chilled-water filled cooler at the end of the ice cream counter. Cigarettes (I bought them most days, for my father) cost 41 cents for a large pack of 25. There were no restrictions on children buying cigarettes in those days.

After the variety store closed, the location became a barbershop run by a man named Fern Jewell. I got my hair cut there for years, until longer hairstyles came into vogue. Mr. Jewell believed that a proper cut involved very short clipped sides.

The store at the N.E. corner of Coxwell/Plains was a pharmacy. Next door to it, going north, there was a small restaurant, The Plains Grille. There may have been a beauty shop in there. Later on, a donut shop and an Italian sandwich shop operated in this location. Loblaw's parking lot was next to this small block of businesses.

There was always a gas station at the corner where ESSO is now. In those days, it cost about $2.65 to fill the tank at the Esso station. Next to the Esso station, on the east side of Coxwell, going south there was a small garbage dump when I was a kid. Certainly, there was some vacant land there for a time. My friends and I played there occasionally. There were construction sites here and there all around the neighbourhood that we explored when construction was not in progress.

Just around the corner on the south side of O'Connor just east of Coxwell, were the offices of Treadway and Hall Real Estate.

On the west side of Coxwell

The Toronto-Dominion Bank was the financial hub of Coxwell commercial strip on Friday afternoons (the Royal Bank wasn't there in those days). In the fifties, banks typically closed for the day at about 3:00 p.m. On Friday's however, the bank re-opened from 4:00 until 6:00 p.m. Mr. Lou Shuttleworth was the manager of that branch. He opened my first bank account at that branch when I was very young, and I still have it!

Fridays were also big shopping days at Loblaws. I distinctly remember my mother, my aunt, and several of the neighbours collecting multi-coloured plastic Melmac dishes that came as free "bonuses" in a certain brand of laundry detergent. The ladies all became quite expert at squeezing the boxes to determine what kind of dish (plate, cereal bowl, etc.) was in that box.

Loblaws also became a hub of activity on Friday afternoons/ evenings, as people completed their weekly food shopping. In later years, after Loblaws left the area and the LCBO moved in, Fridays remained a busy time "up Coxwell." The current signage "Old East York Village" was a later invention/marketing idea from the eighties as part of a community improvement effort for EY commercial strips. It was never called by that name in the community that I remember.

Still on the west side of Coxwell, was another East York fixture – The Drive Restaurant. It was a community favourite for years, especially by the kids from the high school who patronized it extensively. In those days, its premises included only the north half of the current restaurant. It had a typical counter with stools for seating, just inside the door. Booths were located further back, and the kitchen was right at the back.

Eventually, The Drive seemed to take over the back portion of Barry's premises (for a pool table at first, I believe). Eventually The Drive took over the whole of Barry's premises, doubling its frontage on Coxwell to what is now. The name of the restaurant has changed several times over the years, but to a vintage East Yorker, it will always be known as The Drive.

Going farther south, there was a fruit and vegetable store called Restivo's. It was a family business. I particularly remember Mr. and Mrs. Restivo and their sons operating the store for years.

Right next door to the corner store at Plains, going north, there was a shoe store in the early fifties. I do remember being very fascinated by the x-ray machine that they had. You could stand and x-ray your feet right through the shoes, to see if they fit. My feet haven't fallen off yet, so I guess I suffered no major lasting effects from the possibly excessive x-raying that I received then. I don't remember the shoes fitting any better than they did when the salesman simply pressed his thumb on the toe of my shoes to judge where my toes were inside the shoes.

Later on, the store beside it to the north became a restaurant. They sold fish and chips, and I remember that the fellow who cooked the fish and chips usually wore a bright purple sweater (even though it was pretty warm in the shop). In those days, most men's clothes were rather more sombre than this, so the purple colour made an impression on me.

Over the years, of course, many businesses came and went from the strip—but "Up Coxwell" was always centre of commercial activity in the old central part of East York.[19]

East York Village
(Source: blogTO website)

Norm Crone
(Source: East York Foundation)

---

19. Crone, Norm, emails, August 16-November 28, 2016

Woodbine Avenue

Jack Freer has been a barber on the south east corner of Woodbine and Cosburn Avenues since 1951 when he acquired the shop from Bill Watterson, who had barbered at the same site for eighteen years before that. Jack has vivid memories of the businesses on Woodbine during his many years barbering on that corner.

East side of Woodbine from the Danforth to Milverton

On the north east corner of Woodbine and Danforth was the Prince of Wales Theatre, later a Dominion Store and later still a ValuMart.

1017—Silverwoods Dairy stables for their horses – now an apartment

East side of Woodbine from Sammon to Lumsden

1175—Woodbine Heights Baptist

East side of Woodbine from Lumsden to Barker

1233—Greenwood Hardware (Art Greenwood later ran unsuccessfully for Council)

1237—Greenaway's Fish and Chips

East side of Woodbine from Barker to Holborne

1285—Joy Gas Station—one of several such constructed in the shape of a castle

East side of Woodbine from Holborne to Virginia

1313—East York Fire Hall

1329—George's Grill—George and Olga Trayanoff great community volunteers with the "Happy Gang"

East side of Woodbine from Virginia to Cosburn

1347—Jack Freer barber

East side of Woodbine from Cosburn to O'Connor

1485—Hollinger Bus Lines and garage—later purchased from the TTC by East York—now the Trillium Apartments

West side of Woodbine from Wolverleigh to Queensdale
1038—Rogers Memorial Presbyterian Church
Church of Resurrection

West side of Woodbine from Frater to Mortimer
1198—Kanes Dry Goods
1202—Community Theatre—with a popcorn machine outside

West side of Woodbine from Mortimer to Dunkirk
Woodbine United Church (later assisted family apartments)
1244—Rock and Rye Carbonated Beverages—owned by Whipper
    Billy Watson, now a Beer Store

West side of woodbine from Barker to Plains
1304—Ponzo Fruit
Yearly and Reed Construction

West side of Woodbine from Plains to O'Connor
Canadian Martyrs Church, School and Seniors' Home
1500—Dominion Store, now a Shopper's Drug Mart [20]

Badges Hardware 1930s   Community Theatre on Woodbine Avenue 1937
(Source: East York Foundation)   *(Source: Historic Toronto Website)*

20. Interview with Jack Freer, August 18, 2016

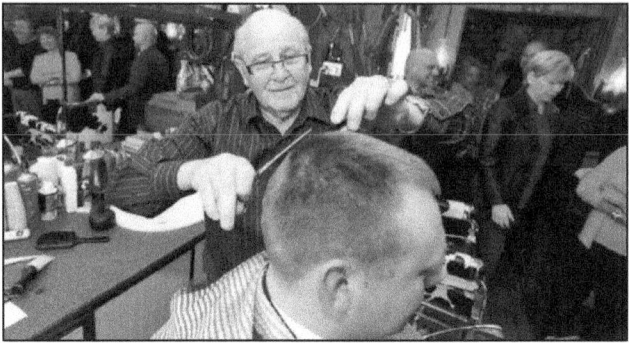

Jack Freer Barbershop
(Source: Inside Toronto)

Joy Gas Station Woodbine Ave
(Source: East York Foundation)

St. Clair / O'Connor

John and Joan Ridout moved to 27 Denvale Road in Parkview Hills when they were married in 1952, about the time that both St. Clair Avenue East and O'Connor Drive became thriving shopping areas. [21]

West side of O'Connor between Sandra and St. Clair
788—Canadian Bank of Commerce

---

21. Interview with Joan and Lyn Ridout, August 17, 2016

West side of O'Connor north of St. Clair

800—Tamblyn Drugs
802—Bank of Nova Scotia
804—Woolworth's
808—Ross Phillips Stores
812—Loblaws

West side of O'Connor north of Curity to Bermondsey

980—Bank of Toronto
Camblin & Stewart Barristers
Merkur Brothers Fruit wholesale
988—S.A. Armstrong Heating
1200—Peek Freans

West side of O'Connor north of Bermondsey

1550—Dominion Regalia
1590—Orange Crush

South east corner of O'Connor

Paul Willison Motors

East side of O'Connor north of St. Clair

797—Mother Goose Drive-In Burgers
801—Reg Brown Service Station—later Mother Goose Drive-In
      Burgers, now the TD Bank
803—Royal Bank
805—Ireton's Pharmacy

Dr. Paul McCutcheon established the East York Animal Clinic and Holistic Centre at St. Clair and O'Connor after he graduated in 1962. Originally, he was located at 2642 St. Clair Avenue East but later moved to the former Ireton Pharmacy on the east side of O'Connor where Dr. Jim Bell, who later became East York's Medical Officer of Health, had his office on the second floor.

807—Dr. J. Stewart Bell
813—Gothard's Shoe Store
833—Taylors Flowers

855—Northways
1401—O'Connor Bowl

St. Clair west of O'Connor
2642—Kerns Jewelry
2648—Hunts Bakery [22]

Jack Bell, the barber on Pape grew up on Main Street and later on St. Clair where his father had a Barber shop at 2855 St. Clair recalls the shopping strip in the 1950s.

South side of St. Clair from O'Connor to Rexleigh
Paul Willison Motors
The Church of St. Columba

South side of St. Clair from Glen Eden to Plaxton
2853—Morningside Park Gospel Church
2855—Bell's Barbershop (Jack's father owned this shop)
2863—Dolbear Hardware
2873—St. Clair Fish & Chips
2879—Brown's Pharmacy
2879A—Dr. Ruth Sky
         Dr. Henry Skykoff[23]

Dawes Road
There is a short shopping strip on Dawes Road extending north to where Dawes joins Victoria Park Avenue, then north on Victoria Park to the Borough's northern limit at North York.

East side of Dawes between Brenton and Gower
391—Holman and Hickey gunsmiths—Today a gunsmith business would be frowned upon but in the 1950s it was strategically located close to the Revolver Club firing range still on the south side of Gower, west of Dawes Road.
397—Uplands Dairies Shops

---

22. Interview with Dr. Paul McCutcheon, August 24, 2016
23. Interview with Jack Bell, August 16, 2016

West side of Dawes north of Gower

468—Clarke's Grocery—Mrs. Clarke told me that when her husband returned from WWII, they settled in East York and opened a grocery store on Victoria Park north of St. Clair but when the rent got too high, they moved to Dawes Road. The tiny store really was a variety store as well with a steady stream of customers to buy a newspaper.

490—Malvern Construction Company Limited. This was the office for R.H. Bob McGregor Construction Company, which built the Woodbine Bridge and a number of apartment buildings.

West side of Victoria Park north of St. Clair

1198—Loblaws

1210—Beauty Salon & Barber

1448—Maple Leaf Mushroom Farm [24]

When the Town of Leaside was merged with the Township of East York to form the Borough of East York in 1967, Leaside had a number of long-established shopping strips.

O'Connor Bowl
(Source: blogto.com)

———

24. Mights Directory 1967

Bayview Avenue

East side of Bayview from Millwood Road to Fleming Crescent
1515—7—Bayview Pharmacy & camera centre and post office
1519—Hunts Bakery
1529—CIBC
1531—Kresges
1541—Loblaws
1573—Dominic's Men's Wear
1575—Gainsborough
1587—Badali's Fruit Market
1591—TD Bank
1597—Bell Credit Jewellers
1599—Aikenhead's Hardware
1613—Sam Hing Fruit Market
1631—Machin & Son Shoe Repair
1635—Hines Meat Market
1639—Frey's Pharmacy
1639B—Dr. Rupert Warren

North of Fleming Crescent to Parkhurst Blvd.
1045—Ann Parker Wool Shop
1689—Jeffery Meat Market
1695—Ayriss Florist
1703—Bassett's Cleaners
1725—Murray's High Grade Footwear
      William Aiken Insurance Agency
      KE Bryant Insurance
1733—Moore's Pharmacy
1737—Norwegian Ski Shop

Badali Brothers
(Source: blogTO website)

Bayview Ave.
(Source: Leaside Fire Dept)

Bayview Theatre
(Source: elocalpost.com)

Millwood Road

North side of Millwood from Rumsey to Airdrie Road
China Food
Hudson's Groceteria
Frank Surovec Leaside Barber / Irene Ann Beauty Parlour

Eglinton Avenue East

North side Eglinton Avenue from Bayview to Bessborough
The Sunnybrook Plaza
660—Tamblyn Drugs
Laura Secord
CIBC
Embassy Cleaners
F.H. Woodworth Ltd. Variety
Hunts Bakery
Sunnybrook Smoke
Anthony Shoes
Power Food Market
Reitman's Ladies Wear
Woodhams Clothes
Scott Hardware
Michaels Ladies Wear
Genova Barber Shop
Ko's Linen—gifts
Sunnybrook Restaurant

North side of Eglinton from Sutherland Drive to Laird Drive

784—Leaside Pharmacy
786—Dr. Lou Anthony
788—Dr. Elmer Hooks
     Dr. Douglas Johnson
802—Adair Shop
812—LCBO
814—Eglinton Furs
824—Leaside Bible Chapel
830—Park Lea Florists

832—Hi—Cue Billiards
838—Frank Arrigo Optometrist
850—Ernest Ferguson Real Estate
876—TD Bank
878—BNS

South west corner of Eglinton and Laird
815—Loblaws [25]

Although the borough's strip shopping areas were still growing and thriving in the 1950s and 1960s, another shopping trend was taking place. The shopping plazas and the shopping malls were moving in. Many, such as Eglinton Square (just across the border in Scarborough), Shoppers World Danforth, and the East York Market Place in Thorncliffe, were indoors, providing protection for the shoppers from cold or wet weather as well as abundant free parking nearby. This drew East York shoppers away from their neighbourhood strip retail stores. The decline in local shopping together with constantly increasing rents has had a deadly effect on the neighbourhood businesses.

Shopping Malls in East York
Sunnybrook Plaza came first. Developed by Principal Investments, it was the initial shopping Plaza in Ontario. Principal Investments was owned by Avie Bennett and his brothers. In 1962, Principal Investments also built the Shoppers World Danforth Plaza at the south west corner of Victoria Park Avenue and the Danforth on the only part of East York south of the Danforth, formerly the site of the Ford Motor Company plant, later the Nash Motor Company, and still later, American Motors. Principal Investments was owned by the Bennett family one of whom Avie, an East York resident, (who later became the owner of McClelland and Stewart book publishers), which was located in the O'Connor industrial area. [26]

In 1967, the Shoppers World Danforth Plaza was home to a large number of retail businesses:

T. Eaton Co.

Firestone Tire and Rubber

---

25. Mights Directory 1967
26. *Globe and Mail*, June 10, 2017, page S12

Canada Trust
Walkers Shoes
Gainsborough Kitchens
Bata Shoes
Mahar Shoes
Reitmans
Tip Top Taylor
Zellers Furniture
CIBC
Eddie Black's Photo Shop
Yolles Furniture
Penningtons Ladies
Shoppers Drug Mart
Singer Company
Sherwin-Williams Paints
Dominion Store

Thorncliffe Park Market Place—Later East York Town Centre

Bank of Montreal
Birrell's Men's Wear
Brewer's Retail
LCBO
TD Bank
Sayvette Dept. Store
Thorncliffe Movie Theatre
Reitman's
SS Kresges—variety
Woman's Bakery
Laura Secord
Bowring Brothers
York Trust
Bowlerama
Thorncliffe Golf Centre—miniature indoor golf
Steinbergs Limited—later Dominion Stores—later Food Basics [27]

---

27. Mights Directory 1967

Sunnybrook Plaza
(Source: The South Bayview Bulldog Website)

Shoppers World Danforth
(Source: Shoppers World Danforth Corp.)

East York Town Centre
(Source: juliekinnear.com)

– Chapter 16 –

TRANSPORTATION

"Transportation in East York at the time of incorporation was almost nil. There were two buses operating; one by a Mr. Pedlar on Broadview Avenue and one by John Hollinger on Woodbine. These were not the first buses, however, quite a few years earlier, a Mr. Featherly had been operating a horse-drawn bus up and down Don Mills Road (Broadview) when it was still unpaved and lined on both sides with very deep ditches, serving as sewers. It was 1920 when John Hollinger started to operate a bus up and down Woodbine as far as Plains Road, where it came to a dead end. Unless one had heard of his experiences first hand, as the writer did, one would never believe the hardship he endured as he ploughed his bus through the snow drifts in the wintertime and the quagmire of mud every spring. When his passengers were scarce, John used his bus to deliver butter and eggs to the neighbourhood housewives. He never took time off for meals; these were carried to him by his young daughter May and son Barclay, through the fields from his home, now the site of the Trillium Apartments. A less energetic man would have doubtless given up the job, but not John—he was of a tougher breed. As more and more roads were paved, and more homes were built, he expanded and later established the Hollinger Bus Lines, which gave the township excellent service. By 1943 his buses were carrying over three million passengers a year.

In 1921, the City appointed the Toronto Transit Commission, which took over the Toronto Street Railway and also the Civic carline on Danforth but the Hollinger buses carried on until 1953 when Metro was formed and the T.T.C. was empowered to take over all transit in the Metropolitan area including the Hollinger Bus Lines. John, who had started on a shoe string, sold out for quite a few shoe strings." [1]

Hollinger Bus Lines Limited

History of Operations

June 1921	Woodbine route started, operating on Woodbine Avenue, from Danforth Avenue to Plains Road.
Mar. 1, 1927	Services on Dawes Road from Danforth Avenue to Peard Road inaugurated by Mr. Hamilton.
August 1928	Service in rush hours started from Danforth Avenue via Woodbine Avenue and Lumsden Avenue to Main Street.
Dec. 27, 1930	Dawes Road operations acquired by Mr. Sefton (Del-Ray Coach Lines).
Jan. 10, 1931	Dawes Road route operating from Luttrell Avenue via Danforth Avenue and Dawes Road to Holland Road.
Nov. 20, 1931	Coxwell Avenue-Main Street route inaugurated from Danforth Avenue via Coxwell, Sammon, Woodbine, and Lumsden Avenues to Main Street. Service inaugurated from Danforth via Broadview, Mortimer, and Donlands Avenues to O'Connor Drive.
Nov. 23, 1931	Routes inaugurated Nov. 20, 1931 are stopped for lack of a permit to operate.
Dec. 16, 1931	Coxwell Avenue-Main Street service resumed.
Feb. 3, 1933	Woodbine Avenue-Dawes Road service inaugurated from Danforth Avenue via Woodbine Avenue, Lumsden Avenue and Main Street to Danforth Avenue.
	Donlands Avenue service inaugurated from Danforth Avenue via Donlands, Mortimer, Linsmore, Sammon, and Coxwell Avenues to Danforth Avenue.

---

1. Bustin, Percy, *Memories: The Early Days of East York*, Self –Published, 1976, 21

Feb. 25, 1933   Donlands Avenue service routed via Monarch Park Avenue instead of Linsmore Avenue.

July 6, 1936   Dawes Road service bought by Hollinger. Operating from Danforth Avenue to Holland Road. Wexford Boulevard service started in rush hours.

July 13, 1936   Woodbine Avenue-Dawes Road service operating from Danforth Avenue via Woodbine, Lumsden, Barrington, Secord Avenues and Dawes Road to Danforth Avenue. Returning via Danforth Avenue, Main Street, Lumsden, and Woodbine Avenues.

Oct. 24, 1937   Woodbine Avenue-Dawes Road and Dawes Road services combine on Sunday to operate from Lumsden Avenue via Main Street, Danforth Avenue, and Dawes Road to Holland Road.

Dec. 5, 1938   High school service started from Woodbine Avenue via O'Connor Drive, Broadview, Mortimer, Pape, Sammon, Donlands, and Cosburn Avenues to Coxwell Avenue.

March 1941   Geco (General Engineering Company, known as GECO Fuse-Filling Plant or GECO Munitions Plant) was a complex of 170 buildings located on 346 acres of Scarborough farmland located at the southeast corner of Eglington and Birchmount Avenues employing 5300 people of which 3400 were women war workers, a great many of them from East York.[2] Service commenced jointly with Danforth Bus Lines. Routes from Danforth Avenue via Dawes Road and Eglinton Avenue to Birchmount Road.

May 22, 1941   Woodbine Park route extended from O'Connor Drive and Woodbine Avenue across the Woodbine Bridge to O'Connor Drive and Glenwood Crescent.

August 1941   Service from Eglinton Avenue and Yonge Street to Geco started.

October 1941   Service from Strathmore Boulevard and Coxwell Avenue to Geco started jointly with Danforth Bus Lines.

---

2. Dickson, Barbara, *Bomb Girls*, Trading aprons for Ammo, Dundurn, 2015

Jan. 5, 1942	Broadview Avenue-Coxwell Avenue service started 9 hours a day.
	Routes from Strathmore Boulevard via Coxwell, Mortimer, Nealon, Jackman Avenues and Broadview Avenue to Mortimer Avenue; returning via Mortimer and Coxwell Avenues.
May 1, 1942	Service from St. Clair Avenue East and Yonge Street to Geco started.
Dec. 20. 1943	O'Connor route inaugurated nine hours a day from Strathmore Boulevard via Coxwell Avenue and O'Connor Drive to Woodbine Avenue.
September 1945	Woodbine Park route extended from Glenwood Crescent via O'Connor Drive to Tiago Avenue.
Oct. 29, 1945	Mount Albert route inaugurated from Gray Coach Terminal at Edward and Bay Streets via Bay, Wellesley, Parliament Streets, Prince Edward Viaduct, Broadview Avenue, O'Connor Drive, Dawes Road, Lansing Road, Don Mills Road through Cedar Valley and Vivian to Mount Albert.
May 5, 1947	Woodbine Avenue-Broadview Avenue rush hour service started from Danforth Avenue via Broadview and Mortimer Avenues to Woodbine Avenue.
	Broadview Avenue-Coxwell Avenue service changed to operate from Danforth Avenue via Broadview, Mortimer and Coxwell Avenues to Strathmore Boulevard.
Aug. 2, 1949	O'Connor Drive route extended from Woodbine Avenue to Amsterdam Avenue via O'Connor Drive.
	Woodbine Avenue-St. Clair Avenue East service inaugurated from Strathmore Boulevard, via Woodbine Avenue, O'Connor Drive, and St. Clair Avenue East to Dawes Road.
	Woodbine Avenue-Tiago Avenue service discontinued from Strathmore Boulevard via Woodbine Avenue and O'Connor Drive to Tiago Avenue.
Jan. 3, 1950	Parkview Hills route inaugurated from Strathmore Boulevard via Coxwell, O'Connor Avenues and St. Clair Avenue East to Woodbine Heights Boulevard.

1951	Parkview Hills route extended to loop via Parkview Hill Crescent., Elswick Road, Hackberry Street, and Woodbine Heights Boulevard to St. Clair Avenue East.
Early 1952	Industrial loop service (rush hours only) started as a portion of the O'Connor Drive service. Looped in A.M. via Curity Avenue, Hollinger Road, Bermondsey Road, and O'Connor Drive. Reverse loop in P.M.
June 1, 1952	Donlands Avenue route rerouted via Coxwell and Mortimer Avenues (formerly operated via Sammon and Monarch Park Avenues).
August 1952	Name of "Geco" route changed to "Eglinton."

The provincial legislation that created the Municipality of Metropolitan Toronto also amalgamated all suburban bus lines including the Hollinger Bus Lines Limited with the Toronto Transit Commission (TTC). The last Hollinger Bus Lines bus rolled into the garage at Woodbine Avenue and O'Connor Drive at midnight on June 30, 1954.[3]

Hollinger Bus Lines (HBL) was a family business. John Hollinger's son, J. Barclay Hollinger, who became president when the founder died in 1951, was a grease monkey as a teenager and drove buses from the day he was old enough to pass his chauffeur's license test. Two of John's daughters, Isabel Macrory and May Vipond, at one time or another headed the office staff. The employees of Hollinger's, some of whom had been with the company for twenty-two years, were all offered employment with the TTC but were no longer entitled to the profit sharing they had received at HBL.

The HBL garage and terminal on Woodbine just south of the bridge, which was acquired with the bus line by the TTC, was purchased by the township in 1955 for $215,000. Subsequently, as Percy Bustin said, it became the site of the Trillium Apartments at 1501 Woodbine Ave.[4]

Five years after it became responsible for public transit in East York, the TTC proposed to build a subway line from Queen Street East north on Pape Avenue to O'Connor Drive. As with so many TTC proposals, this one too was shelved.[5]

---

3. S. Walter Stewart Library, History of Hollinger Bus Line Limited
4. S. Walter Stewart Library, History of Hollinger Bus Line Limited
5. Filey, Mike, The *Sunday Sun*, May 7, 2017

Todmorden Bus Line
(Source: East York Foundation)

Hollingers Bus Depot
(Source: East York Foundation)

Hollinger bus lines, serving the old Township of East York, was a profit-able transit entity until be-ing absorbed by the TTC in 1954. This bus, on Coxwell, just north of Danforth, and would have been on its way to the Bus Terminal on the Danforth that we now know as a breakfast spot.

(Source: Toronto Archives)

Todmorden Bus Line
(Source: East York Foundation)

Hollingers Bus Depot
(Source: East York Foundation)

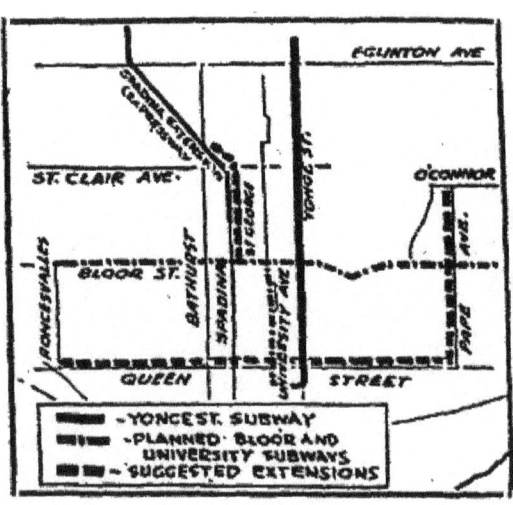

Sun May 7 Queen-Pape subway July 3, 1959
(Source: Mike Filey Toronto Sun)

– Chapter 17 –

THE DON VALLEY

"In the 1950s, a group of East York citizens joined forces to preserve the Don Valley in its natural state. It was a time when threats against the natural beauty of the Valley were multiplying on every side. Pocket sewage disposal plants (one of which was the North Toronto Sewage Treatment Plant in the valley just south of the Leaside Bridge) were so overloaded that raw effluent was being dumped into the Don River and Taylor Creek. There was a threat of factory development where Todmorden Mills now stands. Wooded slopes and wetlands disappeared under heaps of garbage when they were used as municipal dumps. Trees were felled to provide space for a series of lines spanning the Valley. Through a lack of regulations, anyone so minded could despoil the woodlands at will."[1]

"That group of East York citizens which included Roy Cadwell, Charles Sauriol, and Rand Freeland, the owner at the time of Fantasy Farm on Pottery Road, formed The Don Valley Conservation Association (D.V.C.A.) which mounted an intensive conservation campaign to protect

---

1. Sauriol, Charles, *Tales of the Don*, Dundurn Press, November 1984, 23

and beautify the Don Valley. The main areas of concern were pollution, parks, patrolling and aesthetics."[2]

What had brought the valley to this sorry state?

In the 1880s, several gas wells were drilled successfully in the valley. The North Toronto pumping plant used this gas to fuel its steam pump. Then, in 1890, oil and more gas wells were drilled to a depth of 1127 feet in the valley south east of Thorncliffe, this time without success.

Industries in the valley were big offenders. The Taylor Paper Mill, later Smith Fine Papers and then Domtar, was the oldest industry in Metro Toronto. Right beside it was Bate Chemicals and across the valley was the brickworks. Railways, the CPR and the CNR, were laid out and ran through the valley constructed with wood from the trees cut down in the valley itself. The Don Valley Parkway and the Bayview Extension were cut through the valley. Effluent overflowed from the North Toronto Sewage Treatment Plant at the foot of what is now Redway Road. There was also garbage, not only from the dumps (now called land-fill sites of both the former Township of East York and the former Town of Leaside), but garbage dumped over the valley sides for example at 1050 Broadview,[3] where the property was purchased by Franceshini Construction specifically for that purpose. The valley edge on Donlands Avenue leading to the Leaside Bridge was the site of another township dump, which is still being monitored for escaping methane gas.

Hurricane Hazel, which struck Metro Toronto in 1954, was a catalyst for action. The Don Valley was proclaimed a flood plain and buildings there could no longer be occupied as residences. The Metropolitan Toronto and Region Conservation Authority (MTRCA) was established to prevent a similar disaster in the future.

True Davidson was a strong conservationist.

"In her first term on Council, True became chairwoman of the Works Committee and began agitating to dispose of some of the unnecessary land owned by the municipality which she described as 'a liability to us in their present condition.' When she became reeve in 1960, she followed

---

2. Sauriol, Charles, *Tales of the Don*, Dundurn Press, November 1984, 23
3. Interview with Bill Lewis

through on this idea, deeding 245 acres of valley land to the Metropolitan Toronto and Region Conservation Authority as part of its flood control and water conservation scheme. The local paper claimed that this was the largest single block of land ever donated to the authority by a member municipality. Willis Blair approved since East York, with a population of only 72,000, couldn't afford to develop the land into parks."[4]

"A few years later, the Conservation Authority leased the site of what would become Todmorden Mills Heritage Museum and Arts Centre back to East York for ninety-nine years. The restoration of the two old houses and an old brewery, along with the former paper mill, became East York's 1967 Centennial project."[5]

But while East York was giving away 245 acres of Massey Creek and Don River Valley land that it owned, the township had its eye on acquiring the 6.157 acre Goulding estate on Dawes Road on Massey Creek. The Goulding house of Tudor design, situated in valley lands was the home of Walter Massey's daughter, originally a part of the Massey Dentonia Park Farm. The plan was to develop it as a park in conjunction with Donora Park.

In September 1965, East York passed a by-law expropriating the Goulding property. However, before the expropriation by-law was registered in the Land Titles Office, the township planning director learned that Farlinger Developments Limited had purchased the property from Mrs. Goulding on September 8, 1965 for a $30,000 down payment and a mortgage back to Mrs. Goulding for $120,000, interest-free for as long as she continued to live on the property. When Mrs. Goulding sold the property to Farlinger, she was acting on the advice of both her accountant and her lawyer. As such, she was a knowledgeable seller dealing with a knowledgeable buyer, thus, the sale could not be set aside. In order to head off the anticipated apartment development on the site, a special council meeting was immediately convened, not in the council chamber but rather on the lawn of the McLean Estate, which adjoined the Goulding property on Dawes Road north of Massey Creek. The township had purchased the McLean Estate for park land the previous year. That afternoon, Council passed another by-law expropriating the Goulding estate, not from Mrs. Goulding, the former owner, but from the new owner, Farlinger.

---

4. Darke, Eleanor, *Call Me True, A Biography of True Davidson*, Dundurn Press, 1997, 70
5. Darke, Eleanor, *Call Me True, A Biography of True Davidson*, Dundurn Press, 1997, 111

The municipality zoned the Goulding property as public open space but was turned down by the Ontario Municipal Board, who required them to zone it as single family residential land before they would approve the township's Official Plan. But for this OMB requirement, Council would have never agreed to rezone the land as single family residential. The only evidence of value of the land zoned as single family residential was that submitted by Farlinger as compensation for the property in the amount of $360,000. So the Borough of East York Council settled with Farlinger Developments Limited for $360,000 plus costs.

While the matter was being litigated, the borough rented the Goulding House for a period of six years at $10,000 per year, for a total of $60,000. This amount was written off in the cost of changing the sewer system and park maintenance.

The Goulding property was saved from redevelopment and vested in perpetuity to the people of East York as open park land. In January 1978, due to the costs of maintenance, it was sold to the Municipality of Metropolitan Toronto to be included in their parks systems at a cost of $454,730.[6]

The Paper Mill

In 1989, Domtar announced that it would be closing its paper mill in the Don Valley where, under other owners, a paper mill had operated for over 150 years. Their sixteen-acre property was acquired by the Metropolitan Toronto and Region Conservation Authority (MTRCA), marking the beginning of the end for East York's historic valley industries. Bate Chemical and Polyresins Inc., the manufacturer of oil and water-based paint resins and adhesives, was next to go. The Conservation Authority purchased its land and demolished all of the buildings except for the research and development lab that was converted into the Toronto Police dog training facility. The rest of the area was cleaned up and the contaminated soil was removed.[7]

The MTRCA then designated fifty-two hectares (128 acres) on both sides of the valley, from the Leaside bridge to Pottery Road (known as Crothers Wood), as an "Environmentally Significant Area." Crothers

---

6. Wadlow, Stan, *East York Recreation, The Early Years*, Centennial College Press, 1982, 39
7. East York Council minutes, February 1989

Woods was named after George W. Crothers, who founded a manufacturing company called Crothers Caterpillar, which built heavy machinery for the construction and mining industries on the site now known as Redway Road, where a Loblaws store is presently located. Zoned as undeveloped parkland, Crothers Woods consists of woodland, meadows, wetlands, and bicycle trails.[8]

The Brickworks

The Taylors' Don Valley Brick Works was sold to Robert Davies in 1909, resold to Strathgowan Investments in 1928, and sold again to United Ceramics Limited, a German company, in 1956. During these years, the brick works (known as the Toronto Brick Company) prospered as it continued to mine by periodically blasting the north face of the valley for clay and shale. The blasting was understandably a great concern to the residents of Governor's Bridge, as it came closer and closer to their homes built on the table land overlooking the mining operation. At one point, the blasting stopped when the excavation for the Toronto Dominion Centre downtown on King Street hit the same seam of clay that ran north to the brick works. The clay from that excavation proved to be a new supply source for the Toronto Brick Company, but when that supply source was exhausted, the blasting started again.[9]

It stopped permanently, however, in the 1980s, when most of the usable clay and shale had been mined. Then the company decided to offer the land to East York for the sum of $4 million for conservation purposes. But while that was too steep a price for East York, it was just right for a developer called Torvalley Associates Ltd. Proposing to build 756 low-rise housing units on the property, they purchased it for $ 4,001,000.[10]

At this point, the community sprang into action. The Governor's Bridge Ratepayers Association (led by Geoffrey Smith, whose home on Douglas Crescent was almost on the edge of the mining operation), the Leaside Property Owners Association, the Toronto Field Naturalists, together with representatives of the University of Toronto's Department

---

8. The Planning Partnership "Crothers Woods Trail Management Strategy" (PDF) City of Toronto, Archived from original (PDF) on June 7, 2011
http://www.toronto.ca/parks/trails/crothers/
9. Redway, Alan, Recollections
10. East York Council minutes, July 1987

of Geology and Zoology, the Royal Ontario Museum, and Department of Earth Sciences from the University of Waterloo, all urged Council to preserve the site and to designate the North Slope as an historic site.

The Provincial Government intervened by agreeing to provide part of the funding to purchase the site and to designate it as property of archaeological and historic significance under the Ontario Heritage Act. After that, the Metropolitan Toronto and Region Conservation Authority agreed to expropriate the property because it was on a flood plain.[11]

In 1997, the Don Valley Brickworks was officially opened as a geology, nature, farmers' market, industrial education, and conference centre. Thirteen years later, after an expenditure of $55 million, it was reborn as the Evergreen Brick Works.[12]

Thus, the threat of factory development that Charles Sauriol referred to was laid to rest. The North Toronto sewage treatment plant was upgraded and the garbage dumps have become greenbelt and bicycle paths. However, although municipal garbage is no longer dumped in the valley, the problem of litter and river pollution still persists in spite of the efforts of the East York Advisory Committee on the Environment, the City Task Force to Bring Back the Don, and the enormous personal efforts and leadership provided by the late East Yorker, Charles Sauriol. That leadership and those efforts were recognized in 1989 with the dedication of the Charles Sauriol Conservation Reserve in the east valley of the Don River.[13]

Don Valley
(Source: East York Foundation)

11. East York Council minutes, March 1988
12. East York Council minutes, May 1997
13. East Yorker and Council minutes, February 1989

Skating on the Don
(Source: East York Foundation)

Kids swimming in Don River
(Source: Don Valley River Valley Park Website)

Don Valley Paper Mill
(Source: East York Foundation)

Brick Works 2
(Source: East York Foundation)

Brick Works
(Source: East York Foundation)

Don Valley Garbage Dumps
(Source: East York Foundation)

Bellehaven
(Source: East York Foundation)

Joyce Crook
(Source: Panchetta Barnett)

North Toronto Sewage Treatment Plant 1958
(Source: Toronto Archives On Line)

Whitewoods Riding Stables before the 1967 Todmorden Mills Centennial project
(Source: East York Foundation)

Charles Sauriol
(Source: East York Foundation)

Todmorden Mills
(Source: East York Foundation)

Crothers Woods Trail
(Source: City of Toronto website)

Evergreen Brick Works
(Source: Historica Canada Website)

– Chapter 18 –

INDUSTRY

To maintain reasonable property tax rates for residential homeowners, a municipality needs a significant industrial assessment as a proportion of its total property assessment. Since industry requires fewer municipal services than residents do, industrial taxes help to pay for the additional residential services such as libraries, parks, and recreation.

The importance of that was illustrated in the 1960 township report stating, "We appreciate our industrial firms, which with their contribution in taxes and the employment of many of our people, add so much to the economic wellbeing of the community."[1] About the same time, the mayor of Leaside sent a letter to residents of the town: "I hope you will be pleased with the exceptionally low 1962 tax rate... For local requirements, the rate is almost exactly the same as last year. The increase is about 25 cents for the average homeowner."[2] What the mayor failed to credit for the virtually unchanged residential tax rate was the fact that Leaside's industrial assessment was slightly over 50% of the town's total residential and industrial assessment. In stark contrast, at that time, the township's

---

1. Township of East York 1959-1960 Report on Present and Plans for the Future
2. Leaside Mayor Lloyd Dickenson, June 1962 letter to residents

industrial assessment was only 25% of the total. Strengthening the tax base of the new Borough of East York was at least part of the rationale for the merger of the township and the town in 1967.

There had been industry in East York before the Township was incorporated. The Skinners, Helliwells, and Taylors had mills and brickyards in the Don Valley while the Chapmans had brickyards on Dawes Road. Then in 1926, Ford of Canada established its main assembly plant in the township south of the Danforth at Victoria Park Avenue, where it remained throughout the war until, having sold the plant to the manufacturers of the Nash and Rambler automobiles, Ford moved to Oakville in the 1950s. That site became Shopper's World Danforth in 1962. Although there were still industries in the Valley—Toronto Brick Company, Domtar Fine Papers, and Bate Chemical—after World War II, the township's main industrial area was located in the northwest between O'Connor Drive and the rim of the Don Valley.

The township's industrial area north of the Woodbine Bridge and west of O'Connor Drive had been zoned for industrial uses since the bridge had been opened in 1931, but it was not until the arrival of Peek Freans in 1949 that the area began to take off.[3]

Peek Freans was an English firm that was established in 1857. Before World War II, it had opened factories in India and Australia, but not in Canada. After the war, it located at the corner of O'Connor and Bermondsey. The streets in the O'Connor industrial area often took their names from the industries that located on them. Bermondsey is the name of the city in England where Peek Freans' head office was located.[4]

Jack Freer, a long-time barber whose shop is still at the corner of Woodbine and Cosburn, used to cut the hair of the Peek Freans, chief executive officer, then an English ex-pat. When his customer told him where he worked, Jack replied, "Oh, the cookie maker," to which his customer shot back, "That's biscuits, not cookies."[5]

Peek Freans, operating in East York under the name of Associated Biscuits, was purchased by Nabisco in 1982 and is now owned by a holding company, Mondelez International.[6]

---

3. Peek Freans' website
4. Peek Freans' website
5. Interview with Jack Freer, August 18, 2016
6. Peek Freans' website

Peek Freans, Sharpe & Dohme Pharmaceutical (hence the street named Dohme), Yardley's (maker of toilet goods and cosmetics—hence Yardley Avenue), and Kendall, the maker of Curity products (hence the street named Curity) were four of the original industries in the area.[7]

After the township and the town merged, the new Borough of East York had three industrial areas. The Leaside industrial area east of Laird Drive began when Canada Wire and Cable located there in 1913. It was established to make wire for Ontario Hydro but with the beginning of World War I, turned to making artillery shells instead. When the war ended, it got back to the wire and cable business.[8] By 1978, the company had 2,700 employees and sold its products, which now included fibre optics, all over the world. But in 1991, Canada Wire was sold to its giant French competitor, Alcatel. The new owner deliberately limited Canada Wire sales to Canada to eliminate the competition between Canada Wire and Alcatel in foreign markets. With a limited market for its products, Canada Wire was no longer a profitable business. Alcatel closed the plant and sold the property to Mitchell Goldhar of Smart Centres for a big box shopping centre in 1997.[9]

After WWI, and particularly during and after WWII, many other manufacturers followed Canada Wire to the Leaside industrial area, including Durant Motors, Frigidaire, Colgate Palmolive, Canada Varnish, Apco, Lincoln Electric, Sangamo, Canada Varnish, Tremco, Corning Glass, Honeywell, Wajax, E.S.& A. Robinson, Parkhurst Knitting, and Philips Electronics.[10]

When the Ontario Municipal Board awarded Thorncliffe to Leaside, the industrial area expanded to the north side of Overlea Boulevard, where industries such as Barber-Ellis, Coca-Cola, Glenayr-Knit, Magnasonic, and Chetwynd Films located.[11]

Many industries in both the O'Connor Drive and the Leaside area have gone, although some remain. The Toronto Conservation Authority acquired the lands of Toronto Brick Company, Domtar, and Bate

---

7. East York Clerk's Department, 1959
8. Pitfield, Jane, *Leaside,* National Heritage Books, 1999, 39–50
9. Redway, Alan, Recollections
10. Pitfield, Jane, *Leaside,* National Heritage Books, 1999, 50–87
11. East York, Planning Department, 1980

Chemical in the Don Valley, so the original East York industrial area no longer exists.

Each year, from 1977 to 1984, the Borough of East York compiled a list of local industries. In 1984, the following is a partial list of industries located there.[12]

Name	Location
A.B. Dick Co. of Canada Ltd.	60 Overlea Boulevard
Allanson Mfg. Co. Ltd.	33 Cranfield Road
Apco Industries Ltd.	10 Industrial Street
Armstorng, S.A. Ltd.	1400 O'Connor Drive
Barber-Ellis of Canada Ltd.	20 Overlea Boulevard
Bate Chemical Co. Ltd.	44 Beechwood Drive
Block Drug Co. (Canada) Ltd.	36 Northline Road
Bristol-Myers Products Canada	99 Vanderhoof Avenue
Canada Building Materials Co. (Div. of St. Mary's Cement Ltd.)	55 Industrial Street
Canada Wire and Cable Co. Ltd.	
Chevron Asphalt Ltd.	147 Laird Drive
	43 Industrial Street
Coca-Cola Ltd.	42 Overlea Boulevard
Conn Chem. The Group Ltd.	20 Curity Avenue
Corning Canada	135 Vanderhoof Avenue
Crush Canada	1600 O'Connor Drive
Diesel Equipment Ltd.	139 Laird Avenue
Dominion Press (Div. of E. Andrus & Son Ltd.)	15 Gower Street
Dominion Regalia Ltd.	1550 O'Connor Drive
Domtar Fine Papers Ltd.	Don Valley (Beechwood Dr.)
Domtar Inc.	1 Laird Drive
Dorothea Knitting Mills Ltd.	20 Research Road
D R G Incorporated	73 Laird Drive
D R G Sellotape (Div. of DRG Inc.)	10 Esandar Drive
Elliott Research Corp. Ltd.	842 Pape Avenue
Erno Manufacturing Co. Ltd.	19 Curity Avenue
Federal Pioneer Ltd.	19 Waterman Avenue
Floorco Ltd.	120 Wickstead Avenue

------

12. East York, Planning Department, 1984

Glenayr-Knit Ltd.	100 Thorncliffe Park Drive
Kendall Canada Division- CKR Inc.	6 Curity Avenue
Lincoln Electric Co. of Canada Limited	179 Wickstead Avenue
McClelland & Stewart Ltd.	25 Hollinger Road
Mercedes-Benz of Canada Ltd.	849 Eglinton Avenue East
Metals & Alloys Co. Ltd.	205 Wickstead Avenue
O'Connor Tanks Ltd.	15 Bermondsey Road
Pitney Bowes of Canada	19 Curity Avenue
Phillips Electronics Limited	961 Eglinton Avenue East
Polyresins Div. of Bate Chemical Co. Ltd.	44 Beechwood Drive
Regal Greetings and Gifts (Div. of Canadian Corp. Management Co. Ltd.)	939 Eglinton Avenue East
Richvale Block & Ready Mix Co.	S/S Wickstead Avenue
St. Lawrence Sugar Div. of Sucrose Ltd.	225 Wickstead Avenue
Sangano Co. Ltd.	215 Laird Drive
Seven Up Canada Ltd.	12 Cranfield Road
Thornton, G.M. & Son Ltd.	202 Parkhurst Boulevard
Toronto Brick Co. (Div. of United Ceramics)	550 Bayview Avenue
Tremco Canada Ltd.	220 Wickstead Avenue
Twin Offset Ltd.	10 Gower Street

Since maintaining and growing the industrial assessment has been essential to the survival of East York as a separate municipality, the borough conducted a number of studies of both the O'Connor and the Leaside industrial areas, as well as ongoing consultations with the existing industries to encourage more industries to locate there.[13]

It is interesting to note that the Toronto East General Hospital is the borough's largest employer, but pays no taxes.

---

13. East York Council minutes 1972-1996

The main Ford of Canada assembly plant became Shopper's World mall after the company moved operations to Oakville in the 1950s. The loss of jobs and the shift of stores from the street were "a double whammy" for the neighbourhood.

PHOTO COURTESY FORD OF CANADA

(Source: WorldWide Wickens Blog by Stephen Wickens, 2014)

EY O'Connor c1949

(Source: Jim Lister)

EY O'Connor c1970
(Source: Jim Lister)

Canada Wire and Cable Plant at Laird Drive
(Source: Property of Canada Wire and Cable at Laird Dr)

– Chapter 19 –

CLUBS, SOCIETIES, AND ASSOCIATIONS

The East York Garden Club

The East York Garden Club is the oldest continuously active club in East York. It started just a year after the Township was incorporated. Then on November the 1st, 1926, according to the Council minutes, members of the Greenwood Woodbine Horticultural Society came to the meeting complaining about stray horses destroying their lawns.[1]

Renamed the East York Horticultural Society in 1929, the name was changed again to the East York Garden Club in 1968. It has nearly 200 members who meet monthly promoting gardening and beautification in the community by sharing horticultural knowledge and helping to conserve East York's natural resources. The club meetings feature plant and flower shows and sales, discussions on vegetable, plant and flower growing, and workshops on flower arranging. For many years, the junior members of the club flourished under the direction of Mrs. Dorothy Stoneburgh.

----

1. East York Council minutes, November 1926

In 1984, East York's 60th Anniversary, the club played a key role, which it has continued ever since, in organizing and promoting the "Mayor's Blooming Contest." The brain child of a former club member and gardening expert East Yorker Art Drysdale, the contest was initiated by Mayor David Johnson with a view to encouraging borough residents to beautify their properties. [2]

Cosburn Park Lawn Bowling Club

Almost as old as the Garden Club is the Cosburn Park Lawn Bowling Club founded in 1929 when a small group of residents in the vicinity of Cosburn and Coxwell organized the club under the sponsorship of The Township Council. The men's group functioned under Reeve Rupert Leslie while a separate ladies' group was led by Mrs. Grant Jack.

The original clubhouse on the site was a shed with no heating or other facilities. A new clubhouse was built by the members themselves in 1937. The veranda was added in 1952 after the lady members raised the necessary $1,250.00 by holding euchres and a bazaar. The Borough put an addition on the present building in 1971.

Over the years, members of the club have represented East York and won medals in national and provincial lawn bowling champion-ships. [3]

Cosburn Park Lawn Bowling Crest

---

2. East York Garden Club presentation by Malcolm Geast, March 17, 2016, The East Yorker, Inter-view with David Johnson, October 6, 2016

3. Interview with Mike Vince, September 26, 2016; Club 75th Anniversary 1929-2004 book

The Kiwanis Club of East York

In 1943, Walter Stewart, Walter Taylor, Rupert Leslie, Walter Grinnell, Bill Heaton, and Percy Bustin organized the Kiwanis Club of East York. Its charter members also included Harold Donaldson, the Principal of East York Collegiate, Stan Wadlow, Art Dyson, Howard Chandler and Art Greenwood (Greenwood's Hardware, north-east corner of Woodbine and Lumsden).

Over the years, Kiwanis have been a central part of the East York community. Before any libraries were built in the Township, the club provided books for boys and girls libraries in R.H. McGregor, Danforth Park, and William Burgess schools. It followed that up in 1959 by equipping the children's section of the original S. Walter Stewart Library building. The club initiated and substantially funded the construction and operation of the outdoor swimming pool in Cedarvale Park, now Stan Wadlow Park. In co-operation with the "Y," the club built a boys' camp in the Don Valley for local boys deprived of a summer holiday. In addition, the Kiwanis held senior citizens' Christmas parties; sponsored baseball and hockey teams; contributed to the Kiwanis Music Festival; volunteered at the Salvation Army home on Broadview; volunteered with mental patients at 999 Queen Street West; volunteered with patients of the East General Hospital and volunteered with the YMCA youth drop in centre at St. Clair and O'Connor. The club also made a substantial financial contribution to the successful campaign to save the East York Arena roof after the provincial government shut down arenas with roofs similar to that of the Listowel Arena after its roof collapsed killing nine people including several midget hockey players.

While he was living, R.H. (Bob) McGregor, (the former reeve and long-time member of parliament for York East, and a member of the club), presented each guest at the Senior Citizens' Christmas Party with a box of chocolates at his own expense.

In recent years, women not only became club members but several such as Marie Railey and Mary Ellen Trimble have served the club as its president.

Initially, the Kiwanis raised money for their community projects by raffling off two new homes built by club member Fred Baldwin, one on Coxwell Avenue, the other on Glenwood Crescent. It also held a carnival, a Miss East York contest, published and sold a newspaper (1946-1960), sold Christmas trees and cakes, as well as holding concerts and raffles to finance its excellent community work. [4]

East York Kiwanis Club
(Source: kiwanisclubeastyork.ca)

The East York Rotary Club

The East York Rotary Club was founded in 1954 by a number of business and professionals in the St. Clair O'Connor area including: Vern Heslip, a contractor who was the General Manager of Crescent Town for many years, Dr. Paul McCutheon, a veterinarian, John Martin, the owner of O'Connor Bowl, Dr. Jim Bell, later East York's Medical Officer of Health, Whipper Billy Watson, East York's famous wrestler and Jim Vipond, sports writer for the *Globe and Mail*. Originally, the club met at Branch #22 of the Royal Canadian Legion on Woodbine Avenue and later at the Stan Wadlow Club House, among a number of other locations. It has given a financial helping hand to many community organizations including Meals on Wheels and Call-a-Service but its major contribution to East York was the creation of YorkLea Lodges, halfway homes for troubled youth.

The initiative for Yorklea came from the Rev. Gordon King, the Rector of St. Luke's Anglican Church at Coxwell and Cosburn a member of the East York Rotary and another club member, Fred Speer, an East York Board of Education Superintendent. The first Yorklea home was established on Everett Crescent. Rather than sending delinquent boys to jail, the courts sentenced them to a period of living at the Yorklea facility. Later, together with the Leaside Rotary Club, the East York Rotary established a home for girls at another location. The club's main source

---

4. Kiwanis Club of East York History, Self–Published

of funding for these programs was its Rogers Cable TV auction held annually since 1981. [5]

Rotary Club of East York
(Source: eastyorkrotary.org)

The Leaside Lions Club

When the Town of Leaside merged with the Township of East York, the new Borough of East York was enriched by the many volunteers, clubs, societies, and associations that had existed in the former Town for many years. The longest established of these was the Leaside Lions Club.

The club was organized in 1938 by then Leaside Mayor Howard Talbot with the help among others, of the Town Solicitor Stan Schatz later the Honourable Mr. Justice Schatz of the Supreme Court of Ontario. In 1938, Leaside had only 3,000 residents, one school, muddy streets, very few sidewalks and no organized recreational activities for the kids.

The year after they were organized, the Lions opened the town's first playground at Millwood Park, not only providing the equipment but also paying for the supervisors to run the playground. The first summer supervisor was Bert Keene, a teacher at and later the principal of Bessborough School. Millwood Park was renamed for Mayor Trace Manes, another prominent Lion.

In 1941, the first peewee hockey game ever played in Canada pitted a Leaside Lions' team against one from Etobicoke. The following year, the Lions organized a boys' hockey and house league that played on

5. Interview with Paul McCutcheon, August 24, 2016

outdoor natural ice at Millwood Park. Shortly after that, the Lions and the Leaside Rotary Club initiated the efforts to raise the funds to build an artificial ice rink, the Leaside Memorial Community Gardens.

The original kitchens and later the tennis courts at both Rolph Road and Northlea Schools were donated by the Lions. Before the Leaside Gardens pool was built, the first learning-to-swim classes for Leaside kids were organized and paid for by the club, bussing Grade 5 students to the pool at the Glenview Terrace Apartments (now condominiums) on Yonge Street south of Lawrence Avenue.

Between 1941 and 1963, the Leaside Lions boys' marching band and the girls' majorette corps achieved a national and international reputations winning Canadian championships, performing in the Grey Cup and Santa Claus parades in Toronto, as well as parades in Atlantic City and New York City. In the mid-1960s, the Leaside Lions majorettes won the US open majorette corps competition.

During those years, the club sponsored hockey teams at the Gardens, baseball teams at Talbot Park, the 131st Cub and Scout Group, an Air Cadet Squadron and the Sateen Club. Initiated as a weekend dance for teenagers, the Sateen Club drew kids from all over the city. After a live band was replaced by the record player, the site was moved from Rolph Road School to Leaside High, where it grew to almost 1,000 members.

The Lions raised money for their projects by an annual carnival held every June between 1940 and 1961 at Trace Manes Park. The carnival was always opened by a parade led by the Lions marching band and majorettes, followed by cubs, scouts, brownies, girl guides, and numerous floats.

Another major fund raiser were the musicals, such as *Take it Easy*, *Button Busters*, and *The Wizard of Oz*. These were all written, produced, directed, and performed by members of the club. In the beginning, they were held in the auditorium of a local school but as their popularity grew, the productions moved to the Bayview Theatre (now Shoppers Drug Mart) and then during their last five years, the musicals ran for a week downtown at the Royal Alex Theatre.

In 1944, the club held a giant raffle. The first prize was the house at 172 Donlea.[6]

----

6. Redway, Alan, Recollections

Leaside Lions Club Skate-a-Thon Crest
(Source: ebayimg.com)

The Leaside Rotary

The Leaside Rotary Club was chartered in 1940. The original 15 members met weekly on the stage of Lamb Hall in St. Cuthbert's Church. The club was conceived when some local businessmen banded together to contest a local political issue and enjoyed one another's companionship so much they decided to meet on a regular basis.

The club reached its peak membership of 85 in the seventies. Many local endeavours have been initiated or have enjoyed the financial support of the Leaside Rotary. One club member operated a gift store on Bayview where he lent out books, in actuality, a private lending library. In 1945, the Rotary Club, a leased store on the east side of Bayview, and its start-up financing gave birth to the "Leaside Library."

The Leaside Memorial Gardens Community Centre and Arena was a joint venture of the Lions Club and Rotary and at a later date, they contributed to the addition of the swimming pool. Another combined effort, this time with the Leaside Council, was the Trace Manes Park community building. Rotary financed the senior wing and half of the common areas. The Yorklea Lodges and Touchstone for troubled youth have both been Rotary projects.

Todmorden Mills Museum has always had Rotary's support, especially with the rehabilitation of the oldest paper mill in Upper Canada. The building provides premises for the Don Valley Art Club and the East Side Players.

Ongoing local projects include such endeavors as scholarships awarded to all East York secondary schools in recognition of achievement and in support of continuing university or college education.

Rotary conducts weekly Bingo for the veterans at Sunnybrook "K" wing and Saturday morning Bingo at Columbus Hall to raise money to finance its many endeavors.

Each year, Rotary supports a reforestation project in the Don Valley. With the participation of local students, thousands of trees are planted. The club conducts vocational guidance sessions at the high schools, in cooperation with local businesses and as well, they supported foreman skills meetings designed to advance workers of local industry.

At Leaside High School, the Leaside Rotary sponsors interact. Here, the students who are interested become active in Rotary and assist with a variety of events such as the Annual Leaside Rotary Corn Roast. [7]

Rotary Club of Leaside
(Source: eastyorkrotary.org)

Leaside Lawn Bowling Club

In the late 1940s, when Talbot Park was being planned, it was suggested that a bowling green be provided. After a number of meetings were held, Art Donahue, editor of the *Leaside Advertiser* became the first president of the bowling club.

The clubhouse built in 1952 is still standing. In June 1952, Joe Davis, popularly known as "Mr. Bowler," became the president when the club officially opened. A great deal of the club's ongoing success was credited to the forming of an active ladies' section. In 1990, the ladies and men's sections were amalgamated and the following year, Dorothy Ranta was the first lady president of the entire club. This is a busy club with

---

7. Pitfield, Jane, *Leaside,* National Heritage Books, 1999, 157

about 170 members. As well, in winter there are carpet bowling, bridge, and court whist available as activities for members. [8]

Leaside Lawn Bowling Club Logo
(Source: bayview-news.com)

The Leaside-East York University Women's Club

The organization, part of the Canadian Federation of University Women, began in 1956, with True Davidson, (later the Mayor of East York), playing an active role in its initiation. The first president was Mrs. Jean Auger. Beth Nealson (a former mayor of Leaside) also became a member.

The club meets once a month from September to April at Northlea United Church, 125 Brentcliffe Road. Invited speakers address these meetings on a variety of topics with an annual dinner being held in May. Membership is open to all women graduates of accredited universities, with an associate membership also available.

One of the fundamental objectives of the club is the encouragement of young women to pursue post-secondary education and to render financial assistance to deserving students.

Three $500.00 scholarships are presented every year to each of the East York High Schools – East York Collegiate, Leaside High School, and Marc Garneau Collegiate.

As of 1999, the club has 85 members, 64% of whom live in Leaside. [9]

---

8. Pitfield, Jane, *Leaside,* National Heritage Books, 1999, 169
9. Pitfield, Jane, *Leaside,* National Heritage Books, 1999, 161

Leaside Garden Society

Many volunteer organizations have dwindled and disappeared but some have risen again. The Leaside Garden Society was organized in 1950 with 36 members. By 1953, membership had increased to 193 members. They meet monthly except in July, August, and December.

The Leaside Garden Society first planted gardens at the Leaside Library, a garden on Laird Drive and other gardens at traffic intersections. In 1963, for Leaside's 50th anniversary, plaques were placed on various trees. Northern Dancer roses were planted at the library as a centennial project.

Members have participated in several flower shows but in the early 1970s interest dwindled and it was disbanded.

In 1986, a group of gardening enthusiasts started the society again and on June 9, 1988 they were declared a Horticultural Society under the Horticultural Society Act.[10]

East York was a community of volunteers and volunteer clubs, societies and associations. The many of these organizations included the following: [11]

Health Unit	Library Board
Historical and Arts Board	Property Standards
Stan Wadlow Parks and Recreation Complex	Committee of Adjustment
Leaside Gardens Board	Crescent Town Recreational Centre Board
Curling Rinks Board	Planning Board
E.Y. Foundation	Architectural Conservation Advisory Committee
Safety Council	Bayview Business Association
Boy Scouts of Canada	Call-A-Service Inc.
Canadian Cancer Society	Canadian Red Cross Society
Community Care East York Association	Coxwell O'Connor Business and Professional
Don Valley Art Club	Donlands Village Business Association
East Side Players	East York Golden Choir
East York Historical Society	East York Home and School Council

---

10. Pitfield, Jane, *Leaside,* National Heritage Books, 1999, 161
11. East York Clerks Office, 1982

East York Senior Citizens'

East York Symphony Orchestra

Girl Guides of Canada
Chapter

Leaside/East York University
Women's Club

Lions Club of East York (Danforth)
Relations – East York

Meals on Wheels

Neighbourhood Information
Centre (N.I.C.)

Rotary Club of East York

Branch 10 – Ladies Auxiliary

Ladies Auxiliary –Branch 11

Ladies Auxiliary – Branch 22

Ladies Auxiliary – Branch 345

Volunteer Centre of Metropolitan
Toronto, East York Branch

Aerobee's Flying Club (model planes)

Foremen's Club of Leaside
(began in 1952 with John Kennedy
as president)

Leaside Badminton Club

Leaside Bridge Club

Leaside Chapter IODE

Leaside Hockey Association
(Peewee to Minor Midget)

Leaside Lawn Bowling

Leaside Shriner's Club
1954 with Frank Leonard as president)

Scouts and Cubs

Square Dance Club

Sports, Arts and Hobbies at Leaside
Memorial Gardens:

The Business and Professional
Women's Club

East York Volunteer Centre

Heart and Stroke Foundation – East York

Leaside Garden Society

Mayor's Committee on Multicultural and Race

True Davidson Meals on Wheels

Optimist Club of East York

Royal Canadian Legions – Branch 10

Royal Canadian Legion – Branch 11

Royal Canadian Legion – Branch 22

Royal Canadian Legion – Branch 345

Royal Canadian Legion – Branch 626

East York Golden Choir

Art Gallery Group of Leaside

Leaside Atom Baseball Association (boys 9-11)

Leaside Baseball Association (junior teams)

Leaside Camera Club

Leaside Gyro Club

Leaside Horticultural Society

Leaside Rifle and Revolver Club

New Horizons Club (seniors over 60) (began in

Bingo (Wednesday nights, May to August

Free Skating

Leaside Curling Club (formed in 1962)

Leaside Hockey Association for Boys

Toronto Hockey League

The Leaside Debating Club

Ratepayer Associations

Todmorden Ratepayers Association
Eastdale Ratepayer Association
Secord Ratepayer Association
Danforth Park Ratepayer Association
Woodbine Heights and Greenwood Ratepayer Association
Dawes Road Veterans and Ratepayer Association
Central Council of Ratepayer Association
East York Workers Association
East York Home and Property Owners Association
Governor's Bridge Ratepayer Association
Sunshine Valley Community Association
Holland Ratepayer Association
Broadview Heights Improvement Association
Parkview Hills Association
Womens' Electors Association of East York
William Burgess Ratepayer Association
Hartman Jones Ratepayer Association
Federation of Ratepayer Associations of East York
Woodbine Gardens and Morningside Park Ratepayer Association
Collegiate Community Ratepayer Association
Broadview Area Ratepayer Association
Selwyn—St. Clair Ratepayer Association
Leaside—Bennington Heights Ratepayer Association
Leaside Property Owners Association
Ward Three Ratepayer Association
Thorncliffe Park Tenants Association

– Chapter 20 –

EDUCATION

Percy Bustin described the beginning of the East York school system this way:

"One cannot even begin to cover the early days of education in East York without recalling the names of Walter Stewart, William Burgess, Robert McGregor, George Webster, Cosburn, and J.D. Mills, all of whom gave such devoted service to the cause of education before and at the time our present East York Board of Education came into being.

"Let us go back one hundred years ago when the first known schools were built; one in the Todmorden area, and the other on Dawes Road. The Todmorden school was a two-room, brick veneer building, which stood on the north side of O'Connor Drive (then Don Mills Road) in the vicinity of the present Rivercourt Blvd, and as mentioned, the other was on Dawes Road itself. For fifty years prior to the incorporation of East York, the whole area was known as the Township of York School Section No. 7."[1]

By 1937, School Section No. 7 had been divided into five School Sections, Numbers 7, 8, 10, 26, and 27, each administered locally by its

---

1. Bustin, Percy, Memories: *Memories: Early Days of East York*, Self –Published, 1976, 19

own board of three trustees. Secondary education was provided by the East York High School governed by the East York High School Board.[2]

Trustees of EYCI 1929-1930
(Source: East York Foundation)

Lu Ann Fagan said there was an even earlier school in the Secord – Dawes Road area.

"The first school which probably served this area was located just west of the Secord Area (Concession 2, Lot 5) I 1829 or 1830. It was a Common School called Thomas Bingle. It had 26 scholars. The building was log and was replaced by a brick structure after 1847. Another school which may have served the area was Dawes Road School built in 1863. At first it was a cottage type of building, then, in 1876 a frame school building was erected.

These early schools were built by everyone in the neighbourhood. They usually had one teacher and all the grades were in one room. The children used slates and chalk to write because pens and paper were

---

2. East York Township Coronation Service Queen Elizabeth II, Program, June 2nd, 1953

scarce. The seniors had penmanship lessons. They used pens made of sharpened quills. If the students misbehaved they were given homework to do. Many of the boys who lived on farms were only able to go to school for about four months of the year. The rest of their time was spent helping on the farms.

Coleman Avenue Public School

In 1883 The Grand Trunk Railway roundhouse and freight yard were constructed just south of the Secord Area. As a result, a school for the children of the railroad workers called Coleman Avenue School was built. It was also known as Little York Public School after the village in which it was situated. In 1910 the area north of the railroad tracks to Balfour Avenue known as East Toronto and including Little York was joined to the City of Toronto. This included Little York Public School. Thus, the people in the north of Balfour Avenue were without a school. Mr. Bessey, a member of the school board, tried to find a solution to this problem. Finally he did. The existing School Section No. 8 was divided, creating a new school Section known as S.S. No. 26. The area this new school section served was bounded on the east by Scarborough, on the west by Woodbine Avenue, on the south by the city limits and on the north by St. Clair." [3]

Percy Bustin goes on:

"It is all so confusing that perhaps it is best to list the schools according to the dates they were built.

1889	In this year the area west of Donlands became School Section No. 27, and Chester School was built on Broadview Avenue. Its first principal was Mr. J. Latter.
1891	Plains Road School was built. In 1917 it was enlarged to eight rooms, plus two portables to accommodate the then-500 pupils. Plains Road School was later renamed Diefenbaker School.
1907	In this year Coleman Avenue School was built for the area east of Woodbine Avenue, and for a section of the adjacent city. But in 1910 the city annexed the school. Little York

3. Fagan, Lu Ann, *The Secord Area*, East York Board of Education, 1974, 59

left without a school in the area, formed S.S. No. 26 and erected two portables.

1914 Torrens Avenue School was built originally with 12 classrooms, but six more classrooms were added in 1922 and 1928. About the time of incorporation in 1924 its name was changed to the William Burgess School in honour of one who had given faithful service in the area.

1914 Secord School was built originally with 24 classrooms. Mr. D.G. Anderson was the first principal succeeded by Mr. J. Hanley Smith. The original school was later demolished and replaced with a brand new school."[4]

Secord School also had a swimming pool, which was a great attraction not only for the students but for the community as well. Lu Ann Fagan has written:

"In 1920, a Community Centre Committee was formed by the Secord–Danforth Park Ratepayers Associations. By 1921, the community club was thriving with a membership of three hundred adults and teenagers. There were dances on Friday evenings called "At Homes," as well as concerts and readings. The centre had a paid swimming instructor and a paid gym instructor. Mr. John Walker was the swim instructor. He taught Bob and Irene Pirie who later qualified for the Olympics. Mr. Woods ran the gymnastics classes. The gymnastics class performed demonstrations each year called a "circus." As well as swimming clubs for the men and women, there were calisthenics, baseball teams, hockey teams, and boxing displays. Movies were held later in Danforth Park School to raise money for swim trophies and the Education and Entertainment fund. Shows were also put on to raise money to buy dryers, lockers, and equipment for swimming.

"In 1926, the pool was closed from October 31st to May 1st because the attendance was too low. After Danforth Park School was opened with its pool, the attendance at Secord fell off. By 1930, it was decided for the time being to lose the Secord gym and to have all activities at Danforth Park School. This transfer of activities resulted in the development of a thriving community centre there. However, with the coming of the

---

4. Bustin, Percy, *Memories: Early Days of East York*, Self –Published, 1976, 19

Depression, the facilities at Secord were needed again. The pool was opened for two nights and eventually four nights a week to raise money. Friday was the swim club night and they had to pay too. Dances and concerts were held in Secord gym in aid of relief funds. A gym club was formed to keep men who were out of work fit and off the street. A nurse conducted a Well-Baby Clinic on Saturday morning. Later on, the Ratepayers' Association paid the salaries of the swimming instructors out of the Education and Entertainment fund when the Board of Education would not because of lack of funds." [5]

1921   Danforth Park School was built with twenty-four classrooms (later renamed Oak Park Junior High School and now named for East York's long-time director of education, the D. A. Morrison Middle School). Mr. Anderson was the first principal, and was later followed by Col. O.M. Martin, who incidentally, was a close friend of the writer, (Percy Bustin) and whom we much admired. Col. Martin was a proud Canadian of Indian descent. He served in the Second World War with the rank of Brigadier and after the war was appointed a York County magistrate. In 1925, a High School Board was formed and it took over the Continuation School in the basement of Danforth Park. When East York High was opened in 1927, the children went there for high school. They had to cut through Billy MacKay's fields to get there. He used to chase the children from his farm. By 1939, all of the rooms and basement were in use. Three rooms had to be rented from Gledhill School in the City. In 1952, when Oak Park Junior High School opened in Danforth Park School, the remaining eleven rooms were still used by Danforth Park Elementary School. In 1955, Danforth Park Elementary School closed and the younger children south of Lumsden Avenue went to Gledhill Public School.

1922   R.H. McGregor School was opened at Sammon and Coxwell to overcome severe crowding at Plains Road School. Even the twelve rooms at McGregor were not

5. Fagan, Lu Ann, *The Secord Area*, East York Board of Education, 1974, 66

enough. Eight classrooms were needed for the overflow at city of Toronto schools of Earl Beatty and Wilkinson. In 1939, overcrowding sent McGregor students to those two city schools again. In 1946, Stan Wadlow ran the East York Recreation programs from the north end of the gymnasium balcony before moving to the new municipal building when it opened in 1948. A new R.H. McGregor School, including new Board of Education administration offices, was built when the old R.H. McGregor School was demolished in 1972.

1927   East York High School opened as a collegiate and vocational school, but since it had no industrial arts department, it reverted to the name East York Collegiate Institute. While the High School Board of Trustees, which was formed in 1925, was planning EYCI, the high school operated in the basement of Danforth Park School until the new high school building was opened. On completion, the school was officially opened by the then Premier of Ontario, Howard Ferguson. The year earlier, the cornerstone had been laid by the provincial MPP for York East, George S. Henry, who later became the premier of Ontario. The day it opened, one hundred students from Danforth Park basement marched over to their new school. In 1940, an additional five acres to the east of EYCI was purchased from the Anglican Synod (the clergy reserve), for a playing field and in 1948 the East York Collegiate Memorial Stadium was officially opened in that location.

1932   The Hartman Jones Memorial School opened on Carlaw between Floyd and Westwood.

1937   "By special act of the Provincial Legislature, the five school sections of East York Township were united into one board; the East York Board of Education. Members of the first board were Walter Stewart, chairman, George Webster, Fred Hazelton, Albert Croft, and J.D. Mills, all of whom were elected. Three members, R.J. Thompson, William Burgess, and George Leggett, were appointed by York County Council and Mr. Perry was the Separate School representative. The first business administrator was Percy Muir who was followed by William McCordick."[6] When McCordick resigned to become the director of education for the Metropolitan Toronto Board of Education, Dalton Morrison became the East York director of education and Dick McIntosh the business administrator.

The inaugural meeting of the board took place in EYCI but when the additional land east of the collegiate was purchased from the Anglican Church, a new board administration office was constructed at the east end of the site fronting on Cosburn Avenue. It remained there until 1972 when the old McGregor School was demolished and the new McGregor School built. It included new Board of Education administration offices. When Dalton Morrison retired as director of education, he was succeeded by Dick Dodds, who served for many years. When he retired, Eric Lewis was appointed as director of education. Rod Thompson, who succeeded Lewis, was the East York director of education at the time of amalgamation on January 1, 1998. When Dick McIntosh retired as business administrator, he was succeeded by Nora Gray. [7]

Dick Dodds (L) and Dalton Morrison (R)
(Source: Dick Dodds)

Dick McIntosh
(Source: Dick Dodds)

6. Bustin, Percy, *Memories: Early Days of East York*, Self –Published, 1976, 20–21
7. Interviews with Dick Dodds and Dick McIntosh, August 2, 2016

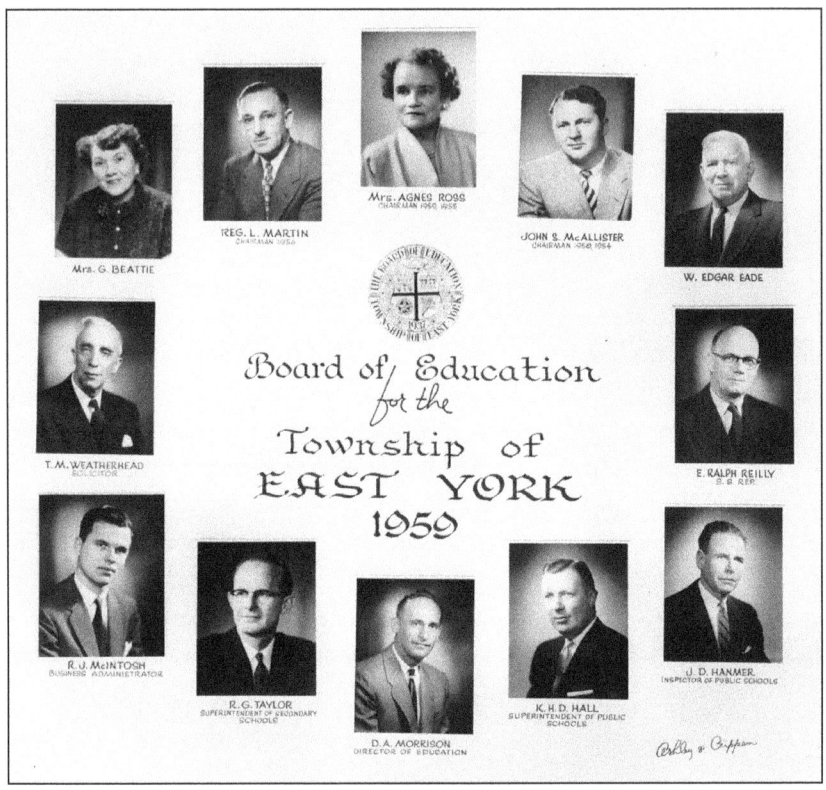

East York B of Ed 1959

(Source: East York Foundation)

1939   The Board of Education found it necessary to rent rooms
        from the city of Toronto Board of Education in Earl Beatty
        and Wilkinson Schools.

        When World War II was ending, the township was experiencing
both a home building and a population explosion, which clearly required
many new schools. [8]

1944   In 1933, Susan Denton Massey, the widow of Walter
        Massey and the namesake of Dentonia Park Farm, sold her
        mansion known by some as "Susan's Foley" to Crescent

8. Bustin, Percy, *Memories: Early Days of East York*, Self –Published, 1976, 22

School, a private school for boys. It was quite a sight for the Dawes Road kids who were raised in the Depression of the 1930s to see the boys arriving at Crescent School in limousines. Crescent School, which opened in 1944, was sold to developers in the late 1960s, when the school was relocated.[9]

1949   Cosburn Public School, 520 Cosburn, was opened. One year later, it became Cosburn Junior High School, and later still, Cosburn Middle School.

1950   Bennington Heights Schools was opened. It was built on the west side of the Don Valley isolated from the rest of the township.[10] Thomas Weatherhead, long-time solicitor for the Board of Education, told the story:

"My law firm has been solicitors for the school board of school section when the R.H. McGregor School was built. Mr. R.H. McGregor M.P., then a young man, was one of our clients. That was about 1921-22 so I was pretty familiar with school law. In December 1925, I saw notices posted on telephone poles that a school meeting would be held at 434 Heath Street East and that new trustees would be elected for our school section Number 10, East York, so I naturally arranged to attend.

"In those days, our school district was governed by three trustees. My wife and I attended the meeting. As I recall it, there were five people present, and I was asked to be the new trustee. I accepted. Our school district took in Governor's Manor and the land lying south of Moore Avenue from the Belt line to the C.P.R. There were about 8 houses north of the C.P.R. and about thirty houses in Governor's Manor. Our street was named Rosemount but as there was a Rosemount in the city, I had the council change the name of our street to Bennington Heights Drive in honour of my wife.

"The very few children of school age in the district attended the nearest city school, which was the very new Whitney School in Moore Park. As the district grew, we chartered a bus from the Grey Coach Lines in Toronto and took the children back and forth two times a day to school.

---

9. Fagan, Lu Ann, *The Secord Area*, East York Board of Education, 1974, 71
10. Bustin, Percy, *Memories: Early Days of East York*, Self –Published, 1976, 23

"In 1935, there was talk of forming a Township Board of Education, and our district was asked to go in on the scheme. We did. That year, a private act was passed by the legislature at Queen's Park providing for the formation of a Board of Education for the township. Formerly, there had been a high school board and a public school board of three trustees in each of the five school districts in the Township of East York. The plan was to have one township area board.

"In 1936, the old boards disbanded, an election was held for trustees for the Board of Education for the Township of East York and five members were elected. The Township Council then appointed two members, the County Council one member, and the Separate School Board, one member, making nine in all.

"I was asked to become the solicitor for the new board and I have remained the solicitor ever since. In those eighteen years, I have seen a large number of trustees come and go. Eventually the county ceased to appoint a member and then the Township Council stopped appointing two members, so now the board only has six members, where before it had nine.

"Gradually, over the years, as more and more families moved into Governor's Manor and into the district east of Moore Park, the school bus became more and more crowded and Whitney School no longer could accommodate the children from east of the Belt Line.

"As solicitor for the Board of Education, it was one of my duties to buy new school sites. The board commissioned me therefore to begin to buy a site for a new school east of the Belt Line. I looked the situation over carefully and decided on the land around where our present school stands. Some folk living south of the railway in Governor's Manor thought the new school site should be down there. At last, one night, about eight o'clock in summer, two or three car loads of trustees and councillors came over to see where the new school-site should be. They got out of their cars on Bayview and looked over the land lying west of Bayview and then drove down Pottery Road, which was then open, and across the tracks to Governor's Manor. It was a rather rainy night and a northeast wind was blowing. As luck would have it just as the trustees got to the proposed new site in Governor's Manor near the tracks, two great freight trains came along, one from the east and one from the west, smoke belching from their smoke stacks and with a deafening noise. The

smoke swirled down and almost choked the trustees, and when they came out of it, they could hardly gasp. That ended all talk of buying a school site south of the tracks and that night the present site was chosen. I was commissioned to try to buy the necessary lots. The land in this district was very cheap then. Year after year, I bought lots when I could; then we held expropriation meetings and took all the lots across the top of the hill. Later we expropriated or bought the land lying south of Pottery Road and the land lying north of Noel Avenue east of the lots on Bayview.

"The Township of East York owned the lots on the east ravine, while the board owned the lots north of Noel Avenue. I arranged to trade so that the Board got all the lots south of Noel Avenue where the park now is. That enabled us to have Bennington Heights Drive closed just in front of the school.

"I then wished to have Pottery Road closed so that the school site would reach from the railway fence to the north side of Noel Avenue. Noel Avenue was closed from the rear of the lots on Bayview over easterly to the ravine at the time Bennington Heights was closed where it ran north from the school along the easterly ravine. Before we could close Potter Road, it was necessary to partly fill the easterly ravine and make a road southerly from Moore Avenue to the railway crossing. This took many years, for the easterly ravine was very deep. In all I was engaged about thirteen years getting the school site arranged and in its present form.

"Then, about 1950, the young people in this district and in Governor's Manor kept coming to the board and asking for a school. An architect, Mr. Witmer, of the firm Parrott, Tambling, and Witmer, was chosen, and he and I went over the school grounds many times trying to find the best place for a school. We were somewhat hampered because the board did not own Mr. Allen's house. We knew that diesel engines were coming in the near future and thought that if there were lights at the crossing to Pottery Road, the engines would not whistle, so after long deliberation we fixed on the present site and on the present plans. In the future, we hoped the board would buy the Allen house when the Allens grew old and wanted to sell. We also planned that in time Pottery Road could be closed and filled, even right across. This would give easy access to the land now on the south side of Pottery Road and also would do much to prevent the erosion of the north side of Pottery Road.

"So the years went by. To accommodate the children from Governor's Manor a walk was constructed up the hill from the railway to the back door of the school. That path proved too hard to maintain, so the present stairs up the hill were constructed from the new Pottery Road. It was almost no time when so many children came to the school that two more rooms had to be built and perhaps you remember when they were added on the north." [11]

1950   Selwyn Elementary School was opened. In 1952, it became part of the St. Clair Junior High and then in 1956 a stand-alone school again.

1951   Presteign Heights Public School opened at 2570 St. Clair Avenue East.

1952   St. Clair Junior High School was opened in part of Selwyn School. It was renamed Gordon A. Brown Middle School after a long-time teacher, principal, and school board trustee.

1952   Victoria Park Public School at 145 Tiago Avenue opened, replacing three previous country schools that had served the children in the neighbourhood, namely, SS No.8. York Township established in 1861–1883, where our first Canadian-born governor general, Vincent Massey, had gone to school. The school established in 1872 to add to SS No.8 and the Dawes Road School, also known as the Town Line School, built in 1876. Victoria Park School had a number of additions and was completely refurbished in 1996.

1952   Oak Park Junior High School was established in the Danforth Park building. Later it was renamed D.A. Morrison Middle School.

1953   Parkside Public School opened in Cedarvale Park, at 401 Cedarvale Avenue when Danforth Park Elementary School became Oak Park Junior School.

1954   George Webster Public School opened at 2 Cedarcrest Boulevard, named for the long-time school board trustee.

———

11. Weatherhead, Peter & Thomas, Interview April 5, 2013

1955   Westwood Junior High School was opened in the Hartman Jones Memorial School building. Hartman Jones later became a stand-alone school renamed as Chester Public School.

1957   Selwyn Public School, 1 Selwyn Avenue, was opened.

1959   Chester Public School was opened at its present site, 115 Gowan Avenue. A new wing was added in 1972. The original Chester School now known as Estonia House, opened Broadview in 1891.[12]

Leaside Schools

In 1967, when the merger of the township and the town took place, the former existing Leaside schools together with the former township schools formed the new Borough of East York Board of Education. Those Leaside schools were:

1924   Bessborough Public School, formerly called Leaside Public School, opened on Hanna Road but presently addressed 211 Bessborough Drive. This was the first Leaside School.

1939   Rolph Road Public School, 31 Rolph Road, opened taking its name from the street on which it is located which in turn took its name from John Rolph, a supporter of William Lyon Mackenzie in the rebellion of 1838.

1944   Northlea School opened at 305 Rumsey Road north of Eglinton.

1948   Leaside High School opened at 200 Hanna Road.

1961   Thorncliffe Park School opened at 80 Thorncliffe Park Drive.[13]

New Borough of East York Schools built after the merger were:

1969   Valley Park Junior High School was opened at Overlea and Don Mills Road.

1972   Crescent Town School in Crescent Town at 4 Massy Square.

---

12. Bustin, Percy, *Memories: Early Days of East York*, Self –Published, 1976, 21
13. Pitfield, Jane, *Leaside,* National Heritage Books, 1999, 117–129

1972   Overlea Secondary School at Overlea and Don Mills Road, later renamed Marc Garneau Collegiate Institute in 1987 in honour of Canada's first astronaut. Both Valley Park and Marc Garneau were actually built on North York rather than East York land, but the Provincial Ministry of Education designated them as East York schools.[14]

Dick Dodds (L), Puddy Dodds (C) and Marc Garneau (R) at the official renaming of Overlea Secondary School as Marc Garneau Collegiate Institute
(Source: Dick Dodds)

1979   Massey Centre Secondary school program established at the Massey Centre 1102 Broadview Avenue.[15]

1979   The Province of Ontario transferred the property on the southwest corner of Pape and Mortimer, formerly the Ontario Teachers College, to Centennial College for its new East York campus to help meet the post-secondary education needs of the borough residents. College President Bev McCauley established a task force on community education in East York. Chaired by Borough Alderman Gordon Crann, other members included Madge Aalto, Chief Librarian; Audrey Camire, President of the Home and School Council; April Coulton of the Amalgamated Clothing and Textile Workers Union; Carol Fripp of the Leaside Property Owners Association; Joan Harvey of the

14. Interview with Dick McIntosh, August 2, 2016
15. Interview with Dick McIntosh, August 2, 2016

Neighbourhood Information Centre (NIC); Danny Missios of the Pape Avenue Businessman's Association; Harry Rychman, Superintendent, Board of Education; Rev. Len Self, Westminster Presbyterian Church; Don Wadlow, Recreation Director; Jim Buller, Historical and Arts Board; and Mayor Alan Redway. It was to identify the programs and services that would best serve the community.[16]

That property was originally the site of a city of Toronto school, Earl Kitchener Public School, which the city Board of Education built in the township of East York. Apparently, the city never asked for permission to build it and the township never objected as long as East York children could attend it. Both Joyce Crook and Claire Cole went to that school. Joyce who was born in 1926 and grew up on Dilworth Crescent, attended Earl Kitchener from kindergarten to grade eight, before going to Danforth Tech, followed by Shaw Business School prior to working for the Toronto Police Department.[17] Claire, who was born in 1932 and grew up on Mortimer Avenue, attended Kitchener for kindergarten and grades one and two before going on to Chester Public School and EYCI. Years later, she went to university and became a social worker.[18] During WW II, the school was used as an RCAF training school. When the war ended, it became an Ontario teachers college, known at that time as a Normal School.

East York Separate Elementary Schools

Many East York students attended local Roman Catholic Separate elementary schools, some of which were located in East York, while others were located nearby in the old city of Toronto and in Scarborough.

Borough of East York Separate Elementary Schools

1928   Holy Cross School. Although Father Robert Miller was the parish priest, the Toronto Catholic District School Board history records show that the school was established by Father J.F. Coughlin (Holy Cross Parish Priest), opened on Donlands Avenue, south of Cosburn Avenue.

---

16. East York Council minutes, June 1982
17. Interview with Joyce Crook, November 12, 2015
18. Interview with Mrs. Claire Cole, July 27, 2016

1939   St. Anselm's School was established on Bessborough Drive by Father Caulfield at the urging of Archbishop James McGuigan.

1952   Canadian Martyrs School, established by Father Peter Henricks, opened on Plains Road at the corner of Woodbine Avenue.

1962   St. Aloysius School opened on Sammon Avenue. Unlike all other elementary separate schools, it was not part of a separate Roman Catholic parish; however, it was built in order to respond to the rapid population growth in the area. The Metropolitan Separate School Board approached then East York Reeve True Davidson to find a site for the school, which subsequently was built on the site of the former Township Municipal Offices and Works yard at 443 Sammon Avenue. Although there is no official record of how the school acquired its name, Ayolisus Ambrosic, later Cardinal Ambrosic, was the parish priest at the nearby Holy Cross Church at the time. The school was closed in 2002 due to declining enrolment.

As well as these four schools located in the borough, East York students also attended the following nearby separate elementary schools:

1921   St. Brigid's School opened

1924   St. Dunstan School opened

1953   Our Lady of Fatima School opened

1969   St. Bernadette School opened

While a Separate School Board was elected by Separate School supporters to deal with elementary school matters, Separate School representatives were elected to the East York Board of Education by Separate School supporters to deal with secondary school matters since the provincial government only supported elementary Separate Schools financially. After 1984, when Ontario Premier Bill Davis announced provincial financial support would be extended to Separate Secondary Schools, Separate School representatives were no longer elected to the East York Board of Education.

Subsequently, the province completely reorganized the school boards, resulting in a Metropolitan Toronto Board, an East York School

Board, a Metropolitan Toronto French Language School Council, a Metropolitan Toronto Separate School Board, and a French Language Section of the Metropolitan Toronto Separate School Board.[19]

East York Collegiate
(Source: wikipedia.org)

Leaside High School
(Source: East York Foundation)

---

19. Archives, Toronto Catholic District School Board

Marc Garneau Collegiate Institute
(Source: 680news.com)

Danforth Park, later Oak Park, now demolished and replaced by
D.A. Morrison Middle School
(Source: East York Foundation)

Bessborough Public School
(Source: susannehudson.com)

William Burgess Elementary School
(Source: East York Foundation)

Secord School
(Source: East York Foundation)

Selwyn Elementary School
(Source: tdsb.on)

Thorncliffe Public School
(Source: theglobeandmail.com)

Cresecent Town Elementary School
(Source: scenesto.files.wordpress.com)

Earl Kitchener Public School
(Source: Jim Lister)

Hartman Jones Memorial Public School
(Source: East York Foundation)

Canadian Martyrs Separate School
(Source: EQAO website)

– Chapter 21 –

MUNICIPAL SERVICES

The First Township Budget
1925

Engineer Dept. – Salaries & Supplies	28,841.00
Roads and Bridges	79,100.00
Waterworks Dept.	14,630.00
Treasurer's Dept.	6,652.00
Clerk's Dept.	4,372.00
Assessment Dept.	5,772.00
Board of Health	3,000.00
Plumbing Dept.	2,260.00
Building Dept.	2,260.00
Police Dept.	8,570.00
Relief Dept.	19,260.00
School Attendance Officer	600.00
General Building Expense	5,687.00
Printing and Stationery	3,500.00
Office Furniture	3,000.00
Election Expenses	1,500.00
Postage and Revenue Stamps	3,200.00

Insurance	500.00
Accounting Fees	1,200.00
Law Costs	3,000.00
High School Grants	2,300.00
Municipal Grants	600.00
Bank Interest	3,500.00
Council Indemnity	4,000.00
General Municipal Expenses	2,000.00
License Inspector	700.00
Corporation's Share of Local Improvements	15,000.00
Land – Corporation payment 1925	1,000.00
Council of York Estimate *	58,000.00
Total	$284,004.00[1]

*Reimbursement to the Township of York for its land, buildings and equipment acquired by the Township of East York when it was created in 1924 having been previously part of the Township of York.

Municipal services in 1925 were provided by outside workers and inside workers as they are now, but by 1997, the number of services and the number of borough staff providing the services had greatly expanded.

Works Department

Of all the municipal staff, the most visible to the taxpayers are those in the Works Department because they do the outside jobs often in freezing temperatures, winter snow storms, teeming rain, or sweltering summer heat.

The Works Department, such as it was in the early days, was run on a shoe string. It occupied a small garage next to the municipal building, but it was much too small to house even the few trucks and equipment it had, which was left out in the open all winter long to rust, and depreciate. With a population of only 20,000 then, in an area of six square miles, it was impossible for the council to provide adequately for all the necessary services, as a result, the township fell far behind in building roads, sidewalks, and worse still—sewers. In wintertime, with just one small plough, they did their best to keep the main roads open, but people living on the side streets had to dig for themselves to get their cars out to the main street. Garbage was collected twice weekly, and burned in an incinerator

---

1. East York Council minutes, April 1925

located in what is now Cedarvale Park, much to the annoyance of the homeowners of the area.

Finding one's way around the township was difficult, especially should one be a stranger. If a street was identified at all, one had to look long and hard before finding the street sign tacked on the side of any building or house that happened to be anywhere in the vicinity of the street corner, and then was lucky if he was able to read it. It was not until the fifties that council corrected this fault, and it decided to have street name plates made in uniform style, and to mount them on posts on every corner, visible to pedestrians and motorists alike. Some council members of the day thought it was a shockingly extravagant idea, pointing out that even the city did not have uniform street signs, which was indeed true at the time, and they voted against it.

It was not until after the Depression of the thirties that the Works Department really got rolling, and was more adequately equipped. When the Hollinger Bus garage became available in 1953, when bus lines were taken over by the Toronto Transit Commission, the township bought it for a works garage. Later, when the property at the corner of O'Connor Drive and Woodbine Avenue (now the site of the Trillium) became too valuable to be occupied with a garage, a modern Works Department building was erected on Northline Road, and today equipment is kept under cover the year round, and properly maintained. Before moving on, we should mention a young feller by the name of Len Swain, the first superintendent, who occupied that position for forty years until his retirement a few years ago.[2]

Garbage, perhaps the most visible of all, was originally collected in open trucks. After the garbage men had picked over for themselves any "treasures" thrown out that day by the residents, the loads were dumped in the Don Valley or wherever there was a depression in a vacant field.[3] Dick Anderson, who worked thirty-two years for East York, told me he furnished his house with those treasures.[4] Later, the open trucks gave way to the garbage packer trucks with two persons to a truck.

When the Town of Leaside merged with the township, the Leaside garbage crews continued to be based at the Leaside works yard on

2. Bustin, Percy, *Memories: Early Days of East York*, Self –Published, 1976, 14–16

3. Interview with Jim Lister, July 25 & December 20, 2016

4. Interview with Dick Anderson, May 15, 2013

Canvarco Road and collect garbage in the former town, while the East York garbage crews based on Northline Road did the same in the former township. Over time, though, they all melded into the Borough Works Department.[5] By the time of the merger, garbage was being trucked to the Metro Transfer Station on Bermondsey from where it went to the Metro landfill site on Beare Road in Scarborough, and still later to the Maple landfill site in Vaughn Township.

When the City of Toronto outside workers went out on strike in 1967 and again in 1972, Metro Toronto closed the Bermondsey Transfer Station for the duration of the strike. East York workers never went out on strike but with the transfer station closed, the borough had no place to take the garbage. They had to stop the collection and lay off the forty or fifty garbage men until the Toronto strike was settled. One East York garbage man told me that while he was laid off, he went to Florida and had a great time. Then, when the strike was settled, he came back and was paid double time to clean up all the bags of garbage piled in Cedarvale Park and Trace Manes Park while the strike was on.

In 1942, the Township of East York workers organized a union, Local 114 of the National Union of Public Employees, which later became the Canadian Union of Public Employees (CUPE). When Bill Buss, the first union president, met with Bill Heaton, the township comptroller, to present the first union proposals, Heaton folded up his papers and walked out. In spite of that rude beginning, from then until amalgamation in 1998, East York employees never went out on strike. During all those years, both the union and management came to realize that it was in their joint best interests to bargain fairly and reasonably. Management understood the reasonable demands of younger workers for pay raises and of older workers for health and pension protection, while the union understood the reasonable needs of management to protect the taxpayers from drastic tax hikes in a municipality with a small industrial and commercial assessment base.[6]

But garbage crews aren't the only groups visible to the residents. When they looked out their windows, they would see Works Department employees filling potholes in winter with cold mix and in summer with

---

5. Interview with Jim Lister, July 25 & December 20, 2016
6. Interview with Jim Lister, July 25 & December 20, 2016

hot mix. They would be repairing ruptured water mains, often in the middle of the night in below freezing temperatures, and of course, the men driving the snow ploughs on the roads and later sidewalks as well, in conditions that you wouldn't walk your dog. Dick Anderson especially enjoyed picking up garbage on Christmas Day at time and a half overtime. Dick, like most old timers in the Works Department, did everything as needed—garbage collection, asphalt, concrete, heavy equipment, and flooding rinks—while the young guys, Dick told me, would say, "That's not my job."[7]

Initially, the Works Department men snow ploughed the roads. Later the job was contracted out to construction firms like Miller Paving, but their contract did not start until December 15. The first winter I served as mayor, 1977–1978, the snow falls prior to that date were enormous and all Miller's equipment was up in North Bay, unavailable to East York. The borough had to rely on one old grader inherited from Leaside. The residents' complaints snowed me under! I seriously believed that my time as mayor would be over after my first two-year term. But snow melts away and so do people's memories.

A few years later, we had several enormous snowfalls. This time, we had the equipment to deal with it, but not fast enough for some of our residents, particularly on the narrow streets lined with parked cars in the southeast community. One day the phone rang in my office with an irate East Yorker demanding to know when the snow would be plowed from his street. The Works commissioner, who had just come into my office, advised me that the equipment would be there in the next five minutes. Shortly afterwards, my phone rang again and I picked it up expecting to be thanked for clearing the snow off the caller's street. Not so—this was the first caller's next door neighbour demanding I get the ploughs off his street because they were costing him tax dollars. So it goes. You can't please everybody.

When Jim Lister was hired by the township in 1952, after he got out of the Canadian Navy, all the outside workers started in the Works Department, but Jim was assigned to the parks (parks and works were all together then). He estimates there were about seventy-five in the works at the time. Jim's first job was to climb a tree at Donlands and Sammon to

---

7. Interview with Dick Anderson, May 15, 2013

trim with a hand saw. There were no bucket trucks then and a ladder was too dangerous, so Jim, who had never climbed a tree before, put on spurs and a safety belt and up he went. No work clothes were issued to township employees at that time, so Jim wore his own clothes, as did all outside workers, until later when clothing became part of a union settlement. As a parks worker, Jim not only trimmed trees, but laid drains, put up fences, painted, cut glass, and removed weeds.[8]

Gradually, the Works Department was divided into various parts, including garbage, roads, water, and sewers, while the Parks Department became a separate entity.[9] In 1964, when Len Swain, who had worked for the Township since it was incorporated on January 1, 1924, retired as Works Department superintendent of operations, Council appointed new officials to head up the departments. Ulo Luksep was commissioner of works, Des Corcoran was parks commissioner, Duncan Little was treasurer, Bill McNinch was chief building inspector, and Jack Cannon was solicitor. That same year, Joe Vernon retired as welfare administrator and was replaced by G. Romanson.[10] Fortunately, this East York position was soon unnecessary when Metro Toronto became responsible for welfare.

Original outside workers 1924 Lloyd Forbes Burnett
(Source: Jim Lister)

---

8. Interview with Jim Lister, July 25 & December 20, 2016
9. Interview with Jim Lister, July 25 & December 20, 2016
10. *East Yorker*, June 1964

EY Waterworks Truck
(Source: East York Foundation)

Excavating Mortimer Rd
(Source: East York Foundation)

Cedarvale Avenue asphalt
(Source: East York Foundation)

Gledhill Trunk Sewage Line
(Source: Jim Lister)

Paving Donlands Ave
(Source: East York Foundation)

Newly completed incinerator
(Source: East York Foundation)

Workmen in incinerator
(Source: East York Foundation)

Inside Workers

Not so visible were the borough employees who were outside sometimes, but often inside. These included the engineers, building and plumbing inspectors, water meter readers, and enforcement officers. Almost invisible to the average taxpayer were the clerk, clerk's department, the treasurer (except at tax time), and the treasury department. As the township's first budget reveals, they were all in place by early 1925.[11]

As the population increased after WW II and East York grew from a rural township to a moderate-sized urban city, the municipal services provided by East York Council grew in number and in sophistication.

Parks and Recreation

In 1945, Premier George Drew's Progressive Conservative Ontario provincial government put in place the Physical Fitness Act, allocating money to municipalities to create and administer community recreation programs. Previously, the only organized recreation was provided by the schools and churches. Now, municipalities could do so as well. East York hired Stan Wadlow as a contract worker to initiate its recreation program. At first, he worked out of his home at 241 Queensdale Avenue, later running his recreation program from the north end of the gymnasium balcony at R.H. McGregor School, then from 995 Cosburn Avenue, and still later from the former Leaside Town Hall at 235 McRae Drive,

---

11. East York Council Minutes, April 1925

before finally settling in the Borough Municipal Offices at Coxwell and Mortimer Avenues.[12]

Stan Wadlow, with the help of service clubs and residents, developed the initial recreation programs and facilities for the township. At the same time, the Town of Leaside had developed similar programs and facilities, originally initiated by service clubs and residents but later further developed and administered by the Leaside Sports and Recreation Directors, Phil Stein and his successor, Bob Davidson.[13] When the merger of the township and the town occurred, the Borough Recreation Department operated with two directors for some time, until Bob Davidson resigned to return to teaching recreation at a community college. In 1968, when Des Corcoran retired as parks commissioner, Stan Wadlow was appointed to succeed him as commissioner of parks and recreation, while Ernie Heyes became director of recreation and Ross Swain became director of parks.[14] After Stan retired, his work as commissioner was carried on by his son Don Wadlow, Bonnie Lindsay, and Claire Tucker-Reid. When Ross Swain retired, he was succeeded by John McGill.[15] Much later, when Claire Tucker–Reid was appointed commissioner of parks, recreation, and operations, David Clark became director of recreation.

Clerk's Department

In 1932, in the depth of the Great Depression, the Township Council appointed Bill Heaton as comptroller with complete control of all the municipal departments and as the point man to deal with the Provincial Supervisor A. B. Gray.[16] After Heaton retired in 1959, his authority was divided among the clerk, the treasurer, the fire chief, and all the other department heads.[17] Each then reported to the Township Council personally, rather than reporting through a comptroller or chief administrative officer (CAO). Apparently, Mayors True Davidson, Willis

---

12. Wadlow, Stan, *East York Recreation, The Early Years*, Centennial College Press, Toronto, 1982, 1–2

13. Pitfield, Jane, Leaside, Natural Heritage Books, 1999, 168

14. Wadlow, Stan, *East York Recreation, The Early Years*, Centennial College Press, Toronto, 1982, 100–101

15. East York Council minutes, October 1993

16. East York Council minutes, January 1932

17. East York Council minutes, April 1959

Blair, Leslie Saunders, Alan Redway, and Dave Johnson found that to be satisfactory, since no CAO was appointed from 1959 to 1994. Staff reports came to Council directly through those responsible for their actions rather than being managed and filtered by a CAO, who could pass any resulting repercussion on to the underlings. The buck stopped with each of them. The position of CAO, which was to come later, merely added another layer of bureaucracy.

Human Resources

An added sophistication occurred when John Hart, the deputy treasurer, a former C.U.P.E. president, and later chief management representative during union negotiations, was appointed a personnel officer, a role that grew into a Human Resources Department.

Planning

Initially, the township had grown without any professional planning. But after the Provincial Legislature passed the Planning Act in 1946, the township appointed its first Planning Board, made up of Reeve Warren and four citizens. In 1958, East York adopted its first Official Plan, prepared for the township by the firm of Urban Planning Consultants.[18] After the opposition to apartment construction of apartments for Rexleigh Boulevard and on the Bayview Ghost property in 1959, the township appointed its first permanent Planning Director, Sandy McWilliams.[19] From then on, the new planning department did the planning for East York rather than consultants. When Sandy retired as commissioner, he was succeeded by Don Baxter, later by Martin Rendel, and still later by Rick Tomaszewicz.

While the Town of Leaside has always been considered a "planned community," it did not adopt an Official Plan and a comprehensive zoning by-law as authorized by the Ontario Planning Act until it was on the verge of merger with the Township of East York. Since Leaside never had its own planning department, those two key documents were prepared for the town by the consulting firm of Project Planning Associates. The Leaside Official Plan and zoning by-law enshrined the actual property

---

18. East York Council minutes, January 1958
19. East York Council minutes, April 1959

uses in Leaside as they existed in 1966. Leasiders have relied upon those documents ever since to defend and maintain the physical character of their community.

Traffic and Parking

The continuing increase of vehicles on East York streets resulted in the appointment of a staff person to deal with traffic issues such as stop streets, road bumps, traffic lights, and speed limits. Because many East York homes had no garages or driveways to park vehicles, the Borough Traffic Department became the Traffic and Parking Department, adding the duties of on-street permit parking and front yard parking. Bo Petroff, originally hired for by-law enforcement, became the first director of traffic and parking.

D.M.Tucker Clerk of EY
(Source: East York Foundation)

Duncan Little EY Treasurer
(Source: East York Foundation)

Bill Alexander
second Borough Clerk
(Source: Alan Redway)

John Hart
(Source: Alan Redway)

Management Restructuring

In 1994, the Borough Council called for proposals to review the structure and management of the municipality. The contract was awarded to George B. Cluff and Associates.[20] Why did they do this? Ray White, who started work in the borough as a summer student in 1976 and later became its director of communications and information technology, told me he felt it was a last-ditch attempt to save East York from amalgamation.[21]

The Cluff report, which the staff and even members of Council such as Case Ootes describes as "a boiler-plate report" similar, if not exactly the same, as Cluff had done for other municipalities,[22] was not well received by the Borough staff.[23] Among other things, Cluff recommended the establishment of a chief administrative officer (CAO), the elimination of sixteen staff positions, as well as the elimination of the Curling Rinks Board, the Leaside Gardens Board, the Stan Wadlow Complex and Community Centre Board, and the Todmorden Mills Board, all of which were staffed by non-paid appointed community volunteers.[24]

When Council approved the appointment of a CAO, lobbying for the appointment between Treasurer Eric Nichols and Works Commissioner Paul Cockburn began immediately. However, after Council appointed Virginia West, an outside applicant to the position, Nichols left the Borough and Council reduced its budget by terminating Cockburn soon after.[25]

Virginia West, the new CAO, recommended a sweeping management and staff reorganization, which Council adopted. Two commissioners, the fire chief, the clerk, and the treasurer, and three directors now reported to the CAO, and the CAO reported to Council—shades of Comptroller Bill Heaton. One commissioner was now in charge of the Parks, Recreation, and the Works Departments.[26]

Bill Alexander, who after joining the Borough in 1972 as the deputy clerk, served as the clerk of East York from January 1, 1977,

20. East York Council minutes, October 1994
21. Interview with Ray White, January 26, 2017
22. Interview with Case Ootes, February 1, 2017
23. Interview with Bill Alexander, January 4, 2017
24. East York Council minutes, January 1995
25. Interview with Bill Alexander, January 4, 2017
26. East York Council minutes, January 1995

until April 1, 1998, when the new megacity staff took over from the Borough staff, which then ceased to exist. Bill told me that each of the East York Commissioners, as well as other senior officials, including himself, were interviewed three times by the provincially appointed amalgamation Transition Committee. Former East York Mayor Willis Blair was a member of that committee. According to Bill, Willis had his eyes closed throughout his interviews. Bill was not hired by the new megacity.[27]

Bill Alexander told me that the Borough staff all felt like family. He says he isn't into tattoos, but if he was, he would have the East York flag as his tattoo.[28] Ray White said that the East York staff were all great friends and always there for the people of East York.[29] Dick Anderson said it was a good feeling being an East Yorker. He always felt like getting up to go to work at the Borough.[30]

Fire Fighters

"Even before incorporation, East York had three volunteer brigades; these were located in the east, centre, and west in areas corresponding to the school district. The firemen's only remuneration was a small annual grant to cover wear and tear of clothing. Three fire trustees were elected annually at a ratepayer's meeting held for the purpose; these posts were later consolidated into a township-wide fire board.

"In the early days, most areas of the township had no piped water supply, so that firefighting consisted of the formation of a bucket brigade from the nearest well. In the east-end, the equipment consisted of what was commonly known as a "banana wagon," a two-wheeled cart with the fire-hose wound around a drum between the wheels. Handles extended at right angles to the drum and the men grasped these to pull the vehicle. During school hours, it was apparently a common sight, when the local siren sounded, to see the boys from the higher grades in the public school rush out to pick up the fire equipment and answer the call.

The west end also boasted a banana cart, but soon felt the need of a truck also. Among the volunteers in this area were R.M. Leslie and John

---

27. Interview with Bill Alexander, January 4, 2017
28. Interview with Bill Alexander, January 4, 2017
29. Interview with Ray White, January 26, 2017
30. Interview with Dick Anderson, May 15, 2013

Warren, both subsequently reeves of the township. It was considered the smart thing to be a volunteer and there was usually a long waiting list.

When the first equipment arrived, it was housed in a garage at the corner of Gowan and Pape Avenues; this was handy since some of the volunteers had their place of business within a stone's throw. Training was carried out under the watchful eye of Chief George Leggett in the basement of William Burgess School and in Rivercourt. The men became proficient with the car and could catch a hydrant, lay a line, and hit a given target in record time. When the Model-T Ford fire-truck arrived, a garage to house it was erected on Gowan Avenue just west of Pape.

In the center section of the borough, the male employees in the Township offices acted as firemen during office hours. A call would come into the switchboard, the operator would pull a switch and the siren would blast forth. Immediately, the male staff would rush for their coats, boots, and helmets, and the operator would call out the address as they dashed by. Meanwhile, the works clerk in the garage office would run out to Sammon Avenue to direct traffic, while one of the draftsmen in the Engineer's Department would start the fire truck, jump into the cab and drive out to the roadway, with the rest of the crew clambering onto the platforms which ran along both sides of the truck.

In 1928, the first permanent force was formed in the borough. This consisted of a fire chief and eight firemen. The Township purchased a fire truck, which was located, along with the crew, in a converted garage situated on Holborne Avenue just east of Cedarvale Avenue. The men were paid twenty-five dollars and they worked eight-hour shifts, seven days a week."[31]

Percy Bustin remembered the development of fire fighting in the central part of the township this way:

At the time of incorporation, the township had no organized fire department; our earliest fighters were all volunteers. Whenever there was a fire, a siren mounted on top of the old municipal building shrieked loud enough to awaken the dead, and the volunteer fire fighters dropped whatever they were doing, and came rushing to the building from all directions. We shall never forget our first sight of the boys in action; they came galloping along the street pulling a hose cart behind them—they never even had a

---

31. Davidson, True, *The Golden Years of East York*, Centennial College Press, 1976, 59

horse. We can call to mind a few of those volunteer firemen; Percy Green, Art Padfield, Jimmy Michael, Fred Smith, and John Warren. In 1929, a fulltime Township Fire Department was established, yet like most of the departments those days, it was poorly equipped. It was not until five years later the first fire hall was built on Cosburn Avenue. The first chief was Tom Paveling; deputy chief, Percy Green; other members were George Rousby, Dave Low, Punch Wilson, Fred Smith, George Leggett, George Wilking, and Gord Shea. Their salary was $25.00, and they worked eight-hour shifts seven days a week. When twenty years later, the writer was first elected to the council and was made chairman of the Fire Committee, there was no fire hall in the east end. An ancient pumper was kept in an old wooden garage on Holbourne Avenue and beneath the garage was a hole in the ground where the firemen spent their eight-hour shifts.[32]

Sid Kerrigan who lived nearby on Gledhill Avenue was one of the firefighters who spent eight-hour shifts in that hole in the ground. He served on the fire department for many years, later as a captain well known for training new recruits who became known as "Sid's kids."[33] "To say we were shocked when with Alderman Chandler, a member of the committee, we inspected it, is putting it mildly; it was unbelievable. Quick action followed, and two years later the firemen moved into a modern fire hall on Woodbine Avenue, and the old pumper was replaced with up-to-date firefighting equipment including an aerial ladder. Today our Fire Department is as good as, or better than, fire departments anywhere, and our firemen are unequaled. In 1958, of all the municipalities in Canada with a population of over 10,000, East York had the lowest per capita fire loss—so said the Dominion Department of Public Affairs.[34]

Secord-area residents recall the beginning of fire fighting in their community this way:

"The Secord Area used to be in Fire Section No. 8 of the County of York. The fire brigade was made up of volunteers from the area who organized themselves to fight any fires. Before part of Little York annexed to East Toronto in the 1890s it had its own Little York fire hall on the west side of Dawes Road north of Danforth Avenue behind Paterson's Grocers,

32. Bustin, Percy, *Memories: Early Days of East York*, Self –Published, 1976, 12
33. Interview with Sid Kerrigan, April 28, 2017
34. Interview with Paul Moffat and Paul Enright, September 9, 2016

which was on the corner. It disappeared from the 1901 directory when the area with the fire hall became part of East Toronto, but on the basis of what we were told in an interview, we believe that this fire hall was still there until 1910 or so.

"Probably in the late 1800s and early 1900s the local people continued to have their own system of protection and did not depend on East Toronto's fire system too much. A shrill whistle on the railway roundhouse blew if there was a fire. It would bleat out so many times depending on the fire's location. Men from all around, including those in the railroad yards would run to get the hand-reel to put out the fire. We believe the hand-reel was kept in the former fire hall on Dawes Road.

"The organized fire brigade which served this area, after the part of Little York south of Balfour Avenue annexed to East Toronto, was called the East Toronto Fire Company. It was based in the fire hall on Main Street south of Gerrard Street. Later in the 1920s the volunteer fire department of Fire Section No. 8 was formed under Chief Seth Mawson. The department's equipment consisted of two hand wagons. The hand wagon was made up of a tongue bar where the hose was wrapped around with two big wheels on either side. It was commonly called a banana wagon. The fire brigade was called the banana brigade, as a result. Sometimes the banana cart was pulled by a team of horses. However, most of the time the volunteers had to pull the banana cart by hand which was hard work. At this time, one of the hand wagons was located on Barker Avenue in Danforth Park and the other was in the girls' schoolyard at Secord School in a hut at the corner of Secord and Barrington.

"The fire brigade was made up of men and boys. The boys' brigade answered fire calls during the day, the men at night. Later on, the boys answered most of the calls, day or night. The siren was located on top of a windmill tower, beside the hut and it would go off when someone opened the door of the hut. One of the members of the Secord boys' fire brigade remembers a period of about three months, when the boys' brigade was called out several times on false alarms. The siren, he recalls, would go off at about 1:30 soon after classes had started, and the boys would be off, pulling the banana wagon. Oddly, the fire was always a long distance away. After running that long distance to the fire, the boys would return slowly, arriving back just in time to be dismissed from school. The fire alarm caused a lot of excitement in the school. Many kids followed the fire brigade to the fire. They thought that it was great fun. They did not think of the fact that some poor family was losing its home. The houses were made of wood and tar paper and burned very quickly. People used to say that the boys got there in time to sift the ashes. There weren't very many hydrants. They had to hook up to the hydrants and then run to the fire. There actually were quite a few hydrants because of the materials which were in the houses. There was a fire almost every night along Chisholm.

"Seth Mawson, chief of the volunteers, held practice drills for his men when the brigade was first formed. However, the first alarm showed that they still had something to learn. It was late Sunday night when Seth heard the siren. Stopping only to put on his rubber coat over his ankle-length night shire, he raced to the wagon, but found no volunteers. After several minutes had passed the men began to arrive, dressed in their Sunday suits, their ties neatly in place at their collars. Their leader was angry. He told them that if the fire had not been a false one, the house would have burnt to the ground by the time they arrived.

"In 1926, the Secord area was taken over by the Danforth Park fire brigade, when a new truck was purchased. It was a very small Model-T Ford, and a fire hall at Barker Avenue in Danforth Park was built to shelter it. Thereafter it was called the Secord-Danforth volunteer fire brigade. Seth Mawson used to turn a hand siren when the truck was on its way to the fire. As a result of the change in area, the siren tower was dismantled and the banana brigade was dissolved. The new truck caused problems between the Secord-Danforth brigade and the Greenwood brigade. It happened that the Greenwood brigade got to their fires more quickly than Chief Mawson's brigade, although they weren't in his district. There were a couple of causes for the delay. Calls to Chief Mawson had to be relayed over the phone and it was not possible to reach him at once, whereas the Greenwood truck was kept at the township offices where people were more likely to phone. Also, the Secord-Danforth brigade did not have qualified drivers like the Greenwood brigade. Sometime they had to send as far as Woodbine Avenue for a driver before the truck could answer an alarm.

"In 1928, the fire sections were joined into one force under full-time Chief Tom Paveling. Full-time drivers for each section were hired from amongst the volunteers. Volunteers were to play a key role in the success of the force until 1945 when the department became fully paid for all positions. The Second World War caused a manpower shortage which brought this about. Since 1967 the fire station serving the Secord area has been on Woodbine Avenue." [35]

"Paveling started as a driver mechanic, being the first full-time employee on the volunteer fire department. As the department grew, he became chief and reorganized the department in 1932 as part-paid and part-volunteer. After WWII, the township had a fully-paid fire service. Tom Paveling served as fire chief from 1928 until his sudden death in 1965. After Paveling died, George Rousby succeeded him as chief until 1967.

George Rousby was succeeded as fire chief by Ernie Bell, who had been Leaside's fire chief from 1929 until the town's merger with East York in 1967. Bell served as East York fire chief from 1967 to 1975. He took two separate and distinct fire departments and molded them into one efficient department.

When Ernie Bell retired, Art Cook became the chief. Art had had a long and distinguished service with East York after his time overseas fighting fires in London, England, during the Blitz. Unfortunately, however, Art Cook, an excellent fire fighter and deputy fire chief, lacked the management skills needed for the role of chief, so Ernie Bell came out of retirement to lead the department again and to mentor Deputy Chief George Kerfoot and Training Officer John Miller, both of whom later became chief of the department, in that order. George served thirty-seven years on the department until he retired after serving as chief from 1980 to 1989. He was succeeded by John Miller, the last East York fire chief.

After the Fire Department became a professional fire-fighting force, it was located in three stations. In the west end, it was at 256 Cosburn Avenue at Donlands, after moving there from Gowan in 1945. The station was completely renovated in 1994. In 1953, the east-end station moved from Holborne Avenue, where it had been located from 1925 to its new location at 1313 Woodbine Avenue. When the township merged with Leaside, the Borough of East York then had its third station at 231 McRae Drive at Randolph Road. That station was attached to the former Leaside Town Hall, which housed the borough's Engineering Department until it was sold as surplus to the municipality's needs in 1980. When the Leaside

---

35. Fagan, Lu Ann, *The Secord Area*, East York Board of Education, 1974, 85

Town Hall was sold, the McRae fire station was legally severed from the town hall and continued to serve as a fire station for the Leaside and Thorncliffe neighbourhoods of the borough.

In 1981, the borough named the Woodbine Station in honour of Tom Paveling and the McRae Station in honour of Ernest N. Bell.[36]

Prior to the township's merger with Leaside, there were fires, explosions, and other tragedies over the years, but some stand out:

1947	A roof fire at a house on Heath Street in Bennington Heights spread to the attic, exploding hundreds of 303 calibre bullets and 12-gauge shotgun shells. "It sounded like a war," said the home owner. "The firemen didn't know what was going on. Luckily, the bullets missed them." The firemen fought the flames for half an hour.[37]
1948	Ten occupants of 118 Donlands Avenue were forced to flee when fire was discovered in the middle of the night. The flames were visible more than a mile away. East York and Toronto firemen battled the blaze for more than three hours before it was brought under control.[38]
1949	A spectacular blaze completely destroyed the clubhouse of the Woobine Golf and Country Club (in today's Woodbine Gardens area).[39]
1949	Two firemen suffered first-degree burns on their hands and face dousing a fire at 184 Chisholm Avenue when trucks from the Cosburn station answered the call.[40]
1954	Firemen and police rescued a CNR section man and his family from the flooded Don Valley during Hurricane Hazel.[41]
1955	A mid-afternoon gas explosion shook the 131 Tiago bungalow separating the porch from the rest of the house.

---

36. East York Council minutes, 1981
37. *Toronto Telegram,* June 1947
38. *Toronto Telegram,* December 29, 1948
39. *Toronto Telegram,* January 8, 1949
40. *Toronto Telegram,* July 8, 1949
41. *Toronto Telegram* October 16, 1954
42. *Toronto Telegram,* March 25, 1955
40. *Toronto Telegram,* July 8, 1949
41. *Toronto Telegram* October 16, 1954

Children in a schoolyard two hundred yards away were showered with cinders.[42]

1956   An explosion blew a six-room brick bungalow in Parkview Hills to pieces. It hurled the shattered roof skyward and blew out the walls, injuring five people who were in the house at the time. The house was heated by oil but a leak in a gas line, which runs down the street, was blamed for the explosion.[43]

1957   Firemen from East York, Leaside, and North York battled thirty-foot flames from a spectacular paper fire in a converted railway roundhouse off Laird Drive owned by E.S. & A. Robinson. At one point, the roof caved in at one end of the building. The fire was still flickering twenty hours after the fire broke out.[44]

1959   A mother and her three children perished in a fire in a house on Woodycrest Avenue on Mother's Day, while the father was working in Oshawa playing piano with a dance band. Investigators found cigarette butts beside the mother's bed.[45]

1962   A natural gas explosion followed by a fire ripped through a Denton Avenue home. The blast blew out one wall, left another bulging, and collapsed the roof. It lifted the sole occupant, a sixty-one-year-old woman with a heart condition, out of her chair as she sat watching TV and tossed her several feet. It also shattered the windows in the homes on either side.[46]

1963   Five attached homes at 12, 14, 16, 18, and 20 Westwood Avenue were gutted by fire, leaving twenty-five persons homeless, including ten children, but none were injured.[47]

1966   Faulty wiring was blamed for a fire on Aldwych Avenue, resulting in the death of four children ages four, three, two, and ten months, while the mother had dozed in front of the

42. *Toronto Telegram*, March 25, 1955
43. *Toronto Telegram*, February 25, 1956
44. *Toronto Telegram*, May 17, 1957
45. *Toronto Telegram*, May 11, 1959
46. *Toronto Telegram*, March 2, 1962
47. *Toronto Telegram*, April 9, 1963

television set and father was at work. Firemen used ladders and breathing apparatus to enter the house. They searched on their hands and knees through deep water in the basement and then applied mouth to mouth resuscitation to one child, who died the following day.[48]

1966   There was no fire involved, but as first responders, East York fire fighters were called to the scene of a disaster at 37 Notley Place. Leonard May's house, likely built on piles of construction fill, had slid into Taylor Creek ravine. Unfortunately, Mr. May, who worked nearby at Rowland Motors, had gone home for lunch that day when he felt the ground shifting. He went out in the backyard to see what was happening. Then the whole house gave way and he was buried under it. Nothing has been built since on that site.[49]

The merger of the East York and Leaside Fire Departments in 1967 was achieved smoothly, not by council or fire officials negotiating the merger, but rather by a meeting of the two fire fighters' union executives. Norm Holmes, Paul Enright, Doug Ranger, George Kerfoot, Bill Judge, John McGurk, and Bob Rankin sat down together and agreed how to merge the East York Fire Fighters' Association Local 418 with the Leaside Fire Fighters' Association Local 1025. It was agreed that the new association would have two executive members from each of the former departments. After the two associations merged, Norm Holmes (from Leaside) became the new president, George Kerfoot (from East York) the secretary, Paul Enright (from Leaside) the Treasurer, and Bill Judge (from East York) as director.[50]

The fire fighters recall many other harrowing times:

The Bate Chemical fire and explosion on Beechwood Drive in the Don Valley stands out in their memory. Bate, which had another plant on Commercial Road in the Leaside industrial area, made resins for paint. The explosion on Beechwood sent plumes of flames and smoke high into

---

48. *Toronto Telegram*, December 1966
49. Interview with Jay and Pat Burford, January 26, 2016
50. Interview with Paul Moffat and Paul Enright, September 9, 2016

the sky. The fire fighters used foam but had to lay hose all the way from Hassard Avenue near Pape and O'Connor, down into the valley to get enough water to fight the fire. The fire lasted so long that several fire fighter platoon shifts took place before it was brought under control.

1980   The fire that was fought under the most frigid winter conditions occurred on Redway Road when the roof caught fire while Teperman Wreckers were dismantling the former Crothers Caterpillar equipment buildings. During the seventeen hours required to put out the fire, the department's pumper trucks froze and Chief Ernie Bell had to bring in steam jennies to thaw them out.

1981   A backhoe used in storm sewer construction caught a gas line by mistake. In the process of warning residents in the area about the subsequent leak, a borough inspector, John Megaw, rang the doorbell at 224 Mortimer Avenue. The resulting spark caused an explosion that destroyed the house and severely damaged the houses on either side, while hurling the inspector right across the road. Fortunately, no one was killed, but the inspector suffered a broken leg.

1981   While the Woodbine Bridge was closed to traffic for almost a year when the bridge was being reconstructed for safety reasons, a fire department pumper truck and firefighters were stationed at Paul Willison Motors on the east side of the Taylor Massey Creek ravine at St. Clair and O'Connor while the bridge was closed. Because there were few fire calls in the area during that time, it was not difficult to get fire fighters to volunteer for duty at the Paul Willison fire station.

1987   The department was the first responder to the collapse of part of Millwood Road south of the railway overpass when a broken water main caused the roadway to slide into the Don Valley. Leaside was cut off and without telephone service for several months. While the telephone service was out, the fire department sent a pumper truck driving through Leaside streets in the event of an emergency.

1989   Another gas explosion destroyed a house on the north-
        east corner of Sprigdale and Coxwell when construction
        equipment hit an unmarked gas line because no locater had
        been requested earlier. The worker went for coffee and the
        house blew up.[51]

In spite of continuing calls to amalgamate the six Metro fire
departments as had been done with thirteen Metro police departments
in 1956, East York maintained a thoroughly trained, efficient, up to date,
and independent fire service until the total amalgamation of Toronto on
January 1, 1998.

At the time of amalgamation, the Borough Fire Department had a
staff of 140 stationed in three fire halls at 231 McRae Drive, 256 Cosburn
Avenue, and 1313 Woodbine Avenue.[52]

Fire Brigade (unidentified)
(Source: East York Foundation)

---

51. Interview with Paul Moffat and Paul Enright, September 9, 2016
52. East York Council minutes, December 1997

1935 EY Fire Chief Tom Pavling 1932
(Source: East York Foundation)

Fire Chief Rousby
(Source: East York Foundation)

Fire Chief Ernie Bell
(Source: East York Foundation)

EY Fire Chief Arthur Cook
(Source: EY Fire Dept)

EY Fire Chief George Kerfoot
(Source: Alan Redway)

EY Fire Chief John Miller
(Source: Alan Redway)

Norm Holmes
(Source: EY Fire Dept)

Paul Enright
(Source: EY Fire Dept)

Bill Judge
(Source: EY Fire Dept)

Sid Kerrigan 1970
(Source: EY Fire Dept)

Holborne Fire Hall
(Source: EY Fire Dept)

Woodbine Fire Hall
(Source: East York Foundation)

McRae Fire Station and
Head Quarters
(Source: East York Foundation)

Cosburn Fire Station
(Source: East York Foundation)

House Fire
(Source: East York Then and Now website)

Diesel Equip Fire Oct 1978
(Source: Fire Dept)

Hydro

"A year or two before East York was incorporated as a separate municipality, Sir Adam Beck, the founder of Ontario Hydro paid a visit to our area, and spoke to a packed gathering in a little mission hall (forerunner of Woodbine United Church) which stood on Gledhill Avenue, now the site of the Oak Park Junior High School, and at the meeting he made a promise that in the very near future electric power would be available to the public at cost. It was not however, until a few years later in 1925 that the East York Commission was set up, and his promise became true."[53]

Prior to May 1, 1925, East York hydro power was supplied by Toronto Hydro. "Since over a half of the East York area was still market gardens, or non-subdivided vacant land awaiting the development that was to come, with thousands of homes occupying the land, customers were few. There were 5,600 domestic accounts, 116 commercial, and just 19 residential. The two best customers were the Don Valley Paper Company, (successors to the Taylor Brothers paper mills,) and the brickyards. Revenue the first year was $168,000.

"The Hydro Commission's first chairman was Mr. Albert Jennings, a postal employee, after whom the present Hydro building is named. Other members of the first commission were; Horace Walsh, and Robert McGregor, then reeve, and ex-officio. At the beginning Hydro had only twelve employees, and the total number of vehicles—one, a horse and wagon. One of the first employees was Mr. Jimmy Wickham, who was not only the first manager, but served in that capacity for over forty years. Others who gave long years of service were; Bruce Wallace, secretary-treasurer for thirty-seven years, Sterling McCleary foreman for thirty-eight years, Robert Humphries forty years, and Helen Beale thirty-six years. Mr. Jennings was a commission member for twenty-two years." [54]

Jim Balmer joined East York Hydro in 1950. There were no bucket trucks to access wires, transformers, or street lights at that time. Hydro linemen had to reach the wires by climbing up with spurs on their boots to dig into the wooden poles to hold them as they shinnied upward secured by a safety belt with hands protected from an electric shock by rubber gloves. This became even more dangerous when the courts decided that it was

---

53. Bustin, Percy, *Memories: Early Days of East York*, Self –Published, 1976, 16
54. Bustin, Percy, *Memories: Early Days of East York*, Self –Published, 1976, 17

legal to staple signs to wooden Hydro poles on municipal property. The staples often ripped the linemen's rubber gloves, providing an opening for electric current to jolt or even electrocute a skilled Hydro lineman.

Balmer himself was seriously injured when he fell thirty feet to the ground on Pape Avenue. At first, he thought he had broken his back, but he landed on his elbow, which was displaced by the fall and driven almost up to his shoulder. It was no fun when the surgeon at East General put it back in place, nor was the weight lifting he did after the surgery that straightened and strengthened his arm.[55]

The East York Hydro office building was constructed at 175 Memorial Park between Coxwell and Durant in 1951. Previously, it had been located next to the original municipal works yard and police station at 443 Sammon Avenue. The storage and main frames were then moved to 3 Dohme at the corner of O'Connor Drive.[56]

When Ontario Hydro converted from twenty-five-cycle to sixty-cycle power in order to standardize the entire province to the same cycle, East York Hydro was directly involved. Each home was surveyed well ahead of time for the appliances that needed attention. Some, such as electric clocks, fans, and small appliances had to be scrapped, but a homeowner could buy a new compatible one for a comparable value. It was a massive and costly undertaking.[57]

Jimmy Wickham recalled his troubles when the first cable was laid underground, "as fast as laid, the ground hogs chewed it up resulting in constant repairs." The Hydro Commission minutes state that the trouble has now been overcome.[58]

Wickham was succeeded as the general manager of Hydro in 1966 by Jack Shand.[59] In 1967, Jack Christie was elected for the first of many times as a hydro commissioner with his own ideas about underground wiring:

Underground Wiring—Not the Way to go

Putting all Hydro wires underground was something I wanted and it seemed that most people in East York agreed. But when Hydro Manager

---

55. Interview with Jim and Charlotte Balmer, October 17, 2015
56. East York Hydro Commission minutes, 1951
57. East York Hydro Commission minutes, 1950
58. East York Hydro Commission minutes, 1966
59. East York Hydro Commission minutes, 1966

Jack Shand explained the high cost factor resulting in increased Hydro rates, I went back to the people at a ratepayers' meeting and explained that placing the cables underground would result in noticeable increases in the Hydro bills. I offered the option of "improved overhead" in which we would be able to remove the ugly cross-arms that marked all the Hydro poles of the day. The crowd of about 200 voted unanimously in favour of improved overhead and that ended my crusade for underground wiring in East York. Later I learned that any underground outages take longer to locate and cost more to repair.[60]

An excellent example of what Jack Christie was speaking about is the underground wiring along Millwood Road from Overlea Drive to the CPR overpass, which has been the source of constant outages and regular traffic disruption resulting from the pavement being torn up and repaired.

Jim Balmer, who worked on the East York-Leaside hydro merger, told me that once that Toronto Hydro learned that the merger was going to take place, it replaced all the new wire in the Hydro vaults under Millwood Road with old used wires. That, says Jim, is the real source of the outages and traffic disruption that continues to this day.[61]

Hurricane Hazel in September 1954 is indelibly imprinted on Jim Balmer's memory. The Hydro Department stored their supplies and equipment in the Don Valley, where the Todmorden Mills historic site is located today. Arriving soon after the storm, Jim marvelled at how wide the Don River had become and to see Hydro poles floating down the river. That day, an East York Hydro crew rescued a man hanging from a tree in the middle of the flooded river.[62]

The merger of the Township with the Town of Leaside presented East York Hydro with another enormous challenge:

"From its incorporation as a town until its merger with the township in 1967, Leaside's electric power infrastructure and its power supply were merely a part of the Toronto Hydro system, whereas, the former Township of East York had discovered early on that it would be less expensive if it built its own electrical supply infrastructure and bought

---

60. Christie, Jack, *The Generation of Change*, Self–Published, 189
61. Interview with Jim and Charlotte Balmer, October 17, 2015
62. Interview with Jim and Charlotte Balmer, October 17, 2015

its power directly from Ontario Hydro rather than from Toronto Hydro. The merger of the town and township meant that in order for all borough residents to receive the same lower electricity costs, the new borough had to buy the Leaside system from Toronto Hydro. While East York taxpayers had to compensate Toronto to the tune of $1.5 million when it bought the Leaside system, no similar compensation was paid to East York taxpayers when Toronto acquired the East York Hydro System at the time of amalgamation in 1998."[63]

When Jim Balmer worked with fellow East York Hydro lineman the famous Fred "Toppy" Topham, V.C., both the park and the street had already been named for him. Later, after Topham had left East York Hydro to work as a lineman for Toronto Hydro, he and East York linemen Jim Balmer and John Shelton worked together separating the Leaside hydro system from Toronto Hydro and connecting it to the East York hydro system. Among other things, that job required Jim and John to climb down a ladder suspended from the side of the Leaside Bridge in order to splice the wires running under the bridge, protected only with their safety belts, which had to be detached and reattached as they moved along. John Shelton never told his wife Elizabeth about that adventure. When Jim Balmer told her after John had passed away, she, most understandably, had a fit. Charlotte Balmer, Jim's wife knew about it at the time but apparently remained calm. Her father had been the chief of the East York Police Department so she had grown up with constant and potential danger in her family.[64]

Before he was elected as a hydro commissioner, Jack Christie had advocated unifying the hydro and the water meter reading. After he was elected, "At one hydro meeting, I proposed merging the hydro and water meter reading procedures to negate the duplicate process and facilitate only one reading every two months. The commission agreed and forwarded the suggestion to the East York Council. They ordered staff to study the proposal. Their report included a rejection because of a negative potential savings (it wouldn't be as great as expected), merging of union contracts would be difficult, the union affected by elimination would strongly object, ratepayers would be adversely affected by receiving their

---

63. Redway, Alan, Recollections
64. Interview with Jim and Charlotte Balmer, October 17, 2015

electricity and water charges on one bill and due at the same time. That ended that proposal, but not forever."[65]

Fortunately, Jack said he made no promises during his election campaign, just statements telling people what aspirations he had and what he would try to accomplish. Later, Jack Christie became the chairman of the Hydro Commission. True Davidson once described Jack as "the most able public servant in Metropolitan Toronto today." In the forward of Jack's book, *The Generation of Change*, I wrote, "Jack was not only extremely knowledgeable, dedicated, hardworking, and trustworthy but he was also one of, if not the best person I ever met in public life, at questioning staff, getting to the root of an issue, and spending tax dollars more carefully then if they were his own." Many times as a Member of Parliament and Minister of Housing, I longed to bring Jack Christie to Ottawa to help straighten out our nation's finances. Hydro General Manager Jack Shand said that he had never seen a commissioner so deeply involved in commission affairs.[66]

When Jack Shand retired, Alex Jordan became general manager in 1987. Alex was succeeded by Murray Lennox in 1990.[67]

At the time amalgamation occurred on January 1, 1998, East York Hydro had one hundred employees, of which seventy-two were members of the International Brotherhood of Electrical Workers Local 636.[68]

Original Staff EY Hydro-ElectricCommission
(Source: East York Foundation)

65. Christie, Jack, *The Generation of Change*, Self–Published, 190
66. Redway, Alan, Recollections
67. East York Hydro Commission minutes, 1990
68. East York Council minutes and East York Hydro Commission minutes, 1997

| Hydro Office 1948-1997 | Jim Balmer |
| *(Source: East York Foundation)* | *(Source: Jim Balmer)* |

Libraries

"Today, it is almost unbelievable that prior to 1950, East York had no public library. In the year 1943, a newly-chartered Kiwanis Club established children's libraries in three of our public schools: McGregor, Burgess, and Oak Park. Realizing that the actual running of these libraries could best be handled by the Board of Education, the Kiwanians handed a cheque for $5,000 to the board, to which the board added another $5,000. The first library was at Burgess School, and was officially opened by the then Premier of Ontario, the Honorable George Drew. This was the beginning of libraries in East York."[69]

In the Township of East York, the need for library service was keenly felt in the days following the end of World War II. On January 1, 1946, at the request of various individuals and groups, the electorate of the township voted to establish a public library. The vote was 4,548 for, 542 against. Later that same year, the first Library Board was appointed. Its members were:

Mr. S. Walter Stewart
Mr. V. McMullen
Mrs. L. Bradshaw
Mr. G. Heaton
Mr. J. Warren

---

69. Bustin, Percy, *Memories: Early Days of East York*, Self –Published, 1976, 20

Planning was soon underway, and in 1948, arrangements were made to have the Toronto Public Library operate the proposed library under the direction and control of the East York Library Board.

The first library, located on the northeast corner of Coxwell and Mortimer Avenues, was officially opened on April 26, 1950, and was an instant success. By the end of the year, there were 2500 registered members and a total of 49,000 books had been circulated. As the years went by, membership continued to grow. It soon became apparent that larger, more spacious facilities would be needed to keep pace with the growing demands for library service.

Accordingly, a site was chosen for a new central library. On October 3, 1960, the S. Walter Stewart Building at Memorial Park and Durant Avenues was officially opened by the Honorable R.H. McGregor, M.P. for York East. Designed by Mr. Harold Witmer, an East York resident, and named in honour of a long-time member of the Library Board and pioneer for library services in the township.[70]

S. Walter Stewart served on the Library Board from 1946 until his death in 1969. In appreciation for the naming of the library in his honour, Stewart donated nine of his A.Y. Jackson paintings to the library.

The building was designed like a flying saucer. The furniture was provided by the T. Eaton Company. There was a large children's room, and the furnishings for that and for the auditorium on the lower level with seating for over two hundred people were donated by the Kiwanis Club of East York. In 1995, the auditorium was named for John S. Ridout in recognition of his many years of service to the Library Board and for tireless supporting and promoting East York history.[71]

Reporting on the opening of the library Nov. 18, 1960, a *Toronto Star* headline read a "Weird Pylon Triples Library Circulation." That weird pylon was the work of avant-garde Toronto sculptor Gerald Gladstone. The Pylon consists of two 35-feet-tall concrete curved columns weighing 105 tons. Curiously, the curved columns resemble the shape of the City of Toronto's new city hall not yet built in 1960. At the bottom of the pylon was a reflecting pond with lights and on top within the two concrete columns was peculiar shaped pieces of bronze.

---

70. East York Library, a History, Publisher, East York Library, 1974, 1
71. Michailidis, John, The East York Mirror, 2008

Today the reflecting pond is filed in with cement and the two concrete columns are showing signs of age.

Reporting about the Pylon, the *Toronto Star* quoted East Yorkers who referred to the odd structure as "a monstrosity" and "a mess of tin cans and bed springs."

East York Reeve Jack Allen defended the Pylon saying, "It's out of this world and exactly what was wanted." Reeve Allen pointed out library book circulation had increased 189 per cent since the new library opened. So curious were people to catch a glimpse of the flying saucer-shaped library and Gerald Gladstone's Pylon that police had to control traffic on the usually sleepy streets of Durant and Memorial Park.[72]

Further expansion of the library occurred the following year when service was extended to the western part of the township with the official opening of the Todmorden Room in October 1961 in the East York Community Centre at Pape and Torrens Avenues. The next year saw the beginning of book service to the senior citizens at East York Acres. Started in December 1962, it was enthusiastically received and has continued to rank high in popularity. Throughout these years before the school library system was developed as it is today, the library cooperated with the East York Board of Education in extending services to boys and girls in the schools. Wherever possible, schools were visited and the library brought to the students.

During the first part of 1966, responsibility for the operations and administrative functions, which had been under contract to the Toronto Public Library, were gradually assumed and taken over by the East York Public Library.[73]

Borough of East York

The amalgamation of the Township of East York and the Town of Leaside on January 1, 1967, marked a new milestone in the library's development. In this year, the two library systems were smoothly and progressively joined together."[74] When the merger took place, the main Leaside Library was located at 165 McRae Drive in what had previously

---

72. Michailidis, John, The East York Historical Society, Tidbits, 2015
73. East York Library, a History, Publisher, East York Library, 1976, 2
74. East York Library, a History, Publisher, East York Library, 1976, 3

been a part of Trace Manes Park with branches in Thorncliffe Park School, Rolph Road School, and Chapel-In-The-Park, as well as a book service for the senior citizens at Central Park Lodge on William Morgan Drive in Thorncliffe.[75]

"In answer to the growing need for library service in the eastern part of the Borough, Woodbine Gardens Branch was officially opened in April 1969 in Harmony Hall at Dawes Road and Gower Street. This was followed a year later with the official opening of the Thorncliffe Branch at 48 Thorncliffe Park Drive on October 5, 1970. Constructed to keep pace with the continuing development in and around that part of the borough, this branch was designed as a multi-purpose building with the library on the upper floor, and day-care and recreational facilities on the lower level." [76]

In 1973, another book service for senior citizens was established at True Davidson Acres.[77] The next year, after the borough purchased the ground floor of a two-storey condominium building at Dawes Road and moved the Woodbine Gardens branch to that location, it become the Dawes Road Library.[78]

Chief Librarians

Town of Leaside

Mrs. Alice Griffiths	1944
Ms. Elizabeth Loosley	1945—1946
Mrs. Eleanor MacAlpine	1947—1962
Mrs. Jean Parriss	1962—1966

Town of Leaside

Miss Dorothy Ashbridge	1950—1965
Mr. Bohus Derer	1965—1966

Borough of East York

Mr. Bohus Derer	1967—1975
Ms. Madge Aalto	1975---?
Mr. Bey Grieve	?--------1994
Ms. Alice Lorriman	1994—1996
Ms. Nancy Chavner	1996—1997 [79]

---

75. East York Library, a History, Publisher, East York Library, 1976, 5
76. East York Library, a History, Publisher, East York Library, 1976, 6
77. East York Library, a History, Publisher, East York Library, 1976, 6
78. East York Council minutes, March 1974
79. East York Library, a History, Publisher, East York Library, 1976, 11

EY Library oringinal NE corner Coxwell & Mortimer
(Source: East York Foundation)

S. Walter Stewart
(Source: East York Foundation)

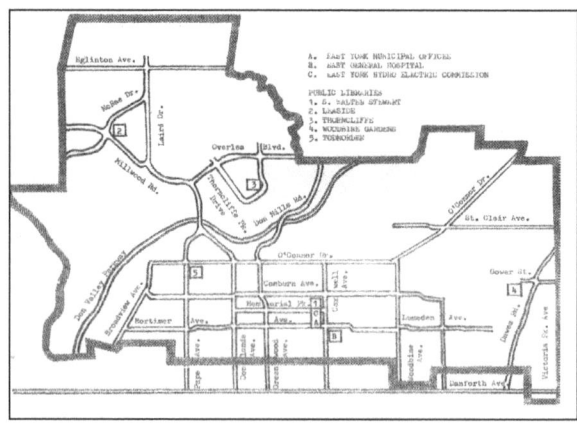

Map of Library Locations
(Source: EY Library)

J.S.Ridout
(Source: East York Foundation)

Health

"The recently incorporated Township of East York appointed a three-member Board of Health to oversee activities of its Medical Officer of Health in 1924. The Public Health Act (Ontario Statutes, 1884, c. 38) made the local board of health responsible for the control of communicable disease, licensing of eating establishments, and the regulation of sanitary conditions related to plumbing and drainage. In the early years the Board of Health involved itself in individual complaints about unsanitary conditions, fumigating houses after the outbreak of a communicable disease, and license applications for the boarding of babies and for eating establishments." [80]

"In the early days of East York there were no comprehensive health services. From time to time, and quite frequently, Medical Officers of Health were appointed by the council, and in one case this writer remembers, the choice was not a very good one. There were no clinics, pre-natal instruction classes, or public health nurses."[81]

Dr. C.E. McLean served as Medical Officer of Health (MOH) in 1939 followed by Dr. Alvin Martin the next year.

"During the 1920s and 1930s, the limited number of staff employed and the rather narrow range of activities administered allowed the Board to participate in the direct enforcement of the Public Health Act. Beginning

80. Bustin, Percy, *Memories: Early Days of East York*, Self –Published, 1976, 16
81. Board of Health, minutes, Archive citation, Fonds 299, Series 1449

in 1939, in co-operation with the Rockefeller Foundation, the Ontario Department of Health and the School of Hygiene at the University of Toronto, the East York Department of Health became a public health demonstration project. This was a significant project which doubled the staff complement and signaled the beginning of increased provincial involvement in the area of public health."[82]

Dr. Bill Mosley became the township MOH in 1942, in addition to being professor of public health at the School of Hygiene at the University of Toronto. The minutes of the Board of Health's first meeting following Mosely's appointment illustrates quite vividly the type of issues he had to deal with at that time:

92 Gledhill Avenue	No water or toilet accommodation in this shack occupied by Mr. Fenscon. Ordered: Allow 30 days to vacate the property which is now condemned by the Board of Health. Property to be placarded.
410 Lumsden Avenue	Building at rear is now vacant and not to be occupied again as a dwelling.
129 Cosburn Avenue	House is vacant and was fumigated.
105 Gamble Avenue	Owner promised that the outhouse would be moved to another spot.
472 Main Street	Septic tank overflowing.
528 Main Street	Outhouse situated in garbage and rubbish, cesspool caving in.
1107 Broadview Avenue	Plumbing connection made and sewer connection made.
844 Pape Avenue	Application to use small store as fish & chip shop. The Board do not feel the building suitable.
1239 Woodbine Avenue & 275 Westlake Avenue	Fish & Chips store licences issued.
Hopedale, Pepler, Woodmount, and Gamble homes	Approved to board a baby in each of these homes. [83]

---

82. Board of Health, minutes, Archive citation, Fonds 299, Series 1449
83. Board of Health, minutes, Archive citation, Fonds 299, Series 1449

Increased provincial funding continued after World War II allowing the East York Health Unit to increase the scope of its work.

In 1947, the name changed to the Board of Health for the East York and Leaside Health Unit to reflect that services were extended to neighbouring Leaside. The composition of the Board at this point changed as two new members of Leaside joined the original three from East York. It changed its name to the Board of Health for the Borough of East York Health Unit in 1967.

Between the 1950s and the late 1990s, the staff of the Health Unit carried out functions which included public-health nurse visits, school immunization, maternal child care, public health education, AIDS awareness, and anti-smoking campaigns, to name a few. During this same period, there was a shift in the activities of the Board. The Medical Officer of Health managed the day-to-day operations of an increasingly professional Health Unit staff. The board became an administrative body largely focused on budgeting, negotiation contracts with unionized staff, board governance models, policies and program development. In 1998, the East York Board of Health merged with the five municipal health boards to form the Board of Health for the amalgamated City of Toronto.[84]

Dr. Bill Mosely, who served as MOH for some thirty years, was succeeded by Dr. Jim Bell, who held that position until 1983, when he retired. Dr. Bell was in turn succeeded by Dr. Richard Schabas. Dr. David McKeown was appointed MOH in 1988, followed by Dr. Gerald Bonham in 1990. Dr. Sheila Basrur was East York's last MOH, serving from 1991 until the amalgamation of the Metro Boards of Health on January 1, 1998.[85]

After the East York Library moved to the new S. Walter Stewart Library building, the health unit leased the former library building at 833 Coxwell Avenue, later moving to the municipal offices and then to the Civic Centre.[86]

---

84. Board of Health, minutes, Archive citation, Fonds 299, Series 1449
85. Board of Health, minutes, Archive citation, Fonds 299, Series 1449
86. East York Council minutes, June 1951

Dr. Mosley MOH
(Source: East York Foundation)

Leaside East York Health Unit
(L to R) Leaside Mayor Beth Nealson, Dr. Mosely, Bill Aitken and
East York Mayor True Davidson
(Source: East York Foundation)

Dr. Stewart Bell, MOH
(Source: East York Foundation)

– Chapter 22 –

MEANWHILE, BACK AT CITY HALL

Both True Davidson and Willis Blair were elected as East York Councillors in 1958. Two years later, True was elected as reeve, serving continuously as reeve of the township until 1967, when she was elected as the first mayor of the new Borough of East York, triumphing over her opponents Beth Nealson, the former mayor of the Town of Leaside, and Township of East York Councillor Roy Brigham. True served continuously as the mayor until she retired in 1972. Meanwhile, Willis continued to be re-elected as a member of East York Council throughout that period. Although he did not always agree with True, but knowing that True had never lost an election, Willis, as an experienced and astute politician, bided his time until True retired.[1]

Jack Christie told Eleanor Darke that by 1972, True knew "she was getting old and might even be too old to reach the end of her term. It was time for someone younger and she had been grooming Willis Blair for years."[2]

---

1. Darke, Eleanor, *Call Me True, A Biography of True Davidson*, Dundurn Press, 1997, 136
2. Darke, Eleanor, *Call Me True, A Biography of True Davidson*, Dundurn Press, 1997, 135

I am sure that Willis never thought he needed any grooming. In fact, Willis had been ready to run in 1969 but backed off when True declared her candidacy. However, in 1972, he declared his intention to run, whatever she decided to do.

He was quoted as saying, "But I would hate to run against True. She deserves to retire undefeated." Willis told Eleanor Darke that she decided against running when her long-time friend, Emily Smith, told her, "It was time to go and warned her that she wouldn't vote for her if she ran in 1972, she'd vote for Willis."[3]

In his biography, Jack Christie recorded his surprise and disappointment when he was not reappointed to the East York Planning Board. But about ten years later Alderman Howard Chandler, who had been involved at the time, told Jack, "True had approached him and was concerned because I appeared to be developing a position from which I could run for mayor, and that besides being strong in my own ward I had the complete backing of Leaside residents. She also was planning to retire and was afraid that I 'would be a shoo-in' for a vacant mayoralty chair. This didn't fit with her plans. She considered Willis Blair as the right man for the job and she wanted him to succeed her. That also meant removing anyone who might stand in the way. Removal from the Planning Board would reduce my exposure."[4]

Mayor Willis Blair

Willis Blair ran and was elected as mayor of the Borough of East York in 1972. Prior to this election, the Ontario provincial government, acting on ratepayer concerns that local councils should be more frequently accountable to their electors, had reduced the term of municipal councils from three to two years. A two-year council would have to listen to the concerns of the residents or it wouldn't be around after the next election. Three-year terms gave the ratepayers less control over their own neighbourhoods and municipal spending priorities than did a two-year term.[5]

During Willis's time in office, the former Township of East York celebrated its golden anniversary as an incorporated municipality with

---

3. Darke, Eleanor, *Call Me True, A Biography of True Davidson*, Dundurn Press, 1997, 136
4. Christie, Jack, *The Generation of Change*, Self–Published, 184
5. Redway, Alan, Recollections

a number of events, including the publication of a history of both the township and the town entitled *The Golden Years of East York*, which was written mainly by True Davidson.[6] Because the bulldog was the symbol of the township, the borough acquired a bulldog puppy named Goliath to mark its fiftieth anniversary. The dog was named for the famous East York Collegiate football team, the Goliaths. But where to keep Goliath was the question; the answer, of course, was at the mayor's house. Unfortunately, dogs don't remain puppies very long, and this bulldog grew to an enormous size. It was so big that when Goliath went out for a walk, it had to be dragged along the sidewalk. It was all anyone could do to take him out. A new home was found for him well before the fiftieth anniversary year was over and that is how Jack Harper, a borough employee, came to be the actual owner of Goliath.[7]

As a result of the merger of the township and the town, the Borough of East York became the home to two municipal curling rinks and curling clubs. Mayor Blair, an enthusiastic curler, was instrumental in East York hosting the first World Junior Curling Championships in 1975. As a member of the Metro Toronto Council and Executive Committee, Mayor Blair worked closely with Metro Chairman Paul Godfrey to bring the Blue Jays Baseball team to Metro Toronto in 1977.

Willis also initiated the East York New Year's Day Levee so that residents could come to the municipal building on January 1 to meet and greet their mayor and members of council at the beginning of the New Year. This became another East York tradition and has been held every year since then, but not always on New Year's Day.[8]

The development applications by Peter Dimitoff were lively issues during Willis Blair's time as mayor. These came under the corporate names of Hemus (high-rise apartments), Claverly (townhouses), and Trimontium (detached-home subdivision), and were all for the same properties on the north side of O'Connor west of Woodbine Bridge. So also was the Sibley Home, a residence for the mentally challenged, which required a zoning change for the southeast corner of Dentonia Park and Sibley Avenues from residential to institutional use. The Sibley Home

---

6. East York Council minutes, June 1974
7. Redway, Alan, Recollections
8. Redway, Alan, Recollections

was approved; Hemus was turned down; Claverly was approved and then reversed after the election of John Flowers as a Ward 2 alderman; while Trimontium was unresolved when Willis resigned as mayor in 1976.[9]

Once again, however, the future fate of East York became the borough's overriding concern when the provincial government appointed the Robarts Royal Commission to review the Metropolitan Toronto system of government. In 1967, East York had escaped amalgamation with the city of Toronto by the skin of its teeth when York East MPP Hollis Beckett intervened with his legislative colleagues and then-Premier John Robarts. They aimed to save East York from permanent extinction by merging the township with the Town of Leaside, thereby creating six Metro municipalities rather than the four as recommended by the Goldenberg Royal Commission. Now again, East York prepared its brief to this new Royal Commission and Mayor Blair made the borough submissions to the commissioner. Then East Yorkers held their breath.[10]

Council's position was bolstered when a borough plebiscite endorsed retaining East York as a separate municipality by a majority of 86.2%. The borough voters in the former Town of Leaside were even more emphatic, endorsing retention by an overwhelming 89%.[11]

However, before the commission announced its recommendations and partway through the final year of his second year term as mayor, Willis Blair announced his resignation. He had been offered and had accepted a provincial appointment to the Ontario Municipal Board. Shortly thereafter, he chaired a Royal Commission inquiry into reform of the property assessment system.[12]

Following Willis Blair's resignation on April 12, 1976, the council, after receiving public representations on the subject, debated whether to hold a by-election or to appoint one of the other Council members to act as mayor for the remaining eight months of the term of office. Years earlier, East York Alderman Leslie Saunders, then a member of Toronto City Council, had been appointed by his council colleagues to complete the term of office of Toronto Mayor Donald Somerville because of his sudden death. After declaring that if selected, he would not stand for the

9. Redway, Alan, Recollections
10. East York Council minutes, January 1975
11. *East Yorker,* 1975
12. East York Council minutes 1976

office of mayor at the next election, Leslie Saunders was appointed by East York Council to serve as mayor for the balance that term. Of course, after being appointed to complete the mayor's term of office that person would have a distinct advantage over their opponents if he or she did run for the same office at the next election.[13]

When Willis resigned, Jack Christie says many of Jack's associates and friends called him to offer their support because they considered him the logical successor as the next mayor, but he had no such aspirations.[14]

The election for mayor for the next two-year council term was hotly contested between Alderman Howard Chandler and Alderman Alan Redway. Howard Chandler had served as a member of council off and on since 1952. In the past, he had run twice for the office of township reeve but had been defeated both by Jack Allen and then by True Davidson. Chandler's friends told Alan Redway that it was Howard's turn this time and that he would have his turn later. Redway was a lawyer who had served on council as an alderman for the past four years.[15]

Alan Redway framed his campaign around the need to maintain the existing physical character of the borough and ensuring that East York remained a clean, safe, caring, and friendly community in which neighbours were concerned for one another. The morning after the election, the headline on the front page of the *Globe and Mail* announced, "Chandler Elected as Mayor of East York." However, much to the astonishment of the *Globe* and many others, Alan Redway—not Howard Chandler—was elected mayor to take office for the next two-year term commencing January 1, 1977.[16]

---

13. East York Council minutes, November 1975
14. Christie, Jack, *Generation of Change*, Self-Published, 184
15. East York Council minutes, November 1976
16. Redway, Alan, Recollections

True Laying on of Hands Willis Blair
(Source: TorontoPublicLibrary.ca)

Mayor Willis Blair
(Source: East York Foundation)

Eleanor Darke with Goliath and Mayor Willis Blair
(Source: Virtualreferencelibrary.ca)

Mayor Alan Redway

Redway placed a great deal of emphasis on communicating with the residents of the borough. He began with a "Mayor Redway Says" column in the *East Yorker*, published quarterly by the borough and distributed to every household in East York. He followed that up by initiating a regular monthly East York mayor's broadcast on Rogers Cable TV, and shortly after that by arranging for live Rogers Cable telecasts of every council meeting. When the property tax bill was issued, Redway held a tax meeting at East York Collegiate for the mayor and councillors to be accountable to the borough residents by explaining in person the decisions made in arriving at the final tax rate. Initially, these annual meetings were hot and heavy sessions, but the crowds dwindled in later years as residents came to understand the decision-making process.[17]

East Yorkers were on pins and needles prior to learning the recommendations of the Robarts Royal Commission, but after the announcement was made, there was, for the most part, a deep sigh of relief. Not only did the Borough survive, but Robarts recommended that its population should be increased by extending its southern boundary

17. Redway, Alan, Recollections 4

to the north side of the Danforth, its north-eastern boundary to Eglinton Avenue, and its eastern boundary to Warden Avenue. However, the Governor's Bridge and Bennington Heights communities were to be lost to the City of Toronto. Needless to say, neither Scarborough, North York, nor the city were happy with those recommendations. Mayor Redway debated Mayor Lastman of North York on the north-east boundary issue at a meeting held in Flemingdon Park, which if Robarts' recommendations were adopted, would become part of East York. Later at Eastminster United Church, Redway debated then-City Alderman John Sewell, whose ward north of the Danforth would have become part of the borough. Ultimately, however, because of the objections of the city, North York, and Scarborough, the provincial government left well enough alone and made no boundary changes in the six Metro municipalities.[18]

Five of the six area municipalities in Metro, including the Municipality of Metropolitan Toronto itself, had their own municipal flag. The exception was East York, so in 1978 Mayor Redway and council set the wheels in motion by holding a contest for a flag design. Redway described the events:

Shortly after I was elected as the mayor of East York and therefore a member of the Metropolitan Toronto Council and Executive Committee, I realized that every one of the six area municipalities which comprised Metropolitan Toronto with the exception of East York had a municipal flag.

So I applied for and received authorization from East York Council to hold a design contest for an East York flag. Now every contest needs a prize but I did not want to burden the taxpayers with the cost so I wrote to each of the industries and businesses in the borough asking for a modest cash donation of $200 each towards the prize. Many companies responded positively. However, 7UP sent me a cheque but indicated they thought this was a foolish idea. I promptly sent back their cheque, reminding them that this was a matter of civic pride for a very special municipality with an incredible community spirit.

Design submissions came from a great many adults but especially from school children, some whose teachers took it on as a class project.

---

18. Redway, Alan, Recollections

The winning design was submitted by a Scarborough resident, Raymond Taylor, who had learned about the contest from East Yorker Blain Till when they ran together daily in Taylor Creek Park. The prize was $1000 for Mr. Taylor and $100 for the winning student design. Thus, our flag was a real bargain. On viewing the design, a number of East Yorkers expressed the opinion that the "Y" on the flag also represented the two branches of the Don River.

Once the design was approved by Council, Diana (Didy) Erb, the wife the Rev. Canon John Erb, the Rector of St. Luke's Anglican Church on Coxwell, made the very first East York flag. Ever after, she was known as East York's Betsy Ross. From then on, the flag (logo) appeared throughout the borough, including prominently on all of our street signs.

Unfortunately, in its efforts to ensure we are all Torontonians first, the amalgamated city started replacing our East York street signs with large Toronto blue and white signs. Fortunately, however, in 2017 Councillors Mary Fragedakis and Janet Davis convinced Toronto City Council to allow the East York logo (flag) on street signs within the former borough boundaries. One way we can help to keep the very special community spirit of our borough alive is by flying the East York Flag.[19]

The flag was part of Redway's plan to provide a new symbol around which to unite long-time residents of both the former township and the former town, and to stimulate a distinct pride in their merged municipality, the Borough of East York, in the same way that the new Canadian maple leaf flag had for Canadians from coast to coast to coast. A further part of that plan was the establishment of the self-funded Mayor's Multicultural Committee aimed at bringing new comers and long-time East Yorkers together.

In keeping with the issues on which Redway campaigned for election as mayor in 1976, the borough developed a housing policy that emphasized approving new construction only if it was in keeping with the physical character of established neighbourhoods, as well as conserving and rehabilitating existing homes. The peace agreement with the owners of the Bayview Ghost property (after its demolition), the Trimontium detached home subdivision, and the new seniors homes, Canadian Macedonian Place and the Mennonite Home—built near St. Clair and

19. Redway, Recollections

O'Connor—and the addition to Central Park Lodge in Thorncliffe, all conformed to that policy.

When Alan Redway was mayor, the provincial government partially shut down both the East York Memorial Arena and the Leaside Memorial Community Gardens until their roofs were replaced and strengthened because an arena with a similar roof design in Listowel, Ontario, had collapsed under the weight of snow and ice killing several people including Midget hockey players. Fortunately, two separate fund-raising campaigns were quickly initiated. Stan Wadlow headed the East York Arena Roof fund while Edna Beange headed the Leaside Arena Roof fund. Both fund-raising campaigns proved overwhelmingly successful. While funds were being raised, the snow and ice buildup on both arenas had to be constantly monitored. The residents pitched in with income tax deductible contributions through the East York Foundation. The construction was done and both arenas were reopened.

There were many stormy council and committee meetings during Redway's time as mayor. Subjects included basement flooding, on-street permit parking, front-yard parking, as well as litter and parking on the Donlands commercial strip. Council initiated a program of sewer separation beginning with the installation of trunk sewers to address the basement flooding problem; polling was conducted on the affected streets to try to answer the permit and front yard parking concerns and greater police enforcement and additional street cleaning ordered to address the parking and litter problems on Donlands. But perhaps the stormiest session of all involved a federal rather than a municipal issue of urea formaldehyde foam insulation (UFFI). Urea had originally been approved to insulate homes by Canada Mortgage and Housing Corporation (CMHC) and many East Yorkers did just that. It was later identified as a health hazard, resulting in lenders insisting that the urea be removed before they would approve a mortgage loan. The borough residents who had insulated with urea were irate. Many came to council to voice their anger. In order to let them address their feelings to the federal government (the source of the problem), Mayor Redway arranged an evening public meeting, but not a council meeting, to take place in the council chamber with the federal Member of Parliament, David Collenette. The council chamber was jammed full of angry residents that night. The crowd overflowed down the stairs and out the door. Such a crowd of protesters had not been seen in East York since the Great Depression and has not been seen since.

Nothing was resolved, of course, but brave MP David Collenette got an ear full that night.

Towards the end of his third two-year term as mayor, Alan Redway announced that he would not run again for the office. Instead, he was seeking the nomination to stand as the Progressive Conservative candidate in the federal riding of York East. Although the federal election was two years in the future, Redway believed it was not morally the right thing for him to run for re-election as mayor if he would have to resign part way through his term when a federal election was called.

Shortly thereafter, the provincial government announced that starting after the next municipal election, the term of office would be three years rather than two years, as it had been for the last five terms (ten years) of municipal office. In 1972, the ratepayers' battle cry was that a shorter municipal term would make councillors more accountable for their actions. But in 1983, the councillors lamented that a longer municipal term was needed to allow them to do proper planning, and that won the day.[20]

In the election that followed Alan Redway's departure, Dave Johnson became the new mayor after defeating his opponent, Councillor Herb McGroarty. Before he ran, according to Jack Christie, Dave had carefully reconnoitred the field:

"When Alan Redway announced that he wouldn't run again but would run for federal office, a number of Leaside residents phoned me to offer support and some even offered to organize fund-raiser parties if I would be a candidate. Alan Redway voiced the opinion that 'I was the logical person' being the only likely candidate who had run successfully across the whole municipality. The sitting councillors who might be considering candidature had only run in their own ward and were unknown across the borough. Councillor Dave Johnson had already announced his retirement from politics to return to his management position at Esso (his leave of absence had expired). I met Dave one day and he greeted me with 'I heard you're running for mayor.' When I told him I had no such plans and no such aspirations, he said, 'If you are sure you are not running, I will.' I assured him he would have my support."[21]

---

20. Redway, Alan, Recollections
21. Christie, Jack, *The Generation of Change*, Self-Published, 259

Mayor Leslie Saunders   C. Howard Chandler
(Source: East York Foundation)   *(Source: East York Foundation)*

Alan Redway Chain of Office
(Source: East York Foundation)

Council 1977-78
(Source: East York Foundation)

Bromley Armstrong
(Source: Canadian Encyclopedia)

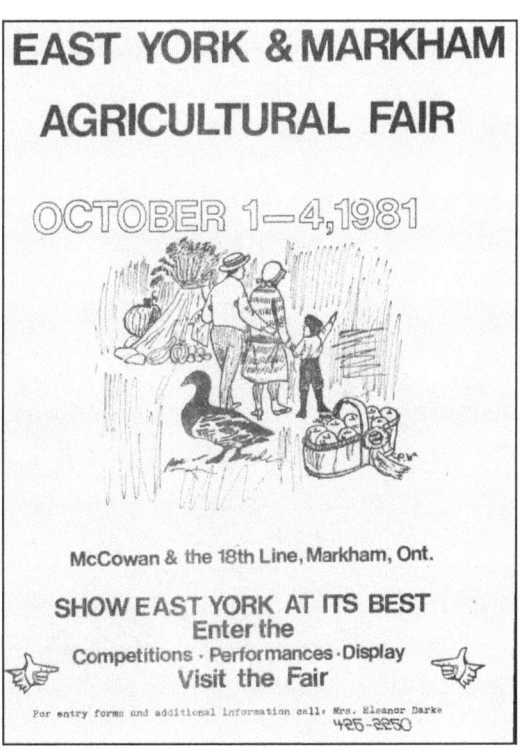

East York Flag

East York Markham Fair 1981
(Source: East York Foundation)

Mayor Dave Johnson

Prior to 1967, the thirteen municipalities that made up the Municipality of Metropolitan Toronto, with the exception of the old city of Toronto itself, had been formerly called towns, villages, and townships. After 1967, again with the exception of the old City of Toronto, the surviving municipalities were all called boroughs. A former mayor of Toronto and later an East York councillor and interim mayor, Leslie Saunders, had advocated unsuccessfully that the City of Toronto should be called the Borough of Queens. However, in 1982, unhappy with its status as a borough, Mayor Mel Lastman and North York Council obtained provincial authority to change its name from the Borough to the City of North York. Etobicoke, Scarborough, and York quickly followed. All were now cities. What was East York to do?[22]

Mayor Dave Johnson favoured city status for East York, but council decided to ask residents for their opinion. The September 1983 issue of the East Yorker put the question to the residents:

Council Wants Your Opinion

The recent change of status of Scarborough, York, and Etobicoke from Borough to City, as are North York and Toronto, has prompted East York Council to investigate changing from a Borough to either a "Town" or a "City." The "Borough" designation was created in 1967 with the amalgamation of the Township of East York and the Town of Leaside. Today East York is the only Borough in Canada.

Those who favour retention of "Borough" status feel that East York should retain its historical Borough status. They feel that the East York community, although 100,000 in population, is not as large or bustling as the other Metro municipalities and the "Borough" designation best reflects this more neighbourly attitude.

Those favouring "City" status feel that the recognized designation for a large, independent urban municipality is City. They feel the term Borough is confusing since it normally identifies a suburb of a City and conversely, City status will make East York equal to other Metro municipalities and may help to ensure East York's independence in the future.

---

22. Redway, Alan, Recollections

Those favouring "Town" status feel that East York has a friendly, slower-paced Town atmosphere. They feel there may be distinction in being the largest Town in Canada. They also point out that some longer-term residents will refer to East York as "Town" or "Township," using the pre-amalgamation terminology.

All three options hope to retain East York as East York without disturbing the distinctive quality of the residential community and without affecting taxes. Finally, there is minimal effect on provincial funding for any one option over the others and the cost of changing to Town or City would be about $5,000 to alter signs and stationary.

Please give the Council your opinion by mailing a completed coupon found on page 3, before September 30, 1983.[23]

Council also asked its staff how much it would cost to change the name from a borough to a city and received the following report from the clerk, the treasurer, and the works commissioner:

If the request were to go forward and be made effective January 1, 1984, to coincide with the sixtieth anniversary of the incorporation of the Township of East York, the estimated administrative costs for change would be approximately $4,000 to $5,000. This amount is to change the names on the borough vehicles, bus shelters, signs in parks, and signs at the entrances to the municipality.

The officials feel that there would be no cost to replace letterheads, business cards, water bills, envelopes, and tax bills, as they have to be replaced as used. Purchases of this type would be dealt with keeping in mind the status being changed. The department heads are studying a new logo incorporating the flag design and a recommendation will be forthcoming in the fall of 1983.

*Recommendation:

That the Council of the Borough of East York request the Minister of Municipal Affairs and Housing to change the status of the Borough of East York to the "City of East York," effective January 1, 1984.[24]

---

23. *East Yorker,* 1983
24. East York Council minutes, February 1983

Their recommendation was approved by a committee of council, but the full council overturned the committee recommendation when it received a mere 741 responses from the 100,121 total residents of East York. "BOROUGH – IT IS" declared the next issue of the East Yorker: "In the last edition of the East Yorker, the council requested the opinion of citizens on changing the status of East York from Borough to City or Town. Here are the results: Borough 448, Town 161, City 132. The council then voted unanimously, according to Dave Johnson, to retain borough status.[25]

The borough staff was not happy with the decision. Six years later, they asked that the issue be revisited.

Recommendation:
That the issue of borough status be reconsidered, in concert with the promotion of the new Civic Centre.
Background:
For some time, department heads have discussed the issue of borough status. We have been concerned that the appropriate image be projected. In our opinion, and based upon discussions with others outside the municipality, the title of borough projects an image of "less than a city" and therefore tends to be a negative image.

The province is about to establish two more boroughs, both in Northern Ontario, and both former Indian reserves. In view of the impending demise of "Canada's Only Borough" and in view of the new Civic Centre Project, we are suggesting Council re-consider the issue of borough status.[26]

"The city of Montreal has nineteen boroughs as well, but Council took no action on this staff recommendation and continued to proclaim that East York was Canada's Only Borough." [27]

The decision to build, and the subsequent construction of the Civic Centre, also took place while Dave Johnson was mayor. Dave opposed

25. *East Yorker*, 1983
26. East York Council minutes, July 1983
27. Redway, Alan, *Governing Toronto: Bringing back the city that worked*, Friesen Press, November, 2014, 238

the idea out of a desire to keep property taxes affordable and because rumours of possible amalgamation were circulating again.[28] But once more, Council asked for public input on the issue by holding an open house for residents to examine the options.

OPEN HOUSE
MUNICIPAL HALL OPTIONS

On July 6, 1987, East York received a consultant's report that studied a number of options with respect to improvements to the Municipal Office facilities.

"A public information 'Open House' has been scheduled for 7:00 p.m. October 8, 1987, in the Council Chambers of the Municipal Offices at 350 Mortimer Avenue to enable the public to receive information on the study process and its conclusions and to provide input to Council on this matter:

All residents of East York are welcome at this informal discussion.

- Do Nothing—limited to essential maintenance and repairs only at a cost of $2,135,070. This was not recommended as anything more than a stop-gap measure.
- Renovation to the existing building at a cost of $7,367,500. This was not recommended.
- Renovations and an addition to the existing building at a cost of $6,962,500. This was not recommended.
- Construct a new building at the present location within Memorial Park at a cost of $6,996,000. The consultants strongly recommend this as the most cost-effective strategy for the borough." [29]

The mayor wanted a question placed on the ballot for the 1988 municipal election requesting the electorate's opinion with regard to constructing a new municipal hall but his efforts were voted down after strong opposition to a referendum was voiced by Councillors Steve Mastoras and Bob Dale. Council minutes recorded the vote as follows:

"Upon the question of the adoption of the foregoing motion by Mr. Johnson, the vote was taken as follows:

---

28. Interview with Dave Johnson, October 6, 2016
29. *East Yorker*, 1987

Yeas: Johnson
Nays: Beange, Buckingham, Dale, Mastoras, Oyler, Reader, Vasilopoulos, Willis

Decided in the negative by a majority of seven."[30]

The project was approved. One touchy issue arose, however, concerning the relocation of the cenotaph, the focus of our November 11 Remembrance Service each year, erected in the Memorial Gardens back in 1948 to commemorate the sacrifices made by veterans of WW I, WWII, Korea, and our Peacekeepers. Fortunately, it was resolved satisfactorily with the involvement of the East York branches of the Royal Canadian Legion.[31] The new Civic Centre was built together with a stand-alone day-care building under the direction of Works Commissioner Paul Cockburn. The former municipal building was demolished and the new Civic Centre was officially opened on September 22, 1990.[32]

According to Mayor Dave Johnson, his toughest meeting concerned the approval of the Touchstone Youth Shelter on Pape Avenue in Ward 3. The meeting, held at William Burgess School, was packed with angry residents. More tried to get in but couldn't because of the size of the crowd. People were shouting at one another and the police had to be called. Ward 3 Councillor Steve Mastoras, who chaired the meeting, was roasted.[33] It went on until two in the morning. Councillor Case Ootes described it as "ugly."[34] In the end, Council approved Touchstone with only the Ward 3 Councillors Steve Mastoras and Helen Kennedy opposed.[35]

The Johnson Council approved seniors' residences on Overlea Boulevard, 955 Millwood Road, 921 Millwood Road, and Westminster Presbyterian on Floyd Avenue with little if any opposition, but when it came to the St. Vincent de Paul assisted family residence at 10 Gower Avenue west of Dawes Road, it was a different story. A stormy meeting on the subject was held at George Webster School. The gym was packed,

---

30. East York Council minutes, February 1987
31. Interview with Case Ootes, February 1, 2017
32. *East Yorker*, 1990
33. Interviews with Steve Mastoras, August 5, 2016 and Dave Johnson, October 6, 2016
34. Interview with Case Ootes, February 1, 2017
35. East York Council minutes, March 1989

standing room only.[36] Ultimately, that too was approved by the OMB after the height was reduced and a community room added.[37] Michael Prue, then a councillor in Ward 1, recalls one other hot meeting, this one in Parkview Hills concerned the East York by-law establishing a floor space index for new home building. It was sparked by the demolition and replacement of many of the original smaller homes in the area with new monster homes. Feelings ran so high that when some people left the meeting, they found their car tires slashed.[38]

During Dave Johnson's time as mayor, the Borough undertook a major sewer separation program to deal with the persistent problem of basement flooding, 80% of the cost was funded by the federal, provincial, and metro governments, while the balance was paid by East York. As in the past, there were issues with permit parking, front yard parking, and traffic control as well.[39]

On December 25, 1983, Anne Sinclair, on behalf of the mayor and assisted by Roly Sheaves and Dave Ellis, organized the first East York Christmas Dinner for three hundred seniors at the Community Centre on Pape Avenue. The event was funded solely by community donations. John Bitove the moving force at Canadian Macedonia Place on O'Connor Drive near St. Clair provided all the turkeys that first year. The Christmas dinner became an annual tradition in East York, as did the Mayor's Blooming Contest, the brainchild of East York's gardening expert Art Drysdale. Held to recognize the best kept gardens in the borough, it too was and still is organized, run, and judged solely by volunteers from the East York Garden Club. Inspired by Metro, Dave Johnson initiated another event that has since become an annual tradition, Environment Day, when free composted soil is available and hazardous waste is collected.[40]

During Dave Johnson's time as mayor in 1988, Case Ootes was elected as a Ward 1 Councillor. Almost from the outset, he urged Council to institute once-a-week garbage collection to help to reduce costs and keep taxes affordable. He kept after that until it was finally approved in 1991 by a vote of 7–2. Shortly after that, he began a campaign to have

---

36. Interview with Case Ootes, February 1, 2017
37. Interview with Michael Prue, April 5, 2017
38. Interview with Michael Prue, April 5, 2017
39. Interview with Dave Johnson, October 6, 2016
40. Interviews with Dave Johnson, October 6, 2016 and Roly Sheaves, January 19, 2017

garbage collection contracted out. The matter came to a head the next year but rather than agree to contract out, Council approved a plan to increase the efficiency of collection that was submitted by its own sanitation workers.[41] Although East York employees were unionized, they were also the neighbours and friends of the residents. It's tough to face your neighbours and friends after you have taken their jobs away. Privatization of garbage collection never came to be in the Borough of East York.

On April 6, 1993, Dave Johnson resigned as mayor of East York following his election on April 1 to the Ontario Legislative Assembly as the Progressive Conservative member for Don Mills Riding. He chaired the council meeting until he announced his resignation as mayor. Then, Councillor John Papadakis, in his capacity as acting mayor, took the chair. As in 1976 when Willis Blair resigned as mayor during his term of office, Council decided, in spite of representations to the contrary by a number of borough residents, to fill the vacancy by appointment rather than hold a by-election. Six of the council members—Case Ootes, Michael Prue, George Vasilopoulos, Bob Dale, Lorna Krawchuk, and Jenner Jean Marie—were nominated to stand to be appointed as interim mayor. Each council member then voted, the one with the fewest votes dropping off the next ballot until someone received a majority. Five ballots later, Case Ootes was the last to be eliminated when Michael Prue received a majority of the votes of the other council members.[42]

Jack Christie had this to say about the process: "On a previous occasion the retirement of Willis Blair, his successor, Leslie Saunders, was appointed on condition that he agree not to run for the mayor's office in the next election. When Council sat to appoint Dave's successor, six councillors announced they would like to be considered. Only one or two would have stood for the post had that condition been attached. Council conducted an open, publically viewed election among themselves. As expected, Michael Prue and Case Ootes were the two finalists and Michael won the final ballot, no conditions attached. Being mayor for that temporary term gave Michael such an "incumbent" advantage that neither Case Ootes nor any other councillor would run against him in the next regular election."[43]

---

41. Interview with Case Ootes, February 1, 2017
42. Interview with Michael Prue, April 5, 2017
43. Christie, Jack, *The Generation of Change*, Self-Published, 196

Dave Johnson Chain of Office
(Source: East York Foundation)

EY Council c1990
(Source: East York Foundation)

Municipal Bldg Construction
(Source: East York Foundation)

Art Drysdale
(Source: google.ca)

Nick Volk
(Source: dignitymemorial.com)

John Tory
(Source: google images)

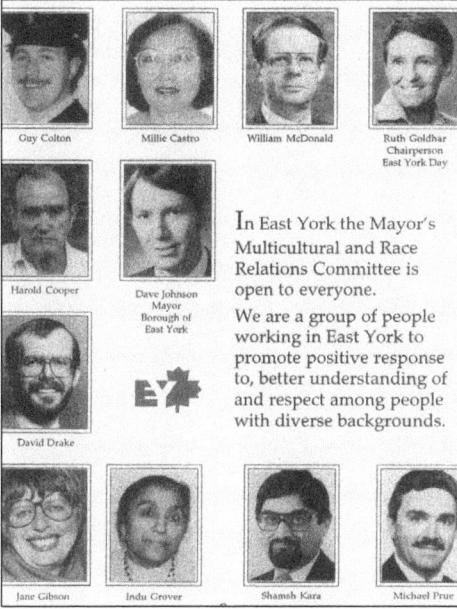

Mayor's Multicultural and Race Relations Committee 1 1990
(Source: Toronto Archives)

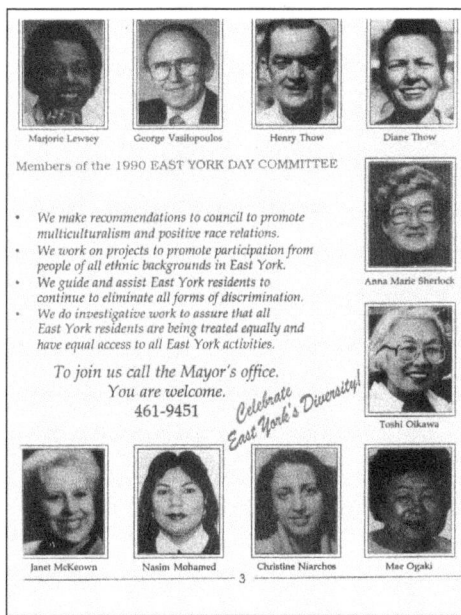

Mayor's Multicultural and Race Relations Committee 2
(Source: Toronto Archives)

Mayor Michael Prue

From the time of its incorporation, the tax rate and the assessment base had always been a central consideration in virtually every decision made by East York Council. When Alcatel, formerly Canada Wire and Cable, the cornerstone of the Leaside industrial area, announced it was shutting down and putting its vast property up for sale, the news came as a major shock to Council, impacting as it did on the financial stability of the borough itself. Since before World War I, when Canada Wire had first located on Laird Drive, it had always been a cash cow first for the Town of Leaside and then for the Borough of East York. The company had paid an enormous amount of business and property taxes, in return for which it had received only a modicum of municipal services. Canada Wire, which made cable and fibre optics for countries around the world, had been sold to its gigantic French competitor, Alcatel. Soon after the acquisition, Alcatel limited Canada Wire's sales only to the Canadian market, knowing full well that the company could not be profitable when restricted to such a small market. Announcing then that Canada Wire was no longer profitable, they shut it down completely. Next, Alcatel sold Canada Wire's high tech, one-of-a-kind machinery and technology for an amount, according to former Canada Wire employees, which exceeded the price Alcatel had paid for the land and the company originally.[44]

Because the land was zoned industrial, there were only a limited number of potential new buyers, so East York Council amended the Official Plan and rezoned the property from industrial to commercial to allow the Smart Centre to establish a huge big-box store shopping centre on the site. Earlier, East York Planning Commissioner Rick Tomaszewicz's reports to Council on the former Phillips Industries property had opened the door for the OMB's decision to allow residential development in the Leaside industrial area.[45] Now, Council enacted Official Plan and zoning amendments based on Tomaszewicz recommendations that changed the former Leaside Industrial area from an exclusively industrial area to partly industrial, partly commercial, and partly residential, meaning that more municipal services had to be provided to the area. Leaside industrial area was no longer a cash cow for East York.[46]

---

44. Redway, Recollections
45. East York Council minutes, January 1997
46. East York Council minutes, March 1997

Ironically, as the Leaside industrial area was dying, the former township industrial area west of O'Connor Drive north of St. Clair Avenue East was getting new lease on life. After talking with John Godfrey (MP for Don Valley West) about fibre optics (now made by Alcatel), Mayor Michael Prue, in his capacity as an East York Hydro Commissioner, convinced the chair of the commission, Jack Christie, that Hydro should install a fibre-optics network through the former township's industrial area. This proved to be an instant success. Vacant industrial buildings there were soon filled with film studios and the like. There were no more vacancies in the former township's industrial area and the borough's financial problems were solved. East York had no increase in its portion of the property tax bill in the four years leading up to amalgamation.[47]

During Michael Prue's time as mayor, there was a major restructuring of the borough staff. Sparked by Councillor Case Ootes' efforts to reduce costs, Council retained as consultants George B. Cluff and Associates to prepare a Structural Management Review. The Cluff report, which some have described as boiler plate, was referred to the senior staff for their comments, following which no action was taken until Council advertised for and subsequently hired a Chief Administrative Officer (CAO) Virginia West.[48]

This was the first major staff reorganization since Bill Heaton retired in 1959. Heaton was appointed as comptroller in 1932, a position with responsibilities similar to that of a CAO. In that capacity, he had complete control over all of the municipal departments.[49] True Davidson said that Bill Heaton ruled the elected officials as well as staff with a firm hand.[50] As an indication of his power, the council minutes record that on June 4, 1959, Bill Heaton turned over the keys to the municipal building and the combination of the safe was changed. When Heaton retired, the position of comptroller was repealed.[51]

The authority of the comptroller was split between two positions. Doris Tucker was appointed as the municipal clerk, Herb Flook as treasurer, and Duncan Little as deputy treasurer. A short time later, Flook

47. Interview with Michael Prue, April 5, 2017
48. Interview with Michael Prue, April 5, 2017
49. East York Council minutes, June 1959
50. Darke, Eleanor, *Call Me True, A Biography of True Davidson*, Dundurn Press, 1997, 70
51. East York Council minutes, June 1959

died suddenly and Little became the treasurer. Until they retired, Doris Tucker and Duncan Little were friendly rivals as to whom was in charge of the East York's inside employees. They would vie with one another, for example, as to who would give the order for the staff to go home early when there was a snow storm. What Mayor Prue and his council may or may not have realized when they opted to hire Virginia West was that without a comptroller or a CAO, Council itself had direct control over the senior staff.[52]

What the new CAO was able to do, however, that Council had been unable to do for itself, was to go forward with restructuring of the senior staff. In the process, Case Ootes insisted that unless the number of commissioners was reduced, it would be impossible to deal with the unionized workers in the next round of collective bargaining. But who was to be let go? That became a controversial issue since it would impact directly on the final restructuring. Ultimately, in spite of his good work constructing the Civic Centre and in dealing with the garbage issue, Works Commissioner Paul Cockburn was the one selected. According to Mayor Michael Prue, this came on the recommendation of Councillor Lorna Krawchuk, although the job of terminating Cockburn fell to the mayor.[53] That led to the interesting decision to place the Works Department and the Parks and Recreation Department both under the direction of former Commissioner of Parks and Recreation Claire Tucker-Reid.[54]

Michael Prue recalls two other controversies while he was mayor. The first concerned the establishment of a mosque on Thorncliffe Park Drive next door to the Cypriot Centre. This required amendments to the Official Plan, and the zoning and parking by-laws. The invasion of Cyprus by the Turkish army a few years earlier did not help the relationship between the two potential neighbours. East York made international news because the council deputations and debates were reported by radio all over the Muslim world. After the mosque was approved, it and the Cypriot Centre became good neighbours.

The second controversy involved Habitat for Humanity's attempt to acquire land to build twenty houses on a former landfill site on Everett Crescent south of the curling rink on Cosburn Avenue. Due to

52. Redway, Recollections
53. Interview with Michael Prue, April 5, 2017
54. East York Council minutes, December 1995

neighbourhood and environmental concerns, the deal fell through and the houses were never built.[55]

A number of initiatives begun by Mayor Dave Johnson were completed by Mayor Michael Prue. One of these was the establishment of the annual Agnes Macphail Award, named for the former borough resident, who was the first woman elected to the Canadian House of Commons and later the first woman elected to the Ontario Legislative Assembly, where she sat as the MPP for the riding of York East. Others included the twinning of East York with Tripolis, Greece;[56] continuing the Provincial Good Neighbour program aimed at encouraging more caring and concerned neighbours and neighbourhoods, in support of the frail, isolated and vulnerable; sewer separation to eliminate basement flooding; and improvements to recreation facilities and traffic calming, otherwise known as speed bumps.

While Michael Prue served as mayor of the borough, East York celebrated the two hundredth anniversary of the founding of the first settlement of Todmorden in 1796. However, hanging over his final time in office was the looming threat of amalgamation.[57]

Dave Johnson placing chain of office on Mayor Prue
(Source: gettyimages.ca)

---

55. Interviews with Michael Prue, April 5, 2017 and Case Ootes, February 1, 2017
56. East York Council minutes, January 1994
57. East York Council minutes, January 1996

Michael Prue
(Source: Michael Prue)

Works Commissioner
Paul Cockburn
(Source: East York Foundation)

Pontian (Greek) Memorial
(Source: insidetoronto.com)

Agnes Macphail
(Source: Agnes Maphail Awards
Committee)

EY Race Relations Committee
(Source: Toronto Archives)

Agnes Macphail Home
(Source: google.ca)

Mayors of EY 4 of 6
(L to R) Dave Johnson, Willis Blair, Alan Redway and Michael Prue
(Source: Donna Lynn McCallum)

– Chapter 23 –

AMALGAMATION

East York's three lives as an incorporated municipality ended on January 1, 1998. It survived the creation of the Municipality of Metropolitan Toronto in 1954. It survived the creation of the Borough of East York in 1967. But at the strike of midnight, 1998, as New Year's Day arrived, the Borough of East York ceased to exist.

The events leading up to the end of the Borough of East York as an incorporated municipality began in 1995 when Ontario Premier Bob Rae established the Anne Golden Task Force. It all seemed innocent enough at the time. After all, the provincial government had appointed an independent reviewer to study and make recommendations concerning the Municipality of Metropolitan Toronto every ten years or so since Metro was created. This time the focus was on the cross border problems between Metro, Peel, Halton, York, and Durham, not on whether to reduce or amalgamate the Metro municipalities.[1]

Before the East York Council brief was delivered to the Golden Task Force, it was discussed and approved by a majority of those who spoke at

---

1. Redway, Alan, *Governing Toronto: Bringing back the city that worked*, Friesen Press, November, 2014, 121

a public meeting called to consider the borough's position. Of course, the brief advocated that East York continue as a separate municipality within Metro Toronto, but it also requested that the boundaries be extended by moving the southern border to the Danforth and the eastern boundary to Warden Avenue and the northern one into North York, as recommended by the 1977 Robarts Royal Commission. Some at the public meeting were concerned, however, that asking for expanded boundaries might bring about the amalgamation option but the majority carried the day.[2]

After presenting the borough brief to the Task Force the Mayor reported to the East York residents.

Mayor's Message

While presenting the borough's position on the Golden Commission Task Force on the future of the Greater Toronto Area, I was asked by a panel member why East York shouldn't just be amalgamated by Toronto.

His question shocked me; my answer shocked him.

East York is a special place to those who live here. It is the municipality where truly everyone can and does participate in civic life. We deliberately foster our "small town" atmosphere even if we are Canada's thirty-fifth largest municipality. All of our committees and council are open to public deputations. Anyone may speak to any issue whether or not it is on the agenda. This year, in the two hundredth anniversary of the founding of the mill at Todmorden, a committee of volunteers from community organizations, businesses, local media, as well as individual citizens and staff from private and public bodies have joined forces to deliver a truly memorable series of events. They have done so wholly thorough fundraising and corporate sponsorships, and without any public monies.

Our borough workforce is among the leanest and most efficient in the country, with just under five staff per one thousand population (in contrast, Toronto has thirteen staff per one thousand population).

Our councillors are the lowest paid in Metro. They have the smallest budgets and together all eight share one administrative assistant. My office has only one full-time staff person, and one assistant who works one day a week.

---

2. The *East Yorker*, 1995

We have managed our finances in a way which has become the envy of almost every municipality in the province. For the fourth straight year, there will be no tax increase. We have not had to rely on "user fees" for 1996 in the same way as our larger neighbours. Our staff are not required to take days off without pay, nor are we forced to close our doors for the period between Christmas and New Year's. East York will even accrue a modest surplus to be added to the 1997 budget. Moreover, for the past six years we have funded capital expenditures from the current budget without incurring any debenture financing (loans). This means that we will be virtually debt-free in just four years. Our reserve accounts are sufficient and growing.

I concluded by telling him that we do not want to be anything less than what we are – a healthy, vibrant, self-assured and successful municipality where everyone can participate. No-one in East York would be satisfied to be something less than we are today.[3]

The Golden Task Force recommendation to replace the five regional governments of Metro, Peel, Halton, York, and Durham with a single Greater Toronto (GTA) regional government and to strengthen local municipalities such as East York upset Mississauga Mayor Hazel McCallion, who didn't like the idea of regional governments at all. Soon, Hazel, joined by Mayors Mel Lastman of North York, Barbara Hall of Toronto, and Nancy Diamond of Oshawa, were advocating that all regional governments in the GTA should be done away with. The new provincial government of Premier Mike Harris initially favourably disposed to implementing the Anne Golden recommendations soon ran into flak from the four mayors and other municipal politicians. That caused the Harris government to review all of the options once again.[4]

The tipping point in favour of total amalgamation actually had occurred unbeknownst to anyone at the time in 1988 when the Ontario government of David Peterson had changed the Metro system of government so that those sitting on Metro Council apart from the Mayors of each local municipality such as the Mayor of East York, would be

3. The *East Yorker*, 1996

4. Redway, Alan, *Governing Toronto: Bringing back the city that worked*, Friesen Press, November, 2014, 123

directly elected by the voters to Metro Council and no longer sit on the six local councils, as before.

When asked why his government had made that change, "Former Premier David Peterson told me that for him, "it was a no brainer. It just evolved." It was of course a no brainer. It was the democratic thing to do; elect the people who represent you at every level of government."[5]

When the Peterson government made that change, "Public involvement on the issue appears to have come only after the province, Metro and the six local councils raised it themselves. Public reaction after the fact was quite modest and certainly not unanimous. For instance, in a letter dated January 20, 1987, Orville Leigh, a past president of the Leaside Property Owners Association, told East York Council it should leave a system that was working well alone and not make any changes."[6]

However, that "no brainer" had a key role in bringing about total amalgamation.

"Former Toronto Mayor David Crombie, known as the defender of neighbourhoods, says it was the key factor that turned him into a supporter of total amalgamation."[7]

But the absolute final decision was made at a meeting arranged by the premier's office, which was held at the Albany Club on October 10, 1996. Present were the Premier Mike Harris, the Minister of Municipal Affairs Al Leach, the Minister of Health and former East York Mayor Dave Johnson, the Premier's election campaign chairman Tom Long, Paul Godfrey and David Crombie. According to Paul Godfrey, the Premier chaired the meeting and opened it by asking: "What should we do about Toronto, leave it or reduce it to four?" David Crombie recalls it somewhat differently. He says Mike Harris only asked about amalgamation. However, both Godfrey and Crombie agree that the Premier first turned to Godfrey and said "Paul you always have a lot to say." According to Al Leach, Godfrey then spoke out strongly in favour of total amalgamation and dominated the discussion. Paul Godfrey told me that in arriving at his decision, the catalyst was the direct election of Metro Councillors.

─────

5. Redway, Alan, *Governing Toronto: Bringing back the city that worked*, Friesen Press, November, 2014, 105

6. Redway, Alan, *Governing Toronto: Bringing back the city that worked*, Friesen Press, November, 2014, 105

7. Redway, Alan, *Governing Toronto: Bringing back the city that worked*, Friesen Press, November,

David Crombie then followed saying, "Paul as a former Metro Chairman, I never thought I would ever hear you say that but I agree with you." The catalyst for Crombie was also the direct election of Metro Councillors. They both said it made no sense to have local municipalities with directly elected Metro Councillors. The 1988 "no brainer" may have been more democratic but by severing the connection between local councils and Metro, carefully crafted by Leslie Frost and Lorne Cumming in 1953, it had destroyed the form of municipal government admired around the world. Leach, Godfrey and Crombie all agree that there was no dissent from anyone in the room. Paul Godfrey warned the Premier he would face major disagreements and to expect to hear every possible reason for not doing it because everyone likes the status quo. Neither Harris nor Leach voiced an opinion but said they wanted to digest what had been discussed. Later at lunch, David Crombie recalls Tom Long saying, "If we are going to do it, we have got to do it fast and bomb the shit out of them before they know what's happened to them.[8]

William Walker, writing in the *Toronto Star* on December 21, 1996, said that according to the unnamed official, "Crombie was the key. When we heard the king of neighbourhoods, the guy who grew up in Swansea, say there won't be damage to neighbourhoods then we felt pretty good about it intellectually. It just put everybody at ease."[9]

For some at least, David Crombie, Paul Godfrey, and Dave Johnson's support for amalgamation was not a surprise. In his 1974 book *The Tiny Perfect Mayor*, Jon Caufield pointed out that both Crombie and Godfrey appeared to favour uniting Metro's boroughs in the long run, into a single political unit governed by a single council. After Al Leach introduced Bill 103 in the Legislature, *Globe and Mail* columnist Colin Vaughan reminded his readers that in 1989, then East York Mayor Dave Johnson predicted in the *Globe and Mail*'s Toronto magazine that Metro would be amalgamated by the turn of the century and was quoted at the time as saying, "It will happen pretty quickly when it comes."[10]

---

8. Redway, Alan, *Governing Toronto: Bringing back the city that worked*, Friesen Press, November, 2014, 154
9. Redway, Alan, *Governing Toronto: Bringing back the city that worked*, Friesen Press, November, 2014, 155
10. Redway, Alan, *Governing Toronto: Bringing back the city that worked*, Friesen Press, November, 2014, 155

Just prior to the public announcement, the six Metro mayors, including Michael Prue, met with Minister of Municipal Affairs Al Leach, who told them total amalgamation was in the works. The mayors then asked for and were given thirty days to come up with their own plan. Their plan resembled in many ways the one previously advanced by Hazel McCallion, Mel Lastman, Barbara Hall, and Nancy Diamond, which should not be surprising since two of the six mayors signed both documents.[11]

At the time, Mayor Michael Prue reported on the six mayors' plan in the East Yorker.

Mayor's Message

For over a month the six mayors, representing the six municipalities make up Metropolitan Toronto, have been fighting the idea of a megacity. These have not been easy times, nor have the decisions that have had to be made. At stake is the very way of life that makes our borough so unique.

Let us all stop and reflect upon why we chose and why we continue to choose to live in East York. Surely, it is not just a fortuitous act of fate which brought us here. We chose East York because it is a unique community in the middle of a very large city. We chose it because it was safe and clean and well run. We admired the many community organizations which contributed so much to our daily life — everything from Meals on Wheels to seniors' care to the baseball, soccer, and hockey associations which service our youth. We chose East York because here people do make a difference. Our council is open and accessible. Everyone is welcome to serve on boards and committees which help run the borough. We are small enough to provide total citizen input and yet large enough to handle all of the big city problems with ease and grace.

Let us also take the time to speculate about a megacity — a city like New York or Los Angeles where decisions are made centrally and where citizens' opinions are registered only at times of elections. Let us see the problems of those places where the citizens have lost control of their neighbourhoods and the downward spiral into crime, violence and urban decay.

---

11. Redway, Alan, *Governing Toronto: Bringing back the city that worked*, Friesen Press, November, 2014, 129 2014, 155

What we are fighting for is our way of life. Cities have been part of the political landscape even before there were provinces. In fact, city governments have exited right back into classical times. They have been built and nurtured by the people of each municipality. Each one is unique and each one reflects the values of those who live there.

The six mayors realize this and are prepared to fight for that which has served us so well. We are not attempting to preserve something negative nor are we trying to save our own jobs as the major media so selfishly portrays.

This debate is about so much more!

Our plan would make government simpler. It would reduce the duplicated services which currently exist between Metro and the municipalities. It would result in modest tax savings and eliminate a whole layer of government.

Most importantly, we are looking to the future. Metro has overgrown the borders set for it in 1953. Whole large communities now exist in Mississauga, Vaughan, and Markham. The urban landscape continues to change with most population growth taking place in the areas outside the Metro boundaries. Our plan recognizes that coordination of intra-municipal services like police, water, and transit must be coordinated not only here, but in the new and sprawling suburban communities which surround us. We have looked to the future and planned for a new relationship with the people of the Greater Toronto Area.

But most of all, this debate is about democracy. Not the kind of democracy where you vote every three years, but about the kind you find in our municipalities. It is the kind of democracy where citizens have the right to hear and to be heard. It is about input and local decision-making.

What we fear most as East Yorkers is that our sense of who and what we are will be swallowed up in the giant maw of a megacity where we will become just a tiny percentage of people with competing interests.

It is for these reasons that we fight on and for these reasons that we must win. East Yorkers overwhelmingly support our continuing existence and have come forward in great numbers to save our borough. Our council cannot and must not fail![12]

---

12. The *East Yorker*, 1996

The dye was cast. An Environics poll concluded that 52% of Metro residents were opposed to amalgamation, although it was enthusiastically supported by the *Toronto Star*, the *Globe and Mail*, and the *Toronto Sun*. The decision led to a citizen revolt across Metro. That was especially true in East York.[13]

As soon as the announcement was made public, a large number of residents from every part of the borough appeared at the next council meeting to protest the provincial decision, including Brian Barron, Kim Scaiff, John Ridout, Edna Beange, Andrea Villiers, Case Ootes, and Allan Gaw. This led to the formation of Team East York.[14]

In early January 1997, the Borough of East York communications director invited some thirty residents to a meeting in the cafeteria of the East York Civic Centre. Team East York was born that evening. Colin MacLeod was chosen as chair to lead the team and the fight. Later, I was appointed honorary chairman and former Mayor Willis Blair was appointed honorary treasurer of Team East York. Colin MacLeod, together with a large dedicated group of East York volunteers, rented an office staffed full time by at least five or six volunteers; held public planning meetings at the S. Walter Stewart Library every Monday night; organized a door to door canvas of residents; supervised the erection of lawn signs reading "Vote No to the Megacity" and initiated a yellow ribbon campaign which was later adopted by the C4LD (the Committee For Local Democracy, a Toronto citizen committee organized by former Toronto Mayor John Sewell) and soon spread right across Metro. They also organized a number of mass meetings including one at East York Collegiate where Jack Christie, the long-time chairman of East York Hydro, publicly ripped up his Ontario Progressive Conservative membership card. East York Council offered start-up funds to anyone who wanted to organize either in support or in opposition to amalgamation. No one who supported amalgamation ever took up the offer even though Mayor Prue spoke to a number of them personally about it. Team East York borrowed $4,000 but soon paid it back in full from public donations, which included the entire reserve fund of the East York Federation of Taxpayers.[15]

---

13. Redway, Alan, *Governing Toronto: Bringing back the city that worked*, Friesen Press, November, 2014, 157

14. East York Council Minutes, December 1996

15. Redway, Alan, *Governing Toronto: Bringing back the city that worked*, Friesen Press, November, 2014, 168

Team East York

...is a volunteer community action group who are working to ensure that East Yorkers all take the opportunity to vote in the referendum on the subject of amalgamation.

TEAM EAST YORK meets every Monday night at 7:00 p.m. at the S. Walter Stewart Library auditorium. Interested individuals and volunteers are very welcome!

TEAM EAST YORK has opened a storefront at 1350 Woodbine Avenue (Woodbine and Cosburn). You can stop by the location to pick up information, yellow ribbon, lawn signs, or drop by and volunteer to help ensure that East York's referendum has a tremendous turnout of voters.

TEAM EAST YORK is pleased to announce that ALL Canada Trust branches in East York are ready to accept donations to help fight the Megacity proposal.[16]

East Yorkers who played a key role as volunteers with TEAM EAST YORK included: Colin McLeod, Peter Scaiff, Kim Scaiff, Edna Beange, Maureen Lindsay, Colleen Peacock, and Donna Lynn McCallum.[17]

All six Metro municipal councils agreed to hold local referendums. The municipalities called this a binding vote. The provincial government said it was a non-binding plebiscite. [18]

Donna Lynn McCallum
(Source: bing.com)

16. The *East Yorker*, 1997
17. Interview with Peter Scaiff, August 29, 2016
18. Redway, Alan, *Governing Toronto: Bringing back the city that worked*, Friesen Press, November, 2014, 171

Team EY
(Source: thestar.comnewsgta2017)

Notice of Referendum

The Council of the Borough of East York at its meeting held on Monday, January 20, 1997 passed a by-law approving the wording for the Mail In Referendum to be held on March 3, 1997.

The question shall read as follows:

Are you in favour of eliminating the Borough of East York and all other existing municipalities in Metropolitan Toronto and amalgamating them into a Mega-City?

Yes

No

Ballots will be mailed out to voters by Friday, February 14, 1997. The ballot is to be returned sealed in the enclosed stamped, self-addressed envelope. This will maintain security so no elector's vote is identified. These ballots must be received at the Civic Centre no later than 8:00 p.m. on Monday, March 3, 1997.

If you do not receive a ballot and you are entitled to be a voter, you may attend at the Clerk's Department at the Civic Centre, 850 Coxwell Avenue on Monday, February 17, 1997 to Friday, February 28, 1997 from 8:30 a.m. until 4:30 p.m. and on Monday, March 3, 1997 from 8:30 a.m. until 8:00 p.m. to complete an application swearing that you should have received a ballot because you have the following qualifications:

During the period from January 3, 1997 to March 3, 1997, resides in East York, or is the owner or tenant of land in East York, or is the spouse of an owner of tenant land in East York; <u>and</u>

- is a Canadian citizen on March 3, 1997, and
- is or will be at least 18 years old on March 3, 1997, and
- is not otherwise prohibited by law from voting.

Persons meeting the above qualifications who have not individually received a ballot, and who would like to vote can apply to the Borough Clerk at the East York Civic Centre, 850 Coxwell Avenue, Monday to Friday, between the hours of 8:30 a.m. and 4:30 p.m. up to and including March 3, 1997, to complete the required prescribed form and receive a ballot. [19]

East York residents voted 81% against the megacity but the Province ignored the vote. In spite of a constitutional court challenge by East York, Toronto, and Etobicoke, total amalgamation of Metropolitan Toronto took effect on January 1, 1998. The Borough of East York was no more.[20]

The last word expressed by now former Mayor Michael Prue in the final edition of the East Yorker was through a Mayor's Message:

Packing up one's desk is the final act of leaving a job. One can do it in bitterness, or one can do it in hope of a new future under different circumstances.

On 10 November, the people of East York gave me the opportunity to go on representing them at the new City of Toronto. It is a responsibility which I will never hold lightly. Moreover, it is a responsibility with which you have entrusted me to ensure that our interests will be safeguarded in a city of 2.4 million people.

This last year has been difficult for all of us, but most especially for the members of East York Council. It is a tribute to their integrity and their stamina that we have finished our term of office as we started it— with a commitment to provide decent, honest, and affordable government to the people of the borough.

The councillors elected in 1994 probably never imagined that they would be the last people elected to our municipality. Nor did they believe that the demise of our borough would take place against the popular will of our people. But events unfolded in uncharacteristic haste. History will

---

19. East York Council minutes, March 1997
20. Redway, Alan, *Governing Toronto: Bringing back the city that worked*, Friesen Press, November, 2014, 172

be the judge of whether these initiatives will help or hinder the growth of our communities.

Having realized the difficult road that lay before us, our council steadfastly held its course. We balanced our budgets for an unprecedented fifth year in a row. We paid down our debts. There were no new debentures. New industry was brought and older industries were encouraged to spend monies on redevelopment. We set up the New Media Village to explore the myriad ways of bringing high technology to our commercial areas. Parks were upgraded, roads paved, sewers relined and programs maintained, building permits were issued and rezoning applications approved.[21]

Addressing the inaugural meeting of Council in 1962, Reeve True Davidson said, "We need to exercise constant vigilance at the Metro and provincial levels if we are to maintain the community identity we all prize so highly."[22] True knew what she was talking about.

Thirty-five years after True's warning, in spite of our constant vigilance, the province amalgamated the Borough of East York with the megacity of Toronto, but East York community identity continues to live on in Toronto's Garden of Eden.

Anne Golden   Crombie
(Source: Tor Star_Getstock.com)   *(Source: Eglinton_getstock.com)*

21. The *East Yorker,* 1997
22. East York Council minutes, January 1962

Godfrey

(Source: Tor Star_Getstock.com)

Allan Leach

(Source: Allan Leach 2014)

Mike Harris

(Source: Mike Harris 2014)

POSTSCRIPT

Although the Ontario provincial government erased the Corporation of the Borough of East York when it created the Toronto megacity in 1998, the name East York still lives on prominently and proudly displayed on many buildings and by sports teams throughout the community. As well, both the annual First of July celebration organized by the East York Canada Day Committee, headed by Shannon Timms-Ugochukwu and Murray Smith, and the East York Historical Society, headed by President Pancheta (Pat) Barnett and Past President Margaret McRae, provide an ongoing reminder of the borough's rich past. Local Councillors Mary Fragedakis and Janet Davis scored a major victory at Toronto Council, ensuring that the East York logo would continue to be displayed on street signs within the former borough. Justin Van Dette initiated the East York Hall of Fame to recognize the contributions of prominent residents and to promote the display of the East York flag in the community. Two other extremely important organizations with mandates help keep the borough alive, the East York Foundation and the Agnes Macphail Awards Committee.

The East York Foundation was established by an Act of the Ontario Legislature in 1965 at the initiative of then Township Reeve True

Davidson. The act was amended and updated in 1973 after the merger of the former Town of Leaside and the former Township of East York in order to include the new boundaries of the Borough of East York. All of the board of directors, now chaired by Raymond White, must live within the boundaries of the area formerly known as the Borough of East York. The foundation is mandated to hold title to all of the artistic, cultural, and historic articles owned by the Borough of East York at the time of its amalgamation with the city of Toronto. The act also empowers the foundation to make donations for other educational, cultural, and aesthetic purposes within the boundary lines of the former Borough of East York. Because the foundation is a charitable non-profit corporation, financial contributions made to it are income tax deductible. Since amalgamation, among other things, the foundation has helped to fund the multimillion dollar construction of the second ice rink at Leaside Memorial Community Gardens as well as providing funding assistance for the Agnes Macphail Awards Committee and the East York Hall of Fame.

The late Agnes Macphail was once described as "the most important woman in public life that Canada has produced in the twentieth century." In 1921, she became the first woman elected to the House of Commons in Ottawa, and then in 1943, she became the first woman elected to the Ontario Legislature, where she represented East York as the Member for York East.

The Agnes Macphail Award was created by East York Council in 1994 following the fiftieth anniversary of her election as the Member of the Ontario Legislature for York East in order to honour residents of the then-Borough of East York, now residents living within the boundary lines of the former Borough of East York, who have made outstanding contributions as a volunteer and a leader in one or more of the areas championed by Agnes Macphail herself, namely women's rights, fairness to seniors, the criminal justice system and penal reform, international peace and disarmament, adequate housing, health care and education, and more. The ideal recipient lives by Agnes' motto: "Think globally, act locally." The award is now administered by a committee made up of former recipients chaired by former East York Councillor Lorna Krawchuk.

As long as these organizations exist and local councillors who represent parts of the former borough continue to respect and honour the special caring community spirit demonstrated by residents of Toronto's Garden of Eden, East York will never die.

Ray White
(Source: bestofeastyork.com)

Lorna Krawchuk
(Source: leasidematters.ca)

East York Canada Day 2018
(Source: InsideToronto.com)

2017 East York Historical Society board members (front row, left to right) Ron Chamberlain, Ron Brown and Kay Horiszny. Back row (left to right), EYHS President Pancheta 'Pat' Barnett, John Michailidis, Justin Van Dette, Margaret McRae, Val Dodge

(Source: Tony Wright)

Hall of Fame

(Source: EY Hall of Fame website)

Mary Fragedakis
(Source: toronto.ca)

Janet Davis Councillor
(Source: toronto.ca)

Jon Burnside Councillor
(Source: toronto.ca)

APPENDIX A

Township of East York Council

1924	**Reeve:** Robert Barker; **1st Deputy Reeve:** Robert H. McGregor; **2nd Deputy Reeve:** John Galbraith; **3rd Deputy Reeve:** Dennis McCarthy; **Councillor:** H. Chapman
1925	**Reeve:** Robert Barker; **1st Deputy Reeve:** Robert H. McGregor; **2nd Deputy Reeve:** John Galbraith; **3rd Deputy Reeve:** Dennis McCarthy; **Councillor:** H. Chapman
1926	**Reeve:** Robert H. McGregor; **1st Deputy Reeve:** R.M. Leslie; **2nd Deputy Reeve:** J.H. Meighan; **3rd Deputy Reeve:** A. Cheeseman **Councillor:** Charles Legg
1927	**Reeve:** R.M. Leslie; **1st Deputy Reeve:** Dennis McCarthy; **2nd Deputy Reeve:** A.J. Cheeseman; **3rd Deputy Reeve:** Charles Legg Councillor: James Michael
1928	**Reeve:** R.M. Leslie; **1st Deputy Reeve:** Dennis McCarthy; **2nd Deputy Reeve:** A.J. Cheeseman; **3rd Deputy Reeve:** Charles Legg **Councillor:** James Michael
1929	**Reeve:** R.M. Leslie; **1st Deputy Reeve:** A.J. Cheeseman; **2nd Deputy Reeve:** James Michael; **3rd Deputy Reeve:** J.H. Meighan Councillor: John Galbraith
1930	**Reeve:** R.M. Leslie; **1st Deputy Reeve:** A.J. Cheeseman; **2nd Deputy Reeve:** James Michael; **3rd Deputy Reeve:** J.H. Meighan **Councillor:** Joseph Vernon
1931	**Reeve:** R.M. Leslie; **1st Deputy Reeve:** James Michael; **2nd Deputy Reeve:** J.H. Meighan; **3rd Deputy Reeve:** Joseph Vernon **Councillor:** John Hollinger
1932	**Reeve:** R.M. Leslie; **Deputy Reeve:** J.H. Meighan **Councillors:** Joseph Vernon, John Warren, A.J. Cheeseman
1933	**Reeve:** R.M. Leslie; **Deputy Reeve:** John Doggett **Councillors:** Joseph Vernon, John Warren, J. Walker
1934	**Reeve:** John Warren; **Deputy Reeve:** John Doggett **Councillors:** J. Walker, James Michael, A.H. Williams
1935	**Reeve:** John Warren; **Deputy Reeve:** John Doggett **Councillors:** James Michael, Joseph Vernon, J. Walker
1936	**Reeve:** A.H. Williams; **Deputy Reeve:** John Doggett **Councillors:** James Michael, Joseph Vernon, J. Walker

1937	**Reeve:** John Warren; **Deputy Reeve:** John Doggett **Councillors:** John Hollinger, J. Walker, G. Treadway
1938	**Reeve:** John Warren; **Deputy Reeve:** John Doggett **Councillors:** George S. Treadway, John Hollinger, James Michael
1939	**Reeve:** John Warren; **Deputy Reeve:** John Doggett **Councillors:** George S. Treadway, John Hollinger, James Michael
1940	**Reeve:** John Warren; **Deputy Reeve:** John Doggett **Councillors:** George S. Treadway, John Hollinger, James Michael
1941	**Reeve:** John Warren; **Deputy Reeve:** John Doggett **Councillors:** George S. Treadway, John Hollinger, A. Blake
1942	**Reeve:** John Warren; **Deputy Reeve:** John Doggett **Councillors:** George S. Treadway, A. Blake, J Hollinger
1943	**Reeve:** John Warren; **Deputy Reeve:** John Doggett **Councillors:** John Hollinger, George S. Treadway, A. Blake
1944	**Reeve:** John Warren; **Deputy Reeve:** George S. Treadway **Councillors:** Walter S. Taylor, A. Blake, James Michael
1945	**Reeve:** John Warren; **Deputy Reeve:** George S. Treadway **Councillors:** Walter S. Taylor, James Michael, Harry G. Simpson
1946	**Reeve:** John Warren; **Deputy Reeve:** Walter S. Taylor **Councillors:** James Michael, Harry G. Simpson, John Doggett
1947	**Reeve:** John Warren; **Deputy Reeve:** Walter S. Taylor **Councillors:** James Michael, Harry G. Simpson, John Doggett
1948	**Reeve:** John Warren; **Deputy Reeve:** Harry G. Simpson **Councillors:** Walter S. Taylor, Richard John Doggett, James Michael
1949	**Reeve:** John Warren; **Deputy Reeve:** John Hollinger **Councillors:** Richard John Doggett, Walter S. Taylor, Norman Cheeseman
1950	**Reeve:** Harry G. Simpson; **Deputy Reeve:** John Hollinger **Councillors:** Norman Cheeseman, Walter S. Taylor, Walter A. Pugh
1951	**Reeve:** Harry G. Simpson; **Deputy Reeve:** John Hollinger **Councillors:** Norman Cheeseman, John Warren, Marie C. Taylor
1952	**Reeve:** Harry G. Simpson; **Deputy Reeve:** John Hollinger **Councillors:** Marie C. Taylor, Percy S. Bustin, George S. Treadway, C. Howard Chandler, N. McKay
1953	**Reeve:** Harry G. Simpson; **Deputy Reeve:** Marie C. Taylor **Councillors:** Percy S. Bustin, Robert M. Kesten, C. Howard Chandler, John H. McGivney, George S. Treadway

1954	**Reeve:** Harry G. Simpson
	Councillors: Jack R. Allen; Percy S. Bustin, George S. Treadway, John H. McGivney, C. Howard Chandler, Norman Cheeseman
1955	**Reeve:** Harry G. Simpson
	Councillors: C. Howard Chandler, Norman Cheeseman, Percy S. Bustin, John H. McGivney, George S. Treadway, Norman McKay
1956	**Reeve:** Harry G. Simpson
	Councillors: C. Howard Chandler, Norman Cheeseman, Percy S. Bustin, George S. Treadway, Norman McKay, Jack R. Allen
1957 – 1958	**Reeve:** Jack R. Allen
	Councillors: Harry G. Simpson, Percy S. Bustin, Norman Cheeseman, G.S. Treadway, William L. Camblin, Norman McKay (two year term)
1959 – 1960	**Reeve:** Jack R. Allen
	Councillors: True Davidson, Norman Cheeseman, Percy S. Bustin, Royden Brigham, Willis Blair, Norman McKay (two year term)
1961 – 1962	**Reeve:** True Davidson
	Councillors: Leslie H. Saunders, Willis L. Blair, James McConaghy, Percy S. Bustin, Norman Maughan, Norman McKay (two year term)
1963 – 1964	**Reeve:** True Davidson
	Councillors: Leslie H. Saunders, Willis L. Blair, James McConaghy, Royden Brigham, Norman Cheeseman, Norman Maughan (two year term)
1965 – 1966	**Reeve:** True Davidson
	Councillors: Willis Blair, James A. McConaghy, C. Howard Chandler, Norman Maughan, C. Howard Chandler, Royden Brigham, Norman Cheeseman (two year term)

Councils of the Borough of East York
Since 1967

Year	Mayor	Alderman Ward 1	Alderman Ward 2	Alderman Ward 3	Alderman Ward 4
1967 1968 1969	T. Davidson	W. L. Blair J. McConaghy	C.H. Chandler N. Maughan	L.H. Saunders N. Cheeseman (resigned 1969)	V.H. Page J.D. Jagger
1970 1971 1972	T. Davidson	W. L. Blair J. McConaghy	C.H. Chandler N. Maughan	L.H. Saunders J.R. Irwin	V.H. Page J.D. Jagger

Oct. 1970 J. McConaghy (resigned August 31, 1970) was replaced by J. Ridout – elected by Council

2 Year Terms Begin

1973 1974	W. L. Blair	J.D. Johnson W.S. Wadlow	C.H. Chandler N. Maughan	L.H. Saunders J.R. Irwin	O.M. Reicker A.A.S. Redway
1975 1976	W. L. Blair	J.D. Johnson W.S. Wadlow	C.H. Chandler J.F. Flowers	L.H. Saunders R.J. Ireland	A.A.S. Redway J.E. Beange

April 12, 1976 W.L. Blair resigned

L.H. Saunders appointed as Mayor

O.M. Reicker appointed Alderman Ward 3 to replace L.H. Saunders who became Mayor

1977 1978	A.A.S. Redway	J.D. Johnson L.H. Saunders	J.F. Flowers N.S. Crone	R.J. Ireland D. Van Mierlo	J.E. Beange P.E. Oyler
1979 1980	A.A.S. Redway	J.D. Johnson C. Reader	J.F. Flowers N.S. Crone	D. Van Mierlo G.P. Crann	P.E. Oyler H.T. McGroarty
1981 1982	A.A.S. Redway	J.D. Johnson C. Reader	N. Crone M. Wyatt	G. Crann K. Page	P.E. Oyler H.T. McGroarty
1983- 1985	J.D. Johnson	C. Reader R. Willis	N. Crone M. Wyatt	G. Crann K. Page	P.E. Oyler J.E. Beange
1986- 1988	J.D. Johnson	C. Reader R. Willis	B. Buckingham G. Vasilopoulos	B. Dale S. Mastoras	P.E. Oyler J.E. Beange
1989- 1991	J.D. Johnson	C. Ootes M. Prue	B. Buckingham G. Vasilopoulos	H. Kennedy S. Mastoras	L. Krawchuk J. Jean-Marie
1992- 1994	J.D. Johnson	C. Ootes M. Prue	G. Vasilopoulos D. Anderson	B. Dale J. Papadakis	L. Krawchuk J. Jean-Marie

April 7, 1993 D.I. Johnson resigned
M. Prue appointed as Mayor

May 17, 1993 N. S. Crone appointed as Councillor – Ward 1

July 11, 1994 J. E. Beange appointed as Councillor – Ward 4 to replace J. Jean-Marie who died on June 18, 1994

1995-1997	M. Prue	N. Crone M. Tziretas	G. Vasilopoulos P. Robinson	B. Dale J. Antonopolous	L. Krawchuk T. Cholvat

Metro Council Elected

1989 – 1991   P.E. Oyler

1992 – 1994   P.E. Oyler

1995 – 1997   C. Ootes

APPENDIX B

Board of Education Trustees

Township of East York
Board of Education Trustees

1937   Walter Stewart, Fred Hazelton, Albert Croft, J.D. Mills, George Webster, R.J. Thompson, George Leggett, Separate School Rep, C.G. Perry

1938   Walter Stewart, Fred Hazelton, Albert Croft, J.D. Mills, George Webster, R.J. Thompson, George Leggett, Separate School Rep, C.G. Perry

1939   Walter Stewart, Fred Hazelton, J.D. Mills, George Webster, R.J. Thompson, George Leggett, James Fletcher, George Heaton, Separate School Rep, C.G. Perry

1940   Walter Stewart, Fred Hazelton, J.D. Mills, George Webster, R.J. Thompson, George Leggett, James Fletcher, George Heaton, Separate School Rep, Anthony McMullen

1941   Walter Stewart, Fred Hazelton, J.D. Mills, George Webster, R.J. Thompson, George Leggett, James Fletcher, George Heaton, Separate School Rep, Anthony McMullen

1942   Walter Stewart, Fred Hazelton, J.D. Mills, George Webster, R.J. Thompson, George Leggett, James Fletcher, George Heaton, Separate School Rep, Anthony McMullen

1943   J.D. Mills, George Webster, R.J. Thompson, James Fletcher, George Heaton, W. Gottschalk, C.R. Purcell, Separate School Rep, Anthony McMullen

1944   J.D. Mills, George Webster, R.J. Thompson, James Fletcher, George Heaton, W. Gottschalk, C.R. Purcell, Separate School Rep, Anthony McMullen

1945   George Webster, R.J. Thompson, James Fletcher, George Heaton, W. Gottschalk, C.R. Purcell, Separate School Rep, Anthony McMullen

1946   George Webster, R.J. Thompson, James Fletcher, George Heaton, W. Gottschalk, C.R. Purcell, Separate School Rep, Anthony McMullen

1947   George Webster, R.J. Thompson, James Fletcher, George Heaton, W. Gottschalk, C.R. Purcell, Separate School Rep, Anthony McMullen

1948   George Webster, R.J. Thompson, James Fletcher, George Heaton, W. Gottschalk, C.R. Purcell, Separate School Rep, Anthony McMullen

1949   George Webster, R.J. Thompson, James Fletcher, George Heaton, W. Gottschalk, C.R. Purcell, True Davidson, Separate School Rep, Anthony McMullen

1950   George Webster, R.J. Thompson, James Fletcher, George Heaton, W. Gottschalk, C.R. Purcell, True Davidson, Separate School Rep, Anthony McMullen

1951   George Webster, R.J. Thompson, James Fletcher, George Heaton, C.R. Purcell, True Davidson, Separate School Rep, Anthony McMullen

1952   George Webster, James Fletcher, George Heaton, C.R. Purcell, True Davidson, John S. McAllister, Separate School Rep, Mrs. Lillian Arbour

1953   George Webster, James Fletcher, True Davidson, John S. McAllister, Mrs. Agnes Ross, Reg Martin, Separate School Rep, Mrs. Lillian Arbour

1954   George Webster, True Davidson, John S. McAllister, Mrs. Agnes Ross, Reg Martin, Separate School Rep, Mr. Griffin

1955   True Davidson, John S. McAllister, Mrs. Agnes Ross, Reg Martin, Royden Brigham, Separate School Rep, Ralph Reilly

1956   True Davidson, John S. McAllister, Mrs. Agnes Ross, Reg Martin, Royden Brigham, Separate School Rep, Ralph Reilly

1957   True Davidson, John S. McAllister, Mrs. Agnes Ross, Reg Martin, Mrs. Gertrude Beattie, Separate School Rep, Ralph Reilly

1958   True Davidson, John S. McAllister, Mrs. Agnes Ross, Reg Martin, Mrs. Gertrude Beattie, Separate School Rep, Ralph Reilly

1959   John S. McAllister, Mrs. Agnes Ross, Reg Martin, Mrs. Gertrude Beattie, W.E. Eade, Separate School Rep, Ralph Reilly

1960   John S. McAllister, Mrs. Agnes Ross, Reg Martin, Mrs. Gertrude Beattie, W.E. Eade, Separate School Rep, Ralph Reilly

1961   Mrs. Agnes Ross, Reg Martin, W.E. Eade, Mrs. Joyce McAllister, Jack Irwin, Separate School Rep, Ralph Reilly

1962   Mrs. Agnes Ross, Reg Martin, W.E. Eade, Jack Irwin, Dr. Jim Bell, Separate School Rep, Ralph Reilly

1963   Mrs. Agnes Ross, Reg Martin, W.E. Eade, Jim Buller, George Cartwright, Separate School Rep, Ralph Reilly

1964   Mrs. Agnes Ross, Reg Martin, W.E. Eade, Jim Buller, George Cartwright, Separate School Rep, Ralph Reilly

1965   Mrs. Agnes Ross, Reg Martin, Jim Buller, George Cartwright, Charles Clarke, Separate School Rep, Ralph Reilly

1966   Mrs. Agnes Ross, Reg Martin, Jim Buller, George Cartwright, Charles Clarke, Separate School Rep, Ralph Reilly

Borough of East York
Board of Education Trustees

1979-80   Ward 1   Ken Maxted, Ruth Goldhar
            Ward 2   Edith Treadway, Jim Palmer
            Ward 3   Bill Phillips, Margaret Hazelton
            Ward 4   Norman Aspin, Gordon Isbister
            Separate School Reps, Anna Marie Sherlock, Mary Staples
            Metro Separate School Rep, Jack Graham

1981-82   Ward 1   Ruth Goldhar, Gordon Brown
            Ward 2   Jim Palmer, Ken Maxted
            Ward 3   Bill Phillips, Margaret Hazelton
            Ward 4   Steve Overgaard, Michael Globe
            Separate School Reps, Anna Marie Sherlock, Mary Staples
            Metro Separate School Rep, Jack Graham

1983-85   Ward 1   Ruth Goldhar, Gordon Brown
            Ward 2   Jim Palmer, Ken Maxted
            Ward 3   Bill Phillips, Margaret Hazelton
            Ward 4   Dr. Bob Murray, Elca Rennick
            Separate School Reps, Anna Marie Sherlock, Mary Staples
            Metro Separate School Rep, Jack Graham

1986-88   Ward 1   Ruth Goldhar, Gail Nyberg
            Ward 2   Ken Maxted, Connie Culbertson
            Ward 3   Margaret Hazelton, Len Self
            Ward 4   Dr. Bob Murray, Elca Rennick
            Separate School Reps, Anna Marie Sherlock, Mary Staples
            Metro Separate School Rep, Catherine O'Halloran

1989-91   Ward 1   Gail Nyberg, Janet McKeown
            Ward 2   Ken Maxted, Connie Culbertson
            Ward 3   Margaret Hazelton, Len Self
            Ward 4   Elca Rennick, Ruth Goldhar
            Metro French Language School Council Rep, Pierre Touchette
            Metro Separate School Rep, Anna Marie Sherlock
            French Language MSSB Rep, Jean-Guy Saint-Yves, Charles
            Arsenault, Paul S. Rouleau

1992-94   Ward 1   Gail Nyberg, Janet McKeown
           Ward 2   Ken Maxted, Connie Culbertson
           Ward 3   Margaret Hazelton, Bessie Anagnostopoulos
           Ward 4   Elca Rennick, Ruth Goldhar
           Metro French Language School Council Rep, Mohammed
           Brihmi, Veronique Perez-McCall
           Metro Separate School Rep, Paul Fernandes
           French Language MSSB Rep, Jean-Guy Saint-Yves, Charles
           Arsenault, J.E.M. Robert Despatie

1995-97   Ward 1   Gail Nyberg, Cindy Anthony
           Ward 2   Jay Josefs, Elizabeth Rowley
           Ward 3   Margaret Hazelton, Bessie Anagnostopoulos
           Ward 4   Ruth Goldhar, Jane Pitfield
           Metro French Language School Council Rep, Mohammed
           Brihmi, Jean-Marc Couffin
           Metro Separate School Rep, Paul Fernandes
           French Language MSSB Rep, Andre Duclos

APPENDIX C

East York Hydro Commissioners

1925	Albert Jennings Chairman, Horace Walsh, Robert McGregor Reeve
1926	Albert Jennings Chairman, Horace Walsh, Robert McGregor Reeve
1927	Albert Jennings Chairman, Horace Walsh, R. Leslie Reeve
1928	Albert Jennings Chairman, Horace Walsh, R. Leslie Reeve
1929	Albert Jennings Chairman, George Martin, R. Leslie Reeve
1930	Albert Jennings Chairman, George Martin, R. Leslie Reeve
1931	Albert Jennings Chairman, George Martin, R. Leslie Reeve
1932	Albert Jennings Chairman, George Martin, R. Leslie Reeve
1933	Albert Jennings Chairman, George Martin, R. Leslie Reeve
1934	Albert Jennings Chairman, George Martin, John Warren Reeve
1935	George Martin Chairman, Albert Jennings, John Warren Reeve
1936	George Martin Chairman, Albert Jennings, A.H. Williams Reeve
1937	George Martin Chairman, Albert Jennings, John Warren Reeve
1938	George Martin Chairman, Albert Jennings, John Warren Reeve
1939	Albert Jennings Chairman, Ray Law, John Warren Reeve
1940	Albert Jennings Chairman, Ray Law, John Warren Reeve
1941	Albert Jennings Chairman, Ray Law, John Warren Reeve
1942	Albert Jennings Chairman, Ray Law, John Warren Reeve
1943	Albert Jennings Chairman, Charles Legg, John Warren Reeve
1944	F.M. Hazelton Chairman, Charles Legg, John Warren Reeve
1945	F.M. Hazelton Chairman, Charles Legg, John Warren Reeve
1946	Albert Jennings Chairman, Charles Legg, John Warren Reeve
1947	Albert Jennings Chairman, Ray Law, John Warren Reeve
1948	Albert Jennings Chairman, Ray Law, John Warren Reeve
1949	Albert Jennings Chairman, Charles Legg, John Warren Reeve
1950	Albert Jennings Chairman, Charles Legg, Harry Simpson Reeve
1951	Charles Ellerbeck Chairman, Charles Legg, Harry Simpson Reeve
1952	Charles Ellerbeck Chairman, Charles Legg, Harry Simpson Reeve
1953	Charles Ellerbeck Chairman, Charles Legg, Harry Simpson Reeve
1954	Norman Maughan Chairman, Charles Legg, Harry Simpson Reeve

1955	Charles Ellerbeck Chairman, Norman Maughan, Harry Simpson Reeve
1956	Charles Ellerbeck Chairman, Norman Maughan, Harry Simpson Reeve
1957–58	Charles Ellerbeck Chairman, Norman Maughan, Jack Allen Reeve
1959–60	Charles Ellerbeck Chairman, Norman Maughan, Jack Allen Reeve
1961–62	Charles Ellerbeck Chairman, Harry Simpson, True Davidson Reeve
1963–64	Charles Ellerbeck Chairman, Harry Simpson, True Davidson Reeve
1965–66	Charles Ellerbeck Chairman, Harry Simpson, True Davidson Reeve
1967–69	Charles Ellerbeck Chairman, Jack Christie, True Davidson Mayor
1970–72	Charles Ellerbeck Chairman, Jack Christie, True Davidson Mayor
1973–74	Jack Christie Chairman, Al Morgan, Willis Blair Mayor
1975–76	Jack Christie Chairman, Al Morgan, Willis Blair Mayor (a)
Part '76	Jack Christie Chairman, Al Morgan, Leslie Saunders Mayor
1977–78	Jack Christie Chairman, Al Morgan, Alan Redway Mayor
1979–80	Jack Christie Chairman, Al Morgan, Alan Redway Mayor
1981–82	Jack Christie Chairman, Frank Johnson, Alan Redway Mayor
1983–85	Jack Christie Chairman, Frank Johnson, David Johnson Mayor
1986–88	Stan Wadlow Chairman, Frank Johnson, David Johnson Mayor
1989–91	Frank Johnson Chairman, John Flowers, David Johnson Mayor
1992–93	Frank Johnson (b) Chairman, John Flowers, David Johnson Mayor (c)
1993–94	John Flowers Chairman, Jack Christie, Michael Prue Mayor
1995–97	Bob Currie Chairman, Jack Christie, Michael Prue Mayor

(a) Willis Blair resigned as mayor in 1976

(b) Frank Johnson died in 1993. Council appointed Jack Christie

(c) David Johnson resigned as mayor in 1993

APPENDIX D

East York
Members of the Canadian House of Commons

York South

1908–1936	William F. Maclean	Conservative
1926–1935	Robert H. McGregor	Conservative

York East

1935–1962	Robert H. McGregor	Conservative 1935-1940
		National Government 1940-1945
		Progressive Conservative 1945-1960
1962–1972	Steve Otto	Liberal
1972–1974	Ian Arrol	Progressive Conservative
1974–1979	David Collenette	Liberal
1979–1980	Ron Ritchie	Progressive Conservative
1980–1984	David Collenette	Liberal
1984–1988	Alan Redway	Progressive Conservative
1988–1993	Alan Redway	Progressive Conservative
1993–1998	David Collenette	Liberal

Broadview

1968–1978	John Gilbert	New Democrat
1978–1979	Bob Rae	New Democrat

Broadview - Greenwood

1979–1982	Bob Rae	New Democrat
1982–1988	Lynn McDonald	New Democrat
1988–1998	Dennis Mills	Liberal

Don Valley West

1979–1993	John Bosley	Progressive Conservative
1993–1998	John Godfrey	Liberal

Rosedale

1968–1978	Donald S. MacDonald	Liberal
1978–1988	David Crombie	Progressive Conservative
1988–1993	David MacDonald	Progressive Conservative
1993–1998*	Bill Graham	Liberal

1997 Riding now named Toronto Centre-Rosedale

York – Scarborough

1965–1968	Robert Stanbury	Liberal

Don Valley

1968–1972	Robert Kaplan	Liberal
1972–1979	Jim Gillies	Progressive Conservative

APPENDIX E

East York
Members of the Ontario Provincial Parliament

York East

1913–1943	George S. Henry	Conservative
1943–1945	Agnes Macphail	Co-operative Commonwealth
1945–1948	John A. Leslie	Progressive Conservative
1948–1951	Agnes Macphail	Co-operative Commonwealth
1951–1967	Hollis Beckett	Progressive Conservative
1967–1977	Arthur Meen	Progressive Conservative
1977–1986	Robert Elgie	Progressive Conservative
1986–1990	Christine Hart	Liberal
1990–1995	Gary Malkowski	New Democrat
1995–1998	John Parker	Progressive Conservative

Don Mills

1963–1971	Stanley Randall	Progressive Conservative
1971–1987	Dennis Timbrell	Progressive Conservative
1987–1990	Murad Velshi	Liberal
1990–1993	Margery Ward	New Democrat
1993–1998	David Johnson	Progressive Conservative

APPENDIX F

Size and Population of East York

Size:

1924	3,647 Acres
1949	3,742 Acres
1963	3,773 Acres
1967	5,312 Acres or 8.5 square miles

Population:

1924	19,859
1949	56,575
1963	71,139
1967	97,555
1969	98,320
1970	98,657
1974	106,107
1975	104,677
1976	104,096
1977	103,362
1978	102,423
1979	100,857
1980	100,263
1982	99,448
1983	100,121
1985	97,679
1986	101,000
1988	101,085
1990	102,696

The Township of East York was incorporated as a separate Municipality on January 1, 1924 under the Township of East York Act, 1923 (Provincial Statute).

The Town of Leaside was incorporated on May 7, 1913.

On January 1, 1967, the former Township of East York and the former Town of Leaside were amalgamated as the Corporation of the Borough of East York by an amendment to the Municipality of Metropolitan Toronto Act. Various orders of the Ontario Municipal Board implemented the amalgamation (P1900-66 in Clerk's office).

Combined, they cover an area of 8.3 square miles or 5.312 acres. Of this total, 320 acres (1/2 square mile) consist of the total area of public parks and playgrounds found within the Borough limits.

APPENDIX G

East York Street Name Changes

Now	Formerly
Adair Road	Tunstall Avenue
Airdrie Road	
Airley Crescent	
Alder Road	
Aldwych Avenue	Randolph Avenue
Amsterdam Avenue	
Annesley Avenue	
Arundel Avenue	
Aspen Avenue	
Astor Avenue	
Athlone Road	
Avis Crescent	
Avonlea Boulevard	
Balfour Avenue	Isabella Street
Banigan Drive	
Barbara Crescent	
Barfield Avenue	Strathcona Gardens
Barker Avenue	Albert Street
Barrett Road	
Barrington Avenue	Elliott Street
Barron Road	Granville Avenue
Bater Avenue	
Bayview Avenue	Side Road
Bayview Heights Drive	
Beaufield Avenue	
Beechwood Crescent	
Beechwood Drive	
Bennington Heights Dr.	Rosemount Avenue
Bermondsey Road	

Now	Formerly
Berney Crescent	
Bessborough Drive	Edith Avenue
Beth Nealson Drive	
Beth Street	
Binswood Avenue	Sproule Street
Bonnie Brae Boulevard	
Bracebridge Avenue	
Brendan Road	Hillside Road
Brentcliffe Road	
Brenton Street	
Broadview Avenue	Don Mills Road
Browning Avenue	
Bryant Avenue	
Burley Avenue	
Burnham Road	Foy Avenue
Burrell Avenue	
Cadorna Avenue	
Cambrai Avenue	
Cameron Crescent	
Canvarco Road	
Carlaw Avenue	
Cedarcrest Boulevard	
Cedarvale Avenue	
Chapman Avenue	
Chilton Road	
Chisholm Avenue	Oaklands Avenue
Clarke Street	
Coleman Avenue	Lansdowne Avenue
Coleridge Avenue	
Commercial Road	
Copeland Street	
Cosburn Avenue	Bee Street
Coxwell Boulevard	

Now	Formerly
Craig Crescent	
Crandall Road	
Cranfield Road	
Crestland Avenue	
Crewe Avenue	
Crofton Road	
Crofton Road	Baird Avenue
Curity Avenue	
Curran Drive	
Dalecrest Drive	Shewman Avenue
Danforth Avenue	Don and Danforth Road
Davies Crescent	
Dawes Road	
Denton Avenue	Meighan Ave
Dentonia Pk. Avenue	Walnut Avenue
Denvale Road	Haden Park Blvd.
Derwyn Road	Plains Rd. (From O'Connor to Edison)
Dewhurst Blvd.	Jones Avenue
Dewhurst Blvd. N.	
Dieppe Road	Fairview Road
Dilworth Crescent	
Divadale Drive	Mitchell Avenue
Dohme Avenue	
Don Avon Drive	
Don Mills Road	
Don Valley Drive	
Doncaster Avenue	Isabella Street
Donegall Drive	
Donlands Avenue	Leslie Street
Donlea Drive	
Donmore Avenue	Shaughnessey Avenue
Donora Street	Wyatt Street
Doris Drive	

Now	Formerly
Douglas Crescent	Garrett Avenue
Druid Court	
Dunkirk Road	Lumsden Avenue
Durant Avenue	Gordon Avenue
Dustan Crescent	
Eastdale Avenue	Diver Street
Eaton Avenue	
Eden Park Road	
Eglinton Avenue East	
Eldon Avenue	Ethel Avenue
Elmont Drive	
Elmsdale Road	Lassell Avenue
Elswick Road	Rowan Road
Epsom Avenue	
Esandar Drive	
Everett Crescent	
Evergreen Gardens	
Faircrest Circle	
Fairland Road	
Fairside Avenue	
Ferncliffe Court	
Fernwood Gardens	
Ferris Crescent	
Ferris Road	
Field Avenue	
Fleming Crescent	
Floyd Avenue	
Four Oaks Gate	
Frankdale Avenue	Franklin & McCurdy Avenue
Frater Avenue	
Fulton Avenue	
Furnival Road	Jackson Avenue
Galbraith Avenue	Herman Avenue

Now	Formerly
Gamble Avenue	
Garden Circle	
Gardens Crescent	
Gatwick Avenue	
George Webster Road	
Glebeholme Boulevard	
Glebemount Avenue	Rixdale Avenue
Gledhill Avenue	
Glen Albert Drive	
Glen Eden Crescent	
Glen Gannon Drive	
Glen Robert Drive	
Glenbrae Avenue	
Glenburn Avenue	Stephney Street
Glencrest Boulevard	Vetland Road
Glenfield Crescent	
Glenord Road	
Glenshaw Crescent	
Glenvale Boulevard	Pine Park Avenue
Glenwood Crescent	Gleneagles Cres.
Glenwood Crescent	Gleneagles Cres.
Glenwood Terrace	
Goodwood Park Court	
Goodwood Park Crescent	Prospect Avenue
Gough Avenue	Moscow Avenue
Governors Road	Hawthorne Avenue
Grandstand Place	
Greenwood Avenue	Greenwood's Avenue
Hackberry Street	
Haldon Avenue	
Hale Court	
Halsey Avenue	
Hamstead Avenue	Hampstead Avenue

Now	Formerly
Hanna Road	
Hassard Avenue	
Heath Road	
Heath Street	Clarence Avenue
Heathbridge Park Drive	
Heathbridge Park Road	
Heather Road	
Hillside Drive	
Hodder Street	
Holland Avenue	
Hollinger Road	
Holmstead Avenue	Gray Road
Holsborne Avenue	
Hopedale Avenue	Gray Avenue
Hutton Avenue	Thornton Avenue
Industrial Street	
Inwood Avenue	
Jackman Avenue	
Joanith Drive	
Judith Drive	
Kathleen Avenue	
Kenrae Road	
Killdeer Crescent	
Kimbourne Avenue	Goyder Avenue
King Edward Avenue	Delane Road
King's Park Blvd.	McLean Blvd.
Knight Street	
Laird Drive	
Langford Avenue	
Lankin Boulevard	
Lea Avenue	
Leacrest Road	Talbot Road
Leadale Avenue	

Now	Formerly
Leander Court	
Leaside Park Drive	
Leroy Avenue	
Leslie Street	
Lesmount Avenue	
Linsmore Cres. (McCosh to Cosburn)	Prestholme Avenue
Linsmore Cres. (N. of Mortimer)	Strathcona Avenue
Linsmore Cres. (Sammon to Mortimer)	McKay Avenue
Logan Avenue	
Longspur Road	Alexandra Street
Lumley Avenue	Alexandra Street
Lumsden Avenue	Edward St., Croydon Ave., & Valley Road
Machockie Road	
MacNaughton Road	
Main Street	
Malcolm Road	
Mallory Crescent	Mallory Avenue
Marilyn Crescent	
Markham Avenue	
Marlow Avenue	Keene Avenue
Maryland Boulevard	
McKayfield Avenue	Mt. Royal Avenue
McRae Drive	Government Road
Medhurst Road	
Meighen Avenue	Dentonia Avenue
Memorial Pk. Ave.	McCosh Avenue
Midburn Avenue	Midland Avenue
Milepost Place	
Millwood Road	
Milton Road	
Milverton Avenue	Poulton Avenue

Now	Formerly
Minton Place	
Monarch Park Ave. (N. of Sammon Ave.)	Fredonia Avenue
Monarch Park Ave. (S. of Sammon Ave.)	Bathgate Avenue
Moore Avenue	Laird Drive
Moorehill Drive	
Mortimer Avenue	Burgess Avenue
Munford Crescent	
Muriel Avenue	
Nealon Avenue	
Nesbitt Drive	Oakdale Crescent
Newman Avenue	
Noel Avenue	
Norlong Boulevard	
Northbridge Avenue	
Northbrook Road	Gamelin Avenue
Northdale Blvd.	Major Cres.
Northline Road	
Notley Place	
O'Connor & Westview Avenue	Diagonal Avenue
O'Connor Drive	Don Mills (from Broadview to Taylor)
O'Connor Drive	Plains Rd. (Taylor to Derwyn)
Oak Park Avenue	Meagher Avenue
Orchard Green	Meagher
Orley Avenue	Chorley Avenue
Overlea Boulevard	
Palmer Avenue	Palmer Street
Pape Avenue	
Park Vista	
Parkhurst Boulevard	Soudan Street
Parklea Drive	Phippen Avenue
Parkview Hill Crescent	

Now	Formerly
Peard Avenue	Hodgson Avenue
Pepler Avenue	
Plains Road	Globe Avenue
Plaxton Crescent	
Plaxton Drive	
Pottery Road	Todmorden
Presteign Avenue	
Queensdale Avenue	Guestholme & Randolph Avenue
Ralston Avenue	
Randolph Road	
Ravenwood Place	
Red Oaks Cres.	Moore Vale
Rednor Road	
Research Road	
Rexleigh Drive	
Richlea Circle	
Ripon Road	
Rivercourt Boulevard	Bungalow Road
Roblin Avenue	Erland Avenue
Rolland Road	
Rolph Road	
Roosevelt Road	Connor Avenue
Rosevear Avenue	Eastbourne Avenue
Rowe Avenue	Reid Avenue
Roxville Avenue	
Rumsey Road	
Rutherglen Road	Kelway Road
Rykert Crescent	
Sammon Avenue	Cronyn Avenue
Sandra Road	
Savoy Avenue	Burleigh Avenue
Secord Avenue	Laura Secord & Johnston Street
Selwyn Avenue	Johnson Avenue

Now	Formerly
Sharron Drive	Clowes Avenue
Sibley Avenue	
Somers Avenue	
Southlea Avenue	
Southvale Drive	Laird Drive
Springdale Blvd.	Poulton Avenue
Sprucedale Place	
Squires Avenue	
St. Clair Avenue East	
St. Cuthberts Road	Balliol Avenue
St. Hubert Avenue	
Stag Hill Drive	
Stanhope Avenue	
Starbrook Avenue	McKay Avenue
Stevenson Drive	Bennington Heights (N. of Heath St.)
Stinson Circle	
Strathmore Boulevard	Hind Avenue
Sutherland Avenue	Colson Avenue
Tanager Avenue	
Taylor Drive	
Thorncliffe Park Drive	
Thursfield Crescent	
Thyra Avenue	
Tiago Avenue	Vivian Road
Todmorden Lane	
Topham Road	
Torrens Avenue	
Treadway Boulevard	
Trenton Avenue	
Trimontium Crescent	
Tunstall Avenue Adair Avenue	Rowe Avenue
Valley Road	Lumsden Avenue
Valor Road	

Now	Formerly
Vanderhoof Avenue	
Vaughan Street	
Ventnor Avenue	
Vicross Road	
Victoria Park Avenue	
Virginia Avenue	Burleigh & Savoy Avenue
Wallington Avenue	
Warland Avenue	
Warvet Crescent	
Waterman Avenue	
Welby Circle	
Westbrook Avenue	Talbot Avenue
Westlake Avenue	Ormerow Street
Westlake Cres.*	Paylor Cres.
Westview Blvd.	Diagonal Road
Westwood Avenue	Nash Avenue
Weymouth Avenue	Sibley Place
White Pine Avenue	
Wicksteed Avenue	
Wiley Avenue	Calford Avenue
William Morgan Drive	
Windmill Road	
Winsloe Avenue	
Wolverleigh Boulevard	
Woodbine Avenue	
Woodbine Heights Blvd.	Woodbine Ave. (N. from St. Clair W.)
Woodington Avenue	
Woodmount Avenue	St. James' Street
Woodvale Crescent	
Woodville Avenue	
Woodycrest Avenue	
Yardley Avenue	
Youngmill Drive	

* Jim Lister recalls Paylor Crescent this way:

A man by the name of Daniel Eddie, who was a teamster, first cut the road through and built a house on Paylor Crescent, which is now Westlake Crescent. He was an old man in the 1930s. He kept a horse in the rear of his property, which is on the ravine. He had kind of an opening under his house that he used as a stable.

He lived there until about the 1960s when his sister came and took him back to her home in Orillia. I believe they were Canadian Indian decent. One day he disappeared and they found him about ten miles down the highway heading back to his home in East York.

The Office (water revenue where Jim worked for East York) used to send me each fall to make sure he did not disconnect the meter so he could keep the water running, so as not to freeze.

I got to know him fairly well. He was part-Indian and born on a reserve. He told me that when he was a young boy his father and he slept in the same house as Jesse James. In those days, travellers could bunk at a farm for the night.

During the 1930s, we kids would see him riding his wagon along Cosburn east of Woodbine and we used to jump on the back for a ride. He never turned around or paid us any attention.

I always thought the street should have been named Dan Eddie Crescent.

APPENDIX H

The Origin of East York Street Names

Airdrie Road	Mr. John Aird, President of the Bank of Commerce, the Canadian Northern banker. He supported the model town idea.
Alder Avenue	In the Parkview Hills district – were named after trees that grew in the area when it was subdivided.
Annesley Avenue	Fred Annesley, Private Secretary to Sir William Mackenzie, of Mackenzie and Mann.
Ashall Boulevard	Named after the lawyer who acted for developer, W. Pugh, in connection with this subdivision.
Aspen Avenue	In the Parkview Hills district – were named after trees that grew in the area when it was subdivided.
Astor Avenue	Origin not known. The street was to be renamed Mayfair, but the request was denied and the name Astor remained. (Possible the name is after the New York Astor Family from the *Titanic*).
Baird Avenue	Hugh Northcote Baird (industrialist) born July 23, 1877. The street is now called Crofton Road.
Banigan Drive	After J. Banigan, Councillor of former Leaside, 1951, 1953–1955.
Barbara Crescent	Hereby hangs a love tale. One of the first to buy a lot on this street from the Taylor Estates was a young man who was in love with a girl named Barbara, and he asked as a special favor that the street be named for his sweetheart. Taylor Estates obliged, but the young man nevertheless, never married Barbara.
Barker Avenue	After Robert Barker, first Reeve of East York Township.
Barrett Road	After C.M. Barrett, a member of East York Planning Board.
Bater Avenue	After Bater family, early residents of Broadview-Bater area. Operated general store and Todmorden post office for many years.
Bayview Road	Became known as Bayview sometime after 1890. The street ran north from Eglinton. At one time the street was also known as Government Road.
Beaufield Avenue	Not known.
Bermondsey Road	Named after location in England of Head Office of Peek Frean's, whose plant was the first one established on this road.

Berney Crescent	Berney Realty Corporation Ltd., the original owners of the Garden Court Apartment named it. This street was to provide visitor parking for the Garden Court.
Bessborough Drive	Formerly Edith Avenue, in 1913, was named after Governor General Bessborough.
Beth Nealson Drive	After Mrs. Beth Nealson, Councillor of former Leaside. Mayor 1963 to 1966. Also, first woman Councillor.
Brentcliffe Road	Formerly Brentwood Road in 1913. The street was named after Brent Cairns, son of A.B. Cairns, a builder who lived on Rykert Crescent.
Broadview Avenue	Named because of the wide view across Riverdale Park, from where one could see Castle Frank, the home of the former Governor General of Upper Canada, John Graves Simcoe.
Broadway Avenue	Extension of a street from North Toronto.
Canvarco Road	Named after Canada Paint & Varnish Co., located on that street.
Chapman Avenue	Part of the property owned by Halsey Chapman who subdivided land and provided roadways. Councillor 1924-5. Owned brick yard at this location.
Chisholm Avenue	After Wm. Chisholm.
Clarke Street	In the former Town of Leaside. Named after Col F. F. Clarke of the Canadian Northern Railway, who worked for Mackenzie and Mann laying out the model town of Leaside in 1912. It basically separated the industrial area from residential area, the first of its kind in Canada. "Basically, he separated the industrial area from the residential area and by anticipating the automobile, made Leaside a town that it was impossible to speed through." Clarke Street was completed by 1913.
Clowes Avenue	Now Sharron Drive. In 1940, the Post Office changed its name because of confusion with another Close Avenue in Toronto.
Commercial Road	Descriptive of the activity on the street in the Industrial Area.
Copeland Street	Possibly named after a sheet metal fabricator, of Leaside.
Cosburn Avenue	Originally known as Bee Street, it was named later after the Cosburn family who were early settlers in this area, operating market gardens.
Craig Crescent	Thomas Craig (b. 1839) was a Montreal businessman and director of the Montreal and Southern Counties Railway Company and Secretary Treasurer of the Lake Champlain and St. Lawrence Ship Canal Company in 1912. James Craig was the Chair of the Board of Health in 1913.

Crandall Road	Not known.
Cranfield Road	Named after W. Cranfield Harris whose family owned a considerable portion of the property in this area and who granted the land for roadway.
Crewe Avenue	One of group of streets between Oak Park and Chisholm Avenues named after famous English race courses.
Crofton Road	Formerly Baird Avenue.
Curity Avenue	Named after famous trade name of Kendall Company, first industry to occupy land on street.
Davies Crescent	Part of the Robert Davies Estate. Street named after owner.
Denton Avenue	Part of the land formerly owned by the Massey Estate. Denton was a family name.
Dentonia Park Avenue	Along with Crescent Town, and the park, was part of the Massey Estate, and was named after a son of the family, Denton Massey.
Derwyn Road	After Bishop Derwyn T. Owen. This land was part of clergy reserves, and was opened up by the Anglican Church.
Divadale Drive	Formerly known as Mitchell Avenue, the street was named for the Divadale Estate, owned by Capt. Flanagan.
Dohme Avenue	Named after the pharmaceutical firm, Sharp & Dohme, one of the first three firms to locate in the Industrial area.
Don Avon Drive	Originally named Lazard Street.
Doncaster Avenue	One of group of streets between Oak Park and Chisholm Avenues named after famous English race courses.
Donegall Drive	Some have suggested a connection to Ireland, but there is no documented evidence.
Donlea Drive	Connects the Lea family with the Don River. Originally the street was known as Donald Street, after Sir Donald Mann.
Don Mills Road	In the mid-nineteenth century, three Taylor brothers operated grain mills in the valley by the Don, hence the name Don Mills Road.
Don Valley Parkway	The Parkway was opened by Metro Chairman Federick Gardiner in 1960. Building the Parkway was an undertaking of considerable magnitude because standing in its path was the Sugar Loaf Hill around Don Mills Road. The size of the hill can be best visualized by the fact that on the top of it lived a Mr. Manse, who had a market garden there. For over a year, huge earth-moving machines tore into the hill, and the earth was used to provide the foundation for the Parkway raising it above flood level.
Doris Drive	Named after wife of developer of this subdivision, Mr. W. Pugh.

Dunkirk Road	Formerly west section of Lumsden Avenue, and renamed Dunkirk during World War II after the battle of Dunkirk.
Dustan Crescent	Named after a one time local doctor, Dr. Gordon Dustan.
Edith Avenue	Now Bessborough Drive. The name changed in 1932 in honour of the governor general.
Epsom Avenue	One of group of streets between Oak Park and Chisholm Avenues named after famous English race courses.
Esandar Drive	Named after E.S. and A. Robinson Co., located on the street.
Fairland Road	Not known.
Field Avenue	Refers to "the field" where Bessborough Public School now stands.
Fleming Crescent	Robert John Fleming (1854–1925) was an associate of Mackenzie and Mann, the company that laid out the Town of Leaside in 1912. He served as a Toronto alderman and mayor for four terms. As well, he operated the Toronto Street Railway Co. In 1924, the Fleming family bought "Donlands," the 1,000 acre farm of William F. Maclean.
Galbraith Avenue	Named after second deputy Reeve, 1924-5, of the former Township.
Gatwick Avenue	One of group of streets between Oak Park and Chisholm Avenues named after famous English race courses.
Glenbrae Avenue	Not known.
Glenvale Boulevard	Formerly Pine Park Avenue.
Goodwood Park Avenue	One of group of streets between Oak Park and Chisholm Avenues named after famous English race courses.
Governor's Road	Named after lieut. governor's residence formerly located at entrance to such roadway.
Gowan Avenue	Named after A.H. Gowan, former owner.
Grandstand Place	Recognizes the presence of Thorncliffe Racetrack's Grandstand (1920–1952).
Grandstand Place	Names associated with former sit of "Thorncliffe Park Race Track".
Hackberry Avenue	In the Parkview Hills district—were named after trees that grew in the area when it was subdivided.
Halsey Avenue	Named after Halsey Chapman, Councillor 1924–5, operated brick works in this area and eventually subdivided.

Hanna Road	After David Blythe Hanna, V.P. of Canadian Northern Railway. He became its president after the government takeover and ultimately the first president of Canadian National Railways. He supported the "model town" idea. The street was originally named Glenallen.
Heath Road	In 1836, the widow of Brigadier-General Heath and her son, Charles, bought land on the hill where deer still roamed, and styled it Deer Park. Their street was known as Heath.
Heather Road	Not known.
Helliwell Street	Named after the Helliwell family who owned a considerable section of land in this area.
Hollinger Road	Named after Councillor John Hollinger, 1931, 1937–43, deputy reeve 1949–51.
Industrial Street	Descriptive of the immediate industrial area.
Jackman Avenue	Named after Jackman family who were early settlers and who owned a considerable amount of land in this area (also adjoining Toronto).
Junction Road	Became known as Bayview sometime after 1890. The street ran north from Eglinton.
Kathleen Crescent	Part of land subdivided by Walter Pugh. Named after a daughter.
Kenrae Road	Named after two men, Ken and Rae.
Kildeer Crescent	Named after bird. Formerly the street had been Kildare. Originally this street was part of Donlea.
Krawchuk Lane	Named after Lorna Krawchuk, Councillor for East York from 1988–1997.
Laird Avenue	Mr. Laird was the first bank manager at CIBC on Laird.
Lee Avenue Leacrest Road Leadale Avenue	former town took its name.
Machockie Road	Named after developer who opened up this street.
MacNaughton Road	Sarah MacNaughton, a British journalist, wrote glowing articles about William Mackenzie's achievements and "puffed" pieces to attract prospective buyers to Leaside. Originally, the name was spelled MacNaughtan. As part of her payment for writing, they named this street after her.
Malcolm Road	William Lindsay Malcolm, educationalist and civil engineer. Born in Guelph, Ontario, he was involved with the town plan.
Mallory Crescent	Not known.
Marilyn Crescent	Part of land subdivided by Walter Pugh and street named after his daughter.

McKayfield Road	Named after Wm. McKay, large land owner whose property in central part of the borough was taken over for tax arrears and developed. The property was taken over by the Township and Coxwell Avenue was extended northward from Sammon to Cosburn. The whole area, including what is now McKayfield Road, was subdivided for homes and the new Municipal Building and Memorial Park are in the exact center of what were the McKay fields.
McRae Drive	Named in honour of the first mayor of former Leaside, Randolph McRae. 1913–1914
Meighen Avenue	Named after J.H. Meighen, deputy reeve 1926, 1929–32.
Memorial Park Avenue	When the McKay fields were opened up, and the Memorial Park was laid out and dedicated in memory of the men of East York who made the supreme sacrifice in World War I and later both wars.
Merritt Road	Named after Lt. Col. Cecil Merritt who was awarded the Victoria Cross at the Dieppe Raid. Wartime Housing developed this plan.
Milepost Place	Names associated with former site of "Thorncliffe Park Race Track". 1920–1952.
Millwood Road	A North Toronto road that continues into Leaside.
Mitchell Avenue	Now called Divadale Drive.
Mortimer Avenue	After the Mortimer family who owned considerable land in and around Mortimer Avenue.
Munford Crescent	Named after subdivider and developer of that name.
Nesbitt Drive	After Hon. Wallace Nesbitt, who owned property in this area.
Newman Avenue	After early family by this name who settled in this area.
Norlong Boulevard	After subdivider and developer, Norman W. Long, Secretary-Treasurer, Monarch Mortgage & Investments Ltd.
O'Connor Drive	After Senator O'Connor.
Orley Avenue	One of group of streets between Oak Park and Chisholm Avenues named after famous English race courses.
Overlea Boulevard	Away from Leaside (or over or above). Named for the Lea family.
Parklea Drive	Formerly known as Soudan. The street was named for the Parkhurst Clothing Company, a partner with Dorothea Knitting Mitts.
Pine Park Avenue	Is now Glenvale.
Pepler Avenue	Named after a Mr. Pepler who in the days of Todmorden, long before East York was incorporated, ran a bus up and down Don Mills Road (Broadview) from Danforth to the Village of Todmorden.

Pottery Road	Was known as Todmorden Road, it being the only vehicular road —except Don Mills Road (now Broadview Avenue)— leading to the settlement of Todmorden. Its name was changed from Todmorden Road to Pottery Road about 1850.
Randolph Road	After Randolph McRae, first mayor of Leaside, 1913–14.
Redway Road	Alan Redway, mayor of East York (1975–1981), federal politician and resident of Leaside.
Research Road	Research Enterprises was located here.
Richlea Circle	Thought to be connected to the Lea family.
Rolland Road	Named for Senator Jean Damien Rolland who died in 1912. His father founded the Rolland Paper Mills in Quebec. Jean Damien took over the mills and then served as a mayor, and alderman in Quebec and in 1887, became a senator. Many Leaside streets were named for well-known people connected with Quebec because of the connection with Montreal planner, Frederick Todd.
Rolph Road	Dr. Albert H. Rolph, Medical Health Officer for Leaside in 1913. As well, Dr. John Rolph, born in 1792 was a supporter of William Lyon Mackenzie. Rolph Road School is named after him.
Roxville Avenue	Not known.
Rumsey Road	Named for a Mr. Rumsey, a manager employed by the Canadian National Railway who supported Mackenzie and Mann.
Rutherglen Road	In 1956, the street was named Rutherglen (between Southvale and Sutherland) replacing Kelway Road.
Rykert Crescent	John Charles Rykert (1832–1913) had a successful legal and political career in St. Catharines. He served in the first Parliament of Ontario. His hobby was fruit farming.
Sammon Avenue	Named after a family by this name who owned land in the area.
Sharron Drive	Formerly known as Clowes Avenue. The origin of Sharron is not known.
Southlea Avenue	Named in recognition of the Lea family.
Southvale Drive	Originally was called Laird Drive.
St. Columba Place	Named after church located on the street.
St. Cuthbert's Road	Was known as Balliol until 1939, then renamed to recognize St. Cuthbert's Anglican Church.
Sutherland Drive	Hugh Sutherland, promoter of the Hudson Bay Railway which later became the Canadian Northern Railway. He was a friend and associate of Sir William Mackenzie.

Tanager Avenue	Named after bird, the Scarlet Tanager. The builder of the original home on the street named it. Originally the street was Albertson Avenue.
Thorncliffe Park Drive	Recognizes the Racetrack and Thorncliffe Farm.
Thursfield Crescent	Recognizes a building production started on Thursday. The "field" part refers to the meadow with few houses.
Taylor Drive	Named after the Taylor family who subdivided their family holdings in this area.
Topham Road	Named after Second World War V.C. Veteran (part of Wartime Housing Subdivision).
Treadway Boulevard	After Councillor G.S. Treadway, 1937–43, Deputy Reeve 1944–50.
Vanderhoof Avenue	Named for a manager in the Canadian National Railway. This road was completed by 1913.
Village Station Road	Village of Leaside, train station.
Warvet Crescent	Part of Wartime Housing Subdivision. Streets named have a war connotation.
Waterman Avenue	Named after Frank Waterman, former president of Toronto Brick Company.
Westbrook Avenue	One of group of streets between Oak Park and Chisholm Avenues named after famous English race courses.
Westwood Avenue	Named after Perc. Westwood, a home builder, and a resident of Broadview Avenue for many years.
White Pine Avenue	In the Parkview Hills district. Named after trees that grew in the area when it was subdivided.
Wicksteed Avenue	Henry K. Wicksteed, chief engineer of Surveys. Worked under Col. Clarke for Canadian Northern Railway, designer of the Mount Royal Tunnel in Montreal. Wicksteed directed construction of this tunnel in 1912.
William Morgan Drive	Named for William Morgan, politician, former Leaside Councillor, 1943–44, deputy reeve 1945–7, reeve 1948–50 and president of the Leaside Lions.
Winsloe Avenue	Originally Woodbridge Avenue. The reason for the name change is not known.
Valor Boulevard	Part of Wartime Housing Subdivision. Streets named have a war connotation
Vanderhoof Avenue	Named after a prominent official who supported model town plan.
Vicross Road	Vicross – Victoria Cross.

APPENDIX I

Borough of East York
Designated Properties "Ontario Heritage Act"

1477 Bayview Avenue (Garden Court Apartments)
67–93 Douglas Crescent
20–22 Beechwood Crescent (Heritage Easement)
Todmorden Mills Historic Site—67 Pottery Road
The Goulding Estate—305 Dawes Road

1) 1477 Bayview Avenue (Garden Court Apartments)

Reasons for the designation of the Property at 1477 Bayview Avenue.

On land purchased from the Lea family, the Jackson-Lewis Company built this apartment complex in 1939–41.

Known as the Garden Court Apartments, they were designed by the prominent Toronto architectural firm of Forsey, Page, and Steele, based on the "New Concept" of Garden City Planning. The apartments were designed to provide their residents with a maximum of quiet and privacy as well as garden and recreational space in an urban environment. This was accomplished by replacing the standard apartment corridor by several entrances and stairways, each serving four to six apartments. Ventilation was improved by having each dwelling from one side of the building to the other.

The landscaping of the complex was designed by Dunnington-Grubb, one of Canada's most noted landscape architects of that day. His design reflected the work of Mr. Jackson of the Jackson-Lewis Company, who correctly believed that a beautiful, well-designed garden would compensate for any long-after depreciation of the buildings.

The Garden Court apartments and their gardens are recommended for designation on the basis of the extreme architectural importance.

2) 67–93 Douglas Crescent

Reasons for the designation of the Property at 67–93 Douglas Crescent.

The property at 67–93 Douglas Crescent, known as Governor's Manor, was designed by Eustace G. Bird and is recommended for designation for architectural reasons. The two storey main and flanking wings were built in 1928 in the sixteenth century Tudor style to surround a spacious courtyard. The courtyard and distinctive brick and half-timbered facades facing the courtyard comprise a unique example of a Tudor form of architecture in the area.

3) 20–22 Beechwood Crescent (Heritage Easement)

The oldest home in East York. Originally, the home of George Taylor, built about 1840 known as Beechwood.

In 1987, then owner Roseanne Wheler agreed to a heritage designation based on the grant of an easement to East York to the effect that no demolition, construction, alteration, remodelling could be done that would affect the appearance of the façade, without the written approval of East York.

4) Todmorden Mills Historic Site—67 Pottery Road

Reasons for the designation of the Property at 67 Pottery Road (Todmorden Mills).

The property at 67 Pottery Road is recommended for designation for architectural and historic reasons. The Paper Mill, Brewery, Parshall Terry House, William Helliwell House and the Don Station are structures which are representative of early industrial development and settlement in East York. Another feature of the Todmorden Mills Site includes the brick road. The Todmorden Mills Site is an important Landmark in the East York Community.

5) The Goulding Estate—305 Dawes Road

Reasons for the designation of the Property at 305 Dawes Road.

The property at 305 Dawes Road known as the Goulding Estate, is historically significant. The land and structures were part of the Dentonia Park Farm founded by the prominent Toronto family of Walter and Susan Denton Massey as an experimental model dairy farm in 1897. At the turn of the century, sixteen out of every 100 Toronto infants died, many from typhoid fever and tuberculosis caused by drinking contaminated milk. The philanthropic Masseys produced pasteurized milk to help prevent children's deaths at a time when pasteurization was virtually unknown. The Goulding house, the home of Dorothy Massey Goulding and her husband Dr. Arthur Goulding is the only house lived in by a Dentonia Park Massey that still stands on what was once 240 acres of farm land.

The house at 305 Dawes Road is architecturally significant. The house was designed by Ferdinand Marani, a prominent Canadian architect in 1921. As an early example of Marani's work, it ranked as one of the outstanding residences of Canada and Ontario in the late 1920s. The house shows the influence of Eden Smith, whose comfortable, cottage-like designs revolutionized the nature of public housing in early twentieth century Toronto.

20 Beechwood
(Source: Margaret McRae)

Garden Court
(Source: bing.com)

Goulding Estate
(Source: bing.com)

Governors Bridge Apts
(Source: bing.com)

APPENDIX J

Borough of East York Fact Sheet
Coat of Arms

The Borough of East York coat of arms, a shield framed by flowing leaves, is a composite formed upon the amalgamation of the Town of Leaside and the Township of East York in 1967. In a public competition to select a design, the entry of Mr. H. K. Faulks of Brentcliffe Road was selected. Mr. Faulks received a set of borough cuff links at a council meeting in appreciation of his efforts. The coat of arms incorporates most of the symbols from the crests of the two former municipalities.

Standing at the top is the old British bulldog, from East York's coat of arms, signifying the tenacious and courageous early settlers from Britain who first lived in the area. The flower is the White Rose of York, another carry-over of the settlers' homeland.

The beaver, a popular Canadian symbol, was taken from the Leaside coat of arms to represent industry. The beaver held a special meaning in the area, as the Don River was a beaver habitat.

Maple leaves representing Canada were on the coat of arms of both former municipalities.

In 1990, with the opening of the new civic centre, Council approved the crafting of a new depiction of the coat of arms. Talented artist, Nicholas Graven of the Artessa Studio used glazed ceramics to construct the crest now hanging in the council chamber.

The new coat of arms, representing the men and women of East York who built this community, will now remain a visible, respected symbol in the chamber.

February 1991

APPENDIX K

Borough of East York Fact Sheet
Mayor's Chain of Office

The chain of office, worn at official functions by the mayor of the Borough of East York, is a symbol of the dignity, authority, and responsibility of the position of the principal elected municipal official. The chain is designed to show the history, achievements, and aspirations of the community.

In 1967, the former Town of Leaside and the former Township of East York amalgamated to become the Borough of East York. To commemorate the occasion, a new chain of office was designed and presented to then-Mayor True Davidson. Several service organizations undertook this project—East York Kiwanis Club, East York Rotary Club, Leaside Lions Club, East York Lions Club, and East York Kinsmen Club. These clubs jointly presented the chain to the mayor at the October 28, 1968 council meeting.

The chain is comprised of several medallions, the main one hanging from the bottom of the chain. It is the coat of arms of the borough designed to incorporate most of the symbols from the coat of arms of the former township and town *(See appendix entitled "Coat of Arms)*.

The four large medallions in the chain collar are:

centre front   — the house and the rising sun, taken from Leaside's coat of arms

shoulders   — the Ontario shield

centre back   — the names of the donating service clubs.

The smaller medallions in the collar are:

Six white roses of York

Four East York bulldog heads

Two Leaside beavers

Two Ontario maple leaves

The chain rests on a collar of blue and green and when taken with the gold of the medallions, the official community colours of both Leaside and East York are represented: green and gold for Leaside and blue and gold for East York.

May 1991

BIBLIOGRAPHY

East York Council Minutes, 1924–1997

J.C. Boylen. *York Township: An Historical Survey 1850–1954*, Municipal Corporation of the Township of York. Toronto, 1954.

Mary Byers, Jan Kennedy, Margaret McBurney and The Junior League of Toronto, Rural Roots, Pre-Confederation Buildings of the York Region of Ontario. University of Toronto Press, 1976.

Ann Guthrie, *Don Valley Legacy, A Pioneer History*, The Boston Press, 1986.

Canada Mortgage & Housing Corporation, *Housing a Nation: 40 Years of Achievement*, 1986.

Patricia W. Hart, *Pioneering in North York, A History of the Borough*, General Publishing Company Limited. Toronto, 1968.

Bruce West, *Toronto*, Doubleday Canada Limited. Toronto, 1967.

True Davidson, *The Golden Years of East York*, Centennial College Press, 1976.

Jack Christie, *The Generation of Change, The Memoirs of Jack Christie*, 2006.

True Davidson, *The Golden Strings*, Griffin House. Toronto, 1973.

Charles Sauriol, *Remembering The Don, a rare record of earlier times within the Don River Valley*, Consolidated Amethyst Communications Inc. 1981.

Eleanor Darke, *Call Me True*, National Heritage. National History Inc., 1997.

Jane Pitfield, *Leaside*, National Heritage Books. Toronto, 1999.

Eleanor Darke, *A Mill Should Be Built Thereon, an early history of Todmorden Mills*, National Heritage. Toronto, 1995.

East York Public Library, Fascinating Facts about East York, 1996.

Paul McGrath, Last Villages of Toronto,

Charles Sauriol, *Trails of the Don*, Hemlock Press. 1992.

Charles Sauriol, *Trails of the Don*, Hemlock Press. 1992.

Ron Fletcher, *Over the Don*, Self–published. 2002.

Lorne S. Miller, *Our Danforth: one hundred years of memories*, Lorne Miller & Associates Inc. 2008.

Joanne Doucette, *Pigs, Flowers & Bricks: a history of Leslieville to 1920*; Self–published. 2011.

Barbara Myrvold, *An Historical Walking Tour of the Danforth*, Toronto Public Library Board. 1979.

Lucy Booth Martyn, *The Face of Early Toronto*, The Paget Press, Sutton West. 1982.

Goad's 1884 Atlas of Toronto, Map 37 & 38

Charles M. Johnston, *E.C. Druary: Agrarian Idealist*, University of Toronto Press. Toronto, 1986.

Alan Redway, *Governing Toronto: Bringing back the City that works*, Friesen Press, Victoria, B.C. 2014.

Ron Brown, *Toronto's Lost Villages*, Polar Bear Press. Toronto, 1997.

Jim Lister, *East York Incorp: 1924 An Illustrated History*, Self-published. 1983.

Michael P. Dolbey, *A History of Woodbine Gardens*, Self-published. 2015.

D. S. Hough, *Some of My Memories of East York*, The East York Historical Society. 1992.

Percy Bustin, *Memories: Early Days of East York*, Self – Published. 1976.

Lawrence G. Main, *Growing Up in the Old Township of East York*, Self-published. 2013.

Patricia V. Schulz, *The East York Workers' Association: A Response to the Great Depression*, New Hogtown Press. Toronto, 1975.

Lee Ann Fagan, Project Co-ordinator, *The Secord Area*, East York Board of Education. 1974.

Jason Bullard, *The Biggest Little Hospital East of the Don River: The History of the Toronto East General & Orthopedic Hospital Inc.*, Toronto East General Hospital Public Relations. 1994.

John Michaelidis, *East York Tidbits*, East York Historical Society, 2003.

Mark Zuchlke, *Juno Beach*, Douglas & McIntyre, 2005.

W. T. Bernard, *The Queen's Own Rifles of Canada*, The Ontario Publishing Company. Toronto, 1960.

Charles Cromwell Martin, *Battle Diary*, Dundurn Press. 1994.

Rt. Hon. John G Diefenbaker, *One Canada, The Crusading Years 1895–1956*, MacMillan of Canada. 1975.

V.C., Fowke, *Canadian Agriculture in War & Peace, 1935–1950*.

National War Service, RG 44, Vol. 10, History of Voluntary & Auxiliary Services Division, Appendix 6, Reports of Citizens Committee & Co-ordinating Councils.

Len Falkner, *Early Days of Branch 22*, Self–Published.

Jim Lister, *The Building of Branch 22–Royal Canadian Legion 70th Anniversary*, Self–Published. January 1996.

Suzanne Grant, Dr. Anne & Bert C., *With a Box of Tools: The History of Crestview & the Grant Family*, Crestview Investment Corporation. 2014.

Michael McMahon, *Metro's Housing Company, The First 35 Years*, The Metropolitan Toronto Housing Company Ltd. 1990.

Stan Wadlow, *East York Recreation: The early Years*, Centennial College Press. 1982.

Don Wadlow, *The History of Recreation in East York*, 1961.

Anthony Stokes & William Keel, *History & Development of East York*, S. Walter Stewart Library.

S. Walter Stewart Library, Local History, Hollinger Bus Lines & East Toronto Weekly & East York Times, June 24, 1954.

S. Walter Stewart Library, Local History, Historical Designation of Goulding Estate, 1994.

Rev. James G. McDonald, Souvenir Booklet, Don Mills United Church.

Robert W. Ogden, *William Burgess School Then & Now 1914–1994*, East York Board of Education. 1994.

East York Library a History, 1974.

Stan W. Wadlow, *Life's Precious Memories*, Twin-Offset Ltd., [1983?].

Brian Vallee, *Edwin Alonzo Boyd: The Story of the Notorious Boyd Gang*, Doubleday Canada Limited. 1997.

Marjorie Lamb & Barry Pearson, *The Boyd Gang*, Peter Martin Associates Limited. 1976.

Melanie Milanich, *Dawes Road: a Shortcut to the Market and a Natural Resource Base*, February, 2011.

East York Public Library, Fascinating Facts about East York.

Col., C.P. Stacey, *The Canadian Army 1939–1945*, Kings Printer. Ottawa, 1948.

A.E. Safarian, *The Canadian Economy in the Great Depression*, McClelland & Stewart. 1970.

L.M. Grayson & M. Bliss, (Editors), *The Wretched of Canada, Letters to R.B. Bennett 1930–1935*, University of Toronto Press. 1971.

M. Horn, (Editor), *The Dirty Thirties, Canadians in the Great Depression*, Copp Clark. 1972.

B. Broadfoot, *The Ten Lost Years 1929–1939*, Toronto Doubleday. 1973.

J.H. Gray, *The Winter Years*, Fifth House Publishers, 2003.

A Final Report on the Structural/Management Review for the Borough of East York, Cuff, George B., & Associates Ltd. Management Consultants. April 1994.

Mights Directory, 1923–1924.

Atlas of the City of Toronto & Suburbs, Toronto Goods Atlas & Plan 1923 & 1924.

Charles Sauriol, *Remembering The Don, a rare record of earlier times within the Don River Valley*, Consolidated Amethyst Communications Inc. 1981.

Paul Huntley, *City Dairy Toronto*, Self–published. 2011.

Barbara Dickson, *Bomb Girls*, Trading aprons for Ammo, Dundurn, A J. Patrick Boyer Book. Toronto, 2015.

Robert T. Dixon, *We Remember, We Believe: A History of Toronto's Catholic Separate School Boards, 1841 to 1997*, Toronto Catholic District School Board. 2007.

Other Sources

S. Walter Stewart Library, Local History Collection

Dawes Road Library, Local History Collection

Riverdale Library, Local History Collection

Pape Library, Local History Collection

Coxwell Library, Local History Collection

Archives of Ontario, Proceedings & Statutes of the Ontario Legislative Assembly

Canada Mortgage & Housing Corporation, Archives

Institute of Environmental Research Inc., Moore George Associates, Proctor & Redfern Limited, Borough of East York, Culture & Recreation Master Plan, 1983, Volumes 1 & 2

United Church of Canada Archives

Anglican Church of Canada, Toronto Archives

Toronto District School Board Museum & Archives

Lennox & Addington Museum & Archives, Napanee, Ontario

East York Police Souvenir Programme

Toronto Archives

Toronto Reference Library

Todmorden Mills Museum

Toronto Museums and Heritage Services

INDEX OF INTERVIEWS

1. Gord Haslett, February 13, 2013

2. Peter Weatherhead, April 5, 2013

3. Dick Anderson, May 15, 2013

4. Gordon Sherk, February 19, 2014

5. Gert & Doreen Hart, November 27, 2014

6. Natalie Clarke, November 9, 2015

7. Bill Lewis, November 9, 2015

8. Joyce Crook, November 12, 2015

9. Ron Raby, November 18, 2015

10. Stan French, November 24, 2015

11. Isabel Montgomery, December 2, 2015

12. Christopher Salmond, December 3, 2015

13. Joanne Doucette, December 14, 2015

14. George England, December 29, 2015

15. Bert C. Grant, January 11, 2016

16. John, Voula & Bessie Janekas, January 23, 2016

17. Joy & Pat Burford, January 26, 2016

18. George Matthews, February 7, 2016

19. Gail Nyberg, July 20, 2016

20. Mrs. Claire Cole, July 27, 2016

21. Bernie Fowler, August 2, 2016

22. Dick McInosh, August 2, 2016

23. Steve Mastoras, August 5, 2016

24. Jack Bell, August 16, 2016

25. Lyn & Joan Ridout, August 17, 2016

26. Jim & Joanne Fryer, August 17, 2016

27. Jack Freer, August 18, 2016

28. Paul McCutcheon, August 24, 2016

29. Peter Scaiff, Peter Paints, August 29, 2016

30. Cathy Andrews, September 9, 2016

31. Paul Moffat & Paul Enright, September 9, 2016

32. Elizabeth Shelton, September 16, 2016

33. Mike Vince, September 26, 2016

34. Dave Johnson, October 6, 2016

35. Jim & Charlotte Balmer, October 13, 2016, March 5, 2017 (email)

36. Paul Robinson, October 25, 2016

37. Ed Freeman, October 26, 2016

38. Norm Crone, October 31, 2016 (email), November 28, 2016, November 15, 2016, November 23, 2016, August 20, 2016, August 16, 2016

39. Jim Lister, October 19, 2015, December 20, 2016

40. John Michailidis, January 2, 2017

41. Bill Alexander, January 4, 2017

42. Roly Sheaves, January 19, 2017

43. John Swan, January 25, 2017

44. Roy White, January 27, 2017

45. Gary & Vivian Harlow, January 27, 2017

46. Tom Carter, January 30, 2017

47. Colleen Peacock, January 31, 2017

48. Bruce Horner, January 31, 2017

49. Case Ootes, February 1, 2017

50. Mrs. Beckle, March 3, 2017

51. Joan Hinala, March 4, 2017

52. Marshall Leslie, March 23, 2017

53. Michael Prue, April 5, 2017

54. Mrs. Hill, April 10, 2017

55. Kevin Chisholm, April 28, 2017

56. Betty Hicks, May 23, 2017

57. Bob Murphy, May 31, 2017

58. Nora Curran, June 5, 2017

59. Bonnie Askin, August 26, 2017

60. Interview with Howard Birnie, September 24, 2017

61. Interview with Pete Dudley, September 17, 2017

ACKNOWLEGEMENTS

This book would never have been published without the enormous help, enthusiasm and computer expertise of my good friend and former federal Constituency Assistant extraordinaire, Anna Malandrino, who not only transcribed my hand written original draft notes into a manuscript capable of presenting to an editor and publisher and did the indexing but also transformed the photographs into the necessary electronic form which then allowed my wonderful photo editor Tracy Choy to perform her own special miracles.

I am truly and deeply indebted to Percy Bustin, Lu Ann Fagan, Lawrence Main, Don Hough, Jim Lister, True Davidson, Eleanore Darke, Anne Guthrie, Thomas Weatherhead, Charles Sauriol, Gordon Sherk, Stan Wadlow, Don Wadlow, Jack Christie, Michael Dolbey, John Michailidis, Jane Pitfield, Norm Crone and John Janikas for recording in their writings important parts of the East York story. Nor can I overlook the debt I owe to the many others listed in the Index of Interviews shown elsewhere in this book who shared with me their personal recollections and memories.

My special thanks goes to the tremendously helpful staff at the Toronto Archives, John Huzil, Andrea de Shield, Glenda Williams and Lawrence Lee; at the S. Walter Stewart Library, Janet Nanos, keeper of all things East York; at the Todmorden Mills Museum, Ulana Baluk and at Toronto Museums and Heritage Services, Tara Bowyer, Gabrielle

Major, Sahana Rivirajasmgam and Jena Karmali. My grateful thanks as well to the master designer of the cover and maps, Valentine De Landro.

I am indebted as well to the East York Foundation for their assistance with the publication of this book and of course to the helpful staff of the publisher, Emily Macdonald, Dawn Johnston, Emma Pickering, Nessa Pullman, Sammy Paulus, and Dahlia Yuen.

To all who, as I do, cherish the Township of East York, the Town of Leaside and the Borough of East York my deepest and most sincere thanks.

Any and all errors in this history of East York are mine and mine alone and should be attributed to none other.

I am pleased to dedicate this book to my parents Alan and Phyllis Redway, my grandfather, Arthur Turner and all the community volunteers, activists and residents past and present of the Borough of East York, where I grew up, for ingraining in me my strong beliefs in what constitutes a truly livable community together with the importance of participating in the local government decision making process.

INDEX

-T-

ABOUT THE AUTHOR

Alan Redway

Born in Toronto and raised in the former Borough of East York, Alan Redway has a degree in Commerce and Finance from the University of Toronto and a law degree from Osgoode Hall. Mr. Redway served for ten years on the council of the Borough of East York, six of those years as the mayor of East York and a member of Metropolitan Toronto Council and Executive Committee. Later he was elected to the Parliament of Canada where he served for almost ten years as a Progressive Conservative member of the House of Commons and as Minister of State (Housing). He has written for *Leaside Life* and the *East York Chronicle*. In 2014 he published his first book, *Governing Toronto: Bringing back the city* that worked.

CPSIA information can be obtained
at www.ICGtesting.com
Printed in the USA
LVHW02s0601181018
593959LV00003B/3/P